BOWING TO NECESSITIES

W9-BCY-669

BOWING TO NECESSITIES

A History of Manners

in America, 1620–1860

C. Dallett Hemphill

OXFORD
UNIVERSITY PRESS

OXFORD
UNIVERSITY PRESS

Oxford   New York

Auckland   Bangkok   Buenos Aires   Cape Town   Chennai
Dar es Salaam   Delhi   Hong Kong   Istanbul   Karachi   Kolkata
Kuala Lumpur   Madrid   Melbourne   Mexico City   Mumbai   Nairobi
São Paulo   Shanghai   Singapore   Taipei   Tokyo   Toronto

and an associated company in Berlin

Copyright © 1999 by Oxford University Press, Inc.

Published by Oxford University Press, Inc.
198 Madison Avenue, New York, New York 10016

www.oup.com

First issued as an Oxford University Press paperback, 2002

Oxford is a registered trademark of Oxford University Press

All rights reserved. No part of this publication may be reproduced,
stored in a retrieval system, or transmitted, in any form or by any means,
electronic, mechanical, photocopying, recording, or otherwise,
without the prior premission of Oxford University Press.

Library of Congress Cataloging-in-Publication Data
Hemphill, C. Dallett, 1959–
Bowing to necessities : a history of manners in America, 1620–1860
C. Dallett Hemphill.
p. cm.
Includes bibliographical references and index.
ISBN 0-19-512557-6; 0-19-515408-8 (pbk.)
1. Etiquette—United States—History.   I. Title.
BJ1853.H46   1999
395'.0973—dc21   98-43410

Some material from this book has been previously published and is
reprinted here by permission: "Age Relations and the Social Order in
Early New England: The Evidence From Manners," *Journal of Social
History*, 28 (Winter 1994): 271–294; "Middle Class Rising in
Revolutionary America: The Evidence From Manners," *Journal of Social
History*, 30 (Winter 1996): 317–344; "etiquette" in *A Companion to American
Thought*, ed. Richard Wightman Fox and James T. Kloppenberg
(Blackwell Publishers, 1995); and "Class, Gender and the Regulation of
Emotional Expression in Revolutionary Era Conduct Literature" in
An Emotional History of the United States, ed. Peter Stearns and Jan Lewis
(New York University Press, 1998).

1   3   5   7   9   8   6   4   2

Printed in the United States of America
on acid-free paper

For John

ACKNOWLEDGMENTS

The one thing painful about acknowledging all the people who helped me with this book is thinking back that far. This project began many years ago as a research paper for a graduate seminar at Brandeis University, and then became a dissertation. Through those years and since I have been nurtured by the wonderful circle of friends that was the Brandeis history community. Although we may now talk about babies as much as books, I can't forget that Matt Gallman, Tom Pegram, Ruth Friedman, Howard Wach, Susan Tananbaum, Dan Cohen, Dan Dupré, David Sicilia, and others helped make me a historian in the first place. In the research stages I was aided by the dedicated librarians at Brandeis, the Schlesinger Library at Radcliffe, the Boston Public Library, the American Antiquarian Society, the New York Public Library, and the Library of Congress. I am grateful to my relatives the Frisches and the Cálveses for putting me up in New York and Washington. John Demos was a patient dissertation advisor and has also taught me by the superb example of his own scholarship. He has continued to encourage me in the long years between the dissertation and this book. Richard D. Brown and Christine Heyrman have likewise been unfailingly generous over the years with their advice and support.

Ursinus College has helped me mature as a historian by providing an ideal teaching environment. The college also provided two summer research grants and a sabbatical leave. The latter was supplemented by a grant from the National Endowment for the Humanities. Some people at Ursinus College have given special aid: Hugh Clark, by being a supportive friend and chair; Carol Dole, by walking the same road with me many times; Margie Connor, by helping in countless ways but mostly by making me laugh every day; and Paul Stern, by sharing ten years of ideas, projects, and encouragement.

Two historians, one very eminent, one just starting out, played key roles in gently but firmly insisting on what had to be cut out of the book. The first, Richard Dunn, has also been a sustaining force by welcoming me into his unparalleled community at the McNeil Center for Early American Studies. My sabbatical year there, in the stimulating company of Brendan McConville, Konstantin Dierks, Valentijn Byvanck, Judy Van Buskirk, Tom Humphrey, Liam Riordan, and others, really helped me pull things together. I owe them all thanks for ideas and citations. The younger historian, Rodney Hessinger, has turned from student to teacher and I hope we continue to share interests for a very long time. Several other scholars have taken the time to read my work and make essential suggestions; for that I thank Michael Zuckerman, Ken Lockridge, and Peter Stearns.

My large, supportive family has always been there to cheer on my work but has mostly served to remind me how wonderful life is outside of any book. I thank them for the healthy perspective. Evan and Alec Hill have helped—with arms around my neck and sloppy kisses—to remind me where most happiness comes from. I also wish to acknowledge all the women who have helped care for and teach my sons; I would not have had the peace of mind to write this book without their expertise and dedication.

John Hill has been putting up with this book for as long as he has been putting up with its "high-maintenance" author. Neither would have survived without him. He is my hero.

CONTENTS

BOWING TO NECESSITIES

INTRODUCTION

One night about 150 years ago, my great-great-grandfather decided to read an etiquette book. He was worried about his awkward bows and thought the manual might help. I was struck by this decision when I came across it in his diary. Why did he care so much about his bow? Why did he turn to a book to deal with his awkwardness? We rarely bow any more; this made me wonder how manners have changed over time and whether changes could tell us anything about the larger society. In short, reading about his decision prompted me to investigate what manners could teach us about early American history.

My grandfather recorded his decision with some seriousness, and drew a connection between his bad bows and the state of his relations with women. This suggested that manners have played an important role in social relations, that somehow people *need* manners. Historians have begun to recognize this, but we are newcomers to the field.[1] Sociologists and anthropologists, in contrast, have recognized the significance of manners since the birth of their disciplines. They may call it by different names—such as etiquette, ceremonial behavior, social ritual, interaction ritual, or politeness—but all describe the same thing: the rule-bound and symbolic behaviors that we perform in the presence of others. Sociologists have developed what amounts to a theory of manners. From Herbert Spencer to Erving Goffman, they have demonstrated that manners serve three social functions. First, they constitute a subtle but pervasive system of social regulation or control, a form of government

3

that underlies all other forms. Second, manners have a creative function in that they generate the feelings that help people assume their social roles. Third, manners have a communicative function, for they tell us not only about each other but about our place in the social order. All of these functions may be illustrated by the bow that worried my ancestor. It began as a gesture performed by an inferior to a superior, it helps one to feel deferential, and it expresses deference.[2]

The sociological argument is that although the "big rules" of social life—our systems of law, morality, and religion—are necessary if humans are to live in groups, the "little rules" of manners are necessary to enact the larger social order in every encounter. Manners also constitute a mediating level of culture between a society's abstract "ideals" and the varied behaviors of its individual members. These meaning-laden acts and gestures are the signal flags of an encounter, by which we communicate, often nonverbally, who we are and what we expect of each other.

What manners offer historians, then, is a new perspective on society—a street-level panorama of how contemporaries thought society was organized, how power was actually distributed, and how larger changes in cosmology, polity, or economy were being worked out in everyday life. The best window onto this scene is provided by conduct advice literature, defined here as everything printed or imported in America that gave direct instruction on how to behave in the presence of others. Fortunately, these prescriptive materials abound. Manners are social behaviors and have to be learned, whether they are taught orally, as through sermons or parental admonitions, or are learned via books. But even the former left their trace in print. Unfortunately, this literature cannot tell us how people actually behaved.

This is not because the writers promoted customs of their own invention; they had to deal with the inherited repertoire of behaviors. No author would open himself or herself up to the ridicule of inventing a new form of salutation, for example, to replace the customary forms of the time, whether the hand kiss, bow, curtsy, or handshake.[3] When one compares conduct prescriptions with the glimpses of actual behavior offered by diaries and letters, however, it is clear that conduct writers were not discussing all behavior. Rather, they focussed on certain issues, for the benefit of certain groups. As do conduct advisors in our own day, they used their discussions of manners to wrestle with—and propose ritual solutions for—certain cultural problems.[4]

Taken together, their suggestions amount to a loose script of rituals for face-to-face interaction in various situations. As with any set of social norms, some people followed the script carefully, while others were careless or ignorant of it, while still others explicitly defied it. That there was a single script (though with multiple roles) is indicated by the great internal consistency of the conduct literature. That is, in each period the authors nearly always reported the same rules, often in the same words. There may have been competing practices among subgroups in the population—there had to have been, as American society grew ever more heterogeneous over time—but only one set of rituals was sufficiently dominant to be codified.[5]

What we find in conduct works, then, is not behavior but a society's dominant code of behavior, and I use the term code in both its meanings as a set of laws and a set of symbols. The discussions of manners in conduct literature generally consist of a set of rules for behavior. Given this code, related behaviors in real life, whether they conform to the rules or not—whether they are examples of "good" or "bad" manners—constitute a set of symbols that others could read.[6] Conduct works are thus a society's code books. Wherever possible, the random references to these symbolic behaviors that surface in diaries and letters are brought to bear in this book to help us see "manners in action." Each chapter opens with a vignette from real life that is emblematic of the concerns revealed in the period's conduct literature. But only the code books offer access to the entire code.

Over two hundred different works prescribing proper face-to-face behavior were published or imported in northern America before 1861. Among them are sermons, child-rearing guides, etiquette books, and advice books, to name just some of the genres involved; and in many cases specific rules for face-to-face behavior are embedded in more general, abstract, and moralistic advice. The changing nature, authorship, audience, role in teaching manners, and popularity of the various works are important topics in this study. But the basic questions are shaped by the fact that the "little rules" of etiquette regulate social relations and vary according to a person's class, age, and sex. This book is therefore an examination of the changing rules of class, age, and gender relations in early America.

To use published rules for behavior as an optic on society is to use a lens with a powerful but changing focus. In geographic terms, the major market for conduct literature was concentrated between Boston and Washington, the Atlantic and the Mississippi; therefore, my conclusions in all periods pertain most to the northern colonies and states. It is not that southerners read a dramatically different literature or used entirely different rituals; diaries and other records show some of the same gestures and some of the same books on their shelves, especially in the colonial era. Recent work on the book trade confirms that books continued to be funneled from the North to the South in the early republic. But studies of colonial Virginia and the Old South suggest a different pattern of consumption and performance, and the divergence clearly widened as the Civil War approached. The natural explanation of this divergence is the place of race slavery in shaping an increasingly distinctive southern culture. The manners system revealed by antebellum conduct literature, produced as it was by northern writers, reveals a picture of a free labor society with its own distinctive class and ethnic relations. It reveals a society coming to grips with the long shift from a hierarchically to a horizontally conceived social order. Scholars of the South, in contrast, suggest that the defenders of the slave regime clung to hierarchy. A comparative study of manners in the two regions should be undertaken, but such a study cannot be done with the sources examined here.[7]

Before the mid-eighteenth century, in fact, the focus is on New England, as almost all the available conduct literature was published in or imported to Boston. New York did not come into its own as a publishing and book-selling center until much later (only one work of the early colonial period was printed in New York) and would be difficult to treat at any rate, owing to the extreme ethnic heterogeneity of its culture. After 1680, the Quaker colonies—Pennsylvania and West New Jersey—likely shared some of the characteristics of manners in New England, but the dearth of prescriptive evidence only allows some speculations in this vein.

In brief, while at least the first generations of Quakers appeared to reject some Anglo-American social rituals (such as doffing the hat) and to adopt some of their own practices (such as the use of *thou* for the single *you*), our only source of prescriptive evidence for Quaker practices, the works of William Penn, do not present a special Quaker code of behavior. Aside from a slightly greater emphasis on brevity and plainness of speech, his works do not contain instructions that vary significantly from other English and New English works of the period. Moreover, as the Quaker colony matured and the famous Quaker merchants prospered, few elite libraries were without some of the English courtesy works that were also owned, as we shall see, by the New England elite. Although they scorned extreme outward shows of deference, the Quaker elite seem to have shared the hierarchical view of society of their northern and metropolitan counterparts.[8]

I will not be arguing that early New England was representative of the northern colonies; in many ways it had the most unique culture of all the British colonies. Yet the elite at least embraced standards for behavior that transcended (and coexisted with) their particular (religious) culture. The available evidence suggests the Quaker elite were similar. At any rate, after 1750 the mid-Atlantic cities began to rival and then surpass Boston as printing and bookselling centers, and we can begin to read conduct literature for the story of manners in the entire Northeast.

As suggested by the common Latin roots of the words *city* and *civility*, manners are always an optic focused on urban culture. While America remained a predominantly rural society for much of its history, northeastern American towns and cities were where the relevant economic, political, and social changes behind manners happened first; and they were the locations that conduct writers had in mind. Foreign travelers often remarked on the huge difference between manners in eastern cities, with which they were favorably impressed, and those in the West, which they found appalling. Unfortunately, some of the more jaundiced among them downplayed eastern civility and emphasized western rudeness, resulting in a bias that tainted the entire nation. Conduct books, and the urban culture they described, did spread west. Easterners and westerners alike feared the barbarism of the latter region and took steps to combat it. Cincinnati town booster Daniel Drake accordingly took two books with him as he went west: the Bible and Lord Chesterfield, the Bible's equivalent in etiquette. The world refracted in this study, then, was the world of the cities, towns, and country lanes where the word of refinement had spread.[9]

Conduct literature also presents a changing focus on class. The available evidence allows us to look at all levels of society in seventeenth- and early-eighteenth-century New England; after the mid-eighteenth century, when the view widens to include all the northern colonies and states, it narrows in on the prosperous. After the second quarter of the nineteenth century, the lens focuses most clearly on the northern middle class in particular. In all periods, of course, the perspective is that of the prevailing "cultural elite." This does not mean that the conduct literature cannot tell us anything about "working-class" Americans. We learn much, for example, about changing attitudes toward and treatment of servants in the first half of American history. While such information does not come from the viewpoint of the underdog, it does tell us something about the world they confronted.

Anthropologists' studies of body language suggested a framework for the data provided by conduct literature. Within the matrix formed by examination of class, age, and gender relations, the plan roughly followed what might be called the progress of an encounter. First, I asked how much time and contact people of varying statuses were allowed with each other, and how time was to be used in their encounters. Then I examined the "proxemic" angle of interaction by looking at rules concerning the use of space and the physical placement of persons. Having established rules for the duration of an encounter and the proximity of persons within it, I asked about what might be called the components of "first impressions": the general demeanor or "air" of persons in an encounter, their posture and body carriage, and the management of their faces. After facial expression I considered gestures of salutation, those physical acts that serve to frame and punctuate encounters, and then moved from such nonverbal messages to conversation; here I examined general rules for propriety in subject matter, as well as rules on conversation leading, interruption, and language choice. The final stage of interpersonal interaction treated was physical contact. This category is broad, because rules on touching include acts as disparate as spanking and hand-holding. Yet this notion of "the encounter" helped to order and make sense of the huge body of prescriptions found in conduct literature.[10]

STUDYING MANNERS can do three things for the historian that study of other topics and sources cannot do. First, manners provide a unique opportunity to compare and contrast different kinds of relations in a systematic fashion. Not only does this shed light on the changing structure of American society; it also increases our understanding of the individual variables under consideration and thus contributes to specific debates on class, age, and gender relations in American history. Comparison is a useful antidote to the chief disease of social history: the fragmentation it has bred, which has led in some cases to serious distortions as historians examine one variable to the exclusion of others. One of the best examples of this concerns gender relations. Historians usually examine gender in isolation—indeed, they usually focus on either men or, most often, women. But examining the experience of women in isolation has led historians to make statements about the nature of gender relations that do not stand up to comparison with class and age relations. Specifically, comparing the rules for gender relations with those of age and class relations erodes support for historians' frequent proclamations of the primacy of gender inequality. Gender relations are unique, but not in the severity of inequality (age relations take that honor). They are unique because they are always crosscut by the intimacy (for most) of heterosexuality and the fixity (for most) of gender status. Paradoxically, this has meant that while gender inequality has in fact been one of the milder forms of inequality, it has required the most cultural work in some periods because of the permanence of sex difference (you cannot grow or earn your way out of your sex). When Americans embraced the cultural ideal of equality, it was gender inequality that required the most ritual obfuscation.

Second, manners offer a chance to read between the lines of cultural proclamations. The concrete advice for behavior sometimes amounted to a pattern at variance with cultural platitudes, and thus etiquette can help to clarify the operative social hierarchy or nature of power relations. A good example here concerns age relations. While support can be found for the time-honored and biblically sanctioned request to show deference to the aged, most such requests were superficial and the conduct advice points more to deference to the middle-aged. It was only in the pre–Civil War decades, when a new kind of deference had developed to ceremonially obscure the persisting weakness of women, that conduct writers had appropriate deference displays to recommend for use with the elderly. In this and other ways, manners caution historians to draw back from dramatic notions of the social construction of age relations. There was just not a lot of room for change in the treatment of the very young and the very old; here biology limits culture. The age group that saw the most change in status was youth.

The third and most important yield of a study of manners is an understanding of their crucial mediating role in American history—an understanding, in short, of how Americans have needed manners. From the beginning of European settlement, American society has been the site of conflict between cultural ideals and material realities. Social rituals have been necessary to conciliate the two. Here the best example is that of class relations. Seventeenth-century Puritans embraced an ideal of inequality and yet lived in relative social and material equality. Nineteenth-century Yankees cherished democracy and yet lived in a world of increasing economic inequality. These apparent paradoxes have caused historians to make contradictory statements about society in these periods. Some historians have argued that colonial society was essentially democratic, others that it was profoundly oligarchic. Some historians have celebrated the second quarter of the nineteenth century as the era of the common man, others as the age of the business class. The authors of conduct advice were not considering abstractions; they were giving Americans concrete advice on how to get along. But along the way they show historians the complex truth about their visions of society. The class story they illustrate is that of the rise of bourgeois culture in America, that peculiar product of the twin economic and political revolutions that made modern society. This is a familiar story. Where close attention to manners pays off is in showing how the rise of the middle class began earlier than has been supposed—with commercial capitalism, not industrial capitalism; with Enlightenment ideas, not their Republican progeny. More important, the study of manners shows the crucial role they have played in maintaining a class society among a people who did not (and still do not) want to admit it.

The role of manners, then, was and is to help Americans live with the contradictions of their culture. Social rituals did (and still do) this by quietly creating, communicating, and controlling status in the ways social scientists have described.[11] The history of manners can offer powerful suggestions as to how Americans bridged the gap in different situations. In so doing, it can also help to reconcile our own conflicting views of American history.

THE RHYTHMS OF THE conduct literature—in terms of its character, content, and authorship—and the changing functions of manners reveal three distinct periods in the history of manners in America before the mid-nineteenth century. The first, or "early colonial," period ran from the founding of the New England colonies in the early seventeenth century to the middle of the eighteenth century. Puritan New England was largely a face-to-face society, made up of intimate communities in which people of different rank, age, and gender mixed freely. Relative to later periods, there was less stratification of wealth, less institutional demarcation of age groups, and less gender polarity in terms of actual economic, political, religious, and familial roles; and yet the ideal of inequality was pervasive, and overtly expressed. The main function of social ritual in this society was to serve in tandem with the law and other institutions to enact and enforce a hierarchical social order. In early colonial New England, then, the social control function of manners was paramount.

The second, or "revolutionary," period in American manners ran from the middle of the eighteenth century to the third decade of the nineteenth. This period of great change in northern society required the creative function of manners. The old deferential model of behavior was challenged by the rise in status of the middle class, youth, and, to some degree, women; and the main function of manners instruction was to guide the behavior of these newly rising groups.

The third, or "antebellum," period in American manners ran from the second decade of the nineteenth century to the Civil War years. In this period, the communicative function of manners came to the fore. The major task of manners was to help northerners come to terms with the revolutionary era challenges to the old hierarchical social order, by offering rules to guide behavior in a supposedly democratic but actually increasingly unequal society. The resulting rules allowed Americans to deal with the contradiction, largely by espousing one set of values while nonverbally communicating another.

This study ends with the mid-nineteenth century. The story of manners in America did not itself end with the outbreak of the Civil War. The Civil War was a crucial watershed in that it altered the terms of some of the fundamental cultural questions with which Americans were wrestling, whether in their polity, their economy, or their social relations. It brought the end to slavery, the system at the root of southern distinctiveness, and it solidified and spread the nation's economic commitment to industrial capitalism. These changes gradually altered American society: strengthening national cohesion on the one hand, but accelerating class stratification on the other. These new social conditions, and new social problems, would require new ritual responses.

Yet the Civil War is not so much a natural ending point for the changes it would bring as it was for bringing an important chapter of American history to a close. Antebellum Americans grappled with a set of cultural problems that largely revolved around the contradictions of the liberal social order. They succeeded in working out solutions to those problems, or at least ways of living with them; that is what we see in their manners. Class, age, and gender relations would all evolve in certain ways after the Civil War, presenting new challenges for manners to address. But the fundamental work of antebellum manners, with its solutions to the basic class, age, and gender conundrums of a capitalist democracy, persisted. Much of it, for better or worse, is still evident today.

PART I

Hierarchy: Manners in a Vertical Social Order, 1620–1740

MANNERS FOR GENTLEMEN

Perhaps it was the prospect of the long and bumpy journey to New Hampshire that put Massachusetts Governor Joseph Dudley in a testy mood. There were six in his coach, plus their baggage, and one of the four horses was "very unruly." As it was early December, the road may have been covered with snow and ice. Of course it did not take much to irritate the man: Dudley was hot-tempered by nature. And about a mile down the road from Roxbury to Boston, two ordinary citizens provided a spark for his fire.

The governor looked out to see the two men approaching, both leading horse-drawn carts loaded with wood. They were farmers Thomas Trowbridge of Newton and John Winchester of Brookline. At Dudley's request his son William told the men that it was the governor in the coach and "they must give way." But here the stories of the two parties diverge. According to Dudley, the second carter came up to the first "and one of them says aloud, he would not goe out of the way for the Governour." Then Dudley himself stepped down from the coach, and ordered the men out of the way, whereupon "Winchester answered boldly . . . 'I am as good flesh and blood as you; I will not give way; you may goe out of the way,' and came towards the Governor." Dudley drew his sword "and again commanded them to give way," but Winchester again refused. The two men stepped up to each other. Winchester grabbed the governor, took his sword, and broke it.

The farmers told a different story. They insisted that the road split into two paths at the point where they met up with the governor, and they expected him to take the empty branch, as it was better than the one they occupied. Trowbridge explained that "when I came near where the paths met, I made a stop, thinking they would pass by me in the other path." When William Dudley told him to move out of the way, he replied that he "could not conveniently doe it, adding that it was easier for the coach to take the other path." Young Dudley drew his sword and threatened Trowbridge, who fended off the blows with a stick. Then Winchester approached from his own cart behind Trowbridge's. And his account differs markedly from the governor's.

> I asked Mr. Wm. Dudley why he was so rash; he replyed 'this dog wont turn out of the way for the Governour.' Then I passed to the Governour with my hat under my arm, . . . saying 'may it pleas your Exelency, it is very easie for you to take into this path, and not come upon us:' he answered 'Sirrah, you rouge or rascall, I will have that way.' I then told his Exelency if he would but have patience a minute or two, I would clear that way for him. I, turning about and seeing Trowbridge his horses twisting about, ran to stop them to prevent damage; the Governour followed me with his drawn sword, and said 'run the dogs through,' and with his naked sword stabed me in the back. I faceing about, he struck me on the head with his sword, giveing me there a bloody wound. I then expecting to be killed dead on the spot, to prevent his Exelency from such a bloody act . . . I catcht hold on his sword, and it broke; but yet continueing in his furious rage he struck me divers blows with the hilt and peice of the sword remaining . . . I told him twas very hard that we who were true subjects and had bene allways ready to serve him in any thing, should be so run upon; then his Exelency took up my cart whip and struck me divers blows . . .

The governor soon joined his son in bestowing the same on Trowbridge, and had the farmers taken to the gaol. Later in the day, Dudley met Superior Court Justice Samuel Sewall, and told him of the incident "in a great passion; [and] threaten'd to send those that affronted him to England." Sewall went to look at the scene and concluded that the governor's rage was unwarranted, for the place where the carts stood "was a difficult place to turn; and the Gov'r had a fair way to have gone by them if he had pleas'd."

What made Governor Dudley so angry? Why did he react the way he did? To be sure, he was a "passionate" man. But the particular form of his anger is part of a larger pattern. What this scene illustrates is that deference from inferiors was vitally important to the early Massachusetts elite. Giving way to allow superiors to pass was a key principle of manners in this period; so was doffing one's hat in their presence. In contrast to the farmers' account, the Dudleys averred that "during this talk with the carters, . . . nor did they once in the Govrs. hearing or sight pull of their hatts or say they would go out of the way, or any word to excuse the matter." Governor Dudley interpreted the farmers' reasonable request that he take one path as an insult; his affidavit referred to "the ingures offered mee upon the road," even though he was the only one dispensing tangible injuries. But the injury he perceived on the part of the farmers was no less real to him.

Contrary to Dudley's cries, these men were not lowly "dogs" but farmers from respectable families. And yet they did not challenge the idea that even this rather unpopular governor ought to be shown respect. Throughout his account of the governor's attacks, Winchester never failed to refer to him as "Exelency"; and he took care to tell the court that he approached the governor with his hat off. But these men were not willing to take deference to unreasonable lengths. This seemingly casual meeting in the road erupted because it sparked tensions at the center of this society. The sort of deference Dudley wanted was not guaranteed.[1]

From the earliest years of settlement to the mid-eighteenth century, those who were trying to rule New England society were continually fighting challenges to their authority. Their response to those challenges was constant too. They insisted on deferential treatment from their inferiors. When it wasn't forthcoming, they sometimes had difficulty controlling their anger.[2]

Puritan leaders were obsessed with deference because the world was changing in a way that threatened their authority. Society in seventeenth-century Anglo-America was caught in the transition between the medieval world of fixed social orders and the modern world of fluid social classes. Contemporary writers spoke of differences in "quality," "condition," and "station," because rank was still thought to be determined by birth as much as or more than by wealth. And yet the latter certainly mattered. Moreover, while New Englanders brought their understanding of society with them from the mother country, they did not bring all the requisite actors. The English families who embarked on the famous Puritan errand into the wilderness included few aristocrats or paupers. They were generally drawn from the middle band of society, from the lesser English gentry and yeoman stock. These circumstances prompted New Englanders, with their still-hierarchical world view, to develop their own stratification system. The small upper stratum or elite was composed of the ruling class of magistrates and ministers. They were almost all "university-trained gentlemen of good family" but not true aristocrats. After these were the "middling sort": the average farmers, traders, and artisans who had some stake in the community, although this group also included former indentured servants, farm laborers, journeymen, fishermen, and common seamen on its lower rungs. "The lower sort" were primarily indentured servants.[3]

Although the social structure of old England was itself changing rapidly with the growth of commerce, those on top were considerably more elevated by both birth and wealth than the New England elite. On the other hand, independent middling folks made up a smaller proportion of the English population, while those on the bottom were more numerous and more permanently fixed in their station. The deference to authority upon which hierarchical societies depend came easy under such conditions. But the early New England social structure lacked the requisite verticality. The small group of magistrates and ministers at the top of society were assuming power and status to which they had not been entitled in Old England. Moreover, the task of clearing land and building towns where there were none before was sufficiently large to prevent those at the top and bottom of society from having starkly different lifestyles for much of the first century of settlement.[4] And then there was the difficulty presented by the Puritan idea of the covenant, which meant that both church and polity had a contractual or voluntaristic foundation. Despite their initial claims of divine calling, the mundane realities were that ministers were chosen by their congregations and most magistrates were voted into office. Those in the middle or on the bottom of society might not have cared so much about the preservation of inequality in the face of these challenges, although the traditional system did offer all a comforting sense of place in a time of rapid change. But those who found themselves on top in New England had every interest in preserving a hierarchical system because notions of inequality were the basis for claims to power.

The New England elite were acutely conscious of the challenge that the reality of equality posed to their claims to power. This is why they were worried about deference from inferiors, for it was the crucial sign that the social fiction of hierarchy was still holding. The elite sought to fight the eroding effects of the new realities on the old ideas about society by supporting institutions that put the ideal of inequality into practice. In the long run, their efforts to maintain the hierarchy, whether against the challenge from the wilderness they entered or that of the rapidly changing civilization they had left behind, would prove futile.[5] But while engaged in the defense of the old order, manners were one of their chief weapons.

The elite used manners in two ways: they demanded deference from their inferiors and they tried to set themselves off from ordinary folk by adopting a special code of behavior.[6] They were doomed to frustration, however, because the second tactic undermined the first. By keeping much of the code of genteel behavior to themselves, they ensured that they never got as much polite treatment as they wanted from ordinary folk.

While extant evidence only allows us to trace this dilemma among early New Englanders, it is probable that similar frustrations were experienced by leaders in other colonies. While the Puritan colonies were unique in their mission and received fewer highborn Englishmen than some other areas, in no colony during the first generations were the ruling elite secure. Leaders everywhere clung to notions of hierarchy that were steadily battered by waves of opportunity in a new world. This should not surprise—the very claims to power of these men were in themselves signs of that opportunity, as most fell short of the qualifications for high status in the mother country. The southern elite floundered until a new generation caught on to the horrendous New World solution of securing status through chattel slavery; would-be rulers in the middle colonies hardly had a chance to defend the old order before it was swept away in their more diverse and later-established societies. Puritan magistrates and ministers were arguably in the best position to hold their own in the first century of settlement; at the least, their efforts leave the clearest picture of the struggle.

THERE WAS NOT a big difference between social ranks in terms of how early New Englanders learned to behave. Most children were instructed by their parents, masters, and ministers. But there was a big difference between the elite and the lower strata in terms of the emphasis on manners and the precise instructions to be mastered. That proper behavior was important to the New England elite is readily apparent in the few diaries they have left us. Indeed, while some historians have claimed that Puritans hated social ritual as much as religious ritual and objected to the bowing and scraping and kissing of the hand practised in court society, these diaries show that there was plenty of bowing and scraping and kissing of the hand going on in Boston. Interest in manners was perfectly compatible with the pervasive religiosity of this so-ciety, for even the most pious Puritans were social animals concerned (con-sciously or not) with status and its maintenance through symbolic gestures.[7] Unfortunately, the diaries only offer occasional glimpses of manners; the ac-tual components of proper behavior are more easily discovered in the one form of instruction that set the elite off from everyone else: that found in courtesy books.

Only the elite possessed the wealth, education, and leisure necessary to own and read such books. Indeed, book ownership in general distinguished the New England elite from the common folk. Most magistrates and all ministers had private libraries, which they continuously updated with new (and some not so new) works from England. A good number of courtesy books circulated in England at this time, and the most important titles began making their way to New England as early as the settlement of Plymouth colony in the 1620s. These books included translations of older Italian and French works that dis-cussed the attributes of gentility, their English imitations, and parent's-advice-to-a-child books (generally written by English noblemen for their sons). The Continental works found on New England bookshelves were Baldessar Castli-glione's *The Book of the Courtier*; Stefano Guazzo's *The Civile Conversation*; Giovanni Della Casa's *Galateo*; Pierre de la Primaudaye's *The French Academy*; and *Youth's Behaviour*, a work compiled by French Jesuits. The New England elite also owned copies of Richard Brathwait's *The English Gentleman* and *The English Gentlewoman*; Richard Allestree's *The Ladies Calling*; James I's advice to Prince Henry, *The Basilikon Doron*; and Francis Osborne's *Advice to a Son*. The authors of these works were all gentlemen. None were Puritans. What their li-brary inventories tell us, then, is that elite New Englanders were familiar with the Renaissance courtesy tradition. They were clearly concerned with teaching their children polite behavior; these are the works they would have consulted.[8]

It is doubtful that many persons below the elite received or looked for much social instruction directly from books. Despite the increasingly high lit-eracy rate of a society that revered the reading of Scripture, these folk had neither the means nor the time to read courtesy literature. Most households contained only a Bible and a few other religious books; only the rich owned "secular books." Moreover, the courtesy works were not generally intended for ordinary folk, and this society had a variety of mechanisms for reminding them of their place.[9]

Indeed, the reality of relative material equality did not keep the populace from acquiescing in elite-led efforts to erect and maintain institutions designed to preserve traditional inequality. The three key institutions were the family, the church, and the court; together they ensured that all New Englanders were imbued, from birth, with a sense of their station. In part these institutions achieved this task through manners instruction, as will be seen. But they also worked in other ways to buttress the social hierarchy and, indeed, to make manners instruction less necessary in this than in other periods. Seats in the meetinghouse, for example, were assigned according to social rank.[10] The local courts played a huge role in regulating both status and behavior, punishing citizens not only for outright contempt of authority but also for lesser breaches of decorum. Little escaped their notice.[11] In the 1680s, for example, a man did not have to learn from a courtesy book that it was improper to swear or to kiss a woman in the street. He knew that he could be flogged for these acts. Gentlemen were simply fined, another official acknowledgment of status.[12]

After 1651, gentlefolk were also spared presentment for infraction of sumptuary laws, as these, initially designed to discourage fancy dress for all, had evolved to accommodate this society's distaste for acting above one's station. As one contemporary observed, "one end of apparell is to distinguish and put a difference between persons according to their Places and conditions." In the Massachusetts sumptuary law of 1651, the General Court declared their

> utter detestation and dislike, that men and women of mean condition should take upon them the garb of gentlemen, by wearing Gold or Silver lace, or Buttons, or points at their knees, or to walk in great Boots, or Women of the same rank to wear Silk or Tiffany hoods, or scarfes, which, though allowable to persons of greater Estates, or more liberal Education, yet we cannot but judge it intollerable in persons of such like condition.

It was therefore ordered that such apparel could only be worn by persons whose estates amounted to 200 pounds or more, magistrates, public officials, or those with exceptional education. The law was not a dead letter as some historians have assumed; the court records show that individuals without sufficient estate were fined for "excess in clothing" in the ensuing years.[13]

These institutions enforced for contemporaries and reveal to us the visibly stratified nature of this society, despite a much lesser degree of wealth inequality than would prevail in later periods.[14] On one level, they help to explain why the humbler sort would not have aspired to or gotten away with trying to behave like gentlefolk. On another level, their existence suggests that one of the social functions of manners—that of communicating a person's place in a social group—may have been adequately performed for most people by the customs of church and court. Because these core institutions gave an explicit and consistent message about the ordering of society, ordinary people were presumably little concerned with gathering the sort of advice found in books on how to transmit and read these cues in their encounters.

While ordinary folk would not have read the courtesy literature aimed at gentlefolk, the magistrates and ministers who ruled New England still wished them to behave in a manner befitting their station. This is especially clear around the turn of the eighteenth century when Puritan ministers published a flood of tracts and sermons that discussed proper behavior. Indeed, this literature was the expression of an active ministerial campaign of social and moral reform.[15] And while many of its prohibitions were repeated and upheld by the courts, some of its more positive admonitions would be missed if we looked only to the conflict-ridden court records for a portrait of this society. These works included treatises on family relations or "household government," such as Benjamin Wadsworth's *The Well-Ordered Family*; works that addressed the general conduct of life or "whole duty" of a Christian; sermons aimed at specific age groups, such as Benjamin Colman's *The Duty and Honour of Aged Women*; and sermons, such as Cotton Mather's *The Rules of a Visit*, which discussed specific activities. These works were also owned and read (as most were written) by the Puritan elite, but their influence was not confined to the elite, for the teaching of the Puritan code of manners and morals to ordinary folk was one of the elite's primary functions. So these works can help us explore how the common folk of late seventeenth- and early-eighteenth-century New England learned to behave.

Doubtless, ordinary folk, as did the elite, received most of the relevant lessons when young, in the family, and, sometimes, the school. But it is also clear that the population at large got regular doses of conduct advice in Sunday sermons, as well as less formally at other times, from the local minister. The printed sermons of the major New England ministers thus give a glimpse at a largely oral mode of instruction. Further, the ministers who gave conduct advice in their sermons often distributed copies of those sermons during visits with their congregants. Cotton Mather claimed that he gave away around six hundred books a year during his weekly visits, and specifically noted giving away copies of three works that gave conduct advice. Even men who weren't ministers spread their sermons; Samuel Sewall gave away copies of Colman and Mather sermons that touched on manners. And members of Mather's congregation spread his *Rules of a Visit* even further. After asking him to publish it, they sent two copies to every town in New England, one to the local minister and the other with the inscription "to be lent."[16]

Sermons are an important source of conduct advice because of the place of religion in early New England culture. Church attendance was mandatory and ministers were regarded as social leaders. Recent studies have underscored the influence of the ministry as well as the high degree of popular piety and literacy. Although the devout reserved the right to make their own judgments, many listened to and read the ministers' works with a surprising intensity, some even taking notes. It was this willingness to consume their word that encouraged the top ministers to publish.[17]

Ministers advised their flocks on particulars of behavior in the process of driving home more general lessons of morality. They often went to the Bible to find appropriate rules for various situations. As Cotton Mather preached: "The most essential *Rules of Good Manners*, are to be found among the *Laws of our Lord* JESUS CHRIST." It was their examination of what exactly the Bible dictated as right behavior that led them to the admission, sometimes implied, sometimes direct, that the smaller points of manners were important, and possibly the very underpinnings of the social order they were trying to create. Mather went so far as to suggest that good manners were a religious duty: "'Tis very pleasing to our Lord Jesus Christ, that our Children should be well-formed with, and well-informed in the Rules of *Civility*; and not be left a *clownish*, and *sottish*, and *Ill bred* sort of Creatures. An Unmannerly brood is a Dishonour to *Religion*."[18] The sermons clearly show that the elite wanted to pass some lessons on to lesser folk.[19] Cotton Mather was as explicit about his audience as he was about the importance of manners when he claimed that "My Flock does generally consist of people that are in a middle Condition of Life; not very rich, not very poor: such as live Tolerably, yea comfortably."[20]

But if the Puritan elite thought it was important to teach some manners to ordinary folk, they did not think they had to teach everything the imported courtesy books dictated. In general, the ministers revealed their intentions when they discouraged the teaching of rituals other than those associated with deference to superiors. Wadsworth explained:

> A civil, respectful, courteous behaviour, is comely and commendable; and children should be taught such a carriage . . . those who won't put suitable marks of civil respect and honours on others, especially on superiours, or those in authority; don't imitate the commendable Examples of the Godly recorded in Scriptures. . . . But though you should teach your children to be mannerly, I Don't mean, that they should spend all or a great part of their time, in nicely, curiously, critically observing those various, changeable, ceremonious, punctilios of carriage, which some very foolishly affect: this would be time very sinfully spent.[21]

But here is where the ministers tripped themselves up. For while their manners lessons had some good effect, they did not accomplish all that they hoped for, and largely because of the limits that they themselves imposed on their task. Cast upon the rich soil of popular piety and a shared hierarchical world view, the ministerial injunctions did yield a certain level of decent behavior among the populace and a modicum of deference toward themselves. And of course the more egregious instances of misbehavior and disrespect were met with court sanctions. But the ministers failed to teach *enough* good manners to overcome the leveling tendencies of their society and generate the great degree of deference they wished for. By keeping the genteel code to themselves and limiting their sermonizing to demands for deference, they failed to teach the self-controls necessary for truly polite behavior. The leaders of early New England were in a manners double-bind.[22]

BOTH PURITAN TRACTS and courtesy books gave ample evidence of their authors' vertical notions of society. Many instructions were couched in terms of what was proper in the presence of inferiors and superiors. Della Casa insisted that "men of the *highest* and of *ordinary* quality" should not be treated with "the *same* modes and gestures," while Benjamin Wadsworth urged parents to teach their children "to be civil and respectful to all . . . according to their Rank and Station."[23] But the Puritan authors revealed their greater concern about deference when they gave the middling and lower sort even stricter advice than that found in courtesy books on the matter of proper behavior with superiors. That much of this advice was directed to children tells us that the Puritans wished to instill this deference early and that there was some overlap in this society between rank and age relations, an issue that will be explored further later. Sometimes Puritan works simply repeated instructions found in the courtesy works. Boston schoolmaster Eleazar Moody's *School of Good Manners,* for example, gave some of the same instructions found in *Youth's Behaviour* concerning the use of space in encounters with superiors. When walking with a superior, both works advised, "at the first give him the Right hand and stop not till he does and be not the first that turns . . . if he be a man of great Quality, walk not with him cheek by joul but somewhat behind him." Both works added that superiors were to be given the wall side of the street, and both told readers to stand back and leave space for superiors in a narrow place (as when meeting the governor on a narrow country lane). But Puritan injunctions went further than those of the courtesy works. Moody and the English Puritan Robert Cleaver gave children the blanket injunction to "Give always place to him that excelleth thee in Quality"; Moody also told children to sit "where your superiors order you."[24]

While Castiglione warned elite readers not to enter the presence of superiors without invitation, Moody told children to "Enter not into the company of Superiors without command." And Puritan writers wanted servants to respect their masters' complete control of their time. According to Wadsworth, servants who were "much for liberty, . . . to give or receive visits, of their own accord and when they will; liberty to keep what company they please; liberty to be out late on nights, to go and come almost when they will . . . are very wicked." Other evidence tells us both that servants were indeed "much for liberty," and that the elite enforced the rule. Samuel Sewall corrected his servant David "for his extravagant staying out, and for his playing when his Mistress sent him of Errands." Footloose inferiors were also admonished (or worse) by the courts.[25]

The Puritan writers were even more concerned with the demeanor of the lower sort in the presence of superiors. While elite readers might have encountered the passing references of Castiglione and Della Casa to the idea that superiors were to be greeted with reverence, the Puritan authors gave this point far more attention. They gave their flocks stricter advice by telling them to add submissiveness to their reverence. Here schoolmaster Moody suggested explicitly that behavior learned by middling children as appropriate toward a broadly defined body of superiors would fit them as adults in their relations with members of the ruling class:

Be humble, submissive, and obedient to those whose Authority by nature or providence have a just claim to your subjection. . . . Be always obsequious and respectful, never bold, insolent, or sawcy, either in words or Gestures. . . and at length . . . if you arrive at manhood . . . there will remain in your well managed minds no presumptuous folly that may prompt or tempt you to be other than faithful, obedient, and loyal subjects.

One author explained the general principle to readers of the lower sort: "In regard that these Degrees and Distinctions of men are, by God's Wise Providence, disposed for the better ordering of the world, there is such a *civil respect* due to those whom God hath dispensed them, . . . therefore, all inferiors are to . . . *order themselves lowly and reverently to all their betters*."[26] That respect was to be shown magistrates and ministers in particular was a point that few of the clerical conduct writers failed to make when addressing ordinary readers.[27] And in reminding servants that reverence and respect were to characterize their demeanor toward their masters and mistresses, the writers added that "all *Sullenness*, all *Sauciness*, all *Impudence* in your Deportments towards your *Masters* (or *Mistresses*) is to be abominated." Servants were to obey their masters' and mistresses' commands readily and cheerfully, and to bear their reproofs with meekness. Elizabeth Johnson found out the hard way that the elite was prepared to punish such infractions when she was whipped and fined in 1642 for, among other offenses, answering her mistress "rudely and unmannerly."[28]

Renaissance courtiers and Puritan ministers alike agreed that all men should bow and uncover when meeting or leaving superiors, "in sign of *honour* and *veneration,* and to shew their readiness to *listen to* (for by putting off the hat the *ears* are *uncover'd*) and *obey* the *commands* of their *superiors,* & *bow* the *body* in testimony of *submission.*"[29] Unlike the courtesy works, however, the Puritan advice for ordinary folk included a variety of other instructions for showing superiors respect through body carriage and facial expression. Puritan works told inferiors to stand up straight, to avoid looking superiors in the eye, and to refrain from sitting before commanded to.[30]

Similarly, while both courtesy authors and Puritan writers told readers of all ranks to wait for superiors to initiate conversation, to avoid talking too much in their presence, to address them by reverent titles, and to refrain from interrupting or contradicting them, Puritan writers took special pains to warn servants against saucy back talk to their masters.[31] Moreover, servants were "not to discover the concerns of that Family wherein you live; for every mans House is his Castle, and should be as His Cabinet, where nothing should be divulg'd but by his Permission." Much less was a servant to tell "false tales and stories" concerning his master's family, for they might thus "hurt their Masters and Mistresses in their credit, Reputation, and Business." More generally, inferiors were not to discuss matters that were "above" them.[32] Once again, the tone and content of the Puritan elite's instructions to the middling and lower sort (and especially to servants) suggest that they wanted ordinary folk to show them even greater deference than that suggested in the courtesy books.

OR SO THEY HOPED. But the glimpses of actual encounters between elite and ordinary New Englanders with which we began suggest that while the common folk could be counted on to show some deference, they did not always go as far as desired. And so a second function of manners in this society was to bolster elite claims to superiority by communicating their special status and setting themselves off as a superior class. This desire to set themselves off may have been especially acute in this culture where the elite otherwise shared so much with ordinary folk.[33] The elite tried to do it with their bodies, by maintaining the courtesy-book code of behavior among themselves and choosing not to pass on most of its injunctions in their advice to ordinary folk.

There was general agreement among the elite that ministers in particular should have good manners. In a manual for ministers, Cotton Mather recommended "those Ingenuous and Mollifying Arts, which may distinguish you from the Uncultivated Part of Mankind." Mather claimed that ministers ought to pursue civility in order to "Ingratiate" themselves with others so as to better "prosecute Good Purposes" among them. But there were other reasons why ministers needed good manners. Many shared with other members of the elite the insecurities of high status unsupported by high birth. They also suffered a special dilemma in that the high social status that they had attained in the "New World" jeopardized their role as "otherworldly" humble servants of their flocks. Genteel behavior afforded them a nonverbal way of proclaiming their status while leaving them free to make meek speeches. In fact, given the theme of self-mastery that runs through the courtesy literature, the genteel code allowed the ministers to proclaim both their status and their affability through their behavior; for according to the code, to be genteel was to be gentle. The need to appear meek grew even stronger for the high status "second generation" of ministers in the late seventeenth century, who mounted a conscious campaign of "imagebuilding."[34] The public behavior of members of the Puritan elite was an important matter, and if a member failed to uphold the standards, he was swiftly and sternly reminded.

Again we can see these principles at work in Judge Sewall's diary. One afternoon in late November 1710, Sewall was joined at home by two dinner guests: John Leverett, President of Harvard College, and Ebenezer Pemberton, Sewall's pastor. The latter, suffering from a particularly acute case of "Puritan elite touchiness," was very quick to perceive slights. Sewall had just fined two men for libeling Pemberton's fellow ministers, Increase and Cotton Mather. Although Pemberton was not friendly with the Mathers, Sewall thought he would be pleased at this defense of his brethren. But Pemberton was piqued at what he regarded as Sewall's partiality toward the Mathers, for when Sewall "began to relate what had been done, Mr. Pemberton with extraordinary Vehemency said, (capering with his feet) If the Mathers order'd it, I would shoot him thorow." Sewall was surprised and disturbed by the fact that Pemberton was literally hopping mad. Sewall, in fact, upbraided him for his carriage: "I told him he was in a passion. He said he was not in a passion." Sewall reminded Pemberton that he was not behaving in accordance with his status: "I said his Carriage was neither becoming a Scholar nor Minister."

Later, the men walked together to a meeting of the Governor's Council, and Sewall's pain only grew as Pemberton, a fellow gentleman, allowed his lack of control to be witnessed in public: "Mr. Sergeant came into our Company. The President walked on his right hand to the Council-Chamber [note the deference here]; I and Mr. Pemberton went next. In the Way Mr. Pemberton charg'd me again, I was grieved and said, What in the Street! He answer'd, No body hears. But Mr. Sergeant heard so much, that he turn'd back to still us."[35] Thus both Sewall and Sergeant prompted Pemberton to watch his behavior. Their concern was shared by even the earliest Massachusetts leaders, who made conscious efforts to appear dignified before their subjects. In 1636, for example, they agreed not to fight before the people. Indeed, they resolved that "magistrates shall appear more solemnly in public, with attendance, apparel, and open notice of their entrance into the court."[36]

From the beginning, then, the Puritan elite felt that they had certain standards to maintain in their behavior with each other and in public. This is probably why they acquired the courtesy works found in their libraries, for these works cataloged the manners we occasionally witness in their diaries. The period's most elaborate advice concerning behavior in general society or with social peers is found in these works. But the elite only gave some of this advice to the middling sort; and Eleazar Moody, who gave the most, always gave a simpler version. The ministers gave even less of this advice to the lower sort. In other words, the elite wanted to secure deference from their inferiors, but when it came to proper behavior between the common folk, they lost interest.

That the elite were only interested in securing their own social exclusivity is evident in their handling of advice on choice of company. Courtesy works urged gentlefolk to seek the company of their social peers. One author recommended "an equality both in degree and condition" "in our *choice* of *Acquaintance*." While the Puritan elite urged all youth to avoid bad company, they assessed company in terms of behavior and not social status. The courtesy code and the Sewall anecdote above suggest that there was a proto–class consciousness among the elite. The extensive intermarriage among elite families is further evidence of such a group consciousness.[37]

We can ask how monopoly of other rules of the courtesy-book code helped to distinguish the elite from the common sort. The answer lies in the common theme running through courtesy injunctions, namely, self-control. In adopting the courtesy code for themselves, the elite would attempt to exert mastery over their demeanor, body carriage, facial expressions, and talk before others, and to a far greater extent than they would encourage in ordinary folk.[38]

The difference was evident, first, in advice on the use of space in encounters with peers. Most writers suggested that it was good manners to give place to peers "at Play or a fire," to "the last commer," or in one's house. But here, as elsewhere, the most elaborate advice was found in the courtesy works. The authors of *Youth's Behaviour* added that a gentleman was not to regard such treatment as his due, but "ought at the first to refuse it but at the second to accept it though not without acknowledging his own unworthiness." Further on, the authors advised: "Set not yourself at the upper end of the Table but if it be your Due or that the Master of the house will have it so, contend not, lest you should trouble the company."[39] That the New England elite had a finely tuned sense of proper placement in encounters is revealed by the fact that nearly every table described in their diaries had an upper and lower end. Samuel Sewall often recorded who was honored by a seat at the upper end of the table at dinner parties and meetings of the governor's council. Offenders brought before the General Court stood at the lower end of the council table. And when the Indian sachem Miantunnomoh objected to being seated with other Indians at a dinner with the General Court, the gracious Puritans responded by seating him at the lower end of the magistrates' table. There is no better indication of their contempt.[40]

The courtesy writers advised gentlefolk to avoid coming too near or looking over the shoulder of another who was reading or writing, unless requested to do so. They were warned above all not to "approach too near him to whom you talk." While Moody gave these instructions in his schoolbook, the courtesy writers gave a more extended discussion. The authors of Youth's Behaviour added that if one observed the proper distance one would "bedew no man's face with your spittle"; they also warned readers to "lean not upon anyone." Della Casa was more concerned about offending others with one's breath.[41]

Both courtesy book authors and Puritan writers recommended an affable and courteous demeanor with equals, and a middle course between formality and familiarity. But here too the courtesy works gave elite readers the most elaborate advice. Della Casa told gentlemen to "Be not loose in your deportment, nor yet severe, neither all honey,' nor all gall' but let affability and gravity be sweetly temper'd and mixt together." One was to act "with an open and unrestrained familiarity," in the presence of peers, as if they "belonged to the same house." And one was especially to avoid having a sullen or melancholy mien before others. To the degree that any trait was emphasized in advice to the middling sort, it was that one was simply to be courteous to others.[42]

The courtesy works contained relatively complex instructions on genteel body carriage. The goal was gracefulness, but this was only thought possible through self-control. While grace in carriage was supposed to appear natural, the discussions of proper posture and movement suggest that the authors realized that such grace did not always come naturally. Castiglione had advised that the ideal courtier "practice in all things a certain sprezzatura [nonchalance], so as to conceal all art and make whatever is done or said appear to be without effort and almost without any thought about it."[43] A man's walk, it was claimed, was an index of his character, a belief reflected in one author's counsel against strutting: "I have seene even in this one motion, the Gate, such especial arguments of a proud heart, as if the body had beene transparent, it could not have represented him more fully." Gentlefolk were to walk with a controlled gravity. Della Casa gave a particularly full description of what gentlemen were to avoid, although its essentials are found elsewhere:

It is not *comely* to *run* along the *streets*, or to make so much haste that you *pant*, and *blow*, and *sweat*, for that belongs to a *foot-man*, not to *Gentile* persons; Neither let your pace be *slow* like a snail's, nor *lofty* and *affected*, nor *soft* and *effeminate*, but *compos'd* and *modest*. 'Tis *unseemly* to *hobble* as you walk, and to *fling* out your legs, and to *stretch* yourself by *wide* steps, to *hang down* your hands, or to *throw* them *about*, as if you were *sowing corn*.[44]

Courtesy writers considered control of the body as important in sitting and standing as in walking. In their pages gentlefolk were advised to stand upright and not lean on others. They were to refrain from crossing their legs or stooping when sitting. They were to avoid showing disrespect for peers through their posture: they were not to sit when others stood, to turn their backs on others, to "sit *musing* in a dull posture with folded arms," or to shrug their shoulders when others spoke. Of course, in real life, one could manipulate these gestures. Sewall noted occasions when members of his class intentionally slighted others by turning their backs.[45]

Courtesy authors warned against all varieties of fidgeting, such as twisting in one's seat, drumming one's fingers on the table, rubbing one's hands, shaking one's limbs, or pulling one's beard, "for by such *odde ridiculous* gestures we demonstrate, that we have but a small stocke of discretion, and common civility, and that we respect nobody near us." Several writers counseled gentlemen to avoid scratching or handling any part of their bodies "not ordinarily discovered, as are the hands and face." Only Moody gave middling children similar advice concerning body carriage in the presence of equals, and his rules were always less elaborate and demanding than those in the courtesy books.[46] While the elite were advised to control their bodies so as to achieve grace, Moody only counseled the middling sort to control their bodies so as to avoid awkwardness.

Puritan writers did share with ordinary folk the counsels they read in courtesy works against both excessive mirth and severity in facial expression.[47] But they only gave the simplest and most abstract injunctions to this effect and did not pass on the concrete and specific advice of the courtesy works. According to the latter, in addition to keeping their faces pleasant and free of frowns, gentlefolk were to avoid facial contortion of any sort. Two authors thus instructed gentlemen to avoid making "*scurvy* faces," as by puffing up their cheeks, sticking out their tongues, biting their lips, or squinting. In addition, they were to "rowl not the eyes, lift not one eyebrow higher than the other, [and] wry not the mouth." Courtesy works also reminded readers to control their gaze, and neither stare too intently at a person with whom they were speaking nor look at the ground. Moody simply told his scholars not to stare.[48]

Courtesy books and Puritan works both recommended that equals be greeted with gestures of salutation, but only the former gave any details. The general thrust was that with peers one's gestures could be friendly and simple. *Youth's Behaviour* suggested that gentlemen did not have to uncover upon

meeting peers, as "to pull off the Hat when there is no need is affectation."
Della Casa claimed:

> The *English* . . . *embrace* one another in token of *union* and *friendship*;
> and *shake hands* to intimate a *league* and *contract* . . . [of] *mutual de-*
> *fence*; and *clap* one another upon the *shoulder* . . . in token of *familar*
> *acquaintance:* and *kiss the lips* . . . an *expression* of *amitie* and *dearness*,
> . . . and *kiss* the hand . . . in signification of *sacred reverence*.

Scattered diary entries suggest that the Puritan elite fit this description. Sewall recorded handshakes with peers, although the bow and hand-kiss, gestures usually reserved for superiors, were sometimes used to signal special
respect.[49]

Puritan writers and courtesy authors warned all classes against talking too
much. Indeed, the lower sort were frequently reminded that "Government of
the tongue" was important, for it was "an unruly member, it oft breaketh
loose, not withstanding God hath shut it up between two doors." Courtesy
works also urged gentle readers, on the other hand, to avoid being *too* silent,
"for when men are obliged to speak by turns, 'tis just as if one should refuse to
pay his shot at an ordinary."[50] The Puritan elite also did not hesitate to share
injunctions against interrupting, contradicting, or verbally injuring others,
engaging in flattery or boasting, or using obscene or profane language. This
conforms with other scholars' observations that the Puritans were concerned
about disorderly speech. But again it was the courtesy works that gave the
most extended discussion of these rules. In light of Sewall's reaction to
Ebenezer Pemberton's outburst, for example, one is not surprised to find that
it was the courtesy authors who most often urged readers not to give rein to
"passion," in addition to the general warning against arguing with others. The
Sewall example is echoed in other sources. Again and again, we find members
of the elite struggling for self-mastery.[51]

Indeed, Della Casa and *Youth's Behaviour* gave elaborate advice that
essentially directed gentlefolk to exert control over every sound they made.
All "rude" noises, even breathing too loudly, were to be avoided. Coughing,
sneezing, passing wind, sighing, and yawning were all offensive for the noises
that they made, although the last two might also offend by suggesting one was
weary with the company. If unavoidable, these were to be done quietly and
aside. One was also not to hum, sing, whisper, or whistle before others.
Moody gave much of this advice to his scholars, but in simpler form.[52] Courtesy works further advised gentlefolk not to speak too fast or too slowly,
but deliberately. One was to strive for a mean between sharpness and flat-
ness of voice, and to avoid extremes of loudness and softness (Moody repeated only the last point). In one writer's words: "'Tis *uncomely* to *lift up*
your voice so *high* as if you were making a *proclamation*, or to depress it to
so *low a softness* that you cannot be heard by *attentive listening*. And when
you are desir'd to speak something *lowder*, you must not *bawl*, lest it be imagined that you are *incens'd*, and intend to clamor for a *revenge*." Setting the
right tone was important; a gentleman's speech was to be neither "careless"

nor "affected." Moody just advised his charges to speak clearly and to avoid stammering.[53]

Courtesy works included additional suggestions concerning the manner and matter of conversation with peers. Gentlefolk were to suit their talk to the occasion. One was generally to be affable, but "if a man discourse of grave Matters he must adde a certain severitie." One was not to speak of sad things at a time of mirth or be gay when one's companions were in pain. One was to talk business or to reprehend a friend only at appropriate times.[54] Gentlefolk were to be especially circumspect in the matter of jesting and joking, carefully avoiding such "where none take pleasure in mirth." They were in any case to avoid laughing too much or too loudly, and were never to laugh at their own jokes. Moody gave only the last advice.[55]

While the Puritan elite wanted the deference of their inferiors, they did not do everything they could to teach them good manners, for good manners were a sign of elite status. Yet because good manners largely meant self-control, in holding back on manners they ensured that their inferiors lacked the self-control to offer anything more than a deference that was narrow, superficial, and rough. Ironically, the Puritan elite were more successful in securing the submission of servants to ordinary masters, for here they equipped masters with something more than awe-inspiring behavior: the power to compel. Self-mastering servants were not necessary.

INDEED, WHEN IT CAME to discussing proper behavior with inferiors, Puritan tracts intended for ordinary folk gave more extensive instructions than the courtesy works, and most of this advice concerned the maintenance of authority over servants. The Puritan injunctions indicate that this was a matter of special concern in early New England. It may have been another instance of manners being called into play to try to enforce inequality in a society of relatively equal circumstance. The task was large, as Puritan writers were teaching those whom they had taught since birth to defer to their betters how to exercise superiority themselves. Their instructions seem to have been effective, however, for while the court records reveal occasional instances of cruel masters and disobedient servants, recent studies conclude that for the most part master-servant relations were satisfactory.[56]

The Puritan writers began by advising ordinary folk to be active in supervising their servants; they urged masters to keep servants busy and under a "diligent eye." They were not to be too intimate, however, for ill consequences followed when "masters suffer their servants to be their companions, playing, drinking, and reveling with them." Servants would naturally take liberties with such a master or mistress.[57] Courtesy writers and Puritan authors alike warned against both an overly familiar and an overly severe demeanor with servants; only the courtesy writers stressed the need to avoid a harsh manner, while Puritan authors emphasized the need for an air of authority, to inspire a servant's "feare" and "reverence." Familiarity, they warned, "many times breedeth contempt."[58]

In contrast, in their advice on body carriage and facial expression, the courtesy books suggested that the elite were allowed a certain familiarity with servants. As one author explained:

> 'Tis therefore a great error for persons of Honor, to think they acquire a Reverence by putting on a Supercilious gravity, looking oily and disdainfully upon all about them: 'tis so far from that, that it gives a suspicion that 'tis but a pageantry of greatness, som mushrome newly sprung up, that stands so stiff and swells so much . . . On the other side, . . . a kind look or word from a Superior, is strangely charming . . . a friendly salutation is as easie as a frown or reproach.[59]

The courtesy works also advised that one could properly relax somewhat before inferiors. While it was impolite for gentlemen to relax their posture or lie down before an equal or a superior, one author argued, "If a *great* person do such a thing before his *domestick* servant, or an *acquaintance* of *meaner* rank, 'tis not to be interpreted as a token and instance of a *proud* and *insolent* humour; but rather of *familiarity* and *condescension*."[60]

Puritan writers for the common folk, always less concerned about body control and facial expression than the courtesy writers, were more inclined to pursue control of inferiors through rules for conversation. Here too they cautioned against undue familiarity with servants. While masters were to command gently and give praise when due, they were not to be sheepish in commanding, much less to gossip or talk idly with or tell secrets to their servants. They were encouraged to correct their servants, though without anger and harshness.[61] And if a servant was "so foolhardy, high, and stout as not to be mended by Words," then they had to resort to harsher means of correction, namely, a whipping. Courtesy works, in contrast, claimed that it "behoveth wise Maisters to forbeare beating their servants."

That the Puritan elite was ready to suggest corporal punishment if servants did not behave suggests powerfully why they were more successful in securing the obedience of servants than they were in securing the deference of the citizenry. And they clearly meant business. While masters were not to resort to this punishment too often, and were never to administer blows when in a rage or passion, the authors implied that it was proper for masters to strike servants with some vigor. The only limits they placed on this act were that it "must be so moderated with Humanity, that he may not be thereby Killed or Maimed." Local court records show the common folk maintaining these injunctions. When one woman was presented for striking another couple's maidservant, for example, the couple told the court that she was taking their place while they were away and was thus fully empowered to do so, especially since the lass was a bad one.[62] That the servant in question was a "lass" provides a final clue to the greater success in subordinating servants than the populace at large: in early New England, servants were young. As will be seen in the next chapter, service was as much a matter of age as of class.

COMPARING THE COURTESY works on their bookshelves with their sermons to ordinary folk reveals the aspirations of the Puritan elite. The ministers encouraged ordinary New Englanders to show deference to superiors and authority over inferiors. Along with other members of the Puritan elite, they observed a special courtesy-book code of behavior among themselves, in order to set themselves apart and further ensure the deference of the commons. But they did not attempt to instill this code among their flocks. Thus there was a gap in this period between manners for the elite and manners for everyone else. In general, it appears that it was more important for members of the upper stratum to exert self-mastery than it was for the middling and lower sort to do so, because in a vertical social order the elite had the most to gain by the proclamation of their status in this way.

Their interest was probably the reflection of a powerful dilemma: not only were the New England magistrates and ministers aspiring to a status they would not have been able to claim in the mother country, but economic realities in New England threatened to flatten their hierarchical cosmology. Their insecurity probably fueled their efforts to demand deference and to shore up the hierarchy through various means, including, along with other measures, dispensing conduct advice to their inferiors. But they undercut their own efforts to secure the good behavior of the commons by withholding the self-control instructions the latter needed to become truly polite. This is one reason why they had to fall back on the external sanctions of the local court. It is understandable that the elite maintained their exclusive hold on courtesy; perhaps it provided a psychological comfort when insufficiently obsequious farmers were met on country lanes.[63] And while exclusivity undermined a well-mannered populace, at least it served to set the elite off from those below. Their late colonial successors would enjoy no such distinction, for the connection between manners and elite power would crumble along with the hierarchical world view. Before turning to that story, however, the early New English equation of manners with a vision—or dream—of a deferential society can be further illustrated with the acknowledgment that most of the advice to the elite was intended for middle-aged men.

MANNERS OVER MINORS

It would be Samuel Sewall's last visit to his father, for Henry Sewall, at eighty-six, was failing fast. On this May evening, Samuel brought his friend Wait Winthrop along. The two visitors shared social status as well as friendship. Both had attained high positions in middle age (Sewall was forty-eight): they were colleagues on the Massachusetts Superior Court bench and the Governor's Council. Henry Sewall must have been proud of his son. The visitors arrived "a little before sunset," and found the old man in bed. Samuel entered and called Winthrop into the room. Henry greeted them by taking and kissing Winthrop's hand, and then his son's. Winthrop did not return the gesture of deference. Samuel did. The next day, when Samuel entered the room to pray with his father, the latter attempted to rise from his chair. But "I persuaded him to sit still," Samuel recorded in his diary. Henry Sewall died the following day.[1]

Like the incident between Governor Dudley and the carters, this glimpse at the elder and younger Sewalls shows us early New Englanders exchanging gestures that symbolized their respective statuses and gives us clues about their vision of the social order. This scene reveals that the hierarchies of age and social rank were intertwined in this society in such a way as to shape notions of proper behavior in an encounter between middle-aged and aged men. It suggests the place in this society of deference to age.

Social rank, then, was just one of the axes of social relations regulated by manners in early America; another, and one more familiar to the twentieth-century reader, was age. At first glance, age relations might seem less subject to social construction than rank relations because inequality seems inherent in relations between the young and the mature. Yet historians have argued in a variety of ways that early Americans had a different way of construing age relations. They have offered such terms as "miniature adulthood," to describe a relative nonrecognition of the stages of childhood and youth, and "gerontocracy," to describe an extraordinary reverence of old age. The rules for behavior spelled out by the leaders of this society call for a drawing back from these exotic images of age relations. Despite some historians' suggestions to the contrary, the conduct literature reveals that the Puritans' conceptions of the stages of life were not very different from our own. Accordingly, in the following pages the age terms are those that were and are used in both periods: that is, "children," to mean young persons between infancy and puberty (the conduct writers did not generally give rules concerning infants; by "children" they generally meant those past the toddler stage who could walk, read, and go to school); "youth," to mean young persons from their mid-teens to early twenties; "adults," to mean fully mature persons beyond their early twenties; and "the aged," for those over age sixty.[2] The rules for behavior also suggest that then, as now, those who were weak in body (whether from immaturity or decrepitude) were deemed weak in society; and the strong wanted to make that clear.

Puritan conduct works show that their elite authors regarded inequality between age groups as the central framework of the social order, but they also indicate the limits of age inequality. The blueprint delineated by their behavioral code reveals that age inequality did not extend to three levels (the aged over adults over the young), as some historians have supposed; the aged were not automatically of higher status than the middle-aged. Rather, age inequality operated in two tiers, wherein all adults were deemed superior to minors. Two forces shaped this design. One was the effort of the elite middle-aged teachers of the code of behavior to use it to buttress their power (the average age of the Puritan authors was forty-one). They may have wanted to do this because the leveling effects of settlement raised the specter of challenge to their authority on the part of their younger as well as their less privileged subjects. Traditional strains between generations were only heightened in this land-rich, labor-poor, and extremely youthful society.[3] The other force shaping the Puritan system of age relations was that age inequality, like class and gender inequality, was set in a particular overarching social model: early New Englanders built their hierarchy on the model of the nuclear family.[4] Such a model meant patriarchy but not gerontocracy. And the evidence suggests that Puritan efforts to maintain this hierarchy were largely successful.

CHILDREN IN EVERY AGE are exhorted to "mind their manners," and, in this, early New Englanders were no exception. The very pains that the Puritans took to teach their children indicates that they recognized childhood as a separate stage of development; they also recognized youth as a distinct stage by directing special advice to them. The colonists had carefully transplanted the basic English educational triad of family, church, and school in order to teach the young piety and occupational skills, to be sure, but also civility. Most instruction was oral, but the lessons of all three "schools" can be traced in the works of this society's main agents of cultural transmission, the Puritan ministers.[5]

Most manners lessons occurred in the household, the family serving as "a little commonwealth," or model for the larger society.[6] As Cotton Mather declared, "*Well-Ordered Families* naturally produce a *Good Order* in other *Societies*; When *Families* are under an *Ill Discipline*, all other *Societies* being therefore *Ill Disciplined*, will feel that error. . . ." Robert Cleaver agreed: "For if nourture be neglected, then our elders and governours shall not be reverenced: if they bee not reverenced, they will not bee regarded: if they will not bee regarded, they will not be obeyed: and if they bee not obeyed, then steps in rebellion, and everyone will doo what he listeth."[7] These quotes reflect the ministerial mission examined in chapter 1. As regarded ordinary folk, their chief goal was to cultivate deference. The ministers apparently thought that if children learned to defer to their parents, they would be more likely to behave appropriately when grown and crossing paths with a Winthrop, Mather, or Sewall. This is why they focused their efforts on the young and on the regulation of relations between minors and adults, and generally kept the elaborate adult and peer-oriented advice of the courtesy works to themselves.

How can we learn about education that took place within the bosom of the family? To some degree manners training must have occurred without conscious instruction, as children simply observed and imitated the acts of the adults around them. The socialization process was casual and gradual in this society where persons of different age and rank mixed frequently and the household was the center of both social and productive activity. The Puritan divines occasionally noted this themselves when they told parents that teaching their children how to behave properly through their own good example was the most effective means.[8]

The sermonizers were not content with telling parents to set a good example, however, for they constantly reminded parents of their duty to instruct their children directly in manners. Cleaver exclaimed, "What a shame is this for any man to take great care to have his dogge well taught, his horse well broken, his land well husbanded, his house goodly trimmed and richly furnished; and yet to have his childe shamefully rude in manners. . . . Parents must teach their children good manners. . . ." In their sermons the ministers described exactly what parents were to teach. They urged parents to begin early: "'tis the best course to begin *betimes*, and instill precepts of *virtue* and good *manners* into them in their *tender* years, before *vice*, and *folly*, and *evil* customes have taken *firm possession* of their minds." We know from their diaries and letters that elite parents attempted to put these principles into practice; it is likely that "the godly and virtuous" among the common sort tried to do the same. Then as now, the dinner hour was useful. Cotton Mather resolved, for example, that at his table "the Rules of Behaviour [would be] nicely given and used." Mather and his fellow ministers also addressed children directly in their weekly sermons, and they enlisted the aid of other adults. As one writer declared, "School-Masters and all such as have the charge of trayning up young children, must be an helpe to parents in teaching children good manners."[9]

Beyond the training received at home and at meeting, then, some boys and a few girls received further lessons in manners from schools. Most children were taught to read at home, by their mothers, or in Dame schools; but at age seven or eight some boys, particularly those from moderately prosperous households, went to school. However the lessons of school masters, who frequently used teaching as a temporary way station between college and the pulpit, did not likely differ from those of the ministers.[10] The elite and the few middling students in the New England colonies who learned enough Latin would presumably have imbibed the manners and morals teachings of the classical authors and Erasmus that their English peers were reading and that their eighteenth-century successors would read, but we do not know enough about seventeenth-century New England school curricula to confirm this. One scholar's claim that the English grammar schools used treatises specifically devoted to manners is confirmed for New England toward the beginning of the eighteenth century by the importation and American printing of some of these works.[11]

The training of youth in proper social behavior was also performed primarily by family, church, and school (although only a few young men went on to college). In addition to the instruction of their natural parents, many young men and women received instruction in a family setting as servants, from masters and mistresses who acted as surrogate parents under the "putting out" or apprenticeship system. Like the Medieval training of young noblemen in other noble households, of which this practice was at least functionally a vestige, this system served to instruct the young person in social behavior as in work skills away from the bosom of the nuclear family. Ministers confirmed the socializing function in their treatises on family government, where they often included these nonrelated young people of the household in their reminders to parents of their duty to train the young in manners and morals.[12] The ministers also addressed youth directly in their sermons and treatises, and their advice was shaped and supplemented by some imported English Puritan works. Those youth who attended school were further exposed to conduct literature according to their social rank (and sex). Ordinary youth would probably not have read more than the schoolbooks on manners mentioned above, if they got that far. Elite youth would have begun to read the courtesy works addressed to their class.

Manners instruction for adults also varied according to rank. The courtesy works mostly described ideal adult behavior, but whether one read such works in one's late teens or as an adult probably depended most on whether one was born to gentility or attained it after receiving an exceptional education. For the middling and lower sort, who would not usually learn the rules of behavior through literature, sermons on "Man's Whole Duty" often described proper adult behavior—as did those on family relations, especially when discussing the proper behavior of husbands, wives, and parents. Some ministers also offered advice to the aged.

HISTORIANS HAVE LONG AGREED that the elite of magistrates and ministers held power in this society, but they have debated the status of the aged. While some have argued that old age was so exalted as to amount to "gerontocratia," others have suggested that there was considerable ambivalence about old age.[13] These scholars have used a wide variety of evidence to support their arguments, from sermons, to fashion, to law, to demographic reconstructions; but they have not systematically examined how the rules for face-to-face interaction weigh in. What can those rules contribute to our understanding of the tableau of Henry and Samuel Sewall? In fact the code of behavior supports and strengthens the arguments of historians who contend that early New Englanders had mixed feelings about the aged. Indeed, while even these scholars allow that the "normative code of colonial New England was decidedly favorable to old age," the conduct evidence—surely part of the "normative code"—suggests that there too the picture was mixed.[14]

At first glance, the conduct advice appears to support the "gerontocratia" thesis, for the sources were unanimous in instructing all age groups to adopt a reverential demeanor and physical bearing in the presence of the aged. All were to follow the biblical injunction in Leviticus: "Thou shalt rise up before the hoary head, and honour the face of the old man." The authors took this command literally and advised their readers to stand up and bow at the approach of an aged person. They also used this biblical passage to support their argument that old people were to be treated and spoken to with reverence. Young persons were to show respect even if the aged person in question was poor and "decrepit." Adults had opportunities to behave correctly with the elderly when interacting with their parents, for the writers agreed that maturity did not lessen a person's obligation to reverence his parents. Adults were to honor their elderly parents, *at least in private*, even if they, the children, surpassed their parents in wealth or office. As one minister wrote, "Be we *grown up and grown Great*, yet we are never *too big to rise up* and *bow down* to our Parents."[15]

Beyond this, however, the advice was mixed. First, the authors often asked for much less than veneration, while revealing a belief in the actual weakness of old age. They did this when they frequently coupled their general admonition to reverence the aged with more concrete and negative instructions not to slight old people. Eight different authors specifically urged their readers not to despise, contemn, or use unmannerly speech or behavior toward the aged. Some of the authors' condemnations of such behavior disclosed their recognition that while the aged ought to be venerated, in reality they often were not. One minister complained: "Are there not some now-a-days; who put a slight upon the persons of the Aged, that is, who not only refuse to pay them a due Respect, but do even actually discover contempt, by laughing them to scorn, and seeking to move others to do so too!" Increase Mather offered cold comfort to the elderly on this issue: "[T]he Aged Servants of the Lord . . . sometimes think themselves more despised than they are; that's a Natural Infirmity of Age: but suppose they are so, if God does not despise them, it is no matter tho' the World does." Despite the writers' commands that all were to honor the aged, one wonders how much respect they actually expected their readers to render.[16]

Some authors furthered the impression that old people could not always expect veneration when they implied that the aged needed to earn or inspire others' reverence through their own proper behavior. The most important attribute of an old person's demeanor was gravity. The writers believed that a major fault in the deportment of the aged and the biggest obstacle to their proper gravity was their trying to act younger than their age: "It is a great *Misbehaviour,* and unbecoming *Age,* to *affect Youth;* or indulge in it self the *Modes, Liberties* and Customs lawful and decent in Youth."[17] Especially repugnant in older persons were the sins of youth. Thus, while excessive mirth was to be avoided by youth, the authors claimed that this was "a more mean and sickly thing . . . in Elder People, as well as more vile and horrid!" And while they urged all persons to abstain from "smutty talk," they added: "But nothing is more Nauseous or Odious in an Old Man than the Levity of Lasciviousness. For Old Men to talk bawdily and filthily . . . 'tis how incongruous!"[18] On the other hand, the gravity of old age was not to lead to censoriousness but was to be tempered "with a certain gentle and jocund humour."[19]

Second, while we might assume that the advice telling young people to defer to adults applied as well to their interaction with the aged, most of this advice concerned relations with parents and masters, positions in which the aged were less involved.[20] As suggested above, some authors did remind adults that they, too, owed their aged parents deference. But here the evidence becomes more complicated, and clues to the interaction of the two Sewalls are found. For at least two writers frankly expressed what most did not care to say openly, namely, that sometimes a son's higher status or official position might prevent his proper relationship with his parent from being acknowledged in public. As one explained: "I grant that a childe may by some office, and outward dignity be so advanced above his father, as other men may more honour and reverence the childe, and give the upper place to him: and for order sake the childe may and ought to take it in company: but when they are alone, the childe must rather reverence the father."[21] Here, as in Sewall's diary, we see the interaction of the hierarchies of age and social rank.

Third, and most important, the authors gave relatively few admonitions regarding behavior with the aged compared to their rules for other relations. They were content with making the vague claim that the aged were owed reverential behavior and leaving it at that. They devoted far more time and space to the delineation of specific ways in which young persons were to defer to their parents, ministers, masters, and teachers; "elders" all, but generally still in the prime of life.[22]

Thus, although we might at first glance assume that the aged had the most power in this society, the conduct writers both explicitly and implicitly denied this. They devoted far more space to the regulation of relations between young persons and adults and within the contexts of the parent/child and master/servant relations. Because they perceived society in terms of a family model, it was these latter relations that were at the heart of their system of age relations; and, if all the rules were followed, various sorts of "parents," or mature adults, were the group that could expect the most deference. That this was the general pattern in reality is suggested by diaries such as Sewall's and Cotton Mather's. For not only do these men fail to record paying any special deference to aged persons around them; they also do not note any especial deference being paid to them as they aged.[23]

Taken together, these findings underscore the necessity of examining the rules for age relations systematically. Among other things, it is important to acknowledge the difference between patriarchy (rule of fathers) and gerontocracy (rule of the old); and thus to distinguish between "elders" and "the elderly."[24] It is also necessary to examine the content of specific admonitions to respect "elders," and to look at the age of the intended audience for these admonitions. In the past, historians have been misled by seventeenth-century exhortations to venerate the elderly, for, when examined in the context of the rules for other relations, it becomes clear that the advice-givers were merely paying lip service to a time-worn biblical injunction. Clearly, given their vertical view of society, Puritan conduct writers were comfortable with making such proclamations. But that they did not back them up with consistent and extensive prescriptions for deference displays suggests that they wanted to reserve power for their own group—that is, the mature but not aged ministerial and magisterial elite.

THE AMBIGUITY ABOUT old age aside, early New English discussions of manners do support the notion that age inequality between mature adults and minors was the fundamental principle of the social order. One of the chief reasons that historians have concluded that childhood and youth were not much recognized in early America is because this society did not have social (or indeed physical) structures—whether school grades or household nurseries—to spatially segregate the different age groups. Not only did persons of different ages mingle in the daily round of work and play in one-room homes and schoolhouses, but it is also true that progress from youth to maturity was not marked by any abrupt transition. Yet so important was the principle of age inequality to the Puritans that they made sure to reinforce it through their legal and familial institutions for education, discipline, and inheritance. All single youth were required to live in families, for example, and independence was hard to come by without inheriting land.[25] They also tried to compensate for the lack of age grading in their society through the use of ritual. That is, the socially dominant used manners to bring age relations into alignment with rank relations in their promotion of a hierarchical social order, and they did so despite the fact that the courtesy works on their shelves were relatively quiet on the subject of age relations. Indeed, it appears that in the ministers' eyes age inequality was the first principle of the social order. While differences of social rank sorted out the mature, such differences mattered little among children and youth who were inferior by virtue of their age.

We know this because in contrast to their limited and rather general discussion of behavior toward the aged, the Puritan conduct writers gave children and youth extensive instructions on ways to show deference to mature adults. On first analysis, this advice suggests that youth were deemed slightly less inferior to adults than were children, because the latter were given a little more advice. For example, while both children and youth were to "Let the upper place and hand be given to Parents" (that is, to give them the best or most honorable places in sitting and walking), only children were told to "Sit where thou art ordered by the Superiors, Parents, or Masters." Similar differences of degree can be found in the advice to children and youth regarding proper body carriage, facial expression, and conversation with their elders. Both children and youth were instructed to maintain a sober and modest face and posture before their elders, "as may argue due respect," but children were also told to stand erect and to refrain from slouching and sticking their hands in their pockets. They were not to sit until they received permission to do so. Some authors also urged children to control their gaze, neither staring nor looking "boldly or wishfully" in the face of an elder. And while the authors asked both children and youth not to speak to elders until spoken to, and then only with reverent titles and few and respectful words, they gave children more specific instructions on proper titles and additional admonitions to ignore elders' errors and submit patiently to their opinions and corrections.[26]

But there was not a big difference between advice to children and advice to youth. Both groups were to demonstrate their reverence by rising, uncovering, and bowing every time they entered or left the presence of an adult.[27] Moreover, the most important instructions to children and youth were those regarding their overall demeanor before mature adults, and here the writers advised both groups that "you Set Light by your Parents, if you withhold from them, the Reverence that is due unto them" and that "this Reverence must have some Outward Expression of it." Both children and youth were also told that they owed such a demeanor to all "Parents, natural, spiritual, and civil"; that is, that they were to treat schoolmasters, ministers, and masters accordingly. This was the same demeanor one was to adopt before superiors in social rank, but the obligation of children and youth to reverence their elders and particularly their parents was greater than that of any adult, however humble his circumstances and great the rank of those in his presence, for the writers referred to this duty of young people over and over again.[28]

The authors' periodic reminders that youth owed a deferential demeanor to their masters as well as their parents serves to remind us that advice to youth in general was accompanied by advice to youth who were servants. If the relationship between children and adults seems a little more unequal than that between youth and adults, that between young servants and their adult masters would appear to redress the balance, for it was distinctly unequal. Early colonial advice to and about servants is pertinent to the relationship between youth and adults because its frequent appearance in the literature reflected the widespread practice, among all classes, of apprenticing or placing youth out to service in others' families in early New England. As suggested by their advice that masters be treated as parents, the authors most often discussed this relationship in age and familial, rather than class, terms. This advice must therefore be considered in the context of age as well as class relations. Age and class concerns came together in the writers' overall message that a young servant was inferior to his or her master as a young man or woman was to his or her parent—only more so.[29]

Take, for example, the advice concerning the regulation of time in encounters with adults. While youth were merely to allow adults to precede them in various ways, recall that young servants were to respect their masters' complete control of their time.[30] Servants were to be reverential in manner and speech before their masters just as youth were with parents and other superiors. But servants were also warned far more often against displaying "sauciness" and "sullenness" in their demeanor and talk with their masters than were youth concerning their parents. Recall as well that servants were urged not to grumble at their masters' orders or reproofs, or to speak of their masters' affairs to others.[31] Instructions for proper body carriage in the presence of adults also suggest that young servants, like children, were thought more inferior to adults than were youth in general. In addition to the sober and modest comportment of the body that all young people were to have in the presence of their elders, servants, like young children, were also cautioned to stand rather than sit before their masters.[32]

While the authors gave all young persons similar advice concerning behavior toward adults, then, they occasionally gave children and often young servants stricter advice than they gave youth in general. They asked young servants to be more submissive in their demeanor and conversation with their masters than they expected youth to be in their encounters with their parents. They gave both children and servants more elaborate and strict advice than they gave youth in general regarding body carriage in the presence of adults. Thus they considered children and servants more inferior to adults than youth in general.[33] But the differences were not dramatic.

Advice to adults about behavior with young people reflected the same attitudes. It is worth noting, first, that the authors directed nearly all of their advice on behavior with younger persons to the parents and masters of children and youth, and thus to middle-age, not aged, adults. The advice to adults regarding children was a bit more elaborate than that concerning adolescent offspring; but substantively these counsels were more similar than different. The rules for behavior with youth were slightly more relaxed in that less concern was expressed about spoiling them with overindulgent demeanor and carriage.

In order to fulfill their responsibility to teach young children how to behave, parents had to take care to adopt the proper demeanor toward them. Moreover, several authors claimed that a parent's example was more powerful than any conscious teaching. A father was to make sure "That in all his doings he should shewe himselfe grave and modest, and by doing well himselfe, give his children an example to do the like."[34] Parents were repeatedly advised to avoid excessive severity. To terrify one's children was counterproductive to the teaching one needed to give them. Cotton Mather thus advised parents:

> Let not your *Authority* be strained with such *Harshness*, and *Fierceness*, as may discourage your *Children*. To treat our *Children* like *Slaves*, and with such Rigour, that they shall always Tremble and Abhor to come into our Presence, This will be very unlike to our Heavenly Father. Our Authority should be so Tempered with Kindness, and Meekness, and Loving Tenderness, that our Children may *Fear* us with *Delight*.

Parents were thus to govern their families "with a suitable Degree of Mildness." But the authors also warned parents to avoid the opposite extreme of overindulgence. One writer warned, "Don't by your Lightness and Weakness and Folly, suffer them to Trample up on you; but keep up so much *Authority*, that your *Word* may be a *Law* unto them." While parents were to be affectionate when their children were well-behaved, too much affection, or "cockering," would ruin a child.

The conduct writers gave parents similar advice regarding demeanor with adolescent sons and daughters, but they had rather less to say about it. They also displayed less concern over a parent's being too affectionate than they did regarding younger children. As the chief design of proper child-rearing in this era was to gain the affectionate respect of one's offspring, the more relaxed rules for behavior with youth reveals the assumption that at their age the important task of will-curbing was already accomplished, and hence there was less danger in indulgence.[35]

But again advice to adults concerning behavior with servants would seem to return youth to the status of children, for while similar to that concerning adolescent offspring, it was also more strict. For example, the authors told both parents and masters to monitor the behavior of their charges; but the emphasis in the latter case was on the master's duty to prevent and correct servants' misbehavior, while with parents the emphasis was on more positive instruction of youth, and mainly by good example. Parents were to supervise the time and associations of their young adult offspring and to keep their young children from "wandering abroad too much"; but recall that Masters were to exert complete control over their servants' time, and to keep them busy. Masters' control over their servants' time is confirmed by one writer's suggestion that the granting "of Liberty" at certain times be used as a reward for good behavior. Masters were not only to observe; they also were to admonish their servants to do good, and to correct them for their faults.[36]

Moreover, the writers added to instructions to masters something they did not counsel parents in regard to youth: that they should not spend time with servants as "play-fellows." The authors thought such interaction injurious to the proper conduct of the master-servant relationship. In the same vein, while they advised masters, like parents, to avoid severity in demeanor with youth, they also warned masters not to be overly familiar with servants, something they were much less concerned about on the part of parents with adolescents. A more reserved and authoritative carriage, masters were reminded, was more likely to command respect. Adults needed to be even more reserved in their conversation with servants than with young children. Recall that masters were to command gently and give praise but not to hesitate in giving orders.[37]

Most of the advice to adults on talk with younger persons concerned discipline. Parents and masters were to admonish children and servants to do good and to correct them when they misbehaved. But adults were to be moderate in correction. Parents of young children were to "Let correction be wisely used, as they need it; neither so severely as to disaffect them to you, nor so little as to leave them in a course of sin and disobedience." Masters were to maintain an "even Temper, not finding fault through the peevishness of [their] own Humour," or casting upon servants "all the reproachfull names that they can call to mind," or speaking harshly to servants, "as tho' they were another sort of creatures, different from themselves." As these comments indicate, correction was to be timely, and, above all, never given in anger. Constant and harsh chiding would only breed "stubbornesse, frowardnesse, and contempt." Still, it was agreed that "When all fair Means, Persuasions, and Encouragements prevail not, then there is a necessity of using sharper; and let that first be tried in Words, . . . not by railing and foul Language, but in sober, yet sharp Reproofs."[38]

The authors also agreed that "if words will not prevail with them to mend their Manners, the Rod must then be made use of." It was thought that "some Children are of such Make and Temper that nothing but the Rod of correction will cause their folly to depart from them," and that striking was "a remedy which may do good when nothing else can." The authors often referred to the biblical injunction in Solomon that parents who spared the rod would spoil their children. "These Scriptures show," the authors claimed, "that God hath put the rodde of correction in the hands of the Governours of the familie; by punishment to save them from destruction." To be sure, few of the writers failed to caution that this punishment, too, was never to be administered in a rage, and was to be moderate in dosage. William Gouge suggested that "it is not so meet to use strokes and blowes . . . when children are grown to man-age."[39] But that so many writers warned of the ill consequences of sparing the rod suggests that corporal punishment was thought proper at least until a child attained maturity. Early New England diaries give us a number of glimpses of youth being beaten—at home, at school, and at Harvard College—which confirms both the fact that minors were whipped and the principle that in their minority even elite youth were considered inferior.[40]

There was even less restraint with youth who were servants. Except for one courtesy writer who advised members of the elite not to beat their servants, early colonial writers agreed that masters were to beat young servants when verbal rebukes failed to correct them. Here again the authors urged that such correction be moderate and not delivered in anger, but they gave masters freer rein than they did parents. Recall that such punishment needed only to "be so moderated" that the servant "may not thereby be Killed or Maimed," a limit which presumably allowed a fair number of stripes. That there were limits is proven by the periodic punishment of masters for overly cruel treatment of servants. But a recent historian of the court records has concluded that "no one questioned the right of masters" to beat their servants, and that the "authorities' reactions to cruelty seem oddly mild," indicating the degree to which hitting servants was acceptable. One master was told that it was fine for him to beat his servant, but he really must desist from hanging him up by the heels.[41]

It is possible that the harsher extreme of corporal punishment prescribed for servants than for one's own progeny helps to explain the Puritan habit of placing their youth in others' households. This "putting out" system may have been a method of disciplining young people and enforcing authority over them, by sending them to someone who would beat them harder than a parent would or should. Historians have wondered why the Puritans put their offspring out to service; and while they have offered several suggestions, none of the economic arguments suffices on its own because all classes engaged in both placing and receiving youth. That this was not simply harsh treatment meted out to poor youth is also suggested by the practices of the colleges—the elite counterpart to apprenticeship—where more fortunate youth were also subject to practices explicitly designed to maintain the hierarchy. Errant students were whipped in the seventeenth century and had their ears boxed in the early eighteenth; more often than not, the provoking offense was insufficient deference to superiors.[42]

Historian Edmund Morgan once speculated that the Puritans placed their teenagers out because they feared they would be overindulgent with them. They did not trust themselves to properly subject their feelings of affection to the needs of authority. Puritan manners, with their gentler treatment of adolescent offspring than of servants, support Morgan's idea. The assorted cases of dispute between parents and masters that surface in the records confirm it as well; some parents had difficulty consigning their offspring to others' discipline, even though they apparently went along with the system.[43]

IN TURNING TO BEHAVIOR deemed appropriate not with older or younger persons but with age-mates, we are confronted with a class division in the evidence. For while relations between the young and the mature were a major concern of the Puritan conduct writers who wrote for everybody, and not a chief concern of the Renaissance courtesy works of the elite, as regards relations between age-peers the situation was reversed. The Puritan advisors to the commons were not much interested in advising adults on behavior with peers; they generally limited their remarks to children and, especially, youth. And they were only concerned with certain areas of behavior. The elite-oriented courtesy works were mostly occupied with relations between adults, although they were sometimes addressed to youth (and schoolmaster Moody passed a simplified version of some of their advice along to children). Distinctions in the advice to different age groups regarding peer interaction thus tend to emerge where the Puritans weighed in alongside the courtesy writers in advising youth. When their advice is examined closely, it reveals a further desire to exert control over youth; instead of passing on the elite-oriented body-control advice, the Puritans were mostly concerned to control the demeanor, talk, and associations of youth. Youthful levity, in particular, seemed a challenge to their authority.

The courtesy works gave similar advice to the different age groups in the areas of behavior with which they were most concerned—body carriage and facial expression—and their instructions were generally not disseminated by the Puritan writers. Thus gentle youth and adults were urged to exercise control over their bodies in the company of peers, ceding space when necessary and saluting others with friendly gestures but suppressing all awkward and unnecessary motions "either of thy head, hands, feet, or body" (including, where possible, such acts as nose-blowing and nail-biting). Only Moody passed some of this advice along to schoolchildren, and only one minister, Increase Mather, gave some of this advice in sermons to the commons in his multifaceted attack, addressed to youth, on dancing.[44] It was mostly elite-oriented courtesy works that recommended the maintenance of a "moderately cheerful" facial expression—avoiding the extremes of both dark looks and excessive mirth. Courtesy works alone advised youth and adults that all distortions of the face were to be avoided in the presence of peers. And instructions on gaze management are only found in the courtesy literature and Moody's schoolbook.[45] Clearly this literature, addressed to gentlefolk but describing only one standard of behavior, was intended to serve the cause of class rather than age differentiation.

The advice to different age groups begins to vary in quantity and emphasis in the areas where the Puritan ministers spoke out. While courtesy works advised all ages to seek good company and avoid bad company, for example, Puritan writers stressed this point in advice to or concerning children and youth. They did so because they believed that young people's companions shaped their manners and character. One minister claimed that "Nothing scarce is of greater consequence to Young People, than what company they keep; for they insensibly grow like those, whom they converse with." We know from their diaries and letters that members of the elite constantly gave this advice to their own relations as well as to ordinary youth. While the courtesy works advised elite adults to seek good company, they did not give this advice as often as the ministers did to all young people, and their rationale differed. Elite adults were to avoid bad company because it would tarnish their reputations, not because it would corrupt their behavior.[46]

The Puritan elite recognized that it was impossible for young persons to avoid bad company all of the time, and indeed believed that the entire class of young people by its very nature constituted a dangerous influence, as they often "enticed" and "provoked" one another to misbehavior. One of their answers to this problem was to encourage parents to control the time their offspring spent in others' company. Children were to ask their parents' permission "to go abroad," and parents were to "restrain them from gading, and wandering abroad, with a lawless Liberty." The ministers also addressed young children directly on this issue, charging them not to loiter in the streets or succumb to the bad example of their peers. Apparently these admonitions to young people were generated by real concerns; they were not always heeded, for local court records show that youth did tend to misbehave in groups, and sometimes groups in which notorious "bad apples" led their age-mates into forbidden activities. It is also clear that elite youth mixed freely with "the meaner sorte" in these groups, another indication of the priority of age over rank grouping in this society. Cotton Mather finally resorted to establishing his own youth group to encourage piety, and expressed satisfaction when this group of "Near one hundred serious devout young Men" asked him to publish his "Sermon, about shunning *bad Company.*"[47]

The courtesy works advised all ages to adopt a courteous and affable demeanor before peers and to eschew excessive reserve. The Puritan tracts echoed this advice but were only concerned with teaching it to children and youth. In addition, they repeated and amplified the few suggestions in the courtesy works that youth should also aim for modesty and sobriety in demeanor, warning of the "youthful sin of Haughtiness" or a "frothy and vain" deportment.[48]

Elite-oriented courtesy works and Puritan sermons gave advice concerning talk with peers in which the same pattern holds; that is, the courtesy works gave elite readers of all ages advice to exert self-control in an effort to appear refined, while the Puritan ministers mostly offered advice intended to exert control over youth. Thus, while courtesy works reminded children and adults to suppress unnecessary noises, and asked all age groups to refrain from talking too much, too little, too loudly, too softly, too rapidly, or too slowly, the only Puritan author to speak on the subject simply urged on young persons "the regular Government of their Tongues." While courtesy writers instructed elite youth and adults to pronounce their words distinctly, Puritan ministers concentrated on warning children and youth, especially the latter, against excessive mirth. They advised the young to content themselves with a "civil, sober mirth," one minister explaining: "there's no necessity of being immodest or Profane, idle and Impertinent, in order to be Merry."[49] In their fear of disorderly speech, the Puritan ministers eagerly joined the courtesy writers in reminding all ages not to boast, swear, use obscenities, or antagonize others. But even here some authors expended special effort on youth, claiming that the rash and hasty expression of anger, like that of mirth, was a particular failing of that age group and one that should be suppressed.[50]

In the end, contrasts in early New English advice to different age groups about behavior with age-mates are not great but do confirm the class and age concerns we have already witnessed. Courtesy works generally gave the different age groups the same advice in their efforts to teach the elite proper self-control. Age inequality was not an important issue in these works. But age inequality was vitally important to the Puritans. The Puritan elite did not go so far as to bolster the authority of all adults by endowing them with elaborate behaviors to use with peers to set themselves off from the young. This would have jeopardized the elite's social exclusivity. Instead, they focussed on shoring up age inequality by giving injunctions intended to restrain youth.

ALTHOUGH ONE MIGHT assume that the elderly were on top of the early New English age hierarchy, far more space in the conduct literature was devoted to the regulation of relations between young persons and the middle-aged. The parent/child and master/servant relationships were at the heart of the regulation of age relations, and, if all the rules were followed, the middle-aged could expect more deference than the aged. These observations point to the importance of examining the rules for the regulation of age relations systematically.

Youth in general were less inferior to adults than were children and servants; but there was not a clear difference between adult-young child and adult-youth relationships, because early New English advice about youth did so often concern servants. Indeed, the advice concerning servants reveals a crucial link between the hierarchies of age and rank in the early colonial period. The conduct literature suggests that the Puritans did not want to leave the relationship between adults and youth too relaxed, and used the institution of service as a means of keeping it unequal. Early court records confirm that youth presented a threat to the social order. They also show that this society was generally able to handle the challenge. While some youth misbehaved, most did not, and the rules of service were there to be enforced when problems arose.[51] Service also performed another function: in a society where differences in wealth were relatively small, it was a way of creating differences in rank. The institution of service was a vestige of a more unequal society; it persisted in early New England despite the countervailing pressure of labor shortage. Might the Puritans have maintained the system precisely because it provided a way of imposing inequality on a society where transition to the power of adulthood was gradual and there was relative equality of wealth? The old practice of putting youth out was likely perpetuated because it served the special purpose of putting them in their place.

Early New English rules for age relations, then, like early New English manners in general, served to reconcile natural parental affection and the leveling conditions of settlement with long-held notions of a vertical or hierarchical social order. This is even seen in advice about behavior with age-mates, where Puritan ministers continued to try to control youth. Manners in early New England were thus designed above all to shore up the authority of superiors. It will come as no surprise in the next chapter that not only were the relevant superiors generally elite and middle-aged but they were also male.

THREE

MANNERS MAKETH MEN

Mistress Phillips did not intend to affront the young minister; she simply had a coughing spell. But Jeremiah Shepherd saw it as an insult. Her husband Samuel explained what happened: "In the time of my wife's long and dangerous sickness he came below to look upon her and there took offense that she did not show him respect though my wife affirms that she bowed her head as well as she could being then entering into her ague fit, but he never would come see her though I wished him to do it." Mistress Phillips was a respectable matron of the town of Rowley. Samuel Phillips was himself a minister, but the younger Shepherd was a candidate for the recently vacated position of pastor, that is, as Phillips's superior. Mr. Phillips was supportive of Shepherd, but the latter's inability to please the women of the parish ultimately did him in. Women like Mrs. Phillips could be quite influential, and ministers were wise to curry their favor.[1] Yet even such a matron tried to show deference to the younger minister.

This misunderstanding brings us again to questions about how age and rank relations were intertwined in this society; only now another variable is tossed into the mix: gender. Between that time and our own, deference to women was one of the central themes of good manners, and even today vestiges of the "ladies first" system persist. But such notions were alien to seventeenth-century New Englanders. Deference was something paid to elite men. Even though she was an equal in social rank, even though she was older, even though she was sick in bed, the Reverend Shepherd was looking for a decent bow from Mistress Phillips, and she did her level best to give it.

Historians have painted two kinds of pictures of gender relations in early New England. Some have emphasized male dominance and female subjection, while others have highlighted the degree of partnership and reciprocity between the sexes.[2] The scenario sketched by conduct advice can help to reconcile the two views. The larger context was not unlike that for rank and age relations: the overarching world view of hierarchy built on the metaphor of patriarchy was clearly thought to apply to gender relations. But as with those other relations, this ideal was challenged somewhat by contrary realities, including the physical and material needs of life on the colonial frontier and the ties of affection. While the principle of male superiority and female inferiority was clear in the law, in practice we find women stepping into male economic and legal roles as family needs arose.[3] While gender inequality was supported in some ways by Puritan theology, it was subverted by their notions of spiritual equality and marriage as a voluntary contract. And then as now, sexual ties served to differentiate gender from other kinds of inequality. The conduct literature suggests how the dominant group imagined that contradictory ideals and realities might be brought into harmony in day-to-day life. The picture painted by these elite males, while obviously congenial to their interests, is brighter than some have supposed.

Manners can tell us much about a culture by allowing systematic comparison of relations that are normally examined separately. Nowhere is this clearer than in the study of gender in early New England. When the rules for gender relations are compared to those for rank and age relations, two facts stand out. Women were definitely regarded as inferior to men, but they were not as inferior to men as the lower sort were to the elite or as young people were to adults. Indeed, contrary to the claims of some historians who have focused on women, gender inequality was not the most fundamental form of inequality in this culture; instead, it was the mildest form.[4] The conduct literature also suggests that the reason for this difference was the intimacy of male-female relations.

The role of intimacy in shaping gender relations points to the centrality of marriage in this culture's views of gender. Take Robert Cleaver's summary of the duties of husbands and wives: "The dutie of the husband is, to deale with many men: and of the wives, to talke with fewe. The dutie of the husband is, to be entermeddling: and of the wife to bee solitarie and withdrawne. The dutie of the man is, to bee skilfull in talke: and of the wife, to boast of silence."[5] This passage is typical of the way conduct advice to women revolved around their roles as wives. Note that the description of wifely duties had implications for wives' social behavior. It is certainly clear in conduct advice to women that the construction of women as wives both shaped and greatly limited thinking about their behavior, whether with men in particular or society in general. For beyond the desire to produce good wives, the authors of conduct literature (all male in this period) were not much interested in female behavior. They used far more ink to describe male behavior in what they evidently regarded as a man's world but did not overtly construe as such, for beyond the marriage relation they lost interest in gender difference.[6] This too is hinted in Cleaver's passage, where he occasionally describes men as men and not just as husbands, and proclaims that while women were to be marginal to the social world, men were "to be entermeddling." Closer inspection reveals a class division in advice to men, however, where there was none in advice to women; the most extensive advice on proper male behavior was found in the courtesy works of the elite, while the elite themselves, like Cleaver, were primarily concerned with the proper roles of husbands and wives in their advice to ordinary folk.[7] Again it seems that the elite were only interested in shaping the behavior of ordinary folk to the degree necessary to ensure family—and thus social—order.

VIEWING WOMEN AS WIVES in a culture that preached the biblically sanctioned subordination of wives to husbands helped to ensure female subordination in general. It was not necessary for the conduct writers to spend too many words on the behavior of girls, however, for they shared with male children, youth, and servants the age and class inferiority of those positions. It was upon maturity, when a man escaped at least some of this inferiority, that a woman entered a new inferior position as a wife. Although she gained some power as a mistress and a mother, the male "governour" of the household was still her superior as well as the final authority in dealings with children and servants. More than one author felt it necessary to remind children that reverential deportment toward parents was to be exercised to the mother as well as to the father, "because Persons are more apt to disregard their *Mothers*."[8] By construing women as wives, then, the authors made them inferiors for life, while proper behavior in men varied with age and social rank.

But thinking of women as wives also qualified their inferiority. This becomes clear when advice to women on behavior with men is compared to advice for rank and age inferiors about encounters with their respective superiors. To be sure, some of the advice was similar, confirming women's status as men's inferiors. But the conduct writers neglected to give women all of the advice they gave to other inferiors. More tellingly, they gave women special advice that arose from the intimate nature of their relations with men.

Women were to have an air of reverence and ready obedience when with their husbands, and to this extent their proper demeanor conformed to that of other inferiors. As one author explained, a wife was "to testifie her acknowledgement of her husband's Superiority by some outward obeysance to him." Several authors did make the significant addition, however, that "This is not so to be taken as if no difference were to be made betwixt the carriage of a servant, or childe, and a wife." They were all inferiors, but children and servants of both sexes were more inferior to the household head than was his wife, so "the obeysance of children and servants ought to be more submissive and more frequent." The combination of intimacy with inequality that made the marriage relationship different led the authors to give further instructions to wives. The ministers often added that marriage required a loving, cheerful—yet appropriately modest—demeanor on the part of the wife.[9]

While they told other inferiors to cede control over the timing of their encounters to superiors, the conduct writers did not do so with women. Their advice simply took contact between the sexes for granted, a fact congruent with the glimpses of ordinary life revealed in local court records. These show men and women mixing freely in homes, fields, and even taverns. Young men and women gathered in groups and "sat up" with each other when courting.[10] The authors also neglected to instruct women to yield place to men, again in contrast to other inferiors. Indifference on this issue is seen in Samuel Sewall's discussions of who sat at the head and foot of the table at various dinner parties, which show no discernible gender pattern.[11] Nor were women given the standard advice to inferiors concerning body carriage or gestures toward men. We know from elite diaries that the polite gesture was a curtsy, but the conduct writers did not care enough to discuss it.[12] Women were thus to demonstrate their inferiority chiefly through their demeanor. Surely this indicates that they were regarded as less inferior to men than were young persons to adults or ordinary folk to the elite.

This hypothesis is borne out by advice on conversation, which, while similar in some ways to that given other inferiors, was again less strict. This advice clearly acknowledges that the intimacy of male-female relations entailed special rules. Courtesy writers and Puritan ministers agreed that women, like other inferiors, should refrain from talking too much in the presence of men. Young women in particular were warned that with men their "best Rhetoricke consists in maiden blushes, and bashfull smiles." But while many authors told women that silence was their best contribution to conversation, they did not forbid women all talk in the presence of men. Even those authors who argued that silence was one of the greatest virtues of a good wife recognized that she had a right to speak to her husband. Although a wife's words were to be few, and she, like other inferiors, might properly await her husband's bidding to commence speaking, total silence was also wrong. As one author explained, "shee may in a modest sort shew her mind, and a wise husband will not disdaine to heare her advise."[13]

Like other inferiors, a wife was to show respect in the titles she used to address her husband. Gouge told wives not to use nicknames or familiar terms for their husbands but rather their full names, for example, "Master Smith." Above all, women were not to argue with or use ill language toward their husbands—and local court records tell us that women who did not heed these instructions were punished.[14] Yet while women were to speak little and with reverence, as were other inferiors, they were also advised that the intimacy of their relations with the opposite sex allowed some talk. They needed only to "carefully shunne and avoyde" "any wanton discourse."[15] The advice to women regarding talk with men was thus mixed: it included allusions to both inequality and sexuality.

The difference between the proper behavior of women with men and that of other inferiors with superiors is most evident in advice on facial expression. Here, especially, the advice was driven by a need to regulate hetero-sexual intimacy. This was also a matter to which the authors devoted consid-erable space. Some of the Puritan counsels reveal a desire to preserve marital peace. Women were to preserve a "milde and amiable countenance" in the presence of their husbands, and to refrain from expressing displeasure. "Con-trary to this mildness," one author continued, "is a frowning brow, a lowring eie, a sullen looke, a powting lip, a swelling face, a deriding mouth," all to-kens, according to another, of "a cruell and unloving heart."[16] Other advice respecting women's facial expressions with men centered on the need for modest looks. While modesty was important in a woman's demeanor and con-versation, it was crucial in her face. Women of all ages were thought best adorned by "shamefastnesse." Young women in particular were advised to put on "bashfull smiles" and "maiden blushes." Several authors gave elaborate diatribes against immodest facial expressions or "light countenance" in young women; "Nyce looks," "bewitching looks and smiles," "wanton glaunces," and "bold glances" were all condemned. One author commanded: "So order and dispose your *lookes*, as censure may not taxe you of lightnesse, nor an amorous glance impeach you of wantonesse. Send not forth a tempting *eye*, to take an-other; nor entertaine a tempting *looke* darting from another." And here as elsewhere courtesy works and Puritan tracts sang the same tune.[17]

In addition to the standard rules for behavior with superiors, then, women were given special advice to be modest with men. This advice was in-termingled with counsels that women be respectful in demeanor and talk; it nearly stood alone in advice on proper facial expression. Modesty was to pre-vent women from engaging in obscene talk; it was also to prevent their en-gaging in unchaste body contact, for more often than not the authors joined their condemnations of wanton talk with implicit denunciations of touching or immoral body contact with men. One author explained:

> When we speak of modesty in our present notion of it, we are not to op-pose it only to the grosser act of incontinency, but to all these misbehav-iours, which either discover or may create an inclination to it; of which sort is all lightnesse of carriage, wanton glances, obscene discourse; things that show a woman so weary of her honour, that the next comer may reasonably expect a surrender, and consequently be invited to the assault.

Beyond that women should not dance with men, however, the authors were not specific as to what constituted improper body contact, short of that "grosser act of incontinency." They only declared that women should avoid "familiarity" of any sort and not "permit, much less invite, the Dalliances of any wanton Creatures which may design anything besides what is honourable on her." Once again the Puritan ministers were giving their female congre-gants advice not unlike that found in courtesy books.[18]

Here and there, then, the sexual element of gender relations creeps in to distinguish the relationship between women and men from other inferior-superior relationships. This is also seen in a fear of wantonness expressed in the few remarks that some of the ministers made to both sexes about contact with the opposite sex. Both Increase and Cotton Mather were firm in their condemnation of "that which is commonly called *Mixt or Promiscuous Dancing, viz.* of men and women (be they elder or younger persons) together." "Now this," Increase declared, "we affirm to be utterly unlawful, and that it cannot be tolerated in such a place as *New England*, without great sin. . . . The unchaste Touches and Gesticulations used by *Dancers*, have a palpable tendency to that which is evil." The Mathers cited Scripture in their denigration of dancing, distinguishing mixed dancing from religious dances in the Bible where a person danced alone. It was the tendency toward *"wantonesse"* of mixed dancing that alarmed them. Sure enough, the court records—which show both infraction and enforcement of all these rules—show that when New England youth danced they also drank and experimented with sex.[19] The fear of wantonness also pervaded a few authors' denunciations to both sexes of "lewd Talk, and evil Communication, in any impure or immodest words or Actions." Cotton Mather denounced lewd talk between men and women in particularly strong terms:

> If we would have our *visits* to be, *as it becometh Saints; away with all Filthyness!* . . . *Baudy Talk*, it argues a singular *Baseness* in them that affect it: *Smutty Talk*, it argues a Little, and a Dirty Soul. . . . They who pollute their *Visits* with nasty Ebullitions of Unchastity, they do nothing but *Vomit* where they come. . . . Their *Excrements* come out of their *Mouthes!* I suppose, there is Enough said, to make you *Sick* of such fulsome Levities.[20]

With dancing and unchaste talk denounced in such terms, the authors must have thought it unnecessary to denounce greater violations of chastity.

The relationship between women and men was thus different from other inferior-superior relations in that the requirements of reverence were coupled with those of modesty. And the intimacy of gender relations that made modesty necessary seemed to make this relationship less unequal than other relations. Nowhere is this more clearly illustrated than in two ministers' pleas that women not beat men. Wadsworth argued that if a woman "strikes her Husband (as some shameless, impudent wretches will) . . . she's then a shame to her profession of Christianity." William Gouge argued that a mistress should not beat male servants, claiming that "a man servant will much disdaine to be smitten by a woman." This was advice they never dreamed necessary to give young folks and servants in regard to superiors, but the intimacy of male-female relations brought the danger of challenge to male authority along with the danger of "wantonesse." Samuel Sewall apparently acted on this belief when he "sentenced a woman that whip'd a Man, to be whip'd." He declared that "a woman that had lost her modesty, was like salt that had lost its savor; good for nothing but to be cast to the Dunghill."[21]

THE ADVICE TO MEN regarding their behavior with women complemented that to women concerning men. It was generally similar in courtesy books and Puritan sermons. It described men as women's superiors. It mostly concerned men's roles as husbands. It conformed in many ways to the rules for other superior-inferior relationships. And yet it clearly distinguished gender from other forms of inequality.

The advice to men corroborates some scholars' recent suggestions that a man's position as head of the household was a key component of male identity in this period, and one which leaders wished to reinforce.[22] Yet men were also given special advice urging them to be loving and respectful of their wives, which indicates that there was less inequality here than in rank or age relationships. The sexual nature of the difference between the male-female relationship and other superior-inferior relationships is signaled by the authors' several references to the importance of discreet behavior between husbands and wives.

As was the case with advice to women, most of the advice to men concerning women revolved around rules for demeanor, talk, and body contact. While some rank and age superiors were encouraged to spend time with their inferiors in order to supervise them, men were not given any such advice regarding women. The only advice the authors gave men concerning the propriety of time and place in their encounters with women was advice that asked husbands to refrain from certain behavior before others. In particular, a man was not "to chide or to fawne upon his wife before others." "An husband's gesture ought to be so familiar and amiable towards his wife, as others may discern him to be her husband," but he was to adopt a suitable "husband-like gravity, sobriety, modesty, and decency" with his wife in company.[23] Beyond these stipulations, the authors were little concerned with the framing of male-female encounters.

Acknowledging men's superiority, the authors claimed that it was more incumbent on wives to show respect and reverence for their husbands than vice versa. But husbands needed to "put respect upon their wives" as well. William Gouge explained:

> . . . [I]f a wife manifest her dutifull respect of her husband by any reverend behaviour, gesture, or speech, he ought to meet her (as we say) in the middest of the way, and manifest his gracious acceptance thereof by some like courteous behaviour, gesture, and speech. . . . The courtesie which I speake of as it cometh from a superiour, being a meere voluntary matter and a token of kindnesse and favour, is no abasement of himselfe, but an advancement of his inferiour.

Husbands were also to strive for a gentle and amiable demeanor. While they were the proper governors of their wives, their government was to be mild. As one author elaborated: "his government of his wife should not be with rigour, haughtiness, harshness, severity; but with greatest love, gentleness, kindness, tenderness that may be. Though he governs her, he must not treat her as a Servant, but as his *own flesh*." While all superiors were warned against too much severity, only husbands were thus reminded to be tender. The advice to men on facial expressions with their wives was similar.[24]

While the writers advised women not to talk too much in the presence of their husbands, they put no such restrictions on the latter. They were mostly concerned with the manner of a man's speech toward his wife. Here again, men were advised, like other superiors, to avoid severity; but unlike other superiors, they were further instructed to be gentle, loving, even respectful. A man was to show respect for his wife in his terms of address, not giving her too-lofty titles, "as *Lady, Mistresse, Dame*," and the like; too-casual terms, as "woman" or "wench"; opprobrious names like "*slut*"; or "beastly nicknames." Good titles were "*spouse*," "*love*," or "dove." Men were duty-bound as superiors to admonish, instruct, and reprimand their wives, and to do so gently. But in contrast to those of other superiors, a husband's commands and reproofs were to be "rare," and delivered meekly and privately. Certainly, husbands were to refrain from using "Ill language" and "hard words." Husbands who verbally abused their wives could find themselves before the magistrate.[25]

Finally, the advice to men on body contact with women contrasted greatly with advice to other superiors. The issue of sexuality is only indirectly addressed, for although the authors told women both to restrain themselves and to carefully shun all "dalliances" on the part of men, they were silent on this issue to men themselves. In other words, they did not aim to restrain men in this area. The authors only told married men not to be too physically affectionate with their wives in public. As one writer complained, "Some are never well but when they have their wives in their laps, ever codling, kissing, and dallying with them, they care not in what company, thus they shew more lightnesse, fondnesse, and dotage, then true kindnesse and love." But, he assured them, "much greater liberty is granted to man and wife when they are alone."[26]

In clear contrast to their advice to other superiors, the writers were united in their opposition to corporal punishment of wives by husbands. In their view, a husband's duty toward his wife was "*to admonish hir often, to reprehend hir seldome, but never to lay hands upon hir.*" The consensus was that if a "*Husband is bitter against his wife*, beating or striking of her (as some vile wretches do) . . . he then shames his profession of Christianity." That this belief was acted upon is suggested by the various instances in the court records where men were punished for beating their wives. That male beating of women was also taboo outside marriage is suggested by one author's comment that masters were to leave the physical correction of maid-servants to their wives, as "it is a great reproach for a man to beat a maid-servant."[27] While it was "impudent" for a woman to beat a superior man, however inferior his social rank, it was shameful for a man to beat any member of the "weaker" sex. The discouragement of corporal punishment of women by individual men in "the great flogging age" is the surest sign that gender inequality was not the model for all other forms but rather a special case.[28]

THIS IS NOT TO SUGGEST that men and women approached equality in this society; they did not. Moreover, the conduct evidence suggests that gender inequality, while justified by the inequality of the marriage relation, was by no means confined to that relation, or even interaction between men and women. It was pervasive. Even women of high social status did not get much respect, from either sex. Respect was generally reserved for men. Although Governor Dudley was not happy with the degree of deference shown by the farmers he encountered on the road to Boston, at least they doffed their hats and addressed him with a title. The affluent Madam Knight was unable to inspire any such deference on her trip from Boston to New York in 1704. As she stopped to lodge, a young woman of the house peppered her with questions:

> [S]he then turned agen to mee and fell anew into her silly questions, without asking mee to sit down. I told her she treated me very Rudely, and I did not think it my duty to answer her unmannerly Questions. But to get ridd of them, I told her I come there to have the post's company with me tomorrow on my journey, etc. Miss star'd awhile, drew a chair, bid me sitt.[29]

The conduct literature offers some clues to the difference between this scene and that of Dudley and the farmers, for when examined from both class and gender perspectives some important points emerge. The conduct writers did not make class distinctions regarding proper behavior in women; the special elite code was for men only. Their goals were thus the same for all women, while they wanted men's behavior to vary by rank.

Another and in some ways opposing truth appears in the rules for behavior with persons of the same sex: the conduct writers' vision of society was not one in which gender differences were elaborately delineated. The authors gave almost no advice to women concerning behavior with other women; and while they gave men much advice that pertained to their behavior with other men, they did not often acknowledge it as such. The gender difference seen in Governor Dudley's and Madam Knight's experiences emerges in the advice to men and women concerning behavior in general society (that is, advice where the sex of those in company was not specified). There Puritan ministers made two important choices. They joined with courtesy writers in advising women of all ranks that modesty was to grace their entire comportment, while they neglected to give ordinary men much of the courtesy writer's elaborate advice urging gentlemen to exert control over every aspect of their deportment. These trends in the advice on behavior with persons of the same sex or in general society serve to reinforce the larger picture painted by all advice to men and women. As regarded gender, Puritan ministers and Renaissance courtiers shared the same vision. Society was a male world, divided by rank. Women's status was always marginal and secondary.[30]

That society was thought of as a male world is suggested by advice to women on behavior in general society, because here the authors appear to have been primarily concerned with women's behavior in the presence of men. Their advice differed little from that which explicitly concerned a wife's behavior toward her husband, which confirms that they did not think men's superiority to women was confined to marriage. As if echoing Cleaver's assertion that while men were to "deale with many men," wives were to "bee solitarie and withdrawne"; the writers told women in general to shrink back, to concern themselves for the most part with the private realm of the family and not be fully social beings. The public sphere, the domain of men, was deemed a treacherous place for women, especially young women, who were to watch their step and choose their company wisely. While women were not confined to their homes and were expected to do some socializing as good neighbors, courtesy writers and Puritan authors agreed that the best wives tended to be "keepers at home." Local court records reveal that the populace took these instructions to heart, for "unnecessary gadding from home" on the part of women was both complained about and censured.[31]

Women, like men, were to adopt a friendly and gracious demeanor with others; but ministers and courtiers agreed that females of all ages should tincture their affability with modesty. As one minister wrote: *"Towards her neighbors she is not sower, but curteous, not disdainfull to the basest, but affable, with modestie. . . ."* The courtesy writers stressed the importance of modesty in young women, while Puritan writers urged "a more strict and severe behavior" among older women (indeed, they required more circumspection of aged women than any other group). Modesty was not to be confined to a woman's air; the ministers and courtesy writers agreed that it was to characterize a woman's posture and movements as well, although they did not give too much detail. The writers were a little more forthcoming concerning proper facial expressions and yet kept to the same theme, agreeing that "if boldness be read in her face, it blots all the lines of beauty." They recommended "blushes, and bashfull smiles" instead, arguing over and over again that a "modest shamefastnesse" was "a woman's chiefest Ornament."[32]

Modesty was to dictate the measure of a woman's conversation with others to the degree that many authors recommended silence as her best contribution to conversation. "Be as silent as the night," "silence is the best ornament of a woman," "a woman must have special care to be silent," sang the Puritan and courtesy writers in unison. If they did not go so far as to tell women to be silent, the authors at least asked them not to talk too much, and expressed their great disapproval of women, especially young women, who were excessively loquacious. The authors bemoaned "confidence in Repartees and Railleries," on the part of young women, arguing that "there is scarce anything looks more indecent, then to see a young maid too forward and confident in her talk." Women were told to listen rather than to speak in company, and that "a maides answere should be in a word." While a little more freedom was granted mature women, as it was thought that simple neighborliness would require a certain amount of talk, a matron was not to be "full of wordes pouring out all her minde, and babbling of her household matters, That were more fitter to be concealed, but speaking upon good occasion, and that with discretion." A couple of authors added that she was to "avoide gossepping, further then the Lawe of good neighbourhood doth require."[33]

Modesty was to describe the manner as well as the measure of a woman's speech. Her talk was to be neither bold nor forward but humble and affable. She was to avoid self-praise. It was permissible to exercise "a ready wit," so long as it was agreeably expressed, and not too sharp.[34] But never was a woman to indulge in any "filthie" or "Baudy talk." Indeed, she was never even to "hear any talk that shall not sound innocently, without bestowing the re-buke of at least that which for her sake we stile, a maiden-blush upon it." Of course cursing and swearing were also inconsistent with a woman's proper modesty. One writer claimed, "An oath sounds gratingly out of whatever mouth, but out of a woman's it hath such an uncouth harshness, that there is no noise on this side hell can be more amazingly odious." Again, these points are to be found in both Puritan and courtesy works. And again, individuals who did not obey these rules could end up in court. The records show women who engaged in "foul language" and "filthy" speeches being fined.[35]

Some of this advice to women on their behavior in general society may have applied as well to their interactions with other women. In telling women not to run around much "abroad," the male authors of this literature were in part restricting women's interaction with other women. Presumably the affability and modesty that were to adorn women's behavior with men were equally proper with women. But the authors were not interested in the issue of women's behavior with other women. In their minds the relevant objects of regulated female behavior were men.[36] This is why their advice to women on behavior in general society mostly sounded like their advice to women on behavior with men. Note as well that these authors were men con-trolling the behavior of women (as superiors were supposed to) by advising them in the first place. By telling women to keep at home, they were exercis-ing their right to control the time and movements of these inferiors; by telling women to be silent, they were exercising their rights as superiors to initiate conversation.

In contrast to the neglect of relationships between women, there was a great deal of advice circulating in early New England about behavior between men. Indeed, like the advice for women, most of the advice for men seemed to concern behavior with other men. But the writers did not emphasize the gender connotations of their prescriptions. They simply assumed that a man's social world would mostly consist of other men. Thus, while most advice ap-pears to be directed to men, the authors only acknowledged gender difference when they advised women or told men how to behave with women.

Proper male behavior with other men varied greatly according to the so-cial rank and age of both the actor and the men in his company. A good deal of the advice to men thus concerned interaction with superiors and inferiors in rank and age and has already been considered in previous chapters. Advice to men concerning male equals is mostly confined to the courtesy works owned by the elite. Puritan leaders did not often share these pointers with the populace; it was generally only Eleazar Moody who passed on simple versions of some of them to schoolboys. If the elite did not particularly care how women behaved with other women, then, they also did not seem to care much about how ordinary adult men behaved together. The Puritan ministers had no problem sharing with ordinary women the comments in courtesy works about female behavior, because the Renaissance courtiers also put women in the margins. But they kept most of the elaborate rules for men, with all their distinguishing possibilities, to themselves. These observations all point to the same truth about these writers: their concern was to use manners in the cause of hierarchy, not to regulate behavior between peers.

As the elite code has already been described, we need not review it in detail. But it is instructive to compare in a general way how a gentleman's behavior was to differ from a woman's. Contrary to their advice that women keep much at home and move cautiously abroad, for example, the courtesy writers assumed that gentlemen would mix freely in society and come into contact with many other persons. While women were instructed to let modesty direct their body carriage and facial expressions, gentlemen were given more specific and elaborate instructions that emphasized the importance of body control. Reflecting the expectation that they would be much in society, the courtesy works gave men advice on gestures of salutation and the proper use of place in encounters that no one bothered to give women. Unlike a woman, a gentleman could talk freely (although he was to suppress all "rude noises"), and was to avoid being too silent as well as too talkative. He had to pay attention to his voice, manner, use of titles and choice of topics in conversation; but he did not, like a woman, have to strive for modesty in manner.[37]

There was one category of advice that Puritan ministers did share with ordinary men and women alike: rules concerning disorderly speech. Like women, men were to be careful in their exercise of wit, to refrain from boasting, and to avoid profanity and obscenity.[38] The writers gave men of all ranks special advice, however, concerning the expression of anger. Men were to refrain from speaking harshly or reproachfully to or of anyone. They were to avoid contradicting or quarreling with others. And they were never to give rein to rage.[39] This last advice presents a problem in that historians have claimed that anger was especially forbidden to women in this culture. We do find records of women being prosecuted for "railing" at others. But neither the Puritan ministers nor the courtesy writers warned women against reproachful or angry talk in general society; they only told women not to speak harshly to their husbands. It is likely that angry talk was regarded as bad on the part of both men and women; both sexes certainly figured prominently in this period's numerous slander suits. But the advice casts doubt on the notion that angry speech was regarded as a particularly female problem. A similar issue arises regarding gossip. Some scholars have asserted that gossiping was regarded as a mostly feminine failing, but only a couple of writers urged women not to gossip, and one of them hinted that some gossip was acceptable. Moreover, a couple of authors advised men not to gossip. Apparently Puritan concerns about disorderly speech were not confined to women. Women may have been doubly offensive when speaking out because they were inferior to men and not supposed to talk too much, but the evidence does not confirm that the crime itself was gendered.[40]

The advice to men and women concerning behavior in the presence of their own sex or in general society suggests, then, that the Puritan leaders of early New England had two concerns. They wished for all women to exhibit their secondary status in this man's world by behaving with modesty. They wished for elite men like themselves to justify and communicate their authority by exhibiting a distinguishing self-mastery.[41] But they did not care much about behavior between ordinary men. The Puritan leaders' concern about disorderly speech in all ranks is the exception that proves the rule; for such speech could challenge the hierarchy that was their primary interest.

THE VISION OF GENDER ROLES revealed by the advice literature presents a paradox: while the underlying assumption seems to have been that women were outside the social world, gender differences were not emphasized.[42] The larger question (not fully answerable here) is: How did this relative nonconstruction of gender affect women in reality? It may be that, in gender as in rank relations, the New England cultural elite created other problems in keeping a distinguishing self-mastery to themselves. For in simply urging women to be modest in general and reverential toward their husbands in particular, they neglected to instill further self-controls. Their omission is evident in their need to resort to more drastic measures to deal with the disorderly women who occasionally rear their proud heads in the local records.[43]

Of course there were practical reasons why the authors did not think women required much advice. Women did not need as much instruction as men because proper behavior on their part changed less than that of men over the course of the life cycle. In this sense, manners were like dress; women continued to wear the gowns of childhood, while young men took on breeches as they grew.[44] This may explain why the authors sometimes noted that even in their positions of authority vis-à-vis young persons as mothers and mistresses, women would not succeed in commanding the same deference that men did. Their early "weakness" was thought to follow them through life.

This is not to say that as an adult a woman's inferiority to her husband was as great as her inferiority to her elders when she was young. Because wives were also their husbands' companions, their inferiority was in some ways moderated, and some of the rules for their behavior toward their husbands (and vice versa) were a bit like the rules for interaction between equals. Historians have suggested that it was the simple economy of the early colonial period that served to temper gender inequality by reinforcing the "elasticity" of early modern gender roles, but the manners evidence suggests that even normative ideals of the sort found in sermons and courtesy works were more complex than has been recognized.[45] While some have acknowledged the mixed message of Puritan theology (spiritual equality and marriage as contract versus husband as household priest and household head), the conduct literature points to a less frequently recognized source of ambivalence: it was the sexual tie of marriage that made this relationship different from other inferior-superior relationships and from other peer relationships. Not only were husbands and wives to be more affectionate in their behavior, but some of the rules for male-female interaction were less related to the overt exercise of power than to the regulation and veiling of sexuality.[46] Of course these rules have power attributes of their own, but of a different sort than rules for other relations.

This is important evidence because so many portraits of marriage in early New England have been drawn from the potentially overly negative picture of patriarchal courts dealing with couples in conflict.[47] Taken together with the rules that were supposed to regulate class and age relations, the gender evidence suggests that in the minds of the writers who dispensed conduct advice to seventeenth-century New Englanders, the inferiority of women to men was embedded in several other kinds of inferiorities (i.e., rank and age) in a complicated hierarchy; and instead of being "the very model" of hierarchy, the inferiority of women to men was in fact the weakest inequality of all.[48] This point shows the importance, for social history topics like the history of women, of asking how one social variable, such as gender, compares with others, for example, class or age. Studying manners is one way of doing so.

While female behavior was relatively unconstructed in the cultural sense, so too was that of ordinary men. For while these men had to learn how to exert authority over children, servants, and wives—thereby ensuring social order—the dispensers of advice did not deem it necessary to teach them much else. The elite code that the advisors embraced was confined to men, but it did not apply to all men and therefore did not serve to define maleness in this society. Again, these observations help us to understand the occasional glimpses in local court records of unrestrained behavior on the part of ordinary men and women. Again, they suggest that relative to the dividing lines of rank and age, those of gender fell relatively lightly in this society.

Conclusion: Manners and a Vertical Social Order

We can learn more about the conduct writers' vision of the social order through direct comparison of the rules for different relations. With regard to behavior toward superiors, the strictest advice, or that which demanded the most deference, was given to young servants respecting their masters. This relationship (at the intersection of age and class relations, given the strong correlation between age, service, and rank in early New England) was deemed the most unequal. Next in rigor was the advice to children on behavior with adults. The relationship between youth who were not servants and adults was slightly more relaxed. And adults themselves had still less deference to pay the aged. The relationship between women and men, especially outside of marriage, was not only less strictly regulated than the norm but occasionally subject to special rules as well. While most inferiors were to show deference to superiors by rising and, if male, bowing and uncovering, for example, women were not advised of any equivalent gestures to perform to men. And while the authors gave no advice concerning body contact with superiors in age or rank, they advised women to avoid too-familiar or unchaste touching of men, on the one hand, and too-violent touching, or beating, on the other. Apparently the authors assumed that the possibility of these acts on the part of other inferiors was so remote that they did not even warrant consideration.

Concerning behavior with peers, elite men, or gentlemen, were given the most advice, especially concerning physical carriage, facial expression, and proper conversation. Otherwise, the authors were silent on peer relations. They did not much care about the interaction of ordinary men and women. Indeed, some advice on behavior with peers actually reveals the authors' desire to secure the deference of inferiors. Thus were children and servants advised not to discuss matters "above" them, even among themselves.

Mirroring the rules for behavior with superiors, those for behavior toward inferiors gave the most reinforcement to the superiority of masters over servants. Next in inequality was the relationship between adults and children, followed by that between adults and youth. The superiority of the elite over inferiors in rank was somewhat less reinforced by etiquette, and that of men over women the least. For instance, while men and members of the elite were given little advice on the amount of contact they were to have with women and inferiors in social rank, masters were advised both to control the time of young servants and to spend time with them to supervise their work and behavior. The authors added, however, that masters were not to make their servants their companions, because any familiarity was apt to undermine their authority. If young servants misbehaved they could and should be beaten. Parents were to spend much time with their children, both to supervise their behavior and to teach them; but parents were never warned against making their children their companions. In fact, they were to encourage their children to keep them company, though they were not to spoil them. And adults were not allowed to beat their children as severely as they were allowed to beat their servants.

Husbands were considered their wives' proper governors, and yet the authors did not speak of the necessity of their avoiding too much familiarity, at least in private. The authors did tell husbands that they should always treat their wives in a loving, gentle, and amiable manner. As it was never permissible for men to beat women, it is clear that women were not deemed as inferior to men as children and servants were to parents and masters. But this is not to be taken as a sign of equality between the sexes either, for the reason it was shameful for men to beat women was because the latter were weaker. Of course the notion that it was wrong to bully the weak did not stop the authors from telling masters and parents to beat their servants and children. Relative to other relations, women's position was poised somewhere between equality and inferiority to men.

What, then, can be said of the social hierarchy delineated by early New English rules for social behavior? First, it is clear that servants were at the bottom of the ladder, regardless of their sex. As all ranks put their youth out to service in other households in seventeenth- and early-eighteenth-century New England, the age of servants was more salient to their status than their social rank. Indeed, servants may have served as an artificial inferior class. Just above servants in the social hierarchy were young children living at home, again regardless of their rank or sex. Just above them were youth who were not servants and thus living with their own families, regardless of their sex or rank. Above children and youth of both sexes came mature women, again regardless of their social rank and perhaps also regardless of their age, as elderly women were much circumscribed in their proper behavior. Aged women were told that they could expect the reverence of younger persons on account of their age, but they had to merit such respect by an extremely sober, grave, and restrained behavior. Mature women were clearly superior to children and youth of both sexes, especially in their roles as mothers and mistresses, but they were not as superior to young persons as were fathers and masters.

Above women came ordinary men, and above them came elite men. All adult men were superior to children and youth, especially in their positions as fathers and masters. They were superior to mature women, especially in their roles as husbands. While one might assume that aged men were at the top of the social hierarchy, regardless of their social rank, the authors contradict this order of things—explicitly by telling elite males that they did not need to show reverence to an aged parent in public if they themselves were of a higher rank or official position, and implicitly by giving all other persons much detailed advice on the showing of deference to mature elite males while only telling them in a general way to revere the aged. Further, their advice to all persons not to despise, contemn, mock, or scoff at old people betrays the authors' sense that the aged were in some ways as weak socially as they were physically. In all, it would seem that while aged men were clearly to be reverenced, mature adult men of the elite were at the apex of the social hierarchy. Given the tone and distribution of their advice, it is inconceivable that the authors expected persons to defer more to aged males of the middling and lower sort than to the male magistrates and ministers who made up the upper layer of society in early New England, especially as many of the authors were drawn from that very stratum of the ruling elite.

The social hierarchy just described suggests a general ordering of the principles of social organization. It suggests that the first principle dividing early colonial society in the minds of the Puritans was age. The Puritans devoted far more attention to this issue than did the courtesy authors. Before maturity all persons were inferior, regardless of their rank or sex. The second principle dividing the population was sex. Among mature adults, whether a person was male or female was the most salient factor in their social position. Mature women, regardless of their rank or age, were inferior to mature men.[49] This is what explains Mistress Phillips's efforts to show deference to young Reverend Shepherd. Thus while the manners evidence contests the assertion that gender inequality was the model for all other inequalities, it supports the idea that gender inequality served to encourage ordinary men's commitment to hierarchy. Indeed, ordinary men became men by marrying.[50] The third principle dividing the population was social rank. That is, adult males found their positions in the top quarter of the social hierarchy according to their rank. Thus, the population in general was divided by age, adults were divided by sex, and men were divided by rank.

Having discerned the outlines of the social order depicted in conduct advice, we can now return to the question posed at the outset: what role did the authors wish social ritual to play in seventeenth- and early-eighteenth-century New England? Although the manners they proclaimed played somewhat different roles in each of the different relations, they can be said to have served one common purpose—that of regulating and reinforcing inequality. When Englishmen came to New England in the early seventeenth century they desired to preserve long-held notions about society, despite whatever contrary lessons either the forces of modernization or their new environment tried to teach them. Indeed, it has often been argued that their hunger for order, always part of the human condition, increased in the face of what they perceived as a wilderness. And thus, the evidence suggests that they resorted to ritual to bridge the gap between their hierarchical cosmology and encroaching contrary realities. Of course, as the holders of power, elite men had the most at stake; they had the most to lose if the relative equality of circumstance wrought by immigration and the fluidity of status that was growing with commerce permeated the larger institutions, the "big rules," governing society. So the ruling class tried to use the communicative function of social ritual by adhering to a code of behavior that set them off from the groups they wanted to control. They attempted to employ the social control function of ritual in trying to teach manners to the ruled—manners that would act, along with other institutions, to reinforce their revered but vulnerable inequality.

Thus, manners can tell us something about this society, both by revealing the exact contours of the power structure in the minds of the elite and showing how some of their major concerns might have been ritually expressed and resolved. We can also learn something about this society from what manners were not designed to accomplish. If the primary role of etiquette was to reinforce inequality by regulating the behavior of inferiors in the presence of superiors, and superiors in the presence of inferiors, the roles of the "ruled" were less "constructed" as regarded behavior among themselves. This fits with the fleeting glances of behavior on the part of the common folk that surface in court records and elite diaries. The court records are also testimony to the role of the community in "external" regulation of behavior. Beyond deferring to their betters, it was far less necessary than in later periods for ordinary people to regulate themselves as individuals.

In the end, it must be said, the wishes of the elite would be frustrated. The conditions of the "New World" and the forces of change would continue to erode, and eventually undermine, the foundations of hierarchy. And perhaps the elite, for all their fancy footwork, tripped themselves. For in refusing to share the self-control advice, they limited their ability to reform the commons. The latter would bow under compulsion, but not freely. And when Sewall or some other leader left the scene, so did the need for civility. As we shall see, that the majority did not internalize and exert self-control was a major distinction between this old order and the new one on the horizon.

PART II

Revolution: An Opening of Possibilities, 1740–1820

F O U R

MIDDLE CLASS RISING

I n January of 1759, a young lawyer from Massachusetts recorded a painful self-assessment in his diary. Among other deficiencies, he noted

> I have insensibly fallen into a Habit of Affecting Wit and Humour, of Shrugging my Shoulders, and moving [and] distorting the muscles of my face. My Motions are stiff and uneasy, ungraceful, and my attention is unsteady and irregular. These are Reflections on myself that I make. They are faults, Defects, Fopperies, and follies, and Disadvantages. Can I mend these faults and supply these Defects!

Not only did John Adams examine his own behavior in this fashion; he was also acutely interested in studying others' behavior. The pages of his diary are studded with his observations of "the Air, Countenances, Actions, and Speeches" of others—or his self-chastisement when he neglected to record them. At one point he even chided himself for not observing his parents' "faces, Eyes, Actions and Expressions" more closely during a domestic argument! Adams's diary reveals a level of concern about the body and gracefulness that is not present in earlier diaries, even of the elite. It can be compared, for example, with Samuel Sewall's diary, one of the most detail-laden of the early colonial period. Although the latter reveals an elite preoccupation with proper behavior, it does not reveal the same obsession with control of the body.[1] What does this mean? Although he would rise to fame and fortune, young Adams's family background was undeniably of "the middling sort." The fact of his rise, and that of a number of other "Founders," has been acknowledged by historians. Gordon Wood has even suggested a link between the Founders' interest in deportment and this period of exceptional access to the elite from below. He denies that their interest was the expression of middle-class culture, however, and claims instead that they were simply trying to make up for less than aristocratic birth by learning to behave like aristocrats. This makes sense from their perspective. But it is possible that their actions mean more if we stand back and look at them from the longer perspective of the history of middling folk.[2] From that perspective young Adams's interest in manners seems very much an expression of middle-class culture.

Scholars have insisted that the most important social cleavage in late-eighteenth- and early-nineteenth-century America was between the elite and everyone else: the middling and lower sort were lumped together in contemporary visions of the social order. As we have seen, this was indeed the primary social cleavage suggested by the conduct literature that circulated in early colonial New England. But the conduct literature of the revolutionary era reveals a different picture. The optic of conduct literature offers a view of northern society as a whole after the mid-eighteenth century, as Philadelphia and New York came into their own as centers of book publication and importation. A new class equation is unmistakable in the code of manners circulating in the North in this period because it was different from the old code that prescribed certain behaviors for elite men and deference for everyone else. Contrary to historians' claims about the verticality of most relationships in the revolutionary era, the deferential model of manners, designed to reinforce inequality in the early colonial period, began to be replaced by a new model that focused on relations between equals.[3] As we shall see, the conduct literature that conveyed this new model was different in character and authorship as well as content from the works circulating before. Among other changes, most of the authors were of middling class status.

The changes in manners suggest that overtly patriarchal conceptions of the social order were being challenged by a rise in the status of the middling sort, along with youth and, to some degree, women. An "opening of possibilities" can be discerned in the new etiquette; it was not so much intended to guide the behavior of these groups in reference to their superiors, as had formerly been the case, as it was to help them step into new, less subordinate roles. There were limits to this revolution in manners—the lower sort and young children were not invited to join—but the changes were nevertheless dramatic.

The conduct literature challenges the orthodoxy that middle-class culture only developed in America in the second quarter of the nineteenth century. Those decades were simply when middle-class culture became hegemonic, and it stands to reason that that predominance did not happen overnight. Of course much depends on what is meant by "middle class." Stuart Blumin, the leading student of the antebellum middle class, defines it by occupation, and argues that what distinguished the middling from the lower sort was non-manual versus manual work.[4] It is such a definition that allows him to claim that a middle class did not exist in the eighteenth century, for the vast majority of the population were farmers and artisans. Only a tiny elite did not work with their hands. The class of clerks and professionals was still small. But fixation on occupation denies a truth recognized by an earlier generation of historians who insisted on the middle-class character of this society, and who noted that the groups of farmers, artisans, merchants, and professionals all included persons who were poor, persons who were rich, and many of middling means. These so-called Consensus historians acknowledged the growing gap between the rich and the poor in eighteenth-century cities (although they were not aware just how many poor there were), but they echoed contemporary observations of the moderately comfortable lifestyles, literacy, and self-respect of many Americans. While much of the prosperity of the population was due to its access to farmland, the growth of urban wealth in the eighteenth century produced a bigger middle class than had existed before. One scholar has described, for example, a clear middling merchant lifestyle in revolutionary Philadelphia.[5]

While the folks in the middle in late-eighteenth-century America had different occupations than the increasingly white-collar middle class of the pre–Civil War decades, the conduct literature suggests that they shared other attributes, namely the social values and practices that students of the antebellum period label middle class. The values of self-discipline, hard work, temperance, and so on—those of the "self-made man"—did not arise only in company with the economic changes that gave rise to the antebellum "non-manual" middle class. They had a longer evolution.[6]

The conduct literature thus suggests that the middle class was rising in the revolutionary era. What we see is a new literature that was written for a competitive status system rather than one in which one's place was largely determined by one's birth. Such texts were open to use by the middling sort in a way that was not possible before. The middle class appropriation of this literature does not become completely obvious until the antebellum era. But again, the revolutionary era was one of transition from a hierarchical to a horizontal social order. Historians who insist that the late-eighteenth-century middling sort were still entangled in the claims of a deferential society miss an essential point revealed by the transition, which was the derivative nature of nineteenth-century middle-class culture. The middling sort from whom the middle class emerged were aping the gentry in manners. The code that authors for the middling sort were offering was the old aristocratic code, but in a far more detailed and accessible form. It would simply be still more detailed and accessible in the antebellum period. This is the point that historians miss in insisting on the aristocratic pretensions of the founders. They may have thought they were simply substituting a "natural aristocracy" for one of birth, but when enough people took the same path, a path allowed by the rejection of an ascriptive status system, the pursuit of gentility became an undeniably middle-class act. Manners, then, were little different from the "emulative consumption" that historians describe as accompanying the consumer revolution of the eighteenth century. Along with tea sets and other such notions of gentility, middling folk could also acquire the motions.[7]

It is not simply the fact that middle-class authors were disseminating the old aristocratic code to a broader audience that signals the emergence of middle-class culture. Two other features of the revolutionary code of manners give it a middle-class character. First, much of the new detail in the code of conduct lay in the particular area of physical self-control. The new middle-class authors took this old aristocratic concern to a whole new level and thereby made it their own. As we shall see, many were inspired by the work of an aristocrat, Lord Chesterfield; but they were both more concerned than he was about bodily self-control and more intent on giving elaborate instructions to achieve it.[8] Self-control would help the middling both achieve and assert their worth. Second, the authors expressed a certain middle-class pride by encouraging interaction with equals and cautioning against both affectation and servility. They were far more interested in interaction between peers than in regulating relations with superiors and inferiors. That greater interest in self-control and preoccupation with behavior between equals were strains of an emerging middle-class culture is borne out by the fact that these were the main themes of the manuals that circulated between 1820 and 1860, the period that scholars agree saw the dawn of middle-class cultural dominance in America. The revolutionary-era instructions were thus a harbinger of the culture of self-improvement that would flourish in the later period.

We will understand that culture better if we understand its origins and recognize that the starting point for self-improvement—the repudiation of inherited status so vividly described by that first American testament to self-improvement, Franklin's *Autobiography*—was an eighteenth-century issue. Thus the story of manners in eighteenth-century America is not simply the story of the spread of aristocratic refinement in tension with the republicanism of the rest of the culture, as Richard Bushman has suggested, for the middling repudiated the basis of aristocratic power even as they seized the aristocratic armor of manners and remade it for their own purposes.[9] This helps to explain the "ambivalence" that some contemporaries expressed toward the spread of European notions of refinement in America, an ambivalence that was often expressed as criticism of "Chesterfieldian" behavior. This "republican criticism" was really an expression of middle-class resentment of the aristocratic, even as they acquired gentility. Critics did aim slaps at Chesterfield, but this reminds us that they had all read him! And contemporaries clearly used his work as they transformed the meaning of genteel.[10]

These issues are brought to life in two letters written by another Founder of middling origins, Benjamin Rush. In one, he urged his son to prepare for a life of labor, the lot "of all young men who are not born to inherit large estates" and his own fate since the age of sixteen. He went on to claim, however, that his life had been a happy one and that he would not "exchange his labors for the independent situation of any idle, sauntering, purse-proud citizen of Philadelphia." Notwithstanding this expression of pride in middling status, Rush was keenly interested in manners. In his very next letter he wrote to his daughter that he approved of her suitor, and not the least of his reasons was that he had heard that the man had "'highly polished and attracting manners.'"[11] In the last generation, neo-Progressive historians have taught us that the story of the American Revolution is not complete without recognition of how the lower orders shattered colonial habits of deference.[12] The conduct literature tells us that the middling played a huge role in this—not by challenging the elite head-on in mob actions but by coopting their code of behavior. It would remain to be seen, of course, how democratic their middling revolution really was.

SOME OF THE INSTITUTIONS that had reinforced the old order and therefore made manners less necessary for ordinary people during the early colonial period were either dying out after the mid-eighteenth century or were so substantially altered as to have lost their old social functions. The church and the court began to pay less formal heed to distinctions of rank. Church seating was no longer assigned in the same ways. Community surveillance of behavior and court enforcement of such surveillance weakened as communities grew. Sumptuary laws were no longer enforced. These practices were not falling out of use because American society was growing more equal; social stratification was simply becoming too complex and fluid to serve as a scheme for institutional organization.

The role of the church also declined in the teaching of manners. While well over half of the conduct works of the early colonial period were written by Protestant clergymen, many of them Puritan, less than a fifth came from clerical pens in the revolutionary era, and only half of these were Puritan. Only a handful of sermons appearing early in the period gave direct advice on face-to-face behavior. As religious pluralism and secularization took their toll after the mid-eighteenth century, and as ministers lost some of their earlier authority, northerners took much less social instruction from this source.

Importation and publication figures suggest that Americans were taking more instruction directly from books. The supply of conduct works grew in numbers of titles and editions. Whereas forty-four different works can be identified as having circulated in the north between 1620 and 1738, at least seventy-five works were printed or imported between 1738 and 1820.[13] The average number of editions or importations per title doubled (from five to ten). Book production in general grew dramatically in the revolutionary era. Probate records and magazine subscriber lists show that book ownership and magazine reading were spreading rapidly, especially among the middling. While books were expensive, it appears that the new lending libraries that sprang up in most eastern towns and cities went a long way in making them accessible to the growing middle-class audience. Conduct works in particular were not simply imported and reprinted in the revolutionary era; library records and private papers show that they were repeatedly borrowed, recommended, referred to, and quoted. Whether attributed to their original authors or not, diaries and letters show Americans appropriating the maxims of the conduct writers; Chesterfieldian sentences are even recorded in the back of Samuel Savage's almanac. These works clearly met a need.[14]

Who wrote these books? Not only was less advice coming from Puritan ministers, but the colonists also ceased importing the works of Renaissance courtiers. Most of the literature circulating after midcentury was written by British laymen of middling class status who were writers by profession. Note the contrast with the earlier regime: whereas in the late seventeenth and early eighteenth centuries the Puritan elite consumed courtesy literature and dispensed different advice in sermons to their inferiors, now middle-class British writers were dispensing conduct advice to a much broader audience. As we shall see, these writers were not simply passing along deference advice, like their predecessors, but the whole code of manners. And middle-class authors meant that middle-class readers were no longer simply receiving instruction from on high. These writers, spokespersons for the emerging British professional and commercial middle classes, were seizing cultural authority. At least the prosperous among the American middling sort must have shared their views, since American printers and importers acted to meet the growing demand for their work.[15]

The British authorship of the majority of revolutionary-era works accords with "anglicization" theories of eighteenth-century American culture. The impulse to look to England for models of behavior was facilitated by the increasing economic and political involvement with the mother country and spurred by the contemporary belief in the cultural degeneration of colonial society. It was also spurred by the fact that it was often cheaper for American printer/booksellers to import British works or publish pirated editions of those works than to pay American authors for native productions. Whatever the cause, English conduct literature continued to be popular until the 1820s. Arthur Schlesinger Sr. rightly remarked that this trend "suggests how little political separation affected subservience to the mother country in matters of decorum."[16]

The British authorship of revolutionary-era conduct literature also makes clear that the changes described here in the American context were part of a transatlantic phenomenon. Thus the "revolutionary era" referred to in these pages was that of the larger transformation to modernity at work in Western society, not simply that in the new American polity. Of course owing to American republicanism and the American class structure, the rise of middle-class culture had special power here.

If the Declaration of Independence in 1776 did not in itself cause much of a stir in manners, the nearly contemporaneous American publication (in 1775) of Lord Chesterfield's *Letters of Advice to His Son*, was quite important. Chesterfield was the first English conduct writer to lay heavy emphasis on gracefulness and to give full treatment to the means of attaining it. He ignored the Anglo-American tendency to embed etiquette injunctions in more moralistic and abstract advice, and took the more Continental route of emphasis on the smaller details of behavior. He did not pretend to be more interested in instructing his son in morality and piety than in teaching him how to make his way successfully in the world. This worldliness was the cause of the wave of unfavorable criticism with which the *Letters* were first greeted. The *Letters* were not a systematized code of manners, however (though manners lessons were scattered throughout), and thus while they aroused indignation in their unedited form, English and American publishers quickly came out with works that both excised the offensive parts and made the conduct rules more accessible by categorizing them. In these capsule forms it quickly became the most popular work on conduct, both in its own editions—variously titled, abridged, and arranged—and in selections in school readers and other etiquette works. In fact, Chesterfield's *Letters* and another conduct work, John Gregory's *Father's Legacy to His Daughters*, were two of the three bestsellers of 1775.

The appeal of Chesterfield's work lay in the fact that more than any of its predecessors his was a manual for strivers. His chief message to his son was that he should work to appear a certain way, regardless of his true character, natural endowments, or inner state. His advice was thus to cultivate appearances—even, when necessary, to dissimulate. This was useful advice to those on the rise, those in the process of making themselves. While this message has to have contributed to the moral ambivalence middling Americans felt about Chesterfield, it must also explain why they all read him, again and again, decade after decade. Although many revolutionary-era conduct works continued to flow in the same moralistic and religious vein as had early colonial works, it was Chesterfield's innovations that would persist.[17] Indeed, Chesterfield sowed the seeds for antebellum etiquette. His was the only revolutionary-era work to be reprinted through 1860, and it was constantly referred to. The fact of its first publication in the 1770s is one of many indicators that the revolutionary era in manners was a transitional phase between the more stable systems of the early colonial and antebellum periods.

The continued popularity of Chesterfield's *Letters* into the mid-nineteenth century confirms the utility of this aristocrat's work for the middle class. While he built on older elite-oriented courtesy works such as Della Casa, the middle class could use Chesterfield because he was rather vague about class distinctions. Indeed, he often ridiculed pride in rank and place as well as an overbearing attitude toward servants, who in his opinion were equals in all but material wealth.[18] Other revolutionary-era conduct works shared these traits—even those, like Chesterfield's, that were originally intended for an elite audience. This reflected the fluidity of a class system increasingly based on wealth and Enlightenment thinking about the natural equality of men. In the earlier society of orders the middling and lower sorts did not have the means, ability, or ambition to study the duties and deportment of the ideal gentleman as outlined in the courtesy works. This was no longer the case by the mid-eighteenth century, as many among the middling sort became literate and prosperous, and as older institutions for keeping people in their place fell out of use.

In any event, few of the courtesy works were still imported. Only a tenth of the manuals reprinted or imported in the North were originally intended for an elite audience (as compared to a third of the early colonial works); and most of these were not treatises on the behavior of the ideal gentleman, as had been the case, but rather were works by British aristocrats like Lord

Chesterfield that were addressed to their children. They all shared his more worldly tone and lack of a clear class tag. Some of these works appeared in so many editions—by themselves, bound with one another, or abridged in collections of other works—as to cast doubt on their limitation to an elite audience. Indeed, one sometimes finds these titles recommended in works written by middle-class authors for middle-class readers.[19]

Over two-thirds of revolutionary-era conduct books clearly addressed the middling sort. Some of these works were intended for both the middle class and the upper class, some for the middling sort alone. Because these works and those ostensibly addressed to all classes (about a fifth of the total) were in reality only limited in audience to those who could read and afford them, we can only exclude the humblest folk from their possible audience. That many of the manuals of this group give advice on how to deal with domestic servants but do not address servants themselves further justifies this exclusion. Although these works gave similar prescriptions in terms of manners, they varied in character, style, and other content. There were treatises on the education of youth, general advice works, etiquette books, a few religious works, and works in the parental-advice-to-a-child genre. Among the last were some of the most widely circulated conduct books of the revolutionary era. Dr. Gregory's *Father's Legacy*, for example, went through at least sixty-nine American editions (it was also imported) and was often bound together with Chesterfield's *Letters*. It was excerpted in American magazines; Benjamin Rush sent a copy to John Adams's daughter.[20] Also popular were the etiquette books, half of which were intended for schoolroom use. Some of these were readers with extensive selections from Chesterfield, such as John Hamilton Moore's *The Young Gentleman and Lady's Monitor*, which appeared in at least thirty-seven editions.[21] Others greatly resembled Moody's *School of Good Manners*, which itself continued to be printed during this period, though most of these works were written after 1750. The growing role of etiquette books in conduct instruction is consistent with the growth of a class society, for these works spelled out directly the little rules for behavior in various situations and were accessible to anyone with the means and inclination to follow their prescriptions.

Only five of the conduct works circulating in this period even began to address the lower classes. Of course little of the literature consumed during the early colonial period had been directed to the lower sort. But oral instruction left its trace in many sermons to which they were compelled to listen, and those teachings had been reinforced by laws and other institutions for the upholding of social distinctions and proper behavior. Traces of such forces at work in the second half of the eighteenth and early nineteenth century are harder to find. Institutions for socialization and social control were getting weaker as inequality grew, feeding the more affluent colonists' fears that the ideals of deference, hierarchy, and order were disintegrating. As the poor got poorer, they were also wrestling free from the social control of ministers and magistrates.[22]

Even old patterns of familial dependency, which had helped to insure the subordination of the young and poor laborer (as apprentice or indentured servant), were dying out under the pressures of occasional labor shortage and the increasing inclination of both workers and employers to wage labor. Ironically, the only two pieces of advice literature directed exclusively to the lower sort address that specific group among the poor: the young and dependent servant or apprentice. Three other works addressed servants in the context of discussions of the master-servant relationship.[23] It is simply doubtful that people of limited means and literacy read them. Perhaps a few did, but it is more likely that these books were read primarily by the middling sort, to whom all but the passages to servants were directed. Still, it is worth attending to their prescriptions, to follow the evolution of middling attitudes toward inferiors. Revolutionary-era conduct literature registers an interesting ambivalence about the inequality of the lower sort, in the form of injunctions to the middling to help soften their lot. This suggests that in this time of middle-class elevation, the middling were not greatly concerned with setting themselves off from those below them. Their sights were trained on the barriers to gentility above.

REFLECTING THE WANE of straightforward deference advice and the new concern about behavior with peers, conduct works circulating in revolutionary America offered only a modest amount of advice about proper behavior with social superiors. But even here the period's trends of a more elaborate version of previously aristocratic advice to the middling and an aversion to servility are evident. For example, authors for the elite and those who addressed the middling sort gave similar advice concerning the proper amount of contact with superiors, but the latter gave extra cautions. This advice called for much less deference than the early colonial admonitions that inferiors should allow superiors to initiate encounters. Indeed, authors for both classes recommended seeking out the company of superiors, although some stressed that personal merit, not social status, ought to be the chief criterion for ideal companions. A good number of authors gave both opinions. Lord Chesterfield thus advised his son to "Endeavor as much as you can" to keep company "with people above you," but suggested that wisdom and merit were as important as birth or riches in the assessment of good company. "Mrs. Peddle" expanded on this point for middling readers, cautioning:

> Greater attention is paid to the accidental circumstances of rank and affluence, than to real merit; we should not else so often see people of the middling rank, when flattered by the notice of a superior, so elated with the honor of keeping, what they call good company, when perhaps that superior is conspicuous for almost every vice and meanness. This is a grand mistake surely. . . .

In his diary, John Adams pondered "Who are to be understood by the better sort of People?" and concluded that there was "no difference between one Man and another, but what real Merit creates."[24]

Some writers actually discouraged middling folk from choosing superiors

as companions or paying them visits too frequently. Some claimed that entertaining superiors was unwise, as the provisions would either be too humble for
the guest or too prodigal for the host. Such aiming above oneself in one's
company would make one servile to superiors and contemptuous of inferiors.
One writer thus advised young women to "pursue not the society of women of
higher rank than your own; be not elated by their notice; look not down on
those who enjoy it not." Similarly, the 1806 edition of Fenelon's *Treatise on
the Education of Daughters* advised parents of daughters in "the middle ranks"
to find them company "among those of the same rank."[25]

In many cases, the elite and the middling sort were given similar advice,
but the latter were given a few extra tips. Both classes were told to show respect for superiors through strict attention, but works for the middling sort
added that one could thereby learn from their manners.[26] Both groups were
given the old direction to give superiors the best places in an encounter; but
now only works for the middling sort gave the more detailed instructions to
allow superiors to go first, and to give them the right-hand or wall side when
walking.[27]

Patterns in the rules for body carriage, facial expression, salutations, and
conversation are similar. Both classes were advised to demonstrate respect for
superiors in each of these areas, but more advice is found in works for the
middling sort.[28] And as regarded demeanor, the extra advice to the middling
sort warned against servility. Both classes were to adopt a respectful demeanor
toward superiors. They were not to be overly familiar but, in keeping with the
generally less deferential tone of revolutionary-era advice, to show their respect "in an easy, unembarrassed, and graceful manner." A number of writers
for the middle class, however, showed further ambivalence about excessive respect. John Burton noted that "the respect due to Superiors is so seldom omitted, that it will be superfluous to use any arguments in its recommendation."
The Marquise de Lambert claimed that "there is always a respect due to persons in elevated stations, but it is merely an outward respect: our real respect
and esteem is due only to merit." She and other authors insisted that while a
certain humility was due, one was to avoid a "mean and flattering," "fawn-
ing," "servile," or awestruck demeanor with superiors.[29] The tendency to servility and "low adulation" was one reason some authors advised the middling
sort not to associate much with persons above them.

That similar advice is found in revolutionary-era works intended for
"persons of quality" and works intended for a wider audience suggests that the
gap between the middling sort and the elite so evident in the earlier period
was narrowing. This change is underscored by the one substantive difference
between revolutionary-era advice for the elite and advice for the middling:
the new warnings to the latter not to let their respectful behavior extend to
servility. Clearly some leveling was taking place in the authors' vision of the
social hierarchy.

But the leveling was not complete, for the writers had relatively little advice for the lower sort, and what they did give—mostly to servants concerning their masters—required more deference than asked of the middling or

upper sort. This advice had changed little from the early colonial period: in addition to the signs of respect in manner and talk that all classes owed to superiors, servants were to take extra care to be obliging and submissive in their demeanor, facial expressions, and talk with their masters.[30] If the conduct writers had new ideas about the proper behavior of the middling sort, they did not apply these ideas to servants.

THE ELITE AND THE middling sort were given especially similar advice on behavior with equals—owing, in part, to the great influence of Chesterfield's *Letters* on works for the middle class—but, in a reversal of the early colonial situation, the advice in works for the middling was always more extensive and elaborate than advice intended only for the elite. Sometimes the differences were subtle. Compare Lord Chesterfield's description of the awkward man with that which appeared in John Moore's *Monitor*. Chesterfield wrote: "When an awkward fellow first comes into a room, it is highly probable that his sword gets between his legs, and throws him down." Moore, writing for a broader audience, was uncomfortable with the aristocratic accessory and wished to give further instruction; he wrote: "When an awkward fellow first comes into a room, *he attempts to bow*, and his sword, *if he wears one*, goes between his legs and nearly throws him down" (emphasis added).[31] Similar to its early colonial counterpart, revolutionary-era advice to lower-class persons only repeated the standard precepts in their bare outlines, and on many points, such as awkward entrances, authors for the lower sort were silent.

Concerning the regulation of contact with equals, for example, works for the elite recommended keeping good company and avoiding bad company, to safeguard one's reputation and polish one's manners. Many more writers for the middle class gave advice that was similar but far more elaborate and cautionary in tone. They advised taking time in contracting friendships. Matthew Hale pleaded: "be very wary and shy in choosing . . . any company or companions; be not too hasty in committing yourself to them: Stand off awhile till you have inquired . . . what they are." Writers for the middling also advised against an extensive acquaintance or too many familiar friends.[32] They even warned against too-frequent contact with virtuous and respectable peers. One was not to visit friends too often, or go into company where one was not sure of one's welcome. When visiting, one was not to stay so long as to weary one's hosts; it was better to "leave them with an Appetite" for one's company. As l'Abbé de Bellegarde advised, "Discretion teaches us to be ever ready to quit company, before company quit us."[33] These cautions were far more elaborate than any in earlier advice.

Lord Chesterfield often told his son to pay attention to peers, and many writers passed on this advice to the middle classes. He claimed that "If a man accosts you, and talks to you ever so dully and frivolously, it is worse than rudeness, it is brutality, to show him, by a manifest inattention to what he says, that you think him a fool or a block head, and not worth hearing." He added that "pulling out one letter after another and reading them in company, or cutting and paring one's nails, is impolite and rude. It seems to say, we are weary of the conversation." Benjamin Rush learned this lesson the hard way, and noted for posterity that "I once lost the business of a respectable and worthy family for several years by taking up a newspaper which lay upon a table and reading it while the lady of the house was giving me an uninteresting history of the case of one of her family." Writers who addressed the middling gave further instructions. One could only read or write in company if there was urgent necessity. Chiding servants or discussing domestic affairs were also improper impositions on others' time, as was being late for appointments or taking too long at table.[34]

Writers who addressed the middling both shared and embellished Chesterfield's suggestion that one should take the lower rather than the more honorable places in company, unless bid to do otherwise. Middling readers were told where and why they should observe this rule, but they were also advised not to go too far and "be troublesome in debasing thyself to the lowest." They were further instructed not to turn their backs to others and to apologize for walking between persons. The middling were also warned against crowding others: they were not to lean on another's chair, run against others in a door or passageway, or come too close to those with whom they spoke. Here as elsewhere middle-class authors seized what had been a few lines in old courtesy books and elaborated on them for their own class.[35]

Conduct works for all classes recommended an easy, affable, and courteous demeanor in the presence of equals; all were to avoid the extremes of formality and familiarity. Chesterfield placed enormous importance on demeanor. To him an easy manner was initially more important in relations with equals than one's inner talents and virtues, which took more time to be discovered. Writers for the elite and writers for the middling sort alike recommended a moderate degree of reserve with equals, some repeating Chesterfield's suggestion that "the general rule is to have a real reserve with almost everyone, and a seeming reserve with almost no one." But writers for the middle class again gave both a more detailed version of this advice and further cautions. They warned readers not to appear out of humor, fretful, melancholy, or surly. They recommended a certain modesty in manner; it was better to act as an inferior toward equals than to show airs of superiority. But one was not to be so humble as to fail to preserve one's dignity. Again, one was never to appear servile.[36]

Both works intended only for the elite and works for a broader audience warned against awkwardness and bashfulness. Lord Chesterfield beseeched his son to avoid them. He pronounced it shameful if a person could not enter company without embarrassment. He thought gracefulness the most important attribute of a person's demeanor. Writers for the middling repeated his entreaties but emphasized that one's gracefulness should not seem affected. William Paterson, yet another Founding Father of middling origins, voiced this concern when he wrote in a college essay that "The true gentleman is easy without affectation." John Adams noted that his mentor's "Grandeur" was "diminished by stiffness and affectation." Indeed, Adams often disparaged affectation in others, lamenting of one acquaintance that "Affectation runs thro the whole Man. His Air, his Gate, his Tone, his Gestures, his Pronunciation." These warnings against affectation were not expressions of ambivalence about gracefulness but indications of its importance. Truly graceful behavior was behavior that appeared "artless." The conduct writers did not assume that gracefulness came naturally, for they gave extensive advice about how it might be acquired. In warning about affectation, the conduct writers were reminding the middling that a convincing performance required work. One's manner would appear affected if one had not practiced enough to make it appear natural. Adams's pairing of affectation with stiffness was no accident.

Much of this advice on demeanor had been sketched out, in much simpler form, in early colonial advice to the elite. But Chesterfield gave Della Casa's old recommendation of graceful carriage a whole new importance by making gracefulness the epitome of genteel demeanor. He also injected something entirely new in recommending the maintenance of a disguised reserve with peers. Writers for the middling echoed and amplified both concerns, indicating a willingness (though not necessarily one they would acknowledge) to distinguish between the inner and outer self, and to work on polishing the latter.

Although he claimed that "a thousand little things, not separately to be defined, conspire to form these graces, this je ne scais quoi, that always pleases," most of Chesterfield's advice on avoiding awkwardness was advice concerning body carriage. In focussing on the body he was again borrowing from the old Continental courtesy tradition, but his repeated exhortations elevated the importance of body control. Chesterfield frequently warned his son "against those disagreeable tricks and awkwardnesses . . . such as odd motions, strange postures, and ungenteel carriage." He disapproved of all "Horseplay" and "romping" in the presence of equals; he gave his mocking description of the awkward man, who stumbled upon entering a room, made a mess at table, and never knew what to do with his hands. He remarked that "All this, I own is not in any degree criminal: but it is highly disagreeable and ridiculous in company, and ought very carefully to be avoided." He ended one lecture with the plea: "The Graces, the Graces, Remember the Graces!"

Chesterfield's advice on these matters was directed, in various forms, to both middle- and upper-class readers. But when it came to specifics, writers for the middle classes went even further than he did in the cause of self-mastery. For example, where Chesterfield advised his son never to "walk fast in the streets, which is a mark of vulgarity, ill-befitting the character of a gentleman or a man of fashion, though it may be tolerable in a tradesman," writers who addressed the middling sort did more. Note the different class language and level of detail in the new middle-class-oriented version of Della Casa:

> A gentleman ought not to run, or walk in too great a hurry along the streets, for it is beneath the dignity of a person *of any rank*, and more becoming a running footman or a post-boy: besides that, in running, a man

appears fatigued, perspires freely, and puffs and blows; all which are unbecoming a man *of any consequence*.

Nor yet ought our pace to be so very slow and tortoise like, nor so
stately and affected like that of some lady of quality, or a bride.

To stagger, likewise, or totter about as we walk, and to stretch ourselves out, as it were, with monstrous strides, is foolish and ridiculous.
Neither ought our hands to hang dangling down, nor yet our arms to be
projected or tossed backwards and forwards, like a plowman that is sowing his corn. . . . (emphasis added)

Authors who addressed the middling sort also added that one should always
stand up straight.[37]

As for the act of sitting, Chesterfield observed that "Awkward, ill-bred
people, being ashamed, commonly sit bolt upright, and stiff; others, too negli-
gent and easy . . . but a man of fashion makes himself easy, and appears so,
by leaning gracefully, instead of lolling supinely; and by varying those easy attitudes, instead of that stiff immobility of a bashful booby." While this might
seem elaborate enough, writers for the middling sort gave this advice and
then some. They claimed that graceful sitting was especially important at
table and warned against moving too much in one's seat. Some specified that
one should not cross one's legs but hold them "firm and settled," with the feet
even.[38] The advice on gestures of salutation, still relatively scant in this as in
the early colonial period, nevertheless conformed to the same pattern: works
addressed to the elite alone and works that also addressed the middling sort
gave very similar advice, but the latter included instructions that were more
direct and specific.[39]

As had been true of some of the old courtesy works, consideration of
body carriage in revolutionary-era manuals extended to the smallest of
actions—scratching oneself; drumming the table; biting one's nails; fingering
one's nose or ears, excessive coughing and yawning, and so on. In contrast
with the early colonial period, however, it was writers for the middling sort,
rather than those who addressed the elite alone, who gave the most extensive and detailed advice. Some authors for the middling repeated and elaborated on Chesterfield's proscriptions, others added new cautions. Some
scholars have noted that what was being denounced here was excessive self-
involvement, especially in ways that would detract from one's own dignity
and that of the occasion by highlighting body functions. These concerns help
us to understand John Adams's lament that a friend "scratches his neck, pulls
the Hair of his Wigg, strokes his Beard, rubbs his Eyes, and Lips."[40]

That elaborate advice on body carriage and repeated exhortations to be
graceful were addressed to the middling sort as well as the elite was the major
innovation of revolutionary-era manners. And this advice was more extensive than that addressed to the elite in the old courtesy books. The goal, for
the middling and the great alike, was supposed to be a dignified and "easy"
body carriage. But such a carriage could not have been easy to achieve, and
the authors apparently thought the middling sort had the most work to do.

That they were recommending this body work for the betterment of the middling is revealed by the writers' neglect to give the lower class any advice regarding body carriage before equals.

The middle class was also given similar but more elaborate advice than the elite regarding facial expression; one author went so far as to discuss a woman's proper facial expressions when watching a play. As was true of the advice regarding body carriage, the extra advice to the middling concerning facial expression urged greater mastery. Again Adams's diary suggests that these concerns were current, as when he regretfully observed of another man that he "has too little command of the Muscles of his face." Some control of the countenance was deemed important for all persons, for the face was thought to reveal one's character and the true meaning of one's words. Chesterfield argued that "a certain degree of outward seriousness in looks and actions gives dignity, without excluding wit, and decent cheerfulness, which are always serious themselves." Both the extremes of silly smiles and melancholy or ill-natured expressions were to be avoided, as well as "all unnatural distortions of the face." Benjamin Rush said his son Samuel behaved like a perfect gentleman but for his frown. Works that addressed the middle class warned further against making "ridiculous" faces and repeated some of the injunctions of the old courtesy works to this effect, such as those against "ogling or winking," lifting the eyebrows, or "wrying the mouth."[41]

Very many authors joined Chesterfield in urging upper- and middle-class readers to avoid laughing aloud, an expression "at all times ungraceful." This was another place where Chesterfield greatly expanded on concerns only hinted in the old courtesy works, and to our ears it is one of the strangest of revolutionary-era demands. Chesterfield objected to laughter because it distorted the face and made unpleasant noises. John Kasson has speculated that laughter was threatening because it undermined the self-control that was essential to genteel deportment. The advice to middle-class readers on this point was somewhat varied in strictness, although all agreed that "nothing shows a genteel person more than laughing decently." It was also, once again, more detailed.[42]

Writers for the middle classes also followed and elaborated on Lord Chesterfield's suggestions about controlling one's gaze. Again Chesterfield elevated an old courtesy-book concern by expanding on it. Whereas older writers had advised the elite not to look at the ground when speaking to peers, Chesterfield advised his son to "Always look people in the face when you speak to them; the not doing it is thought to imply conscious guilt; besides that, you lose the advantage of observing, by their countenances, what impression your discourse makes upon them. In order to know people's real sentiments, I trust much more to my eyes than to my ears. . . ." On the other hand, it was rude "to stare any person full in the face . . . as if you saw something wonderful in his appearance." Again writers for the middle classes both shared Chesterfield's advice and added still more. They explained that it was rude to stare at another at table, in the street, or in conversation, "as if you were taking his picture." Some added that it was impolite to "look upon one in company and immediately whisper to another."

A number of authors also followed Chesterfield in warning middle- and upper-class persons to beware of revealing too much in their faces, urging them to "Display as much as you can an unruffled and serene countenance" before others. Chesterfield warned "A man who does not possess himself enough to hear disagreeable things, without visible marks of anger and change of countenance, or agreeable ones without sudden bursts of joy, and expansion of countenance, is at the mercy of every artful knave or pert coxcomb." Chesterfield begged his son to make himself "absolute master" of his countenance, "whatever you may feel inwardly," for "a tell-tale countenance . . . is a great unhappiness."[43] This advice to watch others' faces while keeping a guard on one's own was new. It suggests again the role played by manipulation of the outward self in the developing bourgeois version of gentility.

Revolutionary-era advice concerning conversation, what one historian has called "the culminating genteel art," also fits the patterns traced above. Whether repeating old advice from the courtesy works or passing on Chesterfieldian innovations, writers for the middling gave more detailed versions than works intended only for the elite. This was true of the old warnings to the elite against making unnecessary noises in conversation, as by whispering, yawning or coughing.[44] It was true of advice on how much and when one should talk, which also had its origins in the old courtesy works. While most authors followed Chesterfield, who advised his son to "Talk often, but not long," for "a man may equally affront the company he is in, by engrossing all the talk, or observing a contemptuous silence" (Benjamin Rush and John Adams again echoed this advice, the first when he bemoaned "taciturnity in company," and the latter when he complained of James Otis that "No other Gentleman in Company can find a Space to put in a word"), writers for the middling alone added elaborate discussion of the old command never to interrupt others. Indeed, they described more than half a dozen different forms of this particular sin.[45]

Authors for the middling passed along Chesterfield's denunciations of awkward speech and his insistence on the importance of choosing and pronouncing one's words with care. This was another area where he built on courtesy-book advice. Naturally, one's talk was to be courteous and friendly, but there was more to do. Both the middling and the elite were urged not to bungle others' names or titles. Both were cautioned against using obscure or bombastic expressions. And here, too, works that addressed the middling went a bit further, reminding readers to use fashionable language and to avoid both rude and hackneyed phrases. Yet they also warned against affectation in speech; an "unstudied correctness" was the goal.[46]

While works for the elite and works for a broader audience both included the old advice (formerly addressed only to the elite) to choose conversational topics with the character of the company in mind, the latter works again spelled out this advice in greater detail. Chesterfield and his followers recommended small talk rather than "serious subjects, that might create disputes." Works that addressed the middling sort specified that such topics as literature, philosophy, or history were also safe. Some advice was such that had been given to both groups in the early colonial period but with the more elaborate versions addressed to the elite; now, the more detailed versions were addressed to the middling. Thus writers for both groups agreed that boasting was never proper, while some also warned the middling against fishing for praise or displaying one's superiority in any area. Both groups were urged to avoid gossiping, comparing others, and discussing their own affairs; works for the middling included variations on these tips as well.[47]

Writers for the middle classes were particularly and uniquely emphatic in denouncing profane speech about God or the saints, and, especially, lascivious talk. Over and over again they decried "that *execrable* and *foolish* vice of profane cursing and swearing," "Filthy or obscene talk," and "double entendres." One was not even to listen to improper talk. Benjamin Rush repeatedly associated good manners with abstention from obscene and profane talk, as when he said of John Wilkes, "He was perfectly well bred. Not an unchaste word or oath escaped his lips."[48]

Both the elite and the middling were given a variety of counsels aimed at keeping conversation pleasant, and here too the middling were given more extensive instructions. This was the case with various warnings against excessive or injurious use of wit. It was especially the case with warnings against offending others directly. As in the past, authors for both classes gave the basic advice to avoid contradicting, reproving, or arguing with others, and to stifle all expression of anger. But works addressed to the middling gave the most specific discussions of these rules and contained quite a few additional instructions about how not to abuse others in conversation and how not to take offense if others were abusive.[49]

On the whole, the extra advice for the middling on body carriage, facial expression, and conversation aimed to explain exactly how they should exert self-mastery. The key was to remain "unruffled," to give a convincingly smooth genteel performance. While the theme of self-mastery had been the subtext of prescriptions for gentlemen in the older courtesy works, Lord Chesterfield made it his central concern and brushed aside traditional pieties that one's outward appearance should reflect one's inner state. He openly urged his son to appear better than he really was, to avoid letting others witness any lapses in his self-mastery, and to hide any feelings others might use against him. The message was so cynical that contemporaries balked at it, but they also made Chesterfield a best-seller. Writers for the middle class only elaborated on his message. Yet the authors gave the lower sort almost no advice requiring body control. Apparently they, like early colonial authors, considered the deportment of lower-class persons among themselves a matter of little importance, even as they, unlike earlier authors, deemed that of middle-class persons worth minute consideration.

Moreover, the middling were given some advice that was not addressed to the elite or the lower sort. Amid the cautions that they keep good company, for example, a number of authors specifically advised the middling to choose companions from among social equals rather than superiors or inferiors. The author of *The Polite Lady* claimed: "Without this equality, there may, indeed, be a kind of acquaintance, but there can be no intimacy or familiarity, and, of consequence, no friendship."[50] Only works that addressed the middling advised against a servile demeanor before others. And only those works warned against affectation in demeanor and motions. These instructions hint at a rising self-respect among the middle classes.

REVOLUTIONARY-ERA CONDUCT writers did not waste much ink on the subject of proper behavior with inferiors, but some slight differences in their advice to the different classes on this issue are significant. As in early colonial New England, the most elaborate counsels are found in works that addressed the middle sort; but in contrast to that earlier advice, most of the elaborations asked the middling to be more gentle with inferiors. Because much of this advice referred specifically to behavior with servants, it is likely that the new tone reflected change in the master-servant relation. As wage relations gradually replaced the older forms of apprenticeship and indentured servitude, servants were no longer regarded as one of the family. But of course the early colonial family had been the model of hierarchy. As the growing incidence of contractual labor relations dovetailed with new ideas about the natural equality of man percolating through the culture, the middling began to hesitate in asserting superiority.

This hesitation confirms the role of manners in the revolutionary era. The primary object was not to draw a line between the elite and everyone else, but instead to help the middling assume a new role. Advice for relations with inferiors indicates that the middling were not so much looking behind them, trying to draw lines between themselves and the lower sort, as they were looking ahead trying to become genteel. This cultural stance is confirmed in the temporary political alliances that were formed between the middling and the lower sort in revolutionary cities.[51] For the time being, the middling were inclined to recognize the natural equality of the servant class. They would only change their minds when comfortable with their control of gentility.

The new advice to the middling tended to be interspersed with more traditional advice regarding inferiors, advice that reminds us of the limits of revolutionary-era leveling. For example, both works for the elite and works for the middle class continued to give the old warning against choosing inferiors, especially servants, as companions. Some writers argued that friends of lower rank would ruin one's reputation, others that they would always flatter. Authors who addressed the middle class provided a new, more practical, reason: one's manners are influenced by the company one keeps, and good manners "are not to be expected, where the scantiness of fortune has absolutely excluded the means of education." Much of the advice to the middling assumed that they would spend a certain amount of time dealing with servants, but cautioned that familiarity would make servants contemptuous of authority.

The concern about overfamiliarity, which extended to advice on proper demeanor with inferiors, was an old one; but note the admission of equality in the revolutionary-era warning that a too-friendly demeanor would give inferiors "*just*, but troublesome and improper claims to equality" (emphasis added). Both the elite and the middling were encouraged to show inferiors an affable and benevolent demeanor; a haughty manner, they were assured, would only inspire hatred. This too was traditional advice. But works that addressed middling masters contained a new injunction: they should strive to lighten the burden of servant status because men were by nature equal. James Mott pleaded: "Servitude being established contrary to the natural rights of man, it ought to be softened as much as possible, and servants made to feel their condition as little as may be." John Burton claimed that "the inequality that is betwixt you [and servants] must not make you forget, that it is not nature, but the necessary subordinations of civil life, which have caused this distinction." Not only was this advice not found in works intended for the elite, but it was also a departure from the earlier Puritan emphasis on maintaining inequality between middling masters and their servants. British and American conduct writers were no longer comfortable with the old assertions that inequality of rank was God's doing.[52]

The new sensibility is also revealed in some remarks to the middling regarding the management of time in encounters with inferiors. Hannah Foster suggested that one owed attention to inferiors just as one did to equals and superiors. Mrs. Peddle argued that it was rude to keep waiting any persons who performed services for one. *The Polite Academy* advised young people to wait until servants were at leisure and not busy with something or someone else before asking them for anything. Mrs. Sproat told children not to delay servants by interfering with their work. These four remarks share the same theme—that middle-class superiors, especially young ones, were to show some respect for inferiors' time. This opinion was never expressed in the early colonial literature, nor was it addressed to the upper class.[53]

As for proper conversation with inferiors, here too those who addressed the middle classes urged a greater effort to be kind than those who addressed the elite alone. Both groups of writers recommended courteous and gentle rather than insulting or domineering speech to inferiors. But most advice about talk with inferiors referred to the master-servant relationship; and here, while both the middling and the upper sort were given the old advice to avoid confiding in their servants, middle-class readers were also advised not to "be backward in occasionally speaking, with kindness and affability, respecting their wants" or talking, with affectionate interest, of their affairs. The middling were also urged not to use slighting or reproachful language to servants or to speak contemptuously of them in their presence. Mrs. Chapone's indignation on the latter score suggests the softening that had occured in Anglo-American attitudes toward servants:

> I have often been shocked at the want of politeness by which masters
> and mistresses sometimes provoke impertinence from servants: a gentle-
> man who would resent to death, an imputation of falsehood from his
> equal, will not scruple, without proof, to accuse his servant of it, in

the grossest terms. I have often heard the most insolent contempt of the whole class expressed at table, whilst 5 or 6 of them attended behind the chairs.

Writers for both the middling and the elite were given the old advice to be mild in commanding and correcting servants, and middling authors passed on the old reminder to praise servants when due. The middling sort were further reminded—in the only revolutionary-era advice on body carriage before inferiors—to control their faces. When their servants committed errors, they were to "appear neither surprised nor disatisfied" and especially never to show themselves in angry "fits of passion."[54] Note that verbal reproofs were the only form of correction mentioned. Nowhere do the authors advise beating servants, a significant departure from early colonial advice.

The advice to the middle class reflected changes in the nature of service in late-eighteenth- and early-nineteenth-century America. As indentured service and apprenticeship gave way to wage labor, masters had to treat their servants more carefully. Ideas about equality were also having an impact. Overall, however, the authors were not highly concerned about this relationship.

THE ELITE LOST their former hegemony over proper behavior in the revolutionary era; as middle-class authors embellished the code of behavior that "gentlemen" once used to set themselves off from the masses and taught it to middle-class readers. But middling authors did not labor to preserve old expectations of class deference. They continued to advise lower-class persons to defer to their betters, but they did not waste too many words on this, and it is likely that their efforts were largely ignored. Certainly the advice they gave middling masters and mistresses on relations with servants called for the former to be more gentle than in the past. Instead, and to a far greater extent than their predecessors, middling authors focused on relationships with peers. And the flourishes they added to the old aristocratic code—the elaborate instructions for self-control—make it clear that their goal was to facilitate the rise of those of middling origins.

What was behind these new features of the code of conduct? Why did middling authors embrace and build upon the old aristocratic body-control advice? Some historians, following on the suggestions of anthropologists, suppose that the physical body symbolizes the social body, and thus interpret striving for control of the body as a desire to impose control on society.[55] This may well be true, though such connections are difficult to prove. More evidence is available on the level of the self. The new middle-class man of the revolutionary era (as we shall see, the emphasis on self-control was strongest in advice to men) achieved his status by his own efforts, not by virtue of his membership in a group. Status was now a function of one's personal behavior, as an individual, and thus required self-discipline. Self-discipline entailed, above all, control of physical drives, hence focus on the body. Self-indulgence could be physically and financially ruinous. One's face or talk might convey information best kept from one's social, economic, or political competitors.

Displaying roughness or irascibility might put off a potential client, patient, or customer. Moreover, because the body is house to the self, control of the body was especially important to middle-class men whose self-presentation was central to their maintenance of credit-worthy reputations. They needed to appear in control as well as to be in control. In yet another fit of self-chastisement, John Adams bemoaned losing his temper in a political discussion, berating himself that "A Character can never be supported, if it can be raised, without a good a great Share of Self Government."[56]

Self-presentation was more important than ever at this time when new men were asserting claims to worthiness. It was an infinitely more subtle task than in the past because these same men were throwing out the old regime of deference. It was also more difficult because of the continued development of cities and commerce; one encountered more and more strangers whom one had to convince on the streets of Boston or Philadelphia, without the supports provided by the old institutions that marked social place. Thus self-control became both the sign and the substance of the message; that is, the accomplishment of a new, more challenging self-mastery both signified and justified one's inclusion among the genteel.[57]

The peer orientation of revolutionary-era conduct literature was another sign of the rejection of the traditional hierarchy wherein one's place was determined by birth. The middling folk who were elevating the virtue of self-madeness were finally capitalizing on the fact that economic change had long been eroding the social-material foundations of that old order. In fact it had never had a firm foundation in America, although the seventeenth-century elite had done their best to maintain the idea of it anyway. But over the course of the eighteenth century, as the elite grew more defined by wealth, the ideas began to loosen up, to form a more competitive system; these developments opened the door for men in the middle, ironically, at a time when a few Americans were finally amassing enough wealth to have truly aristocratic lifestyles in the material sense. But the ideas no longer allowed them exclusivity. It was not, then, that Americans were becoming more equal but that in rejecting inherited status they believed they were starting out equal. The manners game was open to all who could compete. We should note that this peer orientation has always been the peculiar fiction of middle-class culture—the feature that would become, in time, what Benjamin DeMott has called "the Imperial Middle." This is the myth that we are all middle class, playing on a level field, and it has a special salience in America.[58] What study of revolutionary-era conduct literature allows us to see is how Americans partook of the challenge to aristocracy mounted by British and American writers in the second half of the eighteenth century and thereby laid the foundations for American manners. To be sure, the revolution opened up possibilities that went beyond what some of the individual strivers, people like Adams or Rush, ever desired. This set the agenda for the future. The tactic in the subsequent, supposedly democratic, age would be to exclude from the social stage all those who could not enter on a footing of equality.

To bring us back to how the concerns of these books expressed the concerns of real people, let us end where we began, with the young John Adams. Consider his regretful description of the local parson:

> But his Air, and Gesture, is still more extraordinary. When he stands, He stands, bended, in and out before and behind and to both Right and left; he tosses his Head on one side. . . . When he walks he heaves away, and swaggs on one side, and steps almost twice as far with one foot, as with the other. When he sitts he sometimes lolls on the arms of his Chair, sometimes on the Table. He entwines his leggs aroud the Leggs of his Chair. . . . When he speakes, he cocks and rolls his Eyes, shakes his head, and jerks his Body about. . . . It is surprizing to me that the Delicacy of his Mind has not corrected these Indecent, as well as ungraceful Instances of Behaviour.

When Chesterfield's *Letters* were published, Adams did the politically correct thing and spoke disparagingly of them. Perhaps revealing another bourgeois strain of sensibility, many American commentators were appalled at Chesterfield's suggestions that his son acquire the graces by seducing Parisian ladies of fashion. But we should not let his and others' indignation at this and other worldly aspects of Chesterfield's advice delude us into thinking that they did not share his concern about the graces. Abigail Adams admitted, for example, that despite the problems, "many excellent maxims and rules for the conduct of youth were strewn throughout the work."[59] If we miss this early affinity of middling folks for Chesterfieldian advice, we will miss the rising of the middle class.

FIVE

YOUTH RISING

Philadelphia botanist John Bartram did not hold back when it came to giving his children advice about parenting. In a letter of 1758 he laid out his method:

> When your Children comes to about the age of twelve or fourteen . . .
> now is the time to lead them out to See the variety of necessary tempo-
> rall affairs like the bees that Lead their young out to the fields. . . .
> [N]ow take them amongst your friends and Relations or other ways
> where your business may call you. . . . [I]t . . . emboldens them and
> makes them more familiar with Strangers and Different branches of
> business and much improves their Carridg and behaviour. . . . [N]ow
> Parents Should be watchfull as well as free with their advice in a pleas-
> ant agreeable familiar way. . . . [T]ell him it is now time to qualify him
> Self for mens Company and take notice of their discourse. . . . [C]all
> him to Come into the Room with your visitors to Speak directly &
> Chearfully to them: then Sit Down on one Side of the Room with a
> Modest pleasant Countinance & harken diligently what the[y] are Dis-
> coursing upon and if Eny questions be asked him let him give a modest
> answer & then be silent. [T]his will please your friends so well that
> the[y] will Delight with talking more with him. . . .

The gist of Bartram's letter strongly resembles that of Chesterfield's *Letters* (which were written about the same time, though published posthumously).[1]

What linked the two fathers was belief in the Lockean system of education. In a nutshell, this was the idea that parents should teach their children by controlling their experiences and appealing to their reason, rather than ruling through fear and coercion. The goal was to present the world with an adult ruled by internal controls rather than external force. The two fathers' letters also reveal another important facet of the Lockean scheme. Not only was the goal to release an independent adult into the world; the method required exposing the youth to that world. Lord Chesterfield and other fathers show us that in practice Lockean education was somewhat like innoculation—one had to be exposed to the disease, in however controlled doses, to develop the appropriate internal defenses.[2] The hold of these ideas was new (seventeenth-century diarists certainly did not convey the same concerns with introducing youth into the world) but they were ubiquitous, both in private letters and popular literature, after the mid-eighteenth century.

The spread of Lockean ideas about adolescence, a fundamental part of what Jay Fliegelman has called "the American revolution against patriarchal authority," has often been linked with another development: the rise of the affectionate, individualistic, and private nuclear family. Certainly the two trends converged in a new respect for autonomy and affection (rather than the old deference and coercion) in relations between parents and children. Moreover, the Lockean system required considerable parental solicitude for its accomplishment.[3] Contemporary diaries and letters amply illustrate the rise in the importance of the nuclear family and warm family ties, and among the adherents of Locke. Benjamin Rush's letters, for example, reveal great affection and concern for his children and a high valuation of domesticity. At one point he lamented to his wife that the conversation of his medical apprentices was no substitute for the companionship of his absent family. Several historians point to the emergence of the nuclear family portrait after 1770 as another and striking sort of evidence of the new family bonds.[4]

But domesticity and Lockean education could also be at odds, because the goal of the latter was to nurture independence, not dependence. There was an inherent tension between the Lockean method of releasing youth from overt parental control and the new stress on close and private family life.[5] The term "affective individualism" often applied to the new ethic is, in this sense, an oxymoron. Whither American youth? The conduct literature that circulated in the northern colonies and states can again offer insights into how contemporaries might have handled such tensions.

It should be noted, first, that revolutionary-era conduct advice reflected contemporary assumptions in distinguishing between young children and youth. John Bartram's letter to his children is one of many indicators that the mid-teens (the age of puberty) were recognized as the start of a new stage of life in this as in the early colonial period. After 1740, to cite another example, censuses designated children before the age of sixteen as "dependent," and those older than sixteen as "productive." Period novels followed Locke's lead and excoriated parents who failed to distinguish between children and youth; and, as if to underscore the point, publishers brought some of them out in differently edited formats for the two age groups.[6]

The close and affectionate family ties that historians talk about are evident in the conduct literature, especially in discussions of the relationship between adults and young children, but they are not prominent. We are reminded again of the transitional character of the era. The new strains in the advice concerning children are outweighed by the persistence of conduct instructions designed to secure their subordination. More important, the advice to the older group of youth, the site of more dramatic change, is almost wholly caught up in the Lockean method of releasing adolescents into the world rather than clasping them to the familial bosom.

In contrast with the early colonial project of keeping youth in their place, then, the revolutionary-era advice, by welcoming youth into the world of adults, reflects a very considerable rise in their status. Late-eighteenth-century Americans no longer had the desire or the ability to exert direct control over unruly youth, as their seventeenth-century counterparts had largely managed to do. This change was likely the result of both new ideas and new material realities; engaged in a political struggle with what they construed as a tyrannical parent country, fathers were no longer willing to try to exert a heavy hand on their children's futures; they were also no longer able to set their children up in traditional ways.[7] The manners evidence suggests again that the hierarchical and patriarchal family model for society was gradually being replaced by a horizontal republican model, but the new model was not necessarily based on a new idea of the family.[8] As with the middle class, the primary object of the advice was to help a rising group step into a new, less subordinate role. The middle-class writers who wished to raise the status of their class apparently wanted to join parents in educating youth to assume a position of rational independence. Their tactic was the same; just as they had coopted the etiquette of the class above them, they elevated youth by teaching them how to behave as adults. It would remain for antebellum Americans to struggle with the fruits of this revolution in age relations.

Some scholars have dissented from the notion of revolutionary change in age relations in this period. One has claimed that Lockean ideas spread slowly and erratically and in tension with older strains, even in child-rearing literature. Others have argued for continuity in age relations. But study of the conduct literature can help reconcile these divergent views and reveal the exact contours of the revolution against patriarchal authority, because it allows us to sort out contemporary thinking about different age groups. While the manners evidence shows considerable change in attitudes toward youth, it shows relative stability in the status of children and the aged. As we shall see, change in the latter areas was slight. Manners thereby reveal the limits of the revolution against patriarchy. They also help us to understand the natural limits of the social construction of age relations. However powerful, revolutionary ideas about age relations cannot overcome the immutable weakness of the very young and the very old.[9] The in-between nature of adolescence makes this life stage far more malleable.

THE RAPID SOCIAL, economic, and cultural development of early-eighteenth-century America strained the institutions that transmitted culture to the young. It has been observed of New England, for example, that the old system designed to train up good Puritans seemed inadequate in a society that was producing young Yankees. Northerners responded by redistributing their allegiance among the traditional modes of instruction. They began to rely on schools and books to share more of the responsibility previously borne by church and family. Apprenticeship, the system whereby young people had learned proper behavior as well as work skills in a surrogate family, began to be less an educational institution than a purely economic one. Benjamin Rush, for example, thought that few masters and mistresses were prepared to give servants proper instruction. Perhaps his ideas are not surprising when we consider that Rush himself remembered learning manners (in the late 1750s) not in another household but in school.

Schools were changing focus in this period. They were becoming more practical and utilitarian, more concerned with teaching reading and writing in plain English to a broader sector of the population than with teaching Latin to a few boys. More schools began to admit girls. The number of schools increased steadily, both in absolute terms and in proportion to the population. By the mid-eighteenth century the number of children in schools began to increase dramatically. Judging from the textbooks, schooling also became more secular. The American Revolution reinforced these trends, for many believed that an educated citizenry was vital to the survival of the new republic.[10]

The growing reliance on the school was to have important consequences. Socialization within the family, the primary mode of the early colonial period, was automatic. The child learned mostly by the example of those around him and easily made the transition from family to community. Schools represented a more "active" stance toward education. Such a stance is reflected in the conduct literature. Mrs. Chapone claimed, for example, that "propriety of behavior must be the fruit of instruction . . . and is to be cultivated and improved like any other branch of knowledge." A significant aspect of the change is that literacy in this period was both on the rise and evolving in character. No longer was the goal simply to read the Bible; now many wished to read to educate themselves. The new literacy stimulated the colonial press, the products of which stimulated the reading audience still further. The more deliberate attitude toward education that these changes engendered was more appropriate to the theoretical openness of an emerging class society than the familial socialization that buttressed the old order.[11] Together with the growth in the quantity of conduct works available, these changes suggest that the middle and upper classes at least were increasingly studying proper behavior from books.

These shifts in importance of the various "schools of good manners" are reflected in the conduct literature for children printed and imported in the northern colonies. The most dramatic change is that relative to the early colonial period much less of it was written by clergymen. Moreover, the only minister to reiterate his earlier counterparts' admonitions to parents to teach their children manners did not tell them what to teach or voice much confidence in their ability to do so: "[I]f Parents be not capable to teach their Children a *decent* and *becoming* Deportment towards Superiors, Inferiors, and Equals themselves, they should seek out such to instruct them in these Things as know what is fit to be done in this Respect. . . ."[12] Ministers only addressed children in four short-lived sermons. After 1763 their works were supplanted by schoolbooks designed to teach manners to children. Works such as *A Little Pretty Pocket Book* or Nancy Sproat's *The Good Girl's Soliloquy* were simple readers for the young. Several of these works were adaptations of Eleazar Moody's *The School of Good Manners*, the most significant of the early colonial works to be reprinted through the revolutionary era. The continuity of Moody's rules both caused and reflected stability in early American attitudes toward the treatment of children.

The changing balance between family, church, schools, and books in the teaching of manners was even more dramatic for youth than for young children. More youth went to college. For the founders of middling origins described in the last chapter, this experience was the key to their acquisition of gentility.[13] But even for non-college-bound youth, the loosening hold of the family (whether the natural family or the surrogate family of apprenticeship and service), the substitution of schooling for education in the home, and the gradual change to what has been called "liberating" literacy suggest that conduct books played a more direct role in teaching youth proper behavior than in the past. The very number of works directed to youth supports this contention. Nearly three-quarters of the works circulating in the revolutionary period addressed youth, and three-quarters of those works were intended exclusively for youth. Thus most of the conduct advice of this period was addressed to youth. Some authors hinted that they were trying to teach young men and women what their families or ministers had failed to teach them. Judging from the number of reprints, their works were in demand.[14]

Advice to youth came in a variety of genres, but three works deserve mention as a totally new species to appear in the North. They were manuals by dancing masters, in which are found very detailed descriptions of proper physical deportment in a variety of situations. These works, printed in New England after the Revolution, were written primarily to advertise their authors' establishments and probably did not achieve wide circulation. But the fact of their appearance in an area where a century earlier ministers were decrying the very practice of "promiscuous dancing" indicates a change. These works are reminders that dancing academies were schools of good manners in their own right. In the early colonial period Puritan ministers had been ambivalent in their diatribes against dancing as to whether it was permissible for parents to employ dancing masters to teach their children "how to carry themselves handsomely in company." But revolutionary-era works echoed Locke in heartily recommending dancing as an avenue to the graces. Lord Chesterfield argued that gracefulness was best attained through dancing. He frequently reminded his son to attend to his dancing master "more to teach you to sit, stand, and walk gracefully than to dance finely." Another writer put the case simply: "Dancing gives a graceful ease of movement, a modest and polite deportment in society, and a respectable and manly address; it is as worthy of attention as any knowledge put within our reach." Surely it was these goals that led Benjamin Rush to urge a young medical student to "spend an hour every day for 3 months in receiving lessons from some principle dancing master."[15] The manuals by dancing masters give a good picture of the lessons they taught, and their publication presumably spread those lessons beyond the dancing academy door. Five other works shared their emphasis on the minute particulars of behavior and were thus the first true exemplars of the etiquette manual type that would become widespread during the antebellum period.

Adults received much less conduct advice during the revolutionary era than did youth. At most, a third of the available titles were intended for adults, and most of these either contained advice for other age groups as well or were intended for both youth and adults. No conduct works imported or printed in the North in this period were directed exclusively to the aged. While old age is not normally a time of much manners learning, we should note that the writers apparently no longer felt the concerns that had prompted at least some Puritan ministers to write works for this group in the earlier period.

WHY THE LACK OF interest in the aged? Some historians have argued that the status of the aged was declining in the revolutionary era. The conduct literature supports this contention but suggests that the change was not dramatic.[16] Very little advice directed young people to defer to the elderly, and the few remarks directed to the elderly themselves (in works for all ages) claimed they needed to earn through proper behavior any deference that came their way. As in the past, young persons were given much more advice to show deference to adults who were middle-aged.

Of course much of the behavior that was due from children and youth to adults was also due to the elderly; but, as before, most of the advice for children specifically concerned parents and schoolmasters. Some authors did tell children and youth to show deference to the aged, but far fewer than before, and they were vague on specifics. Several repeated the biblical injunction that youth should "rise up before the hoary Head, and honor the face of the old Man," but that was it. Moreover, as was true of earlier advice, revolutionary-era advice on behavior with the aged was often ambivalent. While some authors counseled young people not to shun the company of the aged, a few suggested that youth would have a "natural repugnance to the society of old age." While several advised youth to talk with the aged—as the latters' conversation would be useful and instructive—some implied that young people were prone to be disrespectful in their talk with the elderly. The "Countess of Carlysle," for example, told young women to "suffer no harsh expression to mark your impatience" in the company of old people. Mrs. Chapone denounced the youthful practice of mimicking, insulting, and laughing at the aged.[17] To an even greater extent than in the early colonial period, then, revolutionary-era instructions for deportment in the presence of old people were so scanty and ambivalent as to make it clear that the authors did not deem the aged the most powerful age group. This conclusion is corroborated by "negative evidence" from period diaries and letters; neither John Adams nor Benjamin Rush, for example, ever report showing any special attentions to the aged.[18]

The authors confirmed this tenuous status in their bits of advice to the elderly, for their focus was on the behavior the old needed to adopt in order to deserve the respect of younger persons. This, too, was a continuation of early colonial trends, only now the authors' tone was even more stern. As in the past, the aged were admonished to avoid both affecting youth and succumbing to the sins of old age. To play the "fop or a professed merry maker," one author warned, "produces contempt and justly deserves it." And John Bartram echoed the conduct writers when he begged his children to help him "guard against the pevish fretful disposition which so Commonly attends the aged. . . . If . . . you should observe that I begin to give way to this weakness pray Doe in a loving tender manner advise me of it before it [is] too habituall." The message to the aged was that they would only earn the respect of the young by combining affability with dignity.[19] But this was the only advice for the aged. Manners suggest, then, that the status of the elderly had changed little from the early colonial era, and that minor change was not for the better. The conduct writers' impulse to promote reverence for the aged, never very great, only ebbed further with the waning of a hierarchical world view.

IN KEEPING WITH earlier patterns, revolutionary-era writers gave the young much more advice regarding behavior with mature adults, and addressed most of their remarks about dealing with young persons to mature adults. But, unlike the earlier period, the vast majority of this advice was for or about children, and it was far more elaborate and strict than that for or concerning youth. This is the first evidence that the status of children remained fairly stable over this period while that of youth was rising.[20]

In fact the advice to children themselves was virtually unchanged since the earlier period; it was just that adults were encouraged to be a bit more loving and gentle toward children than they had been in the past. Scholars have acknowledged the latter trend. Most historians of childhood have noted the emergence of a more humane attitude toward children over time; and most of them associate this change with the eighteenth century. But because they are not observing this change in the context of all the rules for behavior, they miss the stronger cord of stability in attitudes about young children with which this new thread was intertwined.[21] This stability is what caused printers to bring out new editions and adaptations of Moody's School of Good Manners. Even the growing popularity of Lockean pedagogy did not disturb this trend, because Locke's discussion of the treatment of young children was compatible with older trends. In addition to drawing clear distinctions between the proper treatment of children and youth, Locke recommended much firmer treatment of the former and gradual relaxation of controls on the latter.[22]

Youth were deemed less inferior to adults than they had been in the past; and the milder advice to them was rarely qualified, as it had been previously, by rather severe and exacting rules for and regarding young servants. The practice of putting youth out to service was on the decline in this period, and as it declined, domestic service changed in character. Service was becoming less an institution for the education and socialization of youth and more a class relationship. Period diaries reflect the change. Benjamin Rush actively disapproved the putting out of youth to service in other families, although he acknowledged that poverty and death sometimes made it necessary. John Adams confirmed that service was now regarded as a lower-class fate when he described a man who wished to see his enemy's daughters "sent out to service as Kitchen Maids." Esther Burr, desperate for domestic help, sighed that all the young women she knew considered it "beneath them to go out."[23] Conduct writers responded to this trend by ceasing to discuss the master-servant relationship in the context of the family. In this indirect way they were confirming the narrowing of the nuclear family circle.

Revolutionary-era advice to youth concerning behavior with adults as age superiors was both much less frequent and much less exacting than that addressed to children. While a few writers suggested to youth that they would benefit from spending time with adults, for example, they warned children to respect adults' command of their time. Children were "Never [to] go abroad without liberty from your parents, masters, or guardians; and be sure to return by the time appointed." They were not to enter or leave their parents' or other superiors' presence without permission. Further, children were to be "always ready to wait upon their superiors." They were to wait until their elders were seated before sitting down at the dining table and to wait until their elders began eating before beginning themselves.[24] Whereas youth were vaguely and indirectly encouraged to pay attention to their superiors, children were given clear and specific directions to "hearken diligently to Instruction" and to "attend diligently to the words of the minister."[25] While a couple of authors told youth in a general way to give superiors place and precedence in encounters, authors for children gave more specific instructions—to walk a little behind superiors, to sit where adults told them to or in the "lowest" places, to stand back to allow an elder to pass first in a narrow passageway, to stand behind an adult's chair, and so on.[26] The gap between the advice to youth and that to children had grown since the early colonial period.

Youth received more advice respecting proper demeanor with adults, but, again in contrast to the previous period, it suggested that they could be more relaxed before adults than could children. Both groups were still to have a humble, respectful, and attentive demeanor with adults, especially parents. But some authors also reminded youth to be at ease. A few writers continued to tell young servants to have an obliging as well as a respectful demeanor before their masters and to submit to correction with resignation, although this sort of advice was on the wane. Children, however, continued to receive it.[27]

Children were given much more detailed advice than were youth regarding body carriage and facial expression before adults. In each case a few authors gave youth rather general suggestions, while children were given expanded versions of the advice they were given in the early colonial era. Chesterfield reminded his son that it was rude for a young person to have too relaxed a posture before a superior; another author urged youth to stand before their elders and "not sit unless commanded." Both children and youth were to rise, bow, and uncover upon the approach of an adult. But authors for children gave more detailed instructions about when, where, and how to assume these postures.[28] While youth were only advised to wear an attentive look when with adults, children were asked not to pout or frown at anything their elders said and were given a number of instructions to control their gaze.[29]

Both children and youth continued to be advised not to talk too much in the presence of age superiors, although they were always to answer promptly when addressed. Again, however, we find differences in emphasis and degree. While a few writers advised youth to speak only when spoken to, writers for children were emphatic on this old point; and some writers cautioned youth not to be too silent in the presence of superiors. Both children and youth were to refrain from interrupting adults; but here, as elsewhere, the authors gave children more detailed advice than they gave youth, describing various contingencies at home, at school, at table, in the meetinghouse, or on the street.[30] As in the earlier period, both children and youth were instructed to address parents, masters, and other adults by "some Title of Respect," and to show respect in their talk. But some authors also gave youth new warnings against awkward bashfulness. Chesterfield advised that "you should be full as easy with them, as with people of your own years. . . ." Children were not warned against bashfulness; they were simply to be meek and humble when talking to adults.[31] While the authors continued to tell both children and youth not to insult or argue with adults, here too, their instructions to children were much more detailed and demanding than their suggestions to youth. And only a few older authors continued to address such instructions to young servants.[32]

That children were always given more elaborate advice than were youth might indicate that the authors thought children, because younger, had more to learn and that youth already knew how to defer to adults. But the writers also asked children to show more deference than they asked youth to show. Suggestions that youth be respectful but not bashful tell us that some relaxation was occurring in the relationship between youth and adults.

THESE CONCLUSIONS are supported by the advice to mature adults regarding interaction with the young, especially on the matter of discipline. But advice to adults also reveals a subtle increase in the requirement of affectionate behavior with young children. Unlike the few remarks to the aged, most of the advice to adults was generally concerned with moderating the exercise of an authority over the young that the authors took for granted. However, and in contrast to the early colonial period, almost none of this advice concerned youth. What little there was consisted almost entirely of a few remnants of older advice on dealing with young servants. A few authors continued to warn masters and mistresses not to adopt a haughty manner with servants, for example, but to command them mildly and to correct them soberly. We should not make too much of these scattered references. What is noteworthy is the lack of suggestions that servants, or any other youth, be beaten. Only a few vague pleas to masters that they "not be over rigorous in their Punishments" hint that some beating of servants might have been expected. But such was never specifically stated, much less encouraged. This is important negative evidence. The beating of youth, especially servants, was a perfectly acceptable last resort in the early colonial period. In the revolutionary era, however, more and more adults condemned the use of corporal punishment, whether at home or at school.[33] Apparently the conduct writers agreed, by leaving out any acknowledgment of this disciplinary measure for youth.

The authors gave adults much more advice regarding young children. Most of it dealt with the duties of parents. As in the past, parents were encouraged to teach their children good behavior by example (or, if unable to do so, to entrust this to another adult).[34] While historians have argued that there was a growing acknowledgment of the mother's role in child-rearing in this period, the conduct writers addressed such injunctions to both parents.[35] A number of authors recommended explicitly that parents encourage their children's attendance upon them in a free and familiar association, and not behave in such a way as would "make them avoid your sight." To have much contact was deemed the best way to maintain parental influence, as well as to prevent children from associating with corrupting persons. Even when not physically together, parents were to control their children's use of time and choice of companions. The authors repeatedly urged parents to restrict their children's contact with the corrupting influences of servants and bad company. This was new advice. It was consistent with the Lockean doctrine that parents should control the influences on their children; it is also another sign that servants were no longer regarded as members of the family but as members of a lower class. Benjamin Rush was particularly vocal on the need to keep children from servants.[36]

The authors urged parents to be more affectionate than formal in their manner and conversation with children. In contrast with the advice on demeanor with class inferiors, many authors told parents to avoid a too-reserved and austere behavior with children; instead they were to be friendly, gentle, and mild in manner. Some of this was traditional advice, but new adjectives were creeping in: parents were to be free, familiar, and easy with children. Parents were still urged not to spoil their children—they were to maintain authority and discipline with a steady firmness—but they were always to meet children's failings with patience and "good nature." Many authors told parents not to be severe with children or to seem always angry or out of humor. Some also counseled parents against the display of anger in their faces. "Frowns and ill Looks," or "a Face of Sowrness and Austerity" would only serve to discourage children. "Benevolence of expression" was to be preserved even when punishing children.[37]

These and other authors also gave parents new advice to strive for easy and familiar conversation with their children, and urged them to use "fair acclamation" and encouraging language whenever possible in training them. John Bartram was of like mind. He tried never "to let a good Deed pass without praise." But he and the conduct writers also agreed that when encouragement failed, firmer measures were to be resorted to. Here the advice did carry over from the earlier period: the first thing to be tried were sharp but sober reproofs, though these were to be infrequent and never given in a passion.[38] Further, more often than not revolutionary authors claimed that it was sometimes necessary for parents to beat young children. While two authors thought this less likely than reasoned argument to reform children and more likely to make them stubborn, five condoned it. The latter authors did warn that beating was not to be frequent and was only to be resorted to when all other means of discipline had failed. They gave the old cautions that flogging was to be timely, moderate, and never done in passion. But, they argued, when it was necessary parents could not neglect to use the rod. Thus while conduct writers reflected the contemporary debate over corporal punishment by neglecting to discuss the beating of youth, they suggest that traditional attitudes persisted as regarded young children. Locke himself did not utterly condemn the corporal punishment of young children (though he insisted it should be moderate and rare); the old ideas were not inconsistent with his concerning the very young. And diaries show that parents did beat children. Young mother Esther Burr claimed, for example, that it was very hard to beat one's own child, and worried sometimes whether she whipped her little daughter "more than was needfull." But she had no doubt that "it did her a vast deal of good."[39]

On the whole, it would seem that revolutionary-era authors advocated a somewhat warmer relationship between parents and children than had early colonial writers, a trend congruent with historians' claims about the increasing place of affection in eighteenth-century families. It is difficult to imagine a seventeenth-century father signing a letter to his wife as Benjamin Rush did: "Love as usual and an hundred kisses for our dearest Jack." But otherwise the advice to and about young children had changed little from the early colonial period. The paucity of advice regarding relations with youth, on the other hand, suggests that they were much less inferior to adults than they had been in the past. Unlike their early colonial counterparts, revolutionary-era conduct writers drew a clear distinction between children and youth. In so doing, they were recognizing the same changes articulated more forcefully by the Yale students who waged a six-year campaign in the 1760s to effect the ouster of President Clap. His offense: he had treated them like children, and most infuriatingly by using the rod.[40]

WHEN BENJAMIN RUSH wrote to young Rebecca Smith that "the first object of all young people is to please in company," he summed up a world of assumptions in revolutionary-era conduct advice.[41] Not only was most of this period's advice directed to youth, but most of it concerned relations with peers. Indeed, here is where most of the revolutionary-era changes are found. It was to youth that the authors addressed their new injunctions about avoiding awkwardness and cultivating grace and their paradoxical recommendation of control of the body in order to attain a comportment that was "easy and natural." To be sure, the authors of this advice, Lord Chesterfield and his followers, were adults, and thus could be said to be acting as parents, guiding their young in appropriate Enlightened "hidden hand" style. But that they had little to say about relations with superiors is significant. They taught youth the rules of the world of adults and invited them to act as adults. When young Philip Stanhope turned eighteen, father Chesterfield ceased to address him as "Dear Boy," and began to address him as "Dear Friend."[42] As enlightened as Cotton Mather was for his time, he would never have done the same with young Increase.

Thus the advice to youth concerned behavior not only with other youth but also as the equals of adults in adult society. But while advice for youth was not different from advice for adults, it was much more extensive, because the instructions were intended to help them assume a new position in society. The authors did give young children some advice regarding behavior with peers, and it was sometimes similar to that for youth, but it was far less elaborate. And while it was intended to guide their behavior with other children, it had the effect of reinforcing their inferiority to adults. Revolutionary-era conduct works thus conveyed the same messages Jay Fliegelman observed in late-eighteenth-century versions of Daniel Defoe's novel *Robinson Crusoe*: those intended for children stressed filial obedience, while those intended for youth conveyed the author's original stress on independence.[43]

While the authors advised all ages to be discriminating in their choice of company, for example, they gave this rule the most emphasis in advice to youth. This was also the case in early colonial works, but we should note that it was mostly to youth that the authors directed the new middle-class cautions to take one's time in forming intimacies and to avoid spending too much time even with good company. The Reverend Manesseh Cutler repeated this advice in a letter to his son, adding that "Intervals of company increases the enjoyment." The assumption was that youth would be actively and independently engaged in the serious business of contracting an acquaintance, both among other youth and adults. Cutler wrote his son to "make it a point to see and contract acquaintance with the most respectable young people in the neighborhood," observing that "this depends upon your own management and exertion." John Adams chastised himself as a young man for neglecting "to extend my Acquaintance with young fellows nor young Girls, with Men of figure, Character, nor fortune. Am content to live unknown, poor, with the lowest of all our species for Company."[44] While expecting youth to exercise autonomy and initiative in these matters, the authors intervened directly to restrict children's freedom of association, and largely by repeating old admonitions that they not loiter abroad. Several writers echoed the jingle: "I must not ramble in the street, or play with every boy I meet." The authors thus acted as monitory adults regarding relations between children.[45]

While the differences were sometimes subtle, this pattern—the assumption that youth would control their own behavior while children should continue to receive direction from adults—is evident in other advice on behavior with peers. For example, both groups were advised to give others their undivided attention, and to refrain from reading anything in company. But the authors also warned youth not to fall asleep, pull out their watches, groom themselves, or move about a room, while they simply told children to "ask leave" to read in company when necessity required it.[46] Both groups were to "desire not the highest place," and seek instead to take the lowest places in company. But youth were to find out what were considered the upper places in every situation and to offer such places to others, while children were simply told to sit "in the place appointed for you," and to give up their seats if there were not enough.[47]

The authors gave youth a good deal of advice on demeanor that they neglected to give either adults or children. All were to be affable and courteous with peers, and to avoid a haughty or surly manner. Several authors further recommended a humble air to children. But the more Chesterfieldian suggestions—that an "easy and unembarrassed" demeanor would gain others' favor even before one's true character was known and that it was crucial to avoid an "awkward bashfulness"—were mostly directed to youth. This advice was echoed in private papers. The young John Adams bemoaned his timidity in company; and wealthy New Yorker Philip Schuyler assured his seventeen-year-old nephew Stephen Van Rensselaer that "an improper backwardness" was as "prejudicial" in a young man as "an unbecoming forwardness." It was thus youth who were the main targets of the various revolutionary-era observations that good breeding did not require stiffness and formality but rather ease and freedom (although not an "unbounded latitude"). It was youth, above all, whom the authors urged to maintain a reserve with all persons. All of these extra cautions to youth—which may have originated in Locke's condemnation of bashfulness—bore the special stamp of Chesterfield. They constituted a significant departure from the early colonial calls for a modest demeanor in youth.[48]

It was to youth that Chesterfield and his followers preached the doctrine of gracefulness, with all its implications for demeanor and physical carriage. Thus the diatribes against horseplay, odd motions, and clumsiness were all intended for youth, as well as the prescription of dancing as an exercise well suited to give one "a graceful ease." The authors also reminded youth that affectation of all sorts was to be shunned. This advice is not generally found in works intended for adults or children.[49]

As regarded specific rules for body carriage, the goals for children did not usually exceed the basics outlined by Moody in the early colonial period, while the demands on youth reflected the new standards of gracefulness. While children were not to run and jump but to walk "decently," youth needed to "preserve a certain dignity" in their gait.[50] While the authors simply continued to remind children to sit up straight, they addressed all of the period's tips on graceful sitting to youth.[51] Similarly, the myriad warnings against unnecessary motions of the limbs and self-touching were all intended for youth, while children were only given odd bits of this advice.[52] Youth were thus to exert considerable control over their bodies, although this was not to lead to a stiff immobility; again, the ideal carriage was "natural" and easy.

The extra measure of body control recommended to youth extended to the authors' discussions of facial expressions. All ages were to greet peers with a cheerful face, for example, but youth were given the extra warnings against constant grinning, which made one look ill at ease. The authors also gave youth more extensive warnings against sour expressions than they gave other groups. Chesterfield's pleas for sufficient self-possession to preserve an unruffled countenance were primarily addressed to youth, as were the period's most elaborate denunciations of displays of anger, distress, excessive mirth, or other varieties of facial distortion. Children were given much simpler instructions on these issues. And while the writers urged both children and youth not to stare at others, it was mostly authors for youth who recommended looking at those with whom one spoke, both to show attention and because "their looks frequently discover, what their words are calculated to conceal."[53] Youth were to control their own faces, but they were to take advantage of others' lapses.

One writer proclaimed that salutations were as revealing as faces: "[I]n nothing do we lay ourselves so open as in our manner of speaking and salutation." But neither he nor other authors offered any specific advice on this matter to adults. Nor did the authors have much advice for children. Generally, they only gave children specific instructions about salutations to elders and were vague about those to be performed to other children. They told children to show "love and respect" on meeting other children, for example, but to "uncover thy head . . . and bowing pass by" a schoolmaster. The authors gave youth more, and more genuinely peer-oriented, advice, essentially all that they directed to the middling sort in this period.[54]

Youth were also given the most extensive advice regarding conversation. They received the most elaborate warnings against making unnecessary noises.[55] While all age groups were warned not to talk too much, youth were also urged not to be too silent and to uphold their share of the conversation. They were to answer and address others with ease and to initiate topics of conversation. Authors for children never warned them not to be too silent.[56] Both children and youth were counseled on proper tone of voice and enunciation, but here, too, youth were given the most elaborate instructions.[57] And while all age groups were targets of the middling diatribes against swearing and obscene talk, the authors again singled out youth for further advice on word choice. It was to youth that they directed warnings against both affected language, on the one hand, and vulgar expressions, on the other. Youth were to aim instead for elegance of expression.[58]

The period's more elaborate discussions of how to choose topics of conversation were addressed to youth. As elsewhere, the authors gave youth advice to help them deal with the adult world, while they continued to treat children (as they had all young persons in the earlier period) as subordinate. Both children and youth were cautioned not to discuss their family's affairs, for example, but with youth the implication was that others might use such information against them, whereas with children the emphasis was on the importance of not tattling or discussing affairs above them. Several authors specifically told children not to tell tales out of school.[59]

All age groups were to be cautious in their exercise of wit, taking care never to ridicule others. Authors for children were emphatic about this. Their concern was to keep the peace, for they urged children not to "jeer" at others, and to take others' jests with good humor. Authors for youth, however, gave further instructions and showed an added concern consistent with their larger youth-training project: that youth not appear ridiculous themselves. While they allowed that a certain degree of wit and humor was proper in conversation, the writers insisted that youth abstain from silly jokes, mimicry, waggery, and constant punning.[60] Similarly, all age groups were urged to keep conversation pleasant, and thus not to argue with or speak ill of others; and writers for children seemed keenly interested in keeping the peace between them. But authors for youth once again gave the most elaborate directions for harmonious conversation.[61] The different emphases on keeping the peace among young children and easy social interaction on the part of youth are also found in the period's few references to body contact between peers. While one author told children not to slap, pinch, bite, strike, or kick others, several urged youth to avoid poking others in conversation or jostling them by accident.[62] Here as elsewhere, the primary concern of revolutionary-era conduct writers was to help youth negotiate new terrain and do so smoothly. The secondary goal, of keeping young children in line, had not changed since the early colonial period.

TO A FAR GREATER extent than in early colonial America, conduct advice in the revolutionary era was directed to youth; and while advice to youth in the earlier period was intended to control their behavior, revolutionary-era advice emphasized self-mastery. The conduct literature thereby suggests how Lockean education was applied to youth. The works of Chesterfield and his middle-class imitators, in particular, indicate that the goal of the self-regulated citizen was pursued in part through the cultivation of physical self-control. Thus was the civilizing process adapted to the needs of a democratizing society. That there were limits to the revolution in age relations, however, is suggested by the fact that the authors were less concerned about relations between children and continued to use advice to children, even that concerning peers, to reinforce their inferiority to adults.

The etiquette of age relations in the revolutionary era was thus a mix of old and new. Mature adults, not the aged, continued to be portrayed as the most powerful age group. Advice to children was little changed from the early colonial period. Advice to adults about behavior with children had also changed little; it only suggested a bit more often than in the past that parents be gentle and loving. But the egalitarianism of the new affectionate family ideal was not extended to young children. This is clear in Locke's *Education;* it has been less clear in historians' accounts of the new family ethic. The new ideal did envision the "equalitarianism of grown generations"; hence the significant change in revolutionary-era advice to and about youth.[63] The scant advice to youth about behavior with adults signaled a more relaxed relationship than that between adults and young children, as did the few suggestions to adults about behavior with youth.

The decline of the old invocation of master-servant relations in connection with youth also reflects the hold and purpose of Lockean pedagogy. The goal of nurturing the autonomy of adolescents was to replace external controls over behavior with internal controls. This was to be the answer to the problem of "masterless men" in the new democratic order. Adolescent service had been the solution to masterless men in the past, but it was succumbing to the economic and cultural challenges of revolutionary America. Again, Franklin's *Autobiography*, with its early flight from apprenticeship, was an eighteenth-century story. Jay Fliegelman has noted the same change in contemporary images of the Prodigal Son. In early prints, the returning son is depicted kneeling before the father; in late-eighteenth-century images, the son stands next to the father, who embraces him, and the servant kneels before both. The son thus stands on his own, free from the deferential attitude, and clearly distinguished from the servant.[64]

Youth were breaking away from firmly regulated relations with adults as the ties of family and service loosened. But this does not mean that conduct writers cast them adrift; far from it, since they gave youth the most advice. Indeed, this flood of advice was likely the authors' response—and contribution—to the decline of older institutions for controlling youth. The counsels were not hierarchical in nature, for most of the advice addressed behavior with peers, and it is in this category that most of the new advice of the period is found. The rules for age relations were thus similar to the rules for class relations in that the authors were less concerned with regulating relations that continued to be unequal (where they did they suggested that these be handled a bit more gently than in the past) than they were with instructing a newly rising group on how to behave with all. Class and age relations are also intertwined in the sense that the new treatment of adolescents was a middle-class treatment. The self-control enjoined by the conduct literature was important to parents who could not or would not simply bestow independence upon their children but insisted instead that their children be, like themselves, self-made. The more indulgent child-rearing that some scholars have noticed in some families in this period was likely an upper-class mode.[65] Middling parents relied on self-discipline. At least they hoped that the investment of parental care and affection, in combination with the encouragement of self-control, would suffice to produce a new internal authority. It was surely this internal mechanism that Benjamin Rush hoped to trigger at the end of a letter of advice to his son John, who was about to sail to Calcutta in 1796 as a new doctor:

One more consideration shall close this parting testimony of our affection. Whenever you are tempted to do an improper thing, fancy that you see your father or mother kneeling before you and imploring you with tears in their eyes to refrain from yielding to the temptation, and assuring you at the same time that your yielding to it will be the means of hurrying them to a premature grave.

With efforts no less heavy-handed than the corporal discipline they sought to replace, Lockean parents hoped for the best. But the tension between the desire to bind youth to the family with ties of love and release them into the world to nurture self-control was never resolved in revolutionary-era discussions of behavior between youth and adults. Conduct advice, as we have seen, followed inexorably the dictates of the new pedagogy, and launched youth into the world of adults. Actual parents may have worried about the effects of this method; actual youth may have welcomed or feared the freedom.[66] Only time would show its effects.

WOMEN RISING

A Manual For Julia

1. Hold up your head.
2. Let go your fingers.
3. Look the person you speak to in the face.
4. Speak in a distinct and elevated tone of voice.

Julia Rush was thirteen years old when her father Benjamin wrote these reminders in 1806. What is striking about them, and the same can be said about his letter of advice to Rebecca Smith in 1791, is that he wished to launch these young women into adult society with the same advice that he might give a young man. There is nothing particularly feminine about these injunctions. And yet Rush is reknowned among historians as one of the architects of the special "Republican Mother" role for women, the notion that women's role in the new nation would be confined to the indirect part of rearing virtuous citizens. This way of thinking would become a building block for the nineteenth-century ideology of "separate spheres," which assumed that men and women occupied different realms of thought and activity. At first glance, then, there appears to be a tension between gender integration and gender separation in Rush's thinking about women.[1] But in fact, the more conscious discussions of women's special role in the new republic were dependent on the unconscious integration of women into what had previously been regarded as the world of men. At least this is what happened in the conduct literature that circulated in Rush's time.

Historians have made contradictory claims regarding women's status in the colonial and early national periods. The first generation of women's historians argued that women had substantial latitude for behavior in the early colonial period, that the eighteenth century brought increasing restrictions, that the Revolution did little to change their position, and that they were immured in woman's sphere in the early nineteenth century. The second generation of women's historians argued the reverse, claiming that the Revolution brought real progress for women by causing previously confined roles to be questioned, and that the creation of a special role for women in the nineteenth century was a necessary first step to emancipation. These latter interpretations remain dominant, although they have been refined. Historians are now examining the construction of gender as a cultural process in interaction with other forms of change (economic, political, and so forth) and have been reviewing contemporary texts as sites of that interaction. Along the way they have begun to consider questions about masculinity.[2] The evidence from conduct literature can be helpful here, both in mediating between divergent positions and furthering the inquiry.

Trends in manners suggest that all the historians of women have been partly right, because contradictory assertions are embedded in the rules themselves. Specifically, new proclamations of the differences between the sexes accompanied equally new though perhaps less consciously given advice that women should behave just as men should behave, advice which reveals that women were included in the social world depicted by conduct literature to a much greater degree than before. At the same time, the integration of women into the new world of individuals made them vulnerable to new dangers. Manners reflect that their sexual safety, in particular, was in their own hands. Revolutionary-era works were full of new warnings to women about how they must fend off men's improper advances—which were assumed to be inevitable. And yet women also needed to be attractive. The implied dangers to women in the new society of peers, and the difficulty of their charge, are among several reasons why revolutionary-era developments were not complete. Some cultural problems would not be worked out until the antebellum era.

Still, new definitions of the citizen in this era of revolutionary change had significant gender implications, which were duly registered in conduct prescriptions. New notions of maleness are always difficult to discern; then, as now, contemporaries universalized the male. But by comparing the prescriptions for face-to-face behavior addressed to men with those addressed to women we can uncover the reconstruction of gender ideals. It becomes clear that the new male ideal was the middle-class ideal described in chapter 4, as middling writers and readers took notions that had been confined to gentlemen and both remade and spread them to their class. But the new middle-class woman, while somewhat different from the man, was not his opposite. Both were engaged in new worlds of competition; indeed, her market, the marriage market, may have been the riskier. She needed to veil her sexuality as she stepped onto the stage of society, but step up she did. Manners show, then, that women won a kind of social equality in the new order, despite their accelerating loss of influence in the political and economic realms. This point needs to be considered in the current debate over the liberal public sphere. Jurgen Habermas described how the expansion of that sphere (wherein bourgeois men could debate politics outside of the government) gave birth to democracy; feminists have criticized him for overlooking the exclusion of women. The patterns in manners suggest, however, that the inclusion of women in the social world may have been the way women were accomodated in the emerging liberal order.[3] Only time would tell if this would be sufficient to bridge the glaring gap between the new ideal of equality and women's continuing legal subordination. In the meantime, manners reflect the ongoing groping of Euroamericans for solutions to the contradiction. They also suggest that sexuality proved a stumbling block.

WE KNOW THAT gender expectations were changing in this period because the conduct writers began to address more works to women than to men, a dramatic reversal from the early colonial period. While we cannot assume that the actual readership of these books conformed to the audience suggested by the authors (diaries, letters, and library records remind us that men read these books too), the works clearly reflect a new interest in female education. We have already examined indirectly how men learned to behave in exploring how different class and age groups learned to behave; the change in the literature addressed to women warrants a special look at the female case.

For the most part young women continued to be educated in the home. The cultural mediation of a minister in his pastoral duties or Sunday lectures declined in importance in female manners instruction, as it did in that of young persons generally—there were no sermons among the group of revolutionary-era titles addressed to women. But women, like men, were affected by the increasing roles of schools and of literature itself. Girls were increasingly gaining entry into town schools, and daughters of prosperous families benefitted from the rash of postwar academy founding. That they learned the graces along with other subjects is suggested by the Salem, Massachusetts, school that tried to attract girls in 1774 by offering both to teach the customary subjects and to introduce them into "genteel company." In the next generation young Catharine Beecher learned manners in "Miss Pierce's" Litchfield, Connecticut, school. In addition to receiving oral instruction, these schoolgirls are likely to have read some of the conduct works addressed to them.[4]

In or out of school, when the fact of economic growth is added to that of increasing female literacy (it was rising after midcentury and approached universality among younger women in New England in the years following the Revolution), it becomes clear that in comparison with the earlier period, many more girls and women had the means and ability to read conduct literature.[5] The very quantity of works addressed to women, in both numbers of titles and of editions, suggests that books were becoming an important means of female conduct instruction in middling and elite families. Many of the titles went through multiple editions: Dr. Gregory's *A Father's Legacy to His Daughters*, an immediate best-seller (along with Chesterfield) when it appeared in 1775, went through sixty-nine American editions; Mrs. Chapone's *Letters on the Improvement of the Mind*, thirty-seven; and John Bennett's *Letters to a Young Lady*, twenty-five. Among those who left records of their reading, we find regular mentions and recommendations of these books, often by fathers to daughters. Benjamin Franklin wrote his wife regarding their daughter Sally, for example, "I . . . would have her read over and over again . . . *The Ladies Library*." Library records reveal the popularity of such works as James Fordyce's *Sermons to Young Women* (women especially were attracted to the era's new lending libraries, where they could obtain books more cheaply than buying them). In addition, some works were reprinted, in whole or in part, in American magazines and compilations. The few American works such as Hannah Webster Foster's *The Boarding School* affirm the popularity of the above-mentioned British texts by recommending them within their own pages.[6]

Like conduct works for men, revolutionary era advice for women came in a variety of genres, including the popular parental-advice-to-a-child works, like Dr. Gregory's, and general conduct-of-life advice works, like *The Ladies Library*. But one type had no parallel among either contemporary works for men or early colonial works. These were books on female education. Their appearance indicates the growing importance of female education, and all devoted considerable space to female deportment and demeanor. These were extremely popular books—Fordyce, Chapone, and Bennett number among them—and nearly all went through more than eight editions on northern American presses alone, some many more.

The authors of conduct works for women, like those of all works of this period, were primarily middle-class Englishmen. Only a third were female, only two were American, and only a handful were upper class. The cultural trends of both "anglicization" and the beginnings of middle-class culture thus applied to women as well as men. Despite some postrevolutionary talk on the part of people like Benjamin Rush of the need for a more American system of education, American loyalty to British tutelage persisted. The above-mentioned works continued to be popular into the 1800s. The changes that were taking place in contemporary thinking about women were thus happening on a transatlantic scale. Discussions of "Republican Motherhood" need to take account of this wider context.[7] The few female authors both were and were not a significant development. On the one hand, the pen had been regarded as a man's tool, and it could not have been easy for women to take it up, even though they began, for the most part, by advising their own sex.[8] On the other hand, women did not offer different suggestions for face-to-face behavior than men did. Both male and female authors offered women the same advice to deal with the same new realities.

> Good news Charles, good news! I have arrived to the utmost bounds of
> my wishes; the full possession of my adorable Eliza! . . . I should have

given over the pursuit long ago, but for the hopes of success I entertained from her parleying with me . . . were her delicacy genuine, she
would banish the man at once . . . who attempts to vanquish it! . . .
Julia Granby is expected. . . . Now there's a girl, Charles, I should
never attempt to seduce; yet she is a most alluring object. . . . But the
dignity of her manners forbid all assault on her virtue. Why, the very expression of her eye, blasts in the bud, every thought, derogatory to her
honor; and tells you plainly, that the first insinuation of the kind, would
be punished with eternal banishment and displeasure! Of her there is no
danger!

Thus did Hannah Webster Foster drive home the lessons to women of
revolutionary-era conduct literature in her best-selling novel of 1797, *The
Coquette*. She would follow up the next year with *The Boarding School*, her
own contribution to the more directly didactic genre. *The Coquette* can be
read as a stinging critique of the system of manners and evolving gender
situation that they manifested, but on the surface, as in her conduct book,
Foster served her sex by reiterating the period's cautions.[9]

Revolutionary-era conduct writers did not think of the relationship between women and men the same way they thought of the relationships between class and age inferiors and superiors. Very little of their fairly plentiful
advice to women about encounters with men conformed to the standard suggestions for proper behavior with superiors, as some had in the early colonial
period. Only a few comments to wives about proper behavior toward husbands resembled advice to other inferiors, and these formed only a small part
of revolutionary-era advice to women, again in contrast to the earlier period.
This lack of interest in the marital relationship is another hint that the patriarchal family model for society of the early colonial era was not necessarily replaced by a new familial model (now affectionate and egalitarian), as some
historians have suggested.[10]

Rather than asking women to show deference in their behavior to superior men, as they had in the past, revolutionary-era authors advised them to
behave in such a way as to avoid arousing men sexually. While allusions to
sexuality had served to qualify the inferiority of women to men in the early
colonial period, in the revolutionary era advice telling women to be careful in
this arena was the main theme. That the authors did not tell women to defer
to men as they had before does not mean that they regarded men and women
as equals. Women bore an unequal burden in the relationship. They were to
"oblige without *Invitation*": to both please men and fend off their advances.
This was not an enviable task.

Women's task was tricky, first, because the authors actively encouraged
contact with men. They did so implicitly by giving women much advice on
behavior with men and explicitly by telling women they would be improved
by contact with men. Scholars have emphasized eighteenth-century proclamations of women's influence on men's behavior, but the conduct writers
thought such influence was reciprocal. In Rush's words: "[B]y mingling to-

gether they mutually polish and improve one another." Influence aside, James Fordyce and John Bennett denounced as hypocritical the prude who shunned male company, the latter observing: "This tremblingly modest female, in a company, of which I had lately the honour of making one, on hearing that a number of gentlemen were coming to drink tea, seemed very much alarmed, and pretended to make an apology for retiring. Now this was nothing less than downright hypocrisy. . . . Every woman in the world is fond of our society." Bennett argued that women could very properly "shew a fondness" for being in male company. Several authors bemoaned customs of separating men and women in company, such as women withdrawing to another room after dinner. Certainly period diaries and letters depict an ample degree of mixing between the sexes.[11]

But the writers qualified their approval of contact with men in certain new ways. A few authors discouraged young women from forming intimate friendships with men. More writers simply insisted, like the era's sentimental novelists, that certain kinds of men be avoided. "Coxcombs" were to be "treated with the neglect they deserve." Young women were to steer clear of presumptuous and impudent men, and to "leave him immediately!" if one said or attempted anything improper.[12] In addition, some writers told women to avoid going too often in public, and their reasons had to do with the presence of men. The author of *The Female Friend* claimed that the less often women were seen in public, the more they would be esteemed by men. William Kenrick also claimed that modest women did not frequent "the public haunts of men." And several writers told young women not to appear too often abroad without a chaperone, because they would be besieged by bad men, who would consider them, in Fordyce's words, "as lawful game, to be hunted down without any hesitation." Contemporary diaries occasionally show the "mortification" of young women who happened to find themselves in public situations without protection.

Dr. Gregory clarified the difference between acceptable and unacceptable sites of encounters with men when he told his daughter:

> You may perhaps imagine that the reserved behavior which I recommend to you, and your appearing seldom at public places, must cut off all opportunities of your being acquainted with gentlemen . . . I do not think public places suitable to make people acquainted together. . . . But it is in private companies alone where you can expect easy and agreeable conversation, which I should never wish you to decline.

Similarly, a number of authors requested that women only dance in private companies, or at least that they not dance often in public assemblies, where they risked being introduced to undesirable men. John Adams echoed these sentiments in a letter to his nieces where he deplored the practice of those "Persons of Rank and figure even" who kept their daughters shut in, "concealing them from all Males, till a formal Courtship is opened." He warned the girls "that no Man that is free and can think, will rush blindfold, into the Arms of any such Ladies," and concluded that "You must therefore associate yourselves in some good Degree, and under certain Guards and Restraints, even privately with young fellows." These discussions suggest that the linkage of public and private with male and female spheres that many have associated with the nineteenth century did not yet exist in these writers' minds. They did indeed label certain public spaces as male; but private spaces, the ideal locale for mixing between the sexes, were not regarded as female domain.[13]

The same concerns differentiated other advice to women from standard advice to inferiors. As in the past, women were not asked to give place to men as class and age inferiors were with their superiors. In contrast to the earlier period, women were also not asked, as were other inferiors, to show any special respect to men. Any similarities to demeanor instructions for class and age inferiors were superficial. While women were to adopt a somewhat reserved demeanor and not be overly familiar with men, for example, the rationale was very different from that of like advice to other inferiors. Women were to avoid being overly familiar with men not for fear of showing disrespect but for fear of encouraging sexual advances. Many writers told women to be on guard, for men "will always be ready to take more than you ought to allow them." They were to have a modest, virtuous, and dignified air, as this was thought to protect them from men's familiarities. If a man attempted such improper advances, a woman was to reduce her complaisance in response; but this was a delicate situation, and the authors disagreed as to how severe her response should be. They did agree that women should never allow their reserve to extend to prudery in the presence of worthy men. Prudery, or unwarranted shyness and severity in the presence of men, was affected delicacy; true delicacy allowed women to be sweet, relaxed, and gay with men. Still, women were not to be too easygoing, which might be taken as an invitation to impropriety. In sum, women were to seek a medium between coldness and forwardness with men, advice Eliza Southgate of Maine had clearly taken to heart when she wrote respecting a new suitor: "I will endeavor . . . to steer between the rocks of prudery and coquetry."

This sort of advice was new to the revolutionary era. While some early colonial authors had recommended a pleasant and modest demeanor in women, they were generally speaking to wives. Some revolutionary-era authors argued that even married women ought to remain modest and reserved, but the bulk of their advice was for maidens.[14] In both periods, the sexual element of male-female relations distinguished them from other relations between unequals; yet the disparity had grown in the revolutionary era, along with a widening of focus from marital relations to male-female relations in general.

The revolutionary advice is consistent with historians' observations that women were adopting new self-controls in the area of sexuality. But some scholars have contrasted the modesty called for here with the "passionlessness" or lack of sexual drive attributed to and accepted by proper Victorian ladies, by suggesting that the former was just an act, an affected "demureness" designed by men for their own pleasure. This interpretation is not supported by the conduct advice. Both male and female writers gave this advice, and both warned women against affected modesty. In essence, they were urging women to have an air of real chastity (not passionlessness, hence their de-nunciation of prudes) for their own protection. Such a demeanor would warn "coxcombs" that their efforts would be in vain. Otherwise, the hope was that women would indeed be pleasing to men.[15]

As were their predecessors, revolutionary-era conduct writers were con-vinced that women's facial expressions had a role in determining men's con-duct. *The Ladies Library* insisted, "'tis certain a modest Countenance gives a Check to Lust." Women were to wear "*Looks* that Forbid without *Rudeness*, and oblige without *Invitation*, or leaving room for the Sawcy Inferences Men's Vanity suggesteth to them upon the least Encouragements." A woman was to strive above all to express modesty in her face. The advice was similar to that of the earlier period, but far more extensive. A number of authors discussed blushing, for example, recommending it as an external sign of a woman's modesty and the most effective reprimand for male improprieties. These au-thors denounced the woman who "hath forgotten to blush," but urged women not to affect a blush; it had to reflect real modesty. Women were also to check improper behavior on the part of men by showing a marked disapproval in their faces. If they failed to do this, the authors warned, men would take it as an invitation to continue their offensive behavior. Women were to have a particular guard over their eyes. Lord Halifax urged his daughter to "have a perpetual *Watch* upon your *Eyes,* and . . . remember, that one careless *Glaunce* giveth more advantage than a *hundred words.*" Women were to give men soft and virtuous rather than bold looks and glances. They were not to stare in men's faces, "lest it be interpreted in the worst sense." They were to make sure their eyes did not betray a weakness for any man, as this would en-courage him to act boldly.[16]

While a few authors continued to dispense the older counsels that wives should be quiet, respectful, and modest in conversation with their husbands, most of the advice to women on conversation reflected the period's new focus and concerns. Revolutionary-era conduct writers did not generally advise women as they did most other inferiors (and as had their predecessors) to limit their talk with men or to allow men to control conversation. Women were to regulate their talk with modesty and reserve—all agreed they should not be loud—but they were not to be too reserved; with deserving men their talk was to be lively and unconstrained. Laughter and gaiety were acceptable if they did not push the limits of proper female delicacy. A few writers lauded the soft and sweet manner of speaking that some women adopted to please men.[17]

Much of the advice about conversation did not concern what women would say to men but how women were to react to men's talk. Again the rule was to be careful but pleasant. While some authors told young women to "be on their guard" against male flattery, most told women to bear it with good humor. Rather than answering, they were to show by their looks and manner what they felt about it, and these were to be civil, not disdainful. The best tactic was to change the subject. If a woman's modesty or blushes did not suffice to silence actually immodest talk on the part of men, women were to express their disapproval verbally. If the offense was serious, they were to reply firmly; mild or evasive language would only make men bolder. In contrast to early colonial advice, few authors felt it necessary to condemn indelicate talk on women's part.[18]

The authors must have been cautioning women against improper body contact, however vaguely, when they advised women never to allow "improper familiarities" or "unwarrantable freedoms" on the part of men. Two authors were more direct. Dr. Gregory told his daughters that "It is your interest to keep yourselves sacred from all personal freedoms. . . . The sentiment that a woman may allow all innocent freedoms, provided her virtue is secure, is both grossly indelicate and dangerous, and has proved fatal to many of your sex." Kenrick specified: "Doth he only ask a kiss of thy cheek, indulge not his frequent request; lest the sweetness thereof inflame him to desire, and the poison of his lips descend into thine own bosom." Note these authors' assumptions of a defensive stance among women: whereas early colonial authors urged women not to indulge in improper familiarities with men, revolutionary era authors asked women not to allow them. The only exceptions were a few old-fashioned warnings to wives not to engage in public displays of affection with their husbands.

Advice to women continued to be different from that to other inferiors, then, because it was filled with allusions to sexuality. What was new in the revolutionary era was the dropping of demands for deference to men and the strong message that the burden of controlling men's passions lay on women's shoulders. Women were to make sure that their demeanor, facial expressions, and words admitted of nothing that a man could take as an encouragement for boldness. A woman's modesty, if apparent in her behavior, was thought to go a long way in protecting her from men's advances, especially if she also had the prudence to avoid "dangerous situations." But if, in spite of her precautions, a man was so bold as to attempt improper familiarities, or, worst of all, seduction, she was to refuse and to repel his advances in no uncertain terms.[19]

Revolutionary-era conduct writers thus conveyed to women a sense of danger in mixing with men, especially without the protection of others in men's "public haunts." In so doing, they reflected a reality of seduction that is also refracted onto other evidence of the period, whether court records, newspaper accounts, ballads, stories, or novels. The injunctions to be careful spoke to the central drama of women's lives at this time: the crucial marriage decision. For while they steered clear of courtship per se (behavior with a specific potential partner), the conduct works were to a great degree occupied in giving young women lessons in courting behavior (interaction with men in general). The pressure for women to marry was great, given the the paucity of sanctioned alternatives or indeed viable options for supporting themselves. Their choice of mate was fateful, given their continuing lack of legal rights and limited access to divorce. Yet women were increasingly making this choice alone. While parents had never arranged marriages in America, it had been thought appropriate for them to play a considerable role in influencing and forwarding matches. Now the young were supposed to take the initiative. If a girl made a mistake and went too far with a man who was unwilling to wed, there would be far less community interference to ensure that he did so. So a young woman had to watch out for herself; her capital on the marriage market was in her hands. The conduct works' cautions were for real. Some scholars suggest that her defensiveness would soon become passionlessness, which in turn served as a basis for claims of female moral superiority; but all of that lay in the future, if it happened at all. For now she had to preserve a certain pleasing openness even while protecting herself, lest she fail to attract the right customer.[20]

"BETSY NILES AFFECTS to trip lightly across the floor, to act with a Sprightly Air, and to be polite. But she is under Restraint, and awe, from her Unacquaintance with Company." When young John Adams jotted down these comments about a friend in 1758, he gave us evidence that he simply assumed women belonged in society. So did the conduct writers. Despite the potential dangers of encounters with men, their advice to women on behavior in general society shows that they nevertheless expected women to be active in the social world (indeed, the latter expectation likely fed their fears for women's safety). While a young man would not have even tried to "trip lightly across the floor," the most important of Adams's concerns about Betsy—that she aspired to a polite deportment and that she still behaved awkwardly and affectedly for want of sufficient opportunity to mix in society—were also his own. A few pages later, for example, he regretfully recorded that he attended court but "felt shy." In another place he judged an older woman by the very same criteria he used to evaluate men, including himself: "She seems good Natured, and obliging to[o], but she has so many shruggs, grimaces, affectations of Witt, Cunning, and Humour, as make her ridiculous. She is awkward, shamefaced, bashful, yet would fain seem sprightly, witty, etc."[21] Whether or not he and his contemporaries realized it, their expectations and aspirations for male and female behavior in general society were substantially the same. Advice to women even varied according to the class and age of the persons interacting as much as advice to men did. These expectations suggest a significant change in the place of women since the early colonial period. The very appearance of regular and extensive descriptions of female deportment in men's diaries was new.

As in the early colonial period, however, it is apparent that the authors still regarded "general society" as a man's world. Men were the relevant audience for both male and female performances; the authors remained largely unconcerned about interaction between women. Yet the expectations for female behavior suggest that women now had a place in the social world. To be sure, there were some differences between advice to men and advice to women. Women were to cloak their behavior with modesty, and to display less boldness and assurance than men. Men were given more elaborately detailed advice overall, and much more exacting counsels about control of their bodies in particular. Underneath these surface details, however, lay an important new undercurrent of common expectations that historians have not acknowledged.

Sometimes the authors gave men and women virtually identical advice. They urged both sexes to be prudent in choosing company, for example, and cautious in forming friendships. Women had not received this advice before. Now, no less than a man, a woman was "to converse with those, whose manners and stile of life may polish her behavior, refine her sentiments, and give her consequence in the eye of the world."[22] A difference of emphasis does emerge in advice about how often and where to enjoy others' society. While the authors directed to middle-class men most of their warnings against too much contact with others, they continued to give women the slightly different advice not to go too often in public. They began to encourage women to socialize in private society, however, which suggests that the social world in which women had won a place was located mainly in private spaces.[23]

In many instances the conduct writers gave men and women the same advice regarding their behavior in company; their instructions to men were just more frequent and specific. This was true of the period's reminders to give time, place, and space to others in company. Whereas Hannah Webster Foster advised women that "Inattention in company is a breach of good manners . . . declaring that you have not the least respect for any who are present," Chesterfield raised the subject more frequently and at more length, describing actions that would indicate inattention, among them, "to go away, or be doing something else," all which would convince one's company "that you despise them."[24] The same equation held in many of the counsels regarding body carriage, including discussions of the importance of salutations, proper standing and walking, and the need to avoid excessive motions of the limbs or self-touching. Both sexes were urged to refrain from bobbing their heads, putting their hands inside their clothes, and picking their noses, for example, but men were warned more often than were women and were given some additional reminders.[25] Both sexes were told not to disrupt conversation by whispering or laughing, while men were also reminded not to yawn, cough, and the like. The same overlap occurs in tips on word choice and use of titles.[26] It was also the case in the various admonitions to avoid unpleasantness in conversation. While they instructed both sexes not to speak ill of others, for example, the authors continued to warn men more often than they warned women not to "deal in scandal" (again challenging scholars' reports of an association between women and slanderous speech).[27] That women were often given the same advice as men in these areas is a dramatic departure from the scant advice to women of the early colonial period.

Sometimes revolutionary-era authors appeared to be distinguishing the sexes in their advice, but upon closer inspection this development was superficial, for the substance of the advice to men and women was the same. One writer urged women not to "sit cross-legged," for example, "for such a free posture unveils more of a masculine disposition." But other authors told men not to cross their legs. And both sexes were urged to sit properly, although men were again given a few more tips than were women.[28] Men were told not to make faces in order to amuse others or accidentally, as when yawning; women were told not to distort their faces in an effort to appear lovely or to show affected fear. Yet substantively, the rules were the same. While men were to refrain from thrusting out their lips, twisting their mouths, puffing up their cheeks, and squinting their eyes, for example, women were to avoid pouting, "winking, dimpling of the cheeks, or primming of the lips."[29]

Usually, the use of more detailed advice to men than to women did not suggest different expectations for their conduct, beyond that men had to exert a bit more control over their bodies. Only occasionally are there hints of the rationale for this greater self-control. The hints, best seen in advice on facial expression, suggest that the more instrumental approach to self-presentation pushed by Lord Chesterfield was especially recommended to men. Take the advice on expression of emotion, for example. While the writers implored both men and women to avoid expressing anger, their reasons differed for each sex. They told women that an angry face was unattractive. "Passion is a prodigious enemy to beauty," declared James Forrester, while The Polite Academy warned women that anger gave "a disagreeable sourness to the whole countenance." The constraints on men were even greater, and for a different reason. They not only had to suppress expression of anger, but also of every other emotion, including distress and joy. They were to exercise command over their faces, keeping them as calm and unmoved as possible, and they were to do so on the grounds that it was imprudent to display every thought and feeling. The different rationales point to the different challenges facing middle-class men and women. Women needed to attract marriage partners. Men did too, of course, but were likely striving in other markets as well, where greater facial control would help keep information from competitors.[30]

Similarly, the writers cautioned both men and women not to stare at others but still to show attention by looking conversation partners in the face. The last injunction was addressed to men more often than to women, however, along with Chesterfield's reminder that by looking conversation partners in the eye, one could discover their true feelings. Women were more often advised to show attention to conversation partners with "an illuminated countenance" than to look them in the eye. And some authors further encouraged women to express modesty with "soft" rather than brazen looks.[31]

As hinted in this last advice, the authors' primary strategy in drawing distinctions between feminine and masculine behavior was to build on traditional calls for female modesty. But their efforts were most often superficial and did not lead to substantive differences in expectations for behavior. Beyond invoking the need for modesty in women, the writers otherwise gave men and women the same advice. While a few authors claimed that modesty should prevent a woman from laughing too much, for example, they certainly warned men not to laugh too much, and otherwise gave both sexes the same advice on maintaining pleasant facial expressions.[32] Women were urged to endow every body movement with modesty, and young women were further warned not to jump about "like boys" and to avoid all "manly exercizes" or "buffoon romping plays . . . not altogether becoming of the modesty of your age and sex." But young men were given just as many warnings against horse-play and romping. While women were reminded not "to forget the delicacy of your sex" when dancing, both sexes were frequently reminded of the impor-tance of this activity.[33]

In rules for conversation, too, some apparent gender differentiation fades as one looks at the advice more closely. Some authors suggested that talking too much was worse in women than in men, and a few claimed that modesty forbade it; more authors warned both sexes against both the errors of talking too much and "too great a taciturnity." And men were given more detailed warnings than were women against interrupting others.[34] The same pattern is seen in advice for proper tone of voice. Most writers agreed with the author of The Polite Lady: "Nothing, my dear, is more inconsistent with modesty, than to talk with a loud, shrill, and harsh tone of voice. This is very unbecoming in a man, but much more in a woman." Yet the authors addressed their most constraining instructions on voice and pronunciation to men.[35] Similarly, some authors warned that profane or obscene talk was worse in women than in men, but more writers denounced these sins to men than to women.[36]

The distribution of advice on the subject matter of talk was similar. Women were warned that joking too much or at others' expense were both "incivilities in Manners" and offenses "against Christian modesty." But men were effectively as circumscribed as women by the more extensive cautions about joking addressed to them.[37] Some authors hinted that proper female modesty should lead women to conceal their learning in company, but other authors disagreed, and two told men to conceal theirs! In addition, more au-thors for men than for women decried boasting and talking of oneself. Several authors told women not to talk politics, while only one older work urged men not to. But the same point about steering clear of potentially dangerous topics was made to men in the many recommendations of small talk as unlikely to cause disputes. Otherwise, men and women were given very similar sugges-tions on proper conversational matter.[38]

Further diminishing the delineation of real differences between proper male and female behavior is the fact that the authors did not confine their requests for modesty to women. This is evident in advice concerning proper demeanor in company. In addition to requests that they be cheerful and courteous—neither too formal nor too familiar—both sexes were urged to have a modest manner before others. The word "modest" also appears regularly in contemporary descriptions of both men and women. John Adams praised his wife and also his friend David Rittenhouse for being "soft and modest." Elias Boudinot likewise complimented several men as "modest & diffident." But the recommendations of modesty to women are significant, for the simple reason that conduct writers expended far more ink in recommending modesty to women than to men. It was the most essential quality in a woman's demeanor: one author opined that "where it is wanting everything disgusts."

What difference was female modesty supposed to make? Some authors implied that modesty distinguished proper female from male behavior by im-posing a measure of restraint on the traits that were recommended to both sexes. Modesty thus kept a woman from a too-free behavior or "robust," "bold," and "masculine" airs. Some authors claimed that modesty was the outward expression of inner chastity. Others claimed that modesty was an attractive timidity and diffidence, while they urged men to show "a modest assurance." This difference between female modesty and male assurance reverberated as well in some advice on facial expression and conversation. While women were to strive for a modest look, eschewing especially a "daring" or "unabashed countenance," Chesterfield and his followers deplored men's "being out of countenance" and looking embarrassed in company. Similarly, women were to avoid overly "forward," "confident," or "bold" speech, while Chesterfield and his followers stressed to men the importance of an assured manner of speaking. But the authors did not push bashfulness for women. As one warned: "Do not confound the ideas of modesty and timidity." Far from an awkward bashfulness, some authors claimed, proper modesty entailed dignity of manner. While a woman's modesty and delicacy might cause her to blush, or even, on occasion, "to melt into affectionate sorrow," affected blushing and weeping were going too far.

Still, women were not to strive for a "confidant ease," while men were; and the authors warned men more frequently than they warned women against awkwardness and bashfulness. But these important nuances should not blind us to the equally important fact that, with the exception of boldness, the authors did not urge any traits of demeanor on men that they did not also recommend to women, a dramatic departure from the early colonial situation. And they charged both sexes equally with the final challenge of making their demeanor seem artless. However important, a man's grace and a woman's modesty were never to seem affected. Ironically, the gender differences the authors wished to appear "natural" were the ones on which they expended the most energy.[39] Conduct writers were searching for ways to distinguish the sexes, but their efforts, working against the stronger tide of gender integration, had not proceeded very far.

Revolutionary-era advice to women on behavior in general society was really just an attenuated version of the advice to women that explicitly concerned behavior with men. The common ingredient in all this advice was modesty. These same observations could be made of early colonial advice. The real change in the authors' minds since the earlier period was such that caused them, in most instances, to give women advice similar to that which they gave men. In essence, in the revolutionary era, the authors were asking women to do everything they asked men to do but in a feminine fashion— that is, with modesty, whereas in the early colonial period conduct writers had treated the behavior of mature women as a case apart from that of mature men, and similar in some ways to that of class and age inferiors. The earlier injunctions to modesty had been surrounded by demands for deference.

The revolutionary-era advice is paradoxical, for while counsels to women were much more similar to those for men than they had been in the early colonial period, the authors seem to have had a more gender-differentiated vision of society (hence their warnings to women to avoid a "masculine" deportment and to cultivate "feminine delicacy") than had early colonial authors. Interestingly, in contrast to scholars' recent focus on supposedly misogynistic language as part of male role definition, and, by extension, female role definition, most definitions by opposition in the conduct literature were directed to women.[40] That is, the authors warned women to avoid a masculine behavior, while they rarely warned men against feminine behavior. In fact, diarists were far more likely to praise than to condemn men for "soft" or "delicate" behavior. Perhaps we have made too much of late colonial misogyny.

Women were newly regarded as rightful players in the social world, but how far women had come in the writers' minds depends on the meaning of their increasing recommendations of modesty. The term has always had several meanings. One was chastity. Modesty had meant chastity in the early colonial period as well; but, interwoven as it was with calls for female deference to men, it had also meant submissiveness. In the revolutionary era the emphasis on modesty as chastity was more pronounced; a woman's modesty was to be so strong that it would not only keep her from improper sexual behavior (its function in the early colonial period as well), but it would also prevent men from behaving improperly toward her.

While they did not use the term to invoke submissiveness to men directly, revolutionary-era authors did use it to encourage humility, or the avoidance of excessive self-assurance, in general society. In this sense, the word could apply to men, especially young men, but there it was a qualifier on a stronger injunction to display self-assurance—modesty was simply to keep men from going too far. In any event, revolutionary-era conduct writers were far more insistent that modesty serve to restrain women's behavior. Their invocation of modesty was frequent enough to justify the third meaning of the term, then as now: modesty as "womanly propriety." Indeed, most of the time the authors felt no need to define the attribute; they simply prescribed it. They seemed to be asking women to behave like men were to behave but in an appropriately womanly (chaste and humble) way.

We have seen that while the authors gave men and women similar advice, they gave men a more detailed and exacting version of it, especially as regarded body carriage, facial expression, and talk. Still to be explained is what this emphasis on control of the body meant. The answer has to do with the rise of middle-class culture. Recall that control of the body was the hallmark of the new middle-class version of the old aristocratic code of behavior. Not only did the achievement of status require self-control but self-control was essential in signing one's worth to others.[41] Given their commercial and political roles, middling men simply had a greater need than did women for such displays of restraint.

This linkage of class and gender concerns reminds us that men were the first middle-class subjects, the first individuals in this age of growing individualism. The role of middle-class women followed closely behind, for they, too, were increasingly improving themselves with an eye to successful performance in a market. The relevant market in their case was not usually that of the economy but the analagous and related one of marriage. Hence the primary focus of their self-control was sexual.[42] While a man needed to watch his behavior to demonstrate his self-control and protect his affairs from competitors, a woman needed to watch her behavior to protect herself from men.

Otherwise, the advice to men and women was similar, indicating that women, like youth, were newly regarded as part of the social world. Rules for face-to-face behavior did not construct a particularly domestic, or even familial, role for women (in part because Americans followed British conduct advice, the rules construct no "Republican Mothers" or "Republican Wives"). Scholars have come to associate the rise of middle-class culture with separate spheres and the domestic female; but perhaps they have done so because as far as gender inquiries go, they have focused on the female. Even critics of the hold of the ideology of separate spheres on historians have taken its dominion in conduct literature for granted. But when we read the script provided by their rules for face-to-face behavior, conduct writers actually suggest something different in this era of revolution. They remind us that new notions of male behavior were the first story in the saga of the rise of the middle class.[43] In this period of transition, when women were first gaining entry into the world of men, they did in fact appear as variations on a male theme. To make this observation is not to dismiss or even diminish their rise but simply to acknowledge the enormity of the challenge it presented. This is why so much attention was devoted to female education in this period. Conduct writers, male and female, were wrestling with a new role for women. They had an older aristocratic construction to work with for men, but for the new social woman they had to start from scratch.

The thrust of these findings, then, is to tug at the interpretive strings binding late-eighteenth-century gender change to the rise of separate spheres. The conventional wisdom suggests that separate spheres and a new private family gave birth to the middle class, or at least that they grew together, and they did not begin to do so until the very end of the century. The evidence from conduct literature suggests that this picture is actually a frame from a sequence with earlier beginnings. It appears that middle-class culture began to develop earlier, as part of the struggle against the old order. In the process, its proponents carved first a new role for men. But, true to their ideology of equality, middling men invited middling women to rise with them. They simply had to contend with the problem of sexual vulnerability that this introduced, as women faced the marriage market on their own. Middle-class men and women did appear to support more affectionate and egalitarian family relationships, indeed a new youth-rearing scheme; but children and private life were still far from exclusively feminine preoccupations. One thinks of Benjamin Rush, who extolled the sweetness of the family circle in his parlor to his friend John Adams. The notion of separate spheres lay in the future, the nineteenth century, where historians have focussed on a later phase of such parlor scenes.[44]

THE SOLUTION TO the problem of sexuality in the new world of peers also lay in the future. For while the conduct writers urged women to protect themselves with modesty, they did not make any such demands of men. Revolutionary-era advice to men concerning women was a mishmash of old and new themes. Overall, relations with women do not appear a major concern. It was as if the middling revolutionaries thought women belonged in their world but had not thought through the consequences. Manners thus underscore the common observation that the revolution for women was an unfinished revolution.

The most notable changes from the early colonial period in advice to men about behavior with women are related: very little of the revolutionary-era advice was confined to marriage (recall that most of the earlier advice was designed to encourage a husband's gentle government of his wife), and it bore little resemblance to advice about relations with class and age inferiors (to which the early colonial advice had to some degree conformed). Indeed, revolutionary-era authors occasionally seemed to be advising men that it was up to them to defer to women, not vice versa. But several hints between the lines indicate that it would be wrong to conclude that the situation had gone from one extreme to the other. First, the authors continued to give men very little advice about behavior with women compared to the amount of advice they gave men regarding their behavior in general society—an indication that they did not consider the relationship with women of great importance. Second, their advice is often contradictory, and occasionally ambivalence can be found in the prescriptions of a single author. For instance, Lord Chesterfield, in many ways the originator of the "ladies first" doctrine, was severely criticized for his less-than-respectful attitude toward women, an attitude that often peeks through in his advice. When he advised, "To women you should always address yourself with great outward respect and attention," for example, he felt compelled to add "whatever you feel inwardly."[45] Sometimes his and others' advice betrays assumptions of male superiority that are not stated directly—for example, that men would initiate and control the timing of encounters. Moreover, it is clear that the deference the authors asked men to pay women was not of a piece with traditional deference. It was not a symbolic recognition of another's strength or power. Rather, it consisted only of attentions and protections that the strong were to pay the weak. The revolutionary-era suggestions in this vein were too few to suggest that a dramatic change in attitudes had taken place, but they were a harbinger of things to come.

In the meantime, hints of a new respect for women were undercut by suggestions that men did not have to show much respect and expressions of fear that they would sometimes show women the wrong kind of attention. Some writers suggested that men should devote time to performing favors for women, as by serving them at table, giving them an arm in walking, and ceding place and precedence generally. But otherwise, men were not asked to greatly modify their behavior in the presence of women. The writers simply recommended the courteous and cheerful demeanor that men owed to all. And a few authors felt the need to warn men to abstain from excessive flattery and gallantry or an unchaste manner toward women.[46]

Remarks on conversation were similar. A few writers encouraged men to talk with women with a lively and easy, though always respectful, manner. Some remarks, however, implied that men did not need to show a lot of respect. Chesterfield again showed his ambivalence toward women when he suggested that men's respect should be "playful," and their talk addressed to women's vanity. Franklin demurred a bit, claiming that excessive flattery had contributed to making women "unfit for the rational Pleasures of Society and Conversation." Chesterfield admitted that overly patronizing talk was dangerous. In the end, he suggested that women were "to be talked to, as below men, and above children. If you talk to them too deep, you only confound them . . . if you talk to them too frivolously, they perceive and resent the contempt." Chesterfield believed that the safest talk with women was small talk. In fact, he and his followers claimed that this useful acquirement was chiefly to be learned in female company.[47]

Even suggestions that men should behave nicely in the presence of women described a fairly passive attitude on men's part, by claiming that women would set the tone of their interaction. While most revolutionary-era conduct writers simply assumed that men would spend time with women, a few openly urged men to seek female company for its salutary effects on their behavior. Women's sweetness would soften men's rough edges, these authors claimed, for "It is not easy to talk, or to look obscenely, or even to behave with rudeness and ill manners under such restraint." Benjamin Rush agreed, arguing that the society of "private families" was much better for men than "society in taverns," because in the former "manners are usually kept within the bounds of decency by the company of females."[48]

Significantly, given their cautions to women, revolutionary-era conduct works rarely advised men on the matter of body contact with women. Only one author urged men to abstain "from all approaches to lust." This was not a departure from the past, as early colonial authors had also not asked men to restrain themselves sexually; but it does contrast with the emphasis on self-control in other revolutionary-era advice to men. This tells us that the growing emphasis on male body control was not yet conceived in sexual terms. Physical self-control was important in general society; it was not particularly important in encounters with women. When compared with the advice to women, the sexual double standard is clear. This conclusion is corroborated in other contemporary sources. Local court records show that men were not held responsible for sexual transgressions after the mid-eighteenth century, whereas the earlier community had at least applied external pressures on erring men; the period's new seduction tales tended to depict men as both immoral and unreformable.[49] In all, the scanty advice to men regarding interaction with women is clearly different from advice regarding class and age inferiors, but it does not suggest equality. There are hints of a new deference to women, but only hints; and men were off the hook in the sexual arena. The new script for men in these scenes was incomplete.

THE ETIQUETTE OF gender relations shows once again the revolutionary era authors' interest in instructing a newly rising group, for more of their works were directed to women. Similar to their dissemination and elaboration of the old elite code of behavior to and for the middle class, they gave women much advice formerly given only to men. And, like their advice for youth, their suggestions for women betray a loosening of family bonds; while much more advice was devoted to opposite-sex relations in the revolutionary era than in the first, much less of it was confined to marriage. But it also cannot be said (as it can be of the advice to the middle class and to youth) that the authors were most concerned with instructing women on how to behave properly toward their (gender) peers, other women. The authors continued to display little interest in relationships between women. If not interested in creating a "Republican Wife" per se, the writers were clearly thinking in terms of women as men's companions.[50] The position of women had risen in the authors' eyes; they were no longer overtly branded as inferior to men. But neither were they regarded as men's equals. When read between the lines, the advice to both sexes on interaction with the opposite sex reveals that the authors continued to view men as the stronger sex, while placing the burdens of restraining their advances on women—the unenviable command to "oblige, without invitation." If self-control was the hallmark of the new man, the abnegation of male responsibility in the sexual arena was a way of reminding women that they had not yet earned equal treatment in the moral realm.[51]

Still, women had come a long way. Whereas in the early colonial period they had been considered a permanently inferior case apart from men, in the revolutionary era their behavior was to vary as much as was men's according to their class and age status and that of the persons in their presence. As to their behavior in general society, the writers urged them to let modesty restrain their behavior but otherwise to act similarly to men. In the revolutionary reconsideration of gender roles, women had won an acknowledged place in the social world. This fact would easily escape us were we to focus only on the surface injunctions of modesty or the fears expressed in seduction tales.[52] Moreover, men's behavior was itself effectively restrained by the increasingly elaborate exactions made of it. In some ways the revolutionary-era etiquette of gender relations is ambiguous; old strains of inequality in the few counsels given in regard to husband-wife relations persisted alongside hints of a new kind of deference toward women. In addition, occasional hints of increasing gender differentiation in the advice suggest that the fate of women in the antebellum era would be different from that of youth and the middle class. Like them, women were being incorporated from the margins into the mainstream of society; but unlike them, women were being incorporated with "a difference."

As was true of class and age relations, then, but even more so, the revolutionary era was a time of transition in gender relations. Only time would reveal the outcome. Clearly British and American conduct writers were groping for a place for women in their democratizing worlds. They saw women in their visions of the social scene but were struggling to come to terms with their presence. They tried to sort out male from female behavior, but their efforts were superficial, belied by the deeper imperative of inclusion in this "enlightened" age. But inclusion raised the spectre of equality, which may in turn have fueled the search for difference. The immediate result of this conceptual tug-of-war was a sense of wariness—it seemed that all fathers could do was warn their daughters that their safety was in their own hands. But this was uncomfortable. The search for a better solution would continue.

Conclusion: Manners and the Revolution against Patriarchy

Whereas early colonial conduct writers effectively lumped the lower and middling sort together and drew a line between them and the elite, revolutionary-era authors dropped the line and treated middle- and upper-class persons alike, while leaving out the lower class. Similarly, early colonial advice to youth and children could be lumped together as different from that to adults, while in the revolutionary era the line between adults and youth blurred, and the differences between youth and children grew. And while there had been a clear line between the code of the world of men and the special behavior required of women in early colonial advice, that line, too, became harder to make out in the revolutionary era.

What do these changes tell us about the conduct authors' vision of the social order? Judging from the advice to different inferiors about proper behavior with superiors, the servant/master and child/adult relationships were more traditional and of greater inequality than youth/adult or middle-class/upper-class relations, and certainly more unequal than the relationship between women and men. For instance, in addition to the standard respectful demeanor, the writers recommended that servants display an air of cheerful obedience rather than a sullen manner in the presence of their masters; and they gave children similarly strict advice to display proper submissiveness in the presence of adults. In contrast, a new ambivalence about deference was registered in the advice to middle- and upper-class persons concerning their superiors, and the old ambiguity persisted in the advice to all age groups concerning the aged. Thus, some authors advised upper- and middle-class readers to seek company "above them," but argued that good company was not solely determined by class status. While they counseled youth to seek out the company of the aged, they assumed that youth would be inclined to shun such society.

The advice to women diverged most from the norm of proper behavior to superiors. The authors mainly counseled women to have a modest demeanor in the presence of men, at most an indirect form of respect. And while they were to heed the standard warning against overfamiliarity with superiors, they were to do so for entirely different reasons than were class and age inferiors: such caution was more for their own protection than for the purpose of displaying deference. Rather than to show respect in their faces, as were other inferiors, women were to have modest blushing countenances in the presence of men. Unlike other inferiors, women were counseled never to allow men to take "personal liberties."

The writers addressed most of their advice on proper behavior with peers to young middle-class men. Clearly this advice—the newest and most elaborate of the revolutionary era—was intended to teach new behaviors to a group on the rise. The authors were less concerned about relations between upper-class persons and still less about relations between lower-class persons, adults, children, or women. The advice to the middling was often similar to but more elaborate than that to upper-class persons; that to youth was always more elaborate than that to adults; and that to men concerning encounters with other men was much more extensive than advice to women concerning encounters with other women. The authors did give middle-class women a lot of the same advice they gave to men regarding behavior in general society. Hence the significant others in most advice to men and women were men. This is another sign of the transitional nature of the revolutionary era; the writers gave women's behavior such detailed consideration as to make it clear that women were a part of the social world they envisioned. But it was still a world dominated by men.

Like advice on behavior with superiors, revolutionary-era advice on behavior with inferiors was less elaborate and less uniform than advice on peer relations. It, too, suggests that the authors considered the middle-class master/lower-class servant and adult/child relations the most unequal. They gave adults less advice about relations with youth, and the upper class and the elderly still less about their inferiors. While the authors said little to adults concerning the amount of contact they were to have with youth, for example, they often advised parents to spend time with children (to teach them good behavior and keep them from bad company). They also told middle-class masters to spend time with their servants to supervise their conduct in addition to their work. Masters were not to go so far as to associate familiarly with their servants, however, while parents were urged to have a free and familiar relationship with their children. Unlike masters with servants, parents were to be warm and loving in manner with their children. The authors were silent on the issues of "discipline-talk" and corporal punishment of youth by adults; nor did they mention beating in connection with the master-servant relationship. More often than not, however, they approved of moderate beating of recalcitrant children. This advice reflects the growing gap between the authors' portrayals of adult/youth and adult/child relations. As for the adult/child and master/servant relations, while similar in some respects they were differentiated to a greater extent than in the early colonial period by the authors' association of the first with pedagogy and the second with authority.

The authors gave men advice about relations with women that once again distinguished gender from both class and age relations. While men were encouraged to seek out the company of women, this was just as much for the salutary influence of female company on their behavior as it was for them to influence women. The different nature of gender relations is also signaled by the fact that, in contrast to other superiors, men were to pay some attentions to women. Further, the proper manner of disciplining women was never the issue that it was in regard to other inferiors.

Judging from the overall amount of advice, revolutionary-era authors were less concerned about relationships with inferiors than they had been in the early colonial period. They certainly no longer thought them as similar as they had before. The relationship between adults and youth was becoming different from that between adults and children. The master-servant relationship was losing some of the paternalistic emphasis that had formerly likened it to relationships between adults and young people. And men's proper behavior in the presence of women resembled peer advice more than advice on behavior with inferiors.

The overall lack of uniformity in the rules for class, age, and gender relations suggests the demise of the hierarchical and patriarchal view of society of the early colonial period, where the same sort of deference sufficed in all relations. Most of the change from early colonial advice came in the area of behavior with peers. Advice on behavior with superiors and inferiors had only changed a little, and the changes suggest that the authors viewed these relations as less unequal than their predecessors had viewed them. Inequality and deference were no longer ruling principles in revolutionary-era manners. This is not to deny the persistence of inequality; society continued to be, as it always is, made up of relations between persons of varying power or status. But the power issue became obscured because the authors had come to believe that class, age, and gender relations should be regulated more by affective egalitarian than overtly forceful means, and they were more concerned with relations between peers than those between persons of different status. The question begging to be asked is what relationship their views bore to changes occuring in the wider society.

The event that springs to mind, of course, is the American Revolution. Recall that much of the change in revolutionary-era manners was introduced at about the same time the Revolution was taking place, largely due to the influence of Chesterfield's *Letters*. But this is not to say that the American Revolution—in the narrow sense of the War for Independence—*caused* the changes witnessed in the revolutionary era. For one thing, the body of conduct literature began to change several decades earlier, at midcentury. Moreover, most of the authors of this literature were British, and Americans remained loyal consumers of their works for several decades into the nineteenth century. Changes in revolutionary-era manners were caused by a larger revolution: the changes in social structure and corresponding thinking that had been brewing over the course of a century or more on both sides of the Atlantic, changes that brought about alterations in the rules for social relations on both the microscopic level (changes in manners) and the macroscopic level (changes in polity—among them, the American Revolution). Thus, changes in manners were brought about by the same intellectual, religious, economic, and political challenges to the old order that began to be manifested in the Great Awakening of the mid-eighteenth century and continued through the Revolutionary War. In particular, the rising prosperity of the middle class and spreading currents of Enlightenment thought conflicted with the old exclusivity of the genteel code and the patriarchal control of youth and women.

Manners can tell us some things about the larger revolution. Rules for behavior suggest how their codifiers thought different groups were to accommodate the changes in the "big rules" of economic, political and religious systems in their daily interactions. In one sense manners underscore the possibilities raised by the changes in the Anglo-American world of the eighteenth century. Some groups were clearly meeting with success in challenging their former inequality, because changes were being registered in the ritual of social relations. But manners also suggest the conservative nature of the revolution, in two ways. First, they indicate that the way to advancement for the middle class, youth, and women was not freer behavior but the adoption of self-controls formerly asked only of the elite. Second, as late as the first decades of the nineteenth century the only improvement for lower-class servants and children was that their superiors were asked to be a bit more benevolent in ruling them. It was not at all clear whether the "opening of possibilities" would ever happen for them. The revolutionary era raised questions that remained to be answered in the antebellum period.

Thus the changing facts of and ideas about social relations during the revolutionary era can be seen in the social scaffolding limned by contemporary suggestions for conduct. Revolutionary-era etiquette did not indicate any change in the overall ranking of groups but did suggest that change had occurred in the relative spacing of the ladder's rungs. In essence, the rungs of the middle class, youth, and women had moved quite a bit higher up the ladder, away from those of the lower class and children and closer to those of the upper-class persons, mature adults, and men. Only the working out of a code of manners suitable for the adolescent republic would reveal the height of their climb, whether children and the lower class would follow, and whether women were actually moving to a different scale.

PART III

Resolution: Manners for Democrats, 1820–1860

SEVEN

MANNERS FOR THE MIDDLE CLASS

Sitting in his bedroom on an April evening in 1841, eighteen-year-old Isaac Mickle recorded a decision in his diary.

> I am resolved to read Chesterfield's *Principles of Politeness* forthwith, to the end that I may make my entree into society with becoming flourishes. The first bow that the reader's humble servant ever undertook to perform before ladies—was his last! He caught his feet in the carpet, and fell sprawling upon the floor; and since then, at introductions, recognitions, and salutations, he has never ventured beyond an inclination of the head, or a formal touch of his chapeau. But inasmuch as this stiffness brings great scandal upon him, from the other sex, in general, and the polite part of that sex, in particular, he is resolved to begin de novo, as aforesaid, to wit, by reading Chesterfield.[1]

Little did Mickle know that he was penning a digest of antebellum manners concerns for his descendants. Two items are especially important for the class dimension of the period's manners system. First, in deciding to read Chesterfield, Mickle alerts us that some important revolutionary-era texts, and thus advice, continued to be current among his generation. Second, however, in mentioning his performance at "introductions, recognitions, and salutations," he hints that some previously casual gestures were becoming newly ritualized. In these continuities and new features lay manners' role in mediating class relations in antebellum America.

As we have seen, the American Revolution occurred in the middle of an important period of change in the history of manners, a time when middling authors remade the old aristocratic code of behavior and spread it to their class. They undertook this exercise in cultural cooptation as part of a larger challenge to the crumbling system of orders and aristocratic power. By the end of the period, the middling triumph over aristocratic hegemony was clear. It was evident in political terms with the rejection of the Federalists; it was registered in language, as the term gentleman now simply meant one who was refined. A gentleman was even expected to have an occupation.[2] The changes in manners accompanying this cultural shift prove their liberal potential, as social rituals helped to enact the rise of the middle class.

The question remained how far the social revolution would proceed in the young republic. One would think the possibilities were great, for while the middling project of the revolutionary era was part of a transatlantic cultural sea change, the American Revolution introduced a new political context and new questions of national identity that allowed, indeed forced, Americans to grapple with the the meaning of democracy in their society. In fact, neither contemporary observers nor subsequent historians have been exactly sure how far democracy went in this period of American adolescence. It is, and was, difficult to tell because Americans were actually experiencing two revolutions—the democratic and the market revolutions—and these pulled in different directions. While the political revolution held out the promise of equality, the economic revolution fostered inequality. Once again, manners can help us to see how Americans actually dealt with such cultural conflicts. Unfortunately, they also force us to confront the closing of the door of democratic possibility.

As we saw respecting the early colonial period, manners can serve to erect or maintain as well as to destroy class barriers. They performed the first functions again in antebellum America; only now, the pressure on this physical sign system was greater than ever before, because of the public embracing of democratic ideals. Indeed, manners are what allowed Americans to espouse both democracy and the imperatives of the market; they simply proclaimed the first while acting out the second. In this way, manners communicated nonverbally what was difficult to communicate otherwise.[3]

That antebellum manners signaled class barriers more than they codified democratic opportunity is evident in a number of ways. First, despite some claims that—with the proper behavior—all could be ladies and gentlemen, conduct writers made it clear that this was not a possibility for the lower class. While they balked at acknowledging class differences between the middle and upper classes, they did not hesitate in pushing the lower class to the wings of their social world. To the extent that the serving class was expected on the stage, it was as props. Second, while antebellum conduct writers gave ever more elaborate advice to the middle class, thereby continuing the revolutionary-era task of equipping self-made men and women with the accoutrements of gentility, the nature of the elaboration made the code inaccessible to any who had not in fact "made it." Most of the newly codified rituals of the era—"the introductions, recognitions, and salutations"—were gate-keeping devices to serve the cause of social exclusivity. The new stage directions also involved expensive props—among them domestic servants.

The final clue to the real class functions of antebellum manners emerges from comparison with Britain. Recall that conduct literature consumed in America continued to be of mostly British authorship for several decades after the Revolution. American authors began to declare the need for a special code of conduct suitable for a democratic republic in the decades after 1820. One writer proclaimed, for instance, that "we are beginning to have an American code, in better harmony with the practical and Enlightened common sense of democratical institutions than much that has been dictated by the pompous impudence of aristocratic inclusiveness."[4] And yet the specific advice found in the mostly American-authored conduct works circulating in the decades before the Civil War is shockingly similar to that found in British manuals of the period. What does this mean?

Like rituals point to like conditions. Britain in the age of Victoria was a few steps behind America in the process of democratization, but it was undergoing the same process of cultural bourgeoisification. Similar manners show the primacy of economic forces over political ideals in shaping social realities. The American embracing of democracy simply muddied the cultural waters in such a way as to make the clarifying power of elaborate social ritual all the more necessary. The fact that manners allowed people to act in ways they would not admit openly helps us to understand why manners were so vitally important to middle-class Americans like Isaac Mickle.

CHANGES IN THE conduct literature circulating in northern America around 1820 thus mark the beginning of a new period in manners. The number of titles began to grow more rapidly; over a hundred new works appeared in the next four decades.[5] Changes in the intended audience and authorship of antebellum conduct works were even more dramatic. For the first time, no works were addressed exclusively to the upper class. Roughly 90 percent were addressed to the middle classes; only a few were directed to the lower sort. The manuals were nearly evenly divided as to the sex of their intended audience: about a third were for men, a third for women, and a third for both sexes. As in the earlier periods, most manuals were addressed to youth; but now more than 20 percent were directed to adults, which was double the proportion of the past. Men continued to write most of the conduct literature, but the proportion of female authors grew. Nearly all of the authors were middle-class writers, educators, or clergy by profession, while a few were dancing masters.[6] None were truly upper class, and only one was purportedly a domestic servant and hence a member of the lower class. No longer, then, was the upper class a major force in the instruction of proper behavior; the middle class had completely taken over.

The biggest change in the authorship of antebellum-era works was the change in the nationality of the writers. English authors had always outnumbered Americans, but in the antebellum period the proportions were dramatically reversed. Three-quarters of conduct works were written by Americans. While borrowing from foreign sources, they professed the desire to publish a "truly American and Republican" code of manners. Editors of works by foreign authors began to include a few comments about European usages that were not fitting, or varying practices that were more typical in America. Even unaltered works display subtle changes in the same vein. After numerous editions of varying titles from the mid-1770s, it was only after 1827 that Chesterfield's *Letters* began to appear occasionally as *The American Chesterfield*.

Also significant was change in the relative importance of different genres of conduct advice. While still outnumbered by more moralistic advice books, the proportion of etiquette works grew dramatically in the antebellum decades. Representing less than 10 percent of the early colonial works and 20 percent of revolutionary-era works, between 1821 and 1860 etiquette works amounted to nearly half of the available printed matter that gave northerners specific advice on how to behave in face-to-face encounters. The more general advice books themselves began to give greater treatment to manners than they had in the past. Writers like William Alcott began devoting whole chapters to good manners in such works as his *Young Man's Guide*, departing from earlier counterparts wherein advice on deportment and demeanor was scattered at random.

While the authors of the general-advice works considered a variety of topics—character, work, study, religion—in addition to manners, the etiquette manuals were generally devoted to manners alone. They were not much concerned with the relationship between proper behavior and proper morals; indeed, they built on the Chesterfieldian notion that manners and morals could be separated. Usually the writers paid lip service in their opening pages to the Christian foundation of or general moral principles behind manners and let it go at that.

As Arthur Schlesinger Sr. observed, the handbooks that grew out of the Chesterfieldian tradition were "crisp and to the point. . . . The matter was neatly arranged, nothing was taken for granted, and the precepts were so simply phrased as to be easily remembered."[7] The etiquette works differed from the conduct-of-life advice books in that many were vague as to the age of their intended audience and most were addressed to both sexes. Inexpensive as well as inclusive, these works were intended for a wider audience than ever before. Primarily written for the market and derived from other works, the etiquette manuals were not the expressions of individuals (most of the authors were anonymous or obscure) but collections of rules thought customary in good society, designed for the enlightenment of the uninitiated. Some, like *Beadle's Dime Book of Etiquette* or the publisher Samuel R. Wells's *How to Behave: A Pocket Manual of Republican Etiquette*, were simply hasty compilations published to meet demand.

The roles of family and church as sources of manners instruction continued to decline after 1820 relative to the growing influence exercised by schools and, especially, books. The latter played an increasingly unmediated role in conduct instruction, especially after 1840, when new technologies allowed cheaper printing. Recent studies have concluded that books and reading were cherished parts of middle-class culture. Northerners were more and more likely to treat conduct works in particular as "how to" or "self-help" books, and to use them to teach themselves how to behave. The authors' democratic tone, their solicitation of a wider audience, and their declarations of purpose suggest they regarded themselves as direct partners in the social tutelage of many Americans. Other evidence supports the conclusion that these works had wide circulation as "self-help" books. They were frequently reviewed and recommended in antebellum magazines. Not only did many come out in multiple editions, but we must remember that they could be borrowed as well as purchased, whether from libraries or individuals. Artist John Neagle, for example, recorded lending *The Laws of Etiquette* to six different friends in a two-year period.[8]

Changes in the conduct literature and modes of manners training aside, developments in the social terrain in the 1820s and 1830s alone suggest that the late-eighteenth-century system could no longer have fit society's needs. The North had emerged from the years of young nationhood into a period of growth and self-exploration. The dynamism of the antebellum decades was reflected in growing cities, increasing mobility, new forms of association, movements to reform society, and a "domestic revolution," just to name a few of the trends. Viewed together, these facets of the antebellum period help explain why northerners now felt a desire to work out a new social code to fit new American circumstances. They did develop a new code, but it wasn't *all* new—nor was it uniquely American.

THE COUNTERVAILING political and economic forces at work in antebellum America have caused observers to make dramatically different assessments of this society. Many contemporaries and indeed many past historians viewed this as an egalitarian age—the era of the "common man"—while more recent generations of scholars have stressed the accelerating growth of economic inequality. The latter have proclaimed as myth the general equality of condition, slight differences between classes, and great movement up and down the social ladder that de Tocqueville and others thought they observed.[9]

On the surface, conduct writers shared the "era-of-the-common-man" view with their contemporaries. While none asserted that there was complete equality of condition in America, neither did they describe frankly the increasing wealth stratification and limited mobility that actually prevailed. Indeed, many authors claimed that there was great mobility and equality of opportunity. One claimed, for example, that "In this free land, there are no political distinctions, and the only social ones depend on character and manners. We have no privileged classes, no titled nobility, and everyone has the right, and should have the ambition to be a gentleman. Certainly every woman should have the manners of a lady."[10] These authors asserted that all Americans could become ladies and gentlemen, if only they learned the proper behavior, and viewed their mission as describing the code for the benefit of those who had not learned these rules in childhood.

Despite these democratic affirmations, on second glance the conduct works reflect the contrary economic realities. For while the authors paid homage to the fluidity of American society, they offered advice intended to make class distinctions clear. While proposing in one breath to educate and elevate the uninitiated, in the next the authors reveal their fidelity to the notion that etiquette served as a barrier between the respectable and the rabble. Only a few owned up to this. One writer explained that "True republicanism requires that every man shall have an equal chance—that every man shall be free to become as unequal as he can." Another was even more blunt. In America, he explained, "There is perfect freedom of political privilege, all are the same upon the hustings, or at a political meeting; but this equality does not extend to the drawing room. None are excluded from the highest councils of the nation, but it does not follow that all can enter into the highest ranks of society." While this passage accurately conveys the unspoken message of antebellum social ritual, the author's candor was unique.[11]

None of the works published in this period were addressed exclusively to the upper class. Members of that small group at the top of American society that owned most of the wealth learned how to behave in their youth. The author of one etiquette book asserted, for example, that "In the very highest classes . . . politeness and a good carriage are taught from infancy."[12] If their early training was insufficient, however, members of the upper class could have readily turned to the mass of middle-class literature. For not only had middle-class authors effectively coopted the old aristocratic code in the revolutionary era, but by the antebellum period the advice given in nearly all manuals was such as would, if followed, make a man a gentleman and a woman a lady. At least in the eyes of middle-class conduct writers, then, the middle and upper classes were not greatly distinguished by behavior, however much they may have been distinguished by wealth. While these authors occasionally referred to "rich men," "persons of distinction," "superiors in station," "the person of the highest consideration," and so forth, they did not give different advice for the elite and the middling.

The question is, What did members of the elite make of this literature? While some recent studies suggest that many of the wealthiest Americans espoused bourgeois values and that the homes of the middling and the wealthy were expressions of the same genteel culture (different in degree rather than in character), others suggest that the upper class had unique values and social practices. The experience of Isaac Mickle, for one, suggests that class lines were permeable. As the only son of a family with substantial land holdings, he was comfortable, though sometimes cash-poor. He mixed freely with both the middling and the upper sort. He occasionally mentions events attended by the "best families" of Philadelphia, but his closest friends were mostly Camden artisans. The only clear class line in his diary was between the "respectable" sort and the "rowdies" or "loafers" that he occasionally mentions. While he does not label the latter "lower class," his disdain and sense of class distance are obvious.[13] The conduct works make one thing clear: the carefully wrought distinctions of the seventeenth century between the gentle and the middling sort had been so effectively undermined in the revolutionary era that by the antebellum period the new American middle class had overrun the bastions of gentility and set up camp. This cultural rout was accomplished earlier than historians have acknowledged.[14]

With only a couple of exceptions, all the manuals published in the North between 1820 and 1860 addressed the middle class. Middle-class audience is attributed to these works because of direct statements by the authors (e.g., Mrs. Parke's dedicating her work to "the great middle class") or the general tone and nature of the advice. About a third of these manuals, for example, give advice on how to deal with domestic servants, without addressing the servants themselves. Other clues are found in the writers' assumptions about household layout and furnishings, for recent research suggests that the domestic revolution—which saw the proliferation of the well-upholstered parlors referred to in conduct works—was limited to the middle class. Of course the middle class was changing and growing. Economic development was thrusting up a new group of nonmanual white-collar workers in addition to the old middling group of farmers, merchants, master craftsmen, and professionals.[15] While revolutionary-era advice to the middling met the needs of the more prosperous, better-educated, and socially mobile element of the middling sort, the antebellum advice was pitched to an even broader audience, to include all who aspired to even a modicum of respectability. But it was just as clearly not intended for the lower class.

The lower class continues to escape the historian of manners in this period, as it had begun to do in the revolutionary era. As the Irish poured into northeastern cities, and as the status of free blacks rigidified in the decades after 1830, the lower class took on a more alien character from the elite perspective than it had had in the earlier periods. Owing to new patterns of work, residence, and association, many among the working class lived in an increasingly separate social world within the city. Conduct advice in this more diverse society was no longer reinforced by other institutions that taught social behavior or kept people in their place. Recognition of this fact is one reason middle-class authors did not bother trying to teach the lower sort how to behave.[16] They devoted most of their few efforts to the much smaller Anglo-American sector of the lower class.

What set the more humble ranks of Anglo-Americans apart from other lower-class ethnic groups was the expectation that they could rise to middle-class status. It was these folk who were addressed in a handful of manuals that were directed to all classes or to the lower middle and middle classes. Because these works were written by middle-class authors, were middle-class in tone, and gave advice similar to that of more obviously middle-class works, they are treated with those works.

Only two works were clearly addressed to those of lower class status. These were two general-advice works for domestic servants that discussed work habits, mental, moral, physical, and religious cultivation, and the demeanor and deportment appropriate to their station. One, Robert Roberts's *The House Servant's Directory*, was the work of a house servant, and thus the only title of lower-class authorship in the entire body of conduct literature printed or imported in America before 1860. To the degree that the more humble ranks got behavioral instruction from books, which was probably never very great, it was generally instruction handed down from those higher on the social scale. In whatever guise, it is unlikely that such works had much appeal to servants themselves. A reviewer of the other work for the lower class, *Plain Talk and Friendly Advice to Domestics,* began with the exclamation: "Plain talk to domestics! Yes, indeed! But will they read it? We wish they would. . . . Alas good lady author, we fear . . . you have spent your strength in vain." It is probable that such works appealed more to employers of servants than to servants themselves.[17]

We should not be surprised that so few conduct works were addressed to the lower class, for the simple reason that such works were a commodity they could not afford. While changes in technology had served to halve the price of books since the late eighteenth century, they were still too costly for the poor.[18] We have no published evidence of manners teaching within the lower-class family, and such instruction was likely on the decline as it was among the middle and upper classes. Any manners instruction provided by the schools was advice imposed from above by middle-class teachers. On balance, then, it must be kept in mind that whatever is learned from the conduct literature about class relations in the antebellum North can only be construed as values and behaviors suggested by middle-class writers to middle-class readers. This information does allow us to continue to trace the evolution of mainstream attitudes toward servants. But our optic is focused on middle-class culture; and while it was hegemonic, it obviously did not stand alone. Nor was it uncontested. This was another reason manners mattered so much to the middling.

TO AN EVEN GREATER degree than in the revolutionary era, most antebellum conduct advice concerned behavior with equals, not superiors or inferiors. What remained of deference, then, in antebellum America? When they did discuss relationships with superiors, the middle-class authors of conduct works showed ambivalence about class deference as required of their own class. Their few calls for deference to class superiors were crosscut and attenuated by new obligations of age and gender deference. When compared with British expectations, American authors really did seem to balk at frank acknowledgment of social rank among the middle and upper classes. A more concrete example of the same difference lay in the lack of separate class accommodations in American stages, trains, and boats, contrary to British custom.[19]

But the conduct writers were not ambivalent regarding the inferiority of lower-class servants to middle-class masters and mistresses.[20] They did not— in this "democratic" era—describe this inequality in words; they described it indirectly, but no less clearly, with their assumptions and specific conduct prescriptions to both servants and employers. The master-servant relationship was the only relationship between the middle and lower classes that the conduct writers discussed at any length. Surely reflecting both a desire for exclusivity and a realistic acknowledgment of the limits of their cultural power, the middling authors of conduct advice simply turned their backs on the rest. In antebellum conduct works, then, class deference was something shown primarily by the serving class to middle- and upper-class masters.

To some extent antebellum authors merely amplified reservations about class deference on the part of the middling first voiced in the revolutionary era. In discussions of the need to keep good company, antebellum authors laid greater stress than ever before on merit rather than social status as the appropriate criterion. Taking another tack, Emily Thornwell advised: "It is not necessary that you should select all your associates from the more elevated walks of life, for this would be likely to unfit you for mingling with ease and advantage among the less-refined." Others simply advised against courting the society of "the great."[21] Antebellum writers also repeated and strengthened the revolutionary-era suggestions that one should not forego self-respect in expressing respect for superiors. William Cobbett told youth: "In your manners be neither boorish nor blunt, but, even these are preferable to simpering and crawling."[22] These assertions reflect growing middle-class self-confidence.

When antebellum authors did seem to be invoking the old principle of deference to superiors, their advice to the middle classes was always qualified in some way. Some authors maintained the right of superiors to control the degree of contact with inferiors, for example, by advising middle-class readers not to make the first advances with their betters but to allow the latter to seek their acquaintance. One was to leave it to superiors to do the recognizing on a second meeting and to begin and end encounters on the street. But relatively few writers discussed these practices, and one actually ridiculed them.[23] Moreover, middle-class persons were the only inferiors of the antebellum era who were not told to bestow time—in the form of attentions and services—on superiors.

Similarly, some antebellum authors brought up the old issue of precedence in new contexts. Some claimed that superiors were to be named first in introductions (and inferiors presented to them). But here, too, other writers had reservations. One objected to making such distinctions of rank, another claimed that the custom was less vigorously enforced in America than in England, and a few specified that by superiority they were referring only to "personal distinction."[24] Antebellum authors spelled out the old advice to let superiors go first in a number of other contexts (such as entering or leaving a room); but they paid most attention to this issue in discussing dinner parties, and here again they showed some democratic ambivalence. Most asserted that the host would lead the lady of greatest rank into the dining room first, and the hostess would arrange the remaining couples according to their rank (this was also the British practice). But Robert de Valcourt argued that rank was difficult to determine in America, and nearly all who reported on this custom agreed that the guests' age, sex, and the degree to which they were strangers to the company were at least as important as their rank in determining precedence. Moreover, the authors used vague language rather than explicit class terms when discussing precedence, preferring to talk of "persons of distinction," "distinguished guests," or "those to whom you owe respect." All other things being equal, the authors clearly expected middle-class persons to yield the way to class superiors, but the hedging was significant and distinguished American from contemporary British expectations.[25]

Antebellum conduct writers continued to give the middle class scattered reminders of the traditional advice to yield place to superiors when walking or arranging seats. But these counsels usually involved gender and age considerations as well. This was especially true of the primary discussion of place, again, at dinner parties. Here class considerations were quite literally mixed with those of gender, for the "most distinguished" woman was to be placed next to the host; but this was considered the lower end of the table and the place where guests of less distinction were seated. Meanwhile the honored lady's husband sat to the right of the hostess—at the upper end of the table. The traditional above- and below-the-salt mentality was thus contending with new imperatives. And there were a few notes of outright dissent. One writer argued that age, the degree to which the guest was a stranger to the company, and sex, rather than class, were to determine the disposition of place. Another, writing at the very end of the period, claimed that the "old custom" of placing people by class rank "is by no means slavishly followed by polite society in this country."[26]

In sum, antebellum authors continued to advise the middle class of a number of ways to demonstrate respect for class superiors, but this advice was not as strong as in previous periods. Note that the authors had ceased to advise the middle class to show respect for superiors in their body carriage, facial expression, and talk (and the appropriate gestures of salutation were similar to those expected between peers).[27] Nor was the advice to the middle class as strong, as we shall see, as their advice to other inferiors. It was frequently mixed with rules pertaining to class and age relations. Often the writers directed this advice to men alone and required them to perform an act for women as well as class superiors; or they directed it to young persons concerning age as well as class superiors. And antebellum authors sometimes hesitated in recommending deference to class superiors. Some objected to the recognition of class differences; others continued to remind middle-class readers never to sacrifice their self-respect in showing respect to others.

The mildness of the advice to the middle class is clearest in contrast with advice for the lower class. Here servility was precisely what the authors had in mind, as they addressed most of their advice to those in domestic service. Encounters between employers and servants evidently required a very different set of regulations than those between the middle class and their class superiors. Unlike the middle class, for example, the authors did not advise lower-class persons to seek the society of their superiors; instead, they invoked the older principle that servants were to respect their masters' general control of their time. Robert Roberts argued: "When you hire yourself to a lady or gentleman, your time or your ability is no longer your own, but your employers'; therefore they have a claim on them whenever they choose to call for them." As in the past, servants were not to dally in tasks, loiter on errands, or go out without permission. Other sources confirm that servants had little free time in this period and suffered restrictions on their social lives, a special hardship in the many single-servant households.[28]

Antebellum descriptions of the many ways domestics were to serve their employers occasionally reveal modifications of traditional expectations: rather than allowing their superiors to precede them, for example, servants were to precede entering visitors, to save them the trouble of opening doors. Otherwise, expectations concerning the proper manner, bearing, and talk of inferiors in the presence of superiors had changed little from the past. If anything, the instructions were a bit more detailed and demanding of deference than they had been during the revolutionary era. Servants were to be respectful and attentive, to avoid assuming "airs of familiarity with the family," and to "bear with patience and equanimity the whims and caprices" of their employers. They were to maintain a sober body carriage, always standing erect in the presence of their superiors, and never running in the hallways. They were to refrain from pouting or frowning at their employers and were to keep their eyes to themselves. They were to be quiet, to avoid speaking until spoken to, and then "in as few words as possible." They were to be careful with superiors' names and titles (they were even to use "Mr." or "Miss" with the first names of the young adults of the family). They were never to talk to outsiders of their masters and mistresses. And they were never to contradict superiors but to submit silently to their reproofs.[29] This advice to the lower class, so different from that directed to the middle class, suggests that the major class division in the antebellum conduct world was that between masters and servants.

Antebellum advice hints at an insecure relationship between masters and servants. Gone are the traditional familial aspects of service, where adult masters had a parental relationship with young servants and apprentices. The master-servant relationship was now strictly perceived as one between employer and employee, a class relation shaped by the market. Gone too was the revolutionary-era impulse to "soften" the new relation. That temporary benevolence was replaced by a new ambivalence. One obvious reason for this change was a change in personnel. Whereas in the past, servants came from various social strata (often a boy or girl from the neighborhood), now servants generally came from poor immigrant, especially Irish, families. The new discomfort arose from class and ethnic differences.[30]

In moving away from the patriarchal institution of old, masters lost both power and obligations. Servants escaped patriarchal control, but they lost the advantage of familial intimacy and concern for their welfare. Perhaps out of a sense of loss of the older authority—and in a backlash against revolutionary leveling—middle-class conduct writers attempted to tighten up the master-servant relationship. Masters could no longer beat bad servants, they could only dismiss them. But the authors tried to help them maintain the upper hand by widening the social gap. The loss of the overarching metaphor of the patriarchal family also differentiated this relationship from others; rules for the master/servant relationship began to diverge from rules for other inferior-superior relationships.

Outside the master-servant relationship, counsels to the middle class regarding the lower class were inconsistent. The authors disagreed as to whether middle-class persons should associate with persons of lower class status, although most agreed that one should not refuse to recognize an inferior in public.[31] The authors also disagreed on the class application of the new principle that men should pay attentions to women. Several claimed that "Civility is due to all women; . . . and the greatest man in the land would justly be reclaimed a brute, if he was not civil to the meanest woman." But when describing men's specific duties, most authors did not use the term "women" but "ladies." And sometimes their comments betrayed their belief that the word lady still had a class connotation. One author described the situation frankly:

> When women appear at the door of the coach to gain admittance, it is a matter of some question to know exactly what conduct it is necessary to pursue. If the women are servants, or persons in low rank of life, I do not see upon what ground of politeness or decency you are called upon to yield your seat. Etiquette, and the deference due to ladies, have, of course, no operation in the case of such persons. . . . Such people have nerves considerably more robust than you have, and are quite as capable of riding backwards, or the top, as yourself. . . . If ladies enter, and a gentleman distinguishes them in an instant, the case is altered. . . .[32]

The rules were much clearer regarding servants. Antebellum conduct writers simply assumed the presence of servants in their readers' households. The many offhand references to servants in descriptions of parties and visits suggest, in fact, that middle-class social life depended on them, as both workers and status symbols. In describing these occasions the authors were indirectly telling their middle-class readers how to behave with servants. Moreover, they regularly advised masters and mistresses to teach their servants what to do in these instances. In giving this advice, the writers were both underscoring the middle-class address of their works and reflecting the reality of middle-class existence.[33]

Antebellum authors occasionally addressed the issue of servants directly. Some had a rather jaundiced view. Far from viewing servants as potential equals, as had some revolutionary era writers, or cautioning against undue familiarity with them, as had other, older writers, these writers' nearly viewed servants as a different species. Margaret Conkling observed:

> Like animals and young children, uneducated persons are peculiarly susceptible to all external influences. . . . There are occasions when to *talk* to servants and other employees, make part of a humane bearing towards them. . . . Remember, too, how easily undisciplined persons are frightened by an imperious, or otherwise injudicious, manner on the part of their superiors, out of the self-possession essential to their comprehension of our wants and language.

Another writer sighed, "All that you can do is, to take the most decent crea-ture who applies, trust in Providence, and lock everything up," an ironic ob-servation given historians' findings that it was employers who tended to rob their servants by failing to pay them on time. Occasionally the nativist or racist roots of the authors' feelings become clear in disparaging references to black or Irish servants. Florence Hartley claimed that "Some attention is ab-solutely necessary, in this country, to the training of servants, as they come here from the lowest ranks of English and Irish peasantry, with as much idea of politeness as the pig domesticated in the cabin of the latter." Some com-ments suggest that jaundiced views also resulted from the difficulty of finding and keeping good servants.[34]

Like their predecessors, antebellum conduct writers implicitly encour-aged middle-class persons to spend some time with domestics when they ad-vised them to train their servants. The notion that masters and mistresses were responsible for the morals and education of servants had long since dis-appeared, but many authors evidently agreed with Mrs. Hartley that servants had to be trained in middle-class social rituals. On the other hand, there were times, as when entertaining, that a servant's presence was to be ignored. One was to instruct servants before the guests arrived; if they made any mistakes or had any accidents, one was to appear not to notice. Karen Halttunen has pointed out that undue acknowledgement of the presence of servants de-tracted from the genteel performance in which one was engaged by drawing attention to the mechanics of the household. Ignoring servants' presence, then, effectively relegated them to the sidelines of middle-class social en-counters. They were necessary as stagehands, not as social actors.[35]

Some of the instructions to the middle class regarding inferiors were sim-ply variations on traditional advice. It was assumed that one would control and use servants' time; only a few authors warned young people not to be too demanding.[36] One was to be neither harsh nor too familiar in demeanor and conversation, but kind, courteous, and affable. Some authors did spell out the requirements of politeness to servants a bit more than in the past, adding an air of formality to antebellum master-servant relations. Servants were to be addressed and referred to by their Christian names (if there were several, they might be referred to by the names of their offices, such as nurse, cook, etc.). They were always to be thanked for their services and praised for work well done. They were never to be insulted or reproved before guests—some writers suggesting that this was to avoid embarrassing the servant, others that it was to avoid disturbing the guests. One was always to be the first to salute a ser-vant or other inferior in the street. Several writers implied that a hello "in a kindly voice" was all that was necessary here, although one was bound to re-turn the gesture if an inferior bowed or tipped his hat.[37]

In the end, class deference in antebellum conduct advice was at once a stark and muted matter. While the writers appeared uncomfortable with the traditional class deference of the middling to the upper sort, and therefore un-dermined it in various ways, they clearly wished for deference from lower-class servants to middle-class employers. Between the lines we can detect some discomfort with the latter relationship—not discomfort with the wished-for deference but a sense of distrust and alienation. And this ill ease is from the middle-class authors' perspective—we do not even see the servants' side. The latter must have been even more unhappy, as other sources suggest that they voted with their feet whenever possible.[38] But even if servants did not always comply in showing adequate deference, the middle class still won out; by their simple presence servants served as crucial markers of middle-class status.

THESE RELATIVELY brief discussions of unequal relations aside, the rest of antebellum conduct advice concerned relations with peers. Almost all of this advice was addressed to the middle class, although the authors did not draw distinctions between proper middle- and upper-class behavior as they offered a single code of behavior for all "ladies and gentlemen." They did not include the lower class, however, despite their occasional democratic pronouncements. In the few instances where they did advise the lower class, their attempt to erect a barrier between classes—their own class, the "respectable" sort, and the lower class, the serving sort—was transparent.

Bearing out the argument made in chapter 4 that the origins of middle-class culture are discernible in the conduct advice circulating in the revolutionary era, much of the advice that circulated in the antebellum period continued the trends inaugurated then. We saw that the middle-class authors of the revolutionary era spread the old aristocratic code to their own class but reported it in such a way as to give greater emphasis to the need for physical self-control, especially in interactions with peers. Antebellum advisors passed on the same advice, although they sometimes disseminated still more elaborate versions of it. One reason for the persistence of revolutionary-era body-control advice is that some of the most popular revolutionary-era works, especially Chesterfield, continued to circulate through the antebellum period. But many new authors also repeated the old advice, often word for word.

Antebellum conduct writers did give a lot of new advice—much of it concerning the "introductions, recognitions, and salutations" that Isaac Mickle mentioned. Before treating the new advice, however, it is important to acknowledge the continuities from the revolutionary era, because existing interpretations of the antebellum code imply that it was shaped solely by antebellum conditions. In particular, scholars have linked the code to fears arising from a new urban anonymity, arguing that status had been more reliably communicated and read in the "preindustrial" city. Karen Halttunen has claimed that these antebellum fears coalesced in the spectre of the duplicitous confidence man, and generated a demand for "sincere" performances among the middle class. But to recognize the continuities from the revolutionary era is to recognize the preindustrial origins of middle-class culture and to question the depth of new sincerity concerns in face-to-face performances.[39] To find responses to new antebellum conditions, we must examine, as we will, the new advice of the period. The old advice may have acquired new meanings in new conditions, but it was not created by them. It was created—and perpetuated—by the long-standing desire of people in the middle to assert and gain recognition of their worthiness.

We can briefly review the self-control advice of the antebellum period, noting any new features that might help to explain its role in the new setting. The continuities begin with the advice on giving time to others within interactions. Very many writers repeated the old claims that one always owed others one's full attention and therefore should not read, pull out one's watch, or behave in any way that might communicate boredom or distraction. The only new feature here was the plea of a number of writers that one not be absentminded when walking down a street, lest one neglect to salute one's acquaintances. This tip does hint at the influence of new urban conditions, but only in that it resonates with discussions of "preoccupied" faces in the period's urban exposés.[40]

Antebellum authors gave a little more new advice on the disposition of place within peer encounters. For example, a few authors commented that if one had the wall to one's right when passing equals on the street, one was entitled to keep it. Previously the only discussions of this matter revolved around yielding the wall to show respect to superiors; the new comment revealed a concern with smooth traffic on city sidewalks. Otherwise, the writers just passed along the old warnings against walking between people or turning one's back to others.[41] Alongside older cautions against taking the best place in a room or taking others' seats, a few writers gave new advice concerning seating at parlor visits. One was to avoid taking the chair usually occupied by the master or mistress of the house; and hosts, likewise, were to avoid offering visitors the seats from which they had just risen. This advice suggests that the old principle of deference (take the lowest seat) was being supplemented by a new interest in bodily privacy.[42]

Indeed, while antebellum-era authors gave the middle class the various old warnings against coming too close to others, they made their interest in physical privacy more explicit. Robert de Valcourt claimed, for example, that "around every person there is a certain sphere of repulsion, into which no one ought to intrude. It is an impoliteness, a rudeness; it is even an affront and an outrage to come within a certain distance of any person without permission, expressed or implied. Everybody must keep their distance, and endeavor to know what their distance is." In addition, antebellum authors gave new advice on the use of space when walking with or among others on the street. This too may have been a response to new urban conditions, in the practical sense of dealing with crowds. Readers were urged not to push their way through a crowd or a narrow passageway. Nor was one to block up the way by standing and talking with others in the middle of a sidewalk or at the door of a church. One was to walk carefully so as not to bump into others on the street. Mme. Celnart and others suggested that "One can edge along by turning sideways, contracting his arms, and watching with his eye the direction which it is best to take in order not to come in contact with the person who meets him." One was always to apologize for any accidental jostling. Touching others on purpose was even more egregious. "To run against a man is an act which demands apology," one author explained, "when purposely done, it is a gross affront. To slap a man on the back is a rudeness." Although it reflected a heightened interest in body privacy, even this advice built on antecedents, for antebellum authors also repeated some older rules against poking others in conversation.[43]

There was little change in expectations regarding proper demeanor with peers, as antebellum conduct writers repeated the traditional demands for a polite, kind, and cheerful manner. A number of writers specified that such a demeanor was as important with family members as with guests, and that family relations were an important training ground for manners. These counsels tell us that Victorian homes and culture were not so sharply divided between "front stage" and "back stage" spaces as scholars have suggested, and that self-regulation was necessary even among intimates. Still, many authors implied that proper demeanor was particularly important in encounters with those one did not know well. Building on Chesterfield's old warnings, they reminded the middle class that a "genteel" manner marked one immediately as well bred, whereas it took others time to discover one's true or inner qualities. Antebellum authors thus calmly accepted the difference between a "good impression" and inner character. Cecil Hartley was frank: "If politeness is but a mask, . . . it is a mask which will win love and admiration, and is better worn than cast aside. . . . It will soon cease to be a mask." The authors did continue to warn against affectation, but their demands for an "easy" and "natural" behavior do not evince a particularly antebellum concern for sincerity, as has been suggested, since they first appeared in the revolutionary period. Only rarely did antebellum authors associate affectation with hypocrisy in discussions of face-to-face behavior; they mostly suggested that one's demeanor ought not to *seem* artificial—even if it was. Several authors insisted that manners rules were to be followed even if they were artificial, and that "there is no greater mistake than to suppose that politeness means hypocrisy." The real goal was not a sincere performance but a convincing one, and stiff behavior would give one away. As one author put it: "both sexes should strive to acquire an easy and natural manner, until it becomes habitual." No wonder several antebellum works were entitled *"The Art"* of good behavior.[44]

Antebellum advice concerning the proper degree of familiarity with peers was also just a more elaborate version of earlier instructions, especially those of Chesterfield. Many writers repeated his advice to maintain a disguised reserve with most acquaintances. Antebellum authors were thus not advocating much "openness" with others. In fact, they embellished the traditional advice with extra recommendations of reserve with strangers. Many writers also recommended increased ceremony as the best way to dampen the familiarity of undesirable acquaintance. This implies a fairly instrumental view of demeanor.[45] The pattern was the same regarding other aspects of proper demeanor: antebellum authors generally echoed or amplified Chesterfieldian advice. They repeated his pleas for a dignified manner, stressing the need for self-possession. They warned that proper modesty should not extend to bashfulness. They begged the middle class to shun awkwardness and to cultivate grace, in both demeanor and body carriage.[46]

When it came to specific instructions for sitting, standing, and walking, the antebellum versions were similar to, but far more extensive than, earlier advice. There were many suggestions concerning when it was proper to sit in company, for example, and how to sit in one's chair. A *Manual of Politeness* offered a typical discussion of the matter of what to do with one's legs:

> [T]he knees are generally left one by the other, scarcely separated. Though they should not be turned in, it is highly improper to turn them out in too marked a manner. It is scarcely necessary to say, that to cross them one over the other, and to embrace them with the hands joined, is deemed vulgar. To stretch out the legs while sitting, announces conceit and pride; and to bend them up, gives a timid and frightened air.[47]

Antebellum discussions of standing and walking went into how one should hold one's shoulders, move one's arms, and place one's feet. Two authors offered young women this catalogue of walking sins:

> [S]ome . . . go shuffling along. . . . If it is dusty or sandy, they kick up the dust before them and fill their skirts with it. . . . If I were a gentleman I really do not think I could marry a lady who walked like this: she would appear so very undignified . . . . Some . . . lift up their feet so high that their knees are sent out before them, showing the movement through the dress . . . and others . . . press their arms against themselves as tightly as if they were glued there . . . . But I must stop here, though I have many other things to say about "walking." . . .[48]

Whereas early colonial authors often condemned dancing, and revolutionary-era writers recommended it as beneficial to carriage but best performed in private companies, most antebellum-era authors heartily approved of it. And only some continued to rationalize that dancing was necessary for gracefulness. Other sources confirm that dancing was a popular activity in this period, despite lingering evangelical disapproval. Antebellum conduct advisors did add a few new cautions: one was not to dance if one was unfamiliar with the steps or had a bad ear for music, as one would annoy the other dancers. The writers also gave a fair amount of advice as to proper carriage while dancing, urging readers to move with modesty and grace.[49]

Antebellum conduct writers repeated all of the previous era's warnings against excessive body activity or "odd tricks" in the presence of others—the warnings against fidgeting, touching oneself, excessive coughing, and the like—and again they did so in greater detail.[50] Their advice on proper facial expression likewise consisted almost entirely of more elaborately delineated versions of older counsels. They called for genuine smiles rather than contemptuous expressions, but cautioned against excessive laughter. They warned against distorting the face in any way.[51] They passed on the old dual message that while it was never appropriate to stare at others, one needed to look at those with whom one spoke in order to read their true feelings and intentions.[52] At the same time, one needed to conceal one's own emotions, or, as one author put it, to have "perfect command over the utterance of the countenance." Emotional restraint was surely an important feature of middle-class culture, as scholars have suggested, but this concern was fully developed before the antebellum period. This advice also belies any antebellum concern about sincerity.[53]

Most of the antebellum advice on conversation also had its origins in the past. The writers repeated and elaborated on old warnings against making noise in company, discussions of how much one should talk, and counsels concerning proper enunciation, tone of voice, and word choice.[54] They emphasized the traditional advice to use correct names and proper titles in addressing others. Middle-class readers were especially reminded never to address others by their surnames without the proper prefix (as in "Brown") or by the initial (as in "Mr. B"). Referring to a family of somewhat lower status, Isaac Mickle recorded with some annoyance that "Perhaps if I were only to go once a month they would call me Mr. Mickle" (emphasis his). Names were seemingly more sacred in this period, as quite a few authors advised against proclaiming others' names aloud when meeting them in public.[55]

Antebellum discussions of proper conversational manner and matter were also expanded versions of older advice. One was naturally to be pleasant and courteous, and to choose topics carefully. Some authors encouraged small talk; others specified that the potentially controversial topics of religion and politics were to be avoided, especially in the parlor and at the dinner table. And antebellum-era writers gave all the old warnings against showing off, joking too much or at others' expense, discussing private matters, gossiping, comparing people, verbally abusing others, giving unsolicited advice, contradicting others, arguing, or venting anger. They did take more pains to discourage flattery than had earlier authors. Perhaps Isaac Mickle supplied the reason when he resolved to avoid flattery because it was "a vestige of an age of slavery"; that is, it carried echoes of a more deferential society.[56]

In repeating and expanding on old advice about demeanor, body carriage, facial expression, and talk, antebellum authors were expressing continuing concern about physical self-control. Body management was important for the same reasons it had been: self-presentation was crucial to the maintenance of middle-class reputations. Although the level of detail was new, this too was the continuation of an earlier trend—that of giving more instruction to the previously uninitiated. Some of the details do suggest new concerns of the antebellum decades, namely a new interest in self-management on crowded streets and a new concern for physical privacy. In addition, John Kasson has suggested that in the increasingly heterogeneous American city one's claims to gentility could meet rebuff and thus be shaken, while the increasing codification of rules provided relief from such uncertainties. If one became unsure, one could now look it all up in a book.[57]

But antebellum-era conduct writers did not just disseminate a more detailed version of the old body-control advice. They added something new by embedding the old rules in elaborate "stage directions" to frame and regulate encounters: specifically, rules for introductions, salutations, and various social occasions.[58] They were still building on older traditions of genteel behavior but responding to a need for ever more detailed instructions on how to achieve it: specifically, exactly where, when, and how to execute genteel rituals. In giving this advice, the conduct writers were not generally describing new rituals or forms of interaction—they did not invent the visit or the dinner party. Colonial diaries and letters often mention such occasions. The settings had changed a bit with the increasing elaboration of domestic architecture, but this was change in degree rather than kind, as a growing number of the middling were able to afford nicer homes and parlors. What was new was the need to describe these scenes; the middling now required a complete and uniform script, not simply general guidelines.

The script was necessary for a variety of reasons. Recall, first, that the middle class was changing and growing. The social context was also changing. Urban historians tell us that for the first time residential areas were becoming segregated by class. A similar trend occurred in associational activities. In this "democratic" age, the very wealthy in particular were withdrawing to their own social and residential enclaves.[59] Perhaps the middle class now required more elaborate instructions simply because it was no longer easy to observe "aristocratic" behavior firsthand. Learning how to behave from such instructions was an awkward process—and always invited the ridicule of those who had already mastered the rules—but there was evidently a need, and publishers moved to meet it. Perhaps codification of these rituals was also spurred on by a need to agree on rules as communities broke down, for in setting down the rules for those who would otherwise be ignorant, the conduct writers were systematizing them. The codified rituals were also more elaborate than their more casual predecessors. Indeed, in describing settings more explicitly, the authors were codifying the increasing differentiation of rooms in middle- and upper-class homes.

Codification had mixed implications. On the one hand, to codify and publish the rituals was also to commodify them, to make them truly accessible to all. On the other hand, commodities have a price, and ever more elaborate rituals meant that respectability had a high price of admission in terms of complying with the precise demands of the game (in addition to the high hurdle posed by body management demands). Admission was, of course, the name of the game; several scholars have noted that the new instructions tended to concern what can be construed as "access" rituals; that is, introductions, visits, dinners, and parties were all occasions wherein one attempted to claim membership in a desired social group. But the demanding nature of the system was also its beauty, for it permitted some access to gentility from below without allowing a "vulgar" flood. Thus were class, rather than caste, systems maintained. The high material demands of the system in themselves deterred counterfeit, and thereby lessened the need for the authentification of sincere performances.[60]

Perhaps the most important clue to the forces that shaped antebellum American conduct advice is found in the comparison begged by the American authors' confident proclamations that it was now time for a uniquely American code. Yet their works strongly resembled those circulating in Great

Britain. In England as in the United States, the 1820s marked an important transition in manners, and the ensuing decades saw a flood of new advice works. There, as here, a changing society called for instruction in rituals to make newly ambiguous social relations clearer.[61] Instruction brought codification, and the resulting books described many of the same social practices. The similarities are not so striking in the body-control advice—persisting as it did from the revolutionary era when importation of British advice was the frankly acknowledged norm—as in the new "staging" instructions of the antebellum era. While this challenges the Americans' claim to a republican code of etiquette, the opportunity to compare the two codes and the two contexts helps to explain what the new advice really meant.

The main difference in social context was what it had been from the beginning: English society was "deeper" than American society; it had a true aristocracy and a larger plebian class. Of course the English polity also differed from the American, the main difference being, for our purposes, the longer-lasting restrictions on white male suffrage. England was smaller too, so that "Society" could operate on a national scale with a "Season" followed in a single center (London), which was impossible in America. Indeed, in England, "Society" and politics were interwined in a way they never could be in America. These differences had important consequences for the prevailing codes of genteel behavior in the two places. But more striking are the similarities. Of course the quick answer as to why this was so is that American publishers continued to pirate British material, nationalistic proclamations notwithstanding. It has also been suggested that Americans continued to turn to Europe for guidance because they had no other place to turn. But it was similar conditions that allowed Americans to prescribe parallel social rituals and allowed American book reviewers to accept the results.[62]

In both societies commercial, and then industrial, capitalism were creating an ever larger and more prosperous middle class that was seizing the reins of cultural authority. The similarity of British etiquette reminds us that these economic forces were the insistent cause of the role of manners in antebellum America, despite the democratic assertions of the authors. American conduct writers were not, as has been suggested, merely mediating between democracy and capitalism. They really only had a limited agenda on the former score. By the same token, the similarity between British and American etiquette also reminds us that, however tenacious the hold of the aristocracy on the British social imagination, the forces behind manners there were clearly those of bourgeois assertion. The American experience reminds us that while the middling code originally emulated the aristocratic, in cultural terms the bourgeoisie was now in charge. In the American context, without the lingering legacy of aristocracy, published discussions of manners were more clearly a middle-class concern. This is where the self-conscious democratic assertions played a role—not in including the vulgar but in ignoring the existence of the upper. The frank acceptance and reassertion of a wealthy elite lay in the future, in the post–Civil War rearistocraticization of etiquette.[63]

The socially exclusive or class-communicating functions of antebellum etiquette are evident from the start in discussions of contact with peers. For in addition to giving middle-class readers the time-worn advice about frequenting good company and taking care in forming friendships for the sake of one's manners and reputation,[64] many authors underscored the need for caution in acquaintance-making through extensive advice on introductions. If "proper behavior" was to serve as an unspoken barrier between the middling and the lower sort, we should not be surprised to find devices to exclude the unwanted from one's social circle.[65] The first rule was that one should never introduce two people without knowing whether it was agreeable to both. This had to be ascertained beforehand, unless one was sufficiently intimate with both parties to know that the meeting was desirable. Caution in introductions was indispensable because, once properly introduced, others had a claim on one's goodwill and could not be slighted. One could dodge making any introductions one was not sure about by telling the party requesting it that one was not sufficiently intimate with the other party to take the liberty. Many authors objected to what some called the American practice of introducing everybody who happened to meet in their presence (although this could not have been a uniquely American practice since British manuals offered the same caution!). Thus, they very often advised against introducing people on the street or during visits, unless one knew that both parties desired it. When persons did happen to be named to each other in such a way, they were to understand that such introductions were merely a matter of form, upon which they could not claim acquaintance afterward.

The ritual of introduction was fairly straightforward. When introducing equals, one could simply pronounce the parties' names to each other ("Mr. Jones, Mr. Smith"). Both parties would then say something about how happy they were to make the acquaintance. However simple, Isaac Mickle suggests that there was still an air of formality about this ritual with his tongue-in-cheek remark about a visit to his friend Harry Edwards's family: "a grand introductorial ceremony being gone through with, Harry and I took a sail upon Chester creek." Confirming the access function of this ritual and the visit that followed, he wrote a few days later that "My acquaintance with the Edwardses may now be considered as fairly established."[66]

Antebellum conduct writers also spelled out the proper use of letters of introduction. These had long been in use, but it was only now that that usage was codified in etiquette books. Several authors urged caution in giving out such letters, and recommended refusing if one did not know the person requesting it well enough. Most advised that they be sent rather than delivered in person (unless the introduction was purely for business purposes), as this afforded the recipient a chance to think in private about his or her response. Letters of introduction were to be answered immediately; not to do so was to slight the writer. But it was up to the recipient to decide what hospitalities to extend to the newcomer.[67]

Although it was always proper to render assistance to others without an introduction, antebellum conduct writers urged their readers to avoid interacting with those to whom they had not been properly introduced, especially at places of public amusement. Isaac Mickle confirmed the rule by noting an infraction. After a lecture one evening, he spoke to a pair of sisters and then later recorded that "I spoke to one of the above girls tonight by mistake. I have never been introduced." But one was to converse freely with others without introduction while traveling. This may have been a particularly American rule, for the practice unnerved Charles Dickens on his American tour. He observed of a railroad ride that "Everybody talks to you, or to anybody else who hits his fancy" (he attributed this to American republicanism, however, and claimed not to resent it). One had only to remember that such association always ceased with the occasion and did not entitle one to claim the other's acquaintance afterward. As in Britain, guests were to talk easily and without introduction at a dinner or private party. Most authors explained that the very fact of meeting together in a respectable home served as an introduction for the time, although some recommended getting properly introduced to persons thus met at the first opportunity.[68]

Once properly introduced, middle-class persons were expected to recognize an equal at all future meetings. Refusing to do so, or "cutting" an acquaintance, was only justified in serious cases, such as a strong instance of bad conduct on the part of the person they wished to cut. In the absence of such a reason, one had to recognize the person, however cooly. If one wished to rid oneself of an acquaintance, the authors recommended adopting an ever more reserved and formal manner with that person, in addition to refusing his or her invitations. The writers insisted that such an approach was highly effective; only the densest people would fail to take the hint.[69]

Some authors counseled against encroaching too much on others' time, even when one had been properly introduced. In general, one was never to intrude on others when or where one's presence might not be desired. But most warnings against intrusion concerned meetings in the street. The authors concurred that it was best to avoid stopping and detaining persons in the street in order to talk. If one had to do so, one was to turn and walk with them, so as not to waste their time, and such interviews were always to be short. Several writers suggested that it was awkward to stop and address others in the street when either party was accompanied by others. If one needed to stop a friend who was walking with a stranger, one was to apologize to the stranger and be quick.[70] These rules hint that time was of greater concern in the antebellum era than in the earlier periods; they also served to limit interaction in the street.

Access to others in public was formally granted—or denied—by the gesture of salutation, the signal of recognition that opened the door to interaction. Previously simple signs of deference, these gestures now bore a more complex social burden, and antebellum-era writers accordingly gave far more elaborate counsels than had earlier authors concerning them. Several writers did continue to voice Chesterfield's protest that good breeding did not consist entirely of "low bows and formal ceremony," and a few also expressed their dislike of excessively formal salutations and adieux. Perhaps echoing them, Isaac Mickle claimed that bows were not "necessary to true politeness." But other writers stated explicitly what many implied in their extensive discussions: that such ceremonies were not to be dismissed. Gestures of salutation were of particular importance on first meetings. While a few authors gave elaborate instructions as to how these were to be executed, most either implied or stated that such instruction was the province of the dancing master.[71]

While a few writers suggested that polite persons would bow and shake hands upon introduction, more authors denounced what they considered an American habit of promiscuous handshaking, and told their readers not to give their hands but to simply bow (although if another offered his or her hand, one had to accept it). The authors agreed that when properly introduced persons met thereafter, they were always to salute each other, however slightly. The only time middle-class persons could dispense with salutations was when they met acquaintances subsequent times on the same occasion. Salutations properly varied with the circumstances and the relationship in question, but the general rule was that acquaintances were owed a bow when met in public and another on taking leave. Salutations were also expected upon entering and leaving visits, parties, and balls. Beyond bowing, one could perform a warmer gesture with close friends or relations by shaking hands. A still more intimate form of salutation was the kiss; but this was to be reserved for intimate relations in private situations.[72] All these gestures of salutation were crucial because they raised the curtain for genteel performances. While inferiors could be acknowledged with a condescending hello, peers required the full-fledged gesture which announced that the parties met on equal footing.

The question of social access—am I part of the desired group or not?—must also have been behind the astounding quantity of antebellum advice concerning visiting, a topic that caused little comment in earlier periods. This simple act of social interaction became an institution just as the middle class asserted control over social regulation. Middle-class authors claimed that visiting was essential in maintaining acquaintance. This was nothing new; it had always been the case and always would be, until the arrival of the telephone. New were the many formalized rituals that the authors described, and the fact that the custom had become systematized. The authors suggested that this was in order to allow people to maintain large circles of acquaintances. Some explained further that "morning visits," as they were called, were useful because people could talk of things that were not appropriately discussed in public or at evening parties. But these explanations seem weak in light of the enormous interest in this institution. While the authors do not say so directly, their advice suggests that visiting was important because it served the crucial (but inadmissible) function of defining one's acquaintance by class. Visiting was a ritual performed with social equals, and one's visiting circle constituted a social set defined by class. Isaac Mickle's experience is again illustrative. In one of his self-improvement campaigns he vowed to stop frequenting the local saloon and to start visiting families, professing a wish to form acquaintance with young ladies. But at the same time he decided to stop visiting the daughter of a local livery stable manager. In changing his habits, he was shedding lower-class acquaintance for that of his social equals.[73]

There were two kinds of visits: "ceremonious" and "friendly." Here too, we are seeing a distinction that had long existed but was only now becoming codified. "Friendly" visits, to one's intimate acquaintance, remained for the most part unregulated and could be paid at any time. "Ceremonious" visits, on the other hand, constituted a quick hello to maintain acquaintance. One author explained: "Etiquette is intended to save us from some of the inconveniences attendant on a large acquaintance; and by settling certain points, it enables us to keep a ceremonious acquaintance with a circle too large for friendly visiting, as that consumes far more time than could be given to the number of persons whom you must be acquainted with, if you live in a city." Ceremonious visits were highly ritualized, so that the messages they conveyed would be clear to all. And if the object of one's visit was not at home, the calling card one left would do just as well to signal one's intent. There were rules concerning the type and configuration of calling cards, and some authors described turning down various corners to designate the persons for whom the visit was intended or other messages. Every visit was to be punctually returned, either personally or again by card (although some authors denounced the custom of sending in cards via servants when the persons visited were at home). The obligation to return calls was similar to today's phone etiquette; as one author explained: "A visit and an umbrella should always be returned."[74]

In addition to paying ceremonious visits at regular intervals to maintain an acquaintance, one could also use them to convey messages of condolence, congratulation, welcome, thanks, and leave-taking. Many authors commented on the last two kinds of visits. One was to pay a visit to thank one's hosts after being entertained at a dinner or party. One was to call and leave a card with T.T.L or P.P.C. written on it (To Take Leave or the same in French, Pour Prendre Conge) when going away for a long period. Because the persons to whom one left these cards were expected to visit upon one's return, one could weed out undesirable acquaintance by not sending a card. All of these rules, and most in the following paragraphs, were essentially similar to those current in England.

The message-bearing power of ceremonious visits was such that they did not need to be long; fifteen minutes was generally considered adequate. And while these visits were called "morning visits," they were to be paid in the afternoon; in fashionable parlance, the authors explained, morning meant anytime after noon and before dinner. Thus even the name of these visits was symbolic. As ceremonious visits were made in order to maintain acquaintance, a careful account was to be kept of visits made and received. Here again, one could communicate to others between the lines. Because a visit was to be returned after an interval similar to that which one's acquaintance had taken to return one's earlier visit, one could indicate a lack of enthusiasm for the relationship by gradually delaying one's return and thereby lengthening the interval. First visits, however, were to be returned within a week.

Some of the communication in ceremonial visiting was done by way of a human messenger, the house servant. Servants were to announce one's visit or to receive one's card if their employers were not at home or were otherwise engaged. That only one author did not take the presence of a domestic servant for granted underscores the class limits of this advice. Servants were to be regarded as sentries: if they said the person one had come to visit was not at home, one was not to argue. Some authors opined that if one suspected this was not true, one could only "get the message," retire, and never call again. But the authors were divided as to the visited person's proper conduct in this situation. Some claimed that it was not wrong to send the message that one was not at home if one did not wish to receive a visitor, as it was a generally understood social convention. An only slightly greater number of authors disagreed, instructing their readers to be honest if engaged in household affairs and beg to be excused. It has been argued that the "not at home" message was a device for excluding the unwanted from one's acquaintance, and it clearly was, in the minds of some authors. But the division on this subject suggests an ambivalence about overt snubs. There were other more approved ways of trimming acquaintance.

Some authors advised leaving one's hat, cloak, and umbrella with the servant or in the entry if received for a visit; but more told women to leave their bonnets and shawls on, and men to take their hats and canes into the drawing room with them, as in so doing they signaled that their visit would be short. So ritualized were these visits, then, that there was even a way to silently indicate that one was indeed making a ceremonious rather than a friendly visit—one simply held on to one's hat. Some scholars have observed that these entrance rituals, assisted by the servant, allowed middle-class persons to prepare for the rigorous performance demands of the middle-class parlor. Household geography itself provided what one has called "ceremonial frames" for the individual to pass through on the way to this most explicitly social, and theatrical, zone of the house. Between stepping out of one's carriage in the street and reaching the threshold of the parlor, one learned of one's acceptance, communicated one's intentions, prepared one's appearance, and allowed one's hosts to do the same.[75]

These functions are put in relief through the contrast between ceremonious visits and "friendly" visits, which were much less subject to rules of etiquette. The authors claimed that this was because the individuals involved knew each other well enough to know what was agreeable; but these visits were also less ritualized because status and acceptance did not have to be communicated and negotiated, only maintained. Friendly visits could be made without much dressing up, and at all hours, although some authors warned their readers to be considerate of their friends' time. One did not need to keep account of friendly visits, and one could lay aside one's hat or shawl without asking permission, a liberty one could not take in ceremonious calls. One was not to be too free in making friendly visits, however; some authors advised against going uninvited into the bedchambers of one's companions, and several advised against making a friendly visit if one had not been invited to do so. Thus friendly visits, while less regulated, were not completely unregulated, reminding us that different relations required different levels of "self-management," just as did different regions of the home.[76]

Antebellum conduct writers also taught the middle class how to read and silently respond to various visiting situations, important skills in keeping up an "easy" facade. Neither visitors nor their hosts were to admit it if the call was for some reason inopportune. The visitor who walked in on a party, for example, was to act as if he had been invited, and then leisurely beat a hasty retreat! One author suggested the lengths to which the smooth performance was to be taken:

> Likewise, if you are intending to enter one house, and find that you have got by mistake into another—a blunder very easily and very often committed in Philadelphia, in consequence of the singular uniformity of the houses—it is better, provided you have fairly entered the parlour before perceiving your error, and provided, also, that you are not an utter stranger to the family, it is better, I say, to remain for a short time as if you had intended to pay a visit there and say nothing whatever about the matter; but your visit should not be quite so long, nor your manner so confused, as this sentence.

A number of writers told of signs that indicated it was time to end one's call. One was to take leave if one's hosts allowed the conversation to lapse or rose from their seats (a "tacit invitation to retire"), or if other visitors were announced. It was permissible to stay longer at the host's insistence, but only a short while.[77]

If, as one author observed, visits were the small change of social converse, dinners, evening parties, and balls were the large drafts. Apparently these, too, were similar in Britain and America. Charles Dickens claimed while touring in the 1840s, for example, that with minor exceptions, "I never could find out any difference between a party at Boston and a party in London." He found New York society equally congenial.[78] Like visits, there was nothing new about dinners and dances; what was new was the extensive advice to the middle class concerning the regulation of these encounters.

The authors began by discussing how one was to issue and answer invitations. The extent of this advice underscores the social selection at work in these rituals, it also indicates that face-to-face immediacy had declined in at least some aspects of social communication. Suggestions about how soon before the event dinner and party invitations were to be made varied, but all writers agreed that such invitations were to be answered immediately. Some claimed that one had to give a good reason for declining invitations to dinner; and once one had accepted, one could not properly break such engagements except for urgent cause. Several authors advised hosts to try to invite to dinner only people who were known to each other or who desired to become acquainted, but they claimed an exception could be made with a person of "acknowledged merit." Two writers simply advised hosts to invite persons who would harmonize and get along well. Guests were to be strictly punctual (some authors claimed that punctuality was less important for a ball or a party, but several declared that very late entrances were a vulgar affectation). The concern about quick response to invitations and the timing of arrival is a reminder that middle-class social life was growing increasingly wed to calendar and clock.[79]

Antebellum conduct writers also gave the middle class a precise account of the proper schedule during dinner parties. Their instructions left no doubt about the expected proceedings from entrance hall to drawing room, to dining room, and back to drawing room again, so that their readers would always be assured of knowing what they were to do next, where, how, and with whom. Readers were informed, for example, that when all the guests were assembled in the drawing room, dinner would be announced by a servant, and all were to rise and proceed to the dining room in couples, in the order designated by the hosts. The master of the house would go first, with the female guest of honor, and the hostess would bring up the rear. The writers then gave instructions for proper behavior at the table.[80]

Discussions of dinners were matched by detailed instructions concerning balls and evening parties. The writers paid considerable attention to the proper mode of entering such fêtes, perhaps to help the uninitiated conquer fears (recall as well the persisting Chesterfieldian emphasis on first impressions). *Etiquette at Washington* gave typical advice in claiming that guests "should immediately approach the lady of the house and exchange salutations with her before recognizing any other person in the room, after which they should join their friends and leave her free to receive new visitors." This manual covered every contingency: "If the lady should not at the moment be in the room, the guests may enter into conversation with any one whom they chance to know, and make their salutations on her return." And the manuals gave many other tips, for both guests and hosts.[81]

With such specific instructions, middle-class readers were ready to entertain their peers with irrefutable proof of their social worth. All that these recipes for success required was a little practice . . . well, and a servant . . . a parlor . . . a dining room . . . a few engraved calling cards. . . .

WE SHOULD NOT be surprised, then, that antebellum authors only occasionally directed bits of this vast array of advice to members of the lower class. Conduct writers continued to show little interest in encouraging the humbler sort to exercise control over their bodies; nor were they interested in passing along any of the period's newly elaborate discussions of introductions, salutations, and occasions. In the few areas where they did counsel the lower class, they once again addressed most of their remarks to domestic servants and gave advice intended to keep them in their place. For example, while a few authors recommended that servants adopt a cheerful and polite manner with peers, they mostly intended to encourage a demeanor suited to subordinate status. One author met the issue head-on, telling servants: "It is by no means intended that you should study and endeavor to imitate closely the manners you may have witnessed in ladies at a party, in the parlor, or at a formal dinner. This would be unbecoming your station, and would not be 'good manners' for you."[82]

While several authors gave the lower class rules for conversation that were not unlike some addressed to the middle class—do not swear, gossip, or quarrel with others, for example—this advice is so sparse relative to that intended for the middle class that it could hardly have been significant for lower-class persons themselves. Some advice is revealing, however, of middle-class wishes regarding the lower class. One author advised servants not to refer to their peers as "ladies" and "gentlemen":

> Learn to distinguish properly between the conventional terms "gentleman" and "lady," and the good, worthy, every-day people, who are too sensible to assume names conferred only upon the well-bred and highly educated. Let me be well understood, here, as not derogating from or abating one jot of the value of the true-hearted yeomanry of the country. . . . Your own good sense and observation should teach you the distinction. . . . Do not say "that lady," meaning the washerwoman; or "that woman," speaking of the governor's wife.

And servants continued to be warned not to talk with peers about the families in the homes where they worked.[83]

Comparing antebellum-era suggestions to the different classes about proper behavior with equals lays bare the authors' true intentions. Clearly these middle-class writers wished to teach their own class the code of behavior that had formerly been the preserve of the elite. But their democratic assertions notwithstanding, it is just as clear that they had no intention of helping *all* Americans become "ladies and gentlemen."

SOME SCHOLARS HAVE argued that the antebellum middle class adopted a refinement that was more simple, comfortable, religious, and domestic than the more aristocratic gentility that preceded it. But this interpretation is problematic in light of the major innovation of antebellum etiquette, the highly codified staging rules for social occasions. These rules suggest that antebellum conduct writers, like their British counterparts, were engaged in scripting an elaborate performance designed both to secure and to reinforce bourgeois identity. And there was nothing particularly comfortable, religious, or domestic about it.[84]

It was not just the stage directions that were more complex than ever before; recall that the old body-control advice was also more elaborate. We have considered some of the causes for increasing elaboration in these two areas; there were also more general causes for the overall complication of rituals for face-to-face behavior in antebellum advice. We must remember that this was a period of enormous political, economic, and social transformation. Among other things, the middle and upper classes were enjoying a continually improving standard of living, but the new social order was not yet clear, nor were people's places in it. This much change produces an anomic situation for individuals; the need for social classification becomes acute. The situation was made all the more difficult by urbanization and mobility. The self-presentation that was always important as one encountered strangers became even more so as cities grew larger and one's chances of encountering strangers greater. Judging others by their dress became ever more unreliable with changes in clothing production. Further, as Karen Halttunen has suggested, owing to the emphasis on self-madeness and self-improvement in middle-class culture, a certain liminality was inherent in middle-class status. One was potentially always in the process of becoming, and therefore in constant need of re-presenting oneself. Taken together, these conditions presented confusion, or what anthropologists would call a very "polluted" cultural situation, one ripe for the cleansing power of ritual. And thus did casual old customs become elaborate and meaning-laden rituals, to make the unclear clear.[85]

Perhaps the biggest source of cultural confusion in antebellum America was the embracing of democracy. Rituals of face-to-face interaction were necessary to clarify the emerging social order; they bore the special burden of communicating what it was not possible to say openly. Thus not only did American conduct writers fulfill the revolutionary-era trend of middling cooptation of gentility but they also pursued another goal. In contrast to the earlier period, it was now clear that the behavior of middle-class persons was to serve as an unspoken barrier between themselves and the lower sort.

Some scholars have noted a potential vicious circle here; the rituals grew more elaborate as they were codified and published, but they also became more accessible. Yet the lower class could not have imitated middle-class behavior—even if they wanted to—because polite behavior did not come cheap. If the manual itself could be afforded, the elaborations in the instructions all required further expenditure for various crucial accessories, whether "a stuffed arm chair," a piano, a dining room, or a servant. The rituals themselves thus served to raise the ante to a safely exclusionary level. The middling and the lower sort were becoming increasingly differentiated in occupation and lifestyle in this period; the conduct literature suggests that manners were intended to make the gap evident in individual encounters.[86] Put another way, having confirmed their revolutionary rise, the antebellum middle class wanted to pull the ladder up behind them.

The limits of the authors' democratic vision become quite evident in their discussions of the master-servant relationship, the main repository for class deference in the antebellum era. Here the writers made it clear that they did not consider servants ladies and gentlemen, their democratic proclamations notwithstanding. The lower class was included in their vision of the social order only as it impinged on their middle-class world. Given the growing complexity of class development in the real world, in this sense the conduct writers did manage to simplify the picture.

Some scholars have interpreted middle-class manners and lifestyle as an expression of a middle-class interest that was not explicit in antebellum politics. This is so, but not because "'middle class' meant very little in the political arena," as one suggests. Rather, the burden on the "government" provided by manners was so great because, in this country especially, the direct expression of class in politics was taboo. Scholars have not been sufficiently frank, then, about the essentially political role manners have played. By helping to secure middle-class hegemony and exclusivity in the social and cultural realms, manners undercut the power of electoral democracy.[87] To be sure, manners were a game anyone could play, but only if one could afford the ante. For many, the only option was the sidelines.

The game was so popular and so enduring because it was hugely distracting. Several historians have rightly pointed out that relying on manners to differentiate people had the convenient effect of maintaining the fiction that others were excluded only because their behavior was inadequate. The whole purpose of manners was to silently accomplish the exclusion of the poor.[88] Moreover, because manners were an open game, though with high stakes, they did allow some social mobility. That some could surmount the upholstered barrier dampened discontent. In America, then, manners were the quintessential social safety valve. They served a similar function in Britain. In the end, comparison of America and Britain from the perspective of manners reveals two societies moving in the same direction, albeit from different starting points. Britain wrestled with the stronger grip of the old regime; American society went further in embracing democracy.[89] But both societies were undergoing democratization; both were being transformed by commercial and then industrial capitalism. And it was the latter, above all, that left its stamp on manners.

Why did American authors claim to be giving distinctively American rules when they were giving only slightly more democratic advice than were British authors, and the greater democracy was confined to the claims of their own class? This was simply the antebellum phase of the long distancing campaign that knows no period but is inseparable from the whole project of conduct instruction. Once one has learned how to behave, one wishes to conceal the fact that one was ever unrefined, especially as an adult. One wants one's good behavior to appear the natural emanation of one's good character. One wants especially to deny that one got one's polish from a book. We should not therefore take the period's few scornful comments about excessively "etiquettish" behavior too seriously. In all periods, we find the consumers of etiquette satirizing their own endeavors as a way of distancing themselves from the project. In the antebellum era, proclaiming a new American and democratic code of behavior was just a new way for the authors to deflect the old charges of encouraging European or "aristocratic" refinement.[90] But scholars have paid too much attention to this perennial ambivalence about the pursuit of gentility, too much attention to the noise on the surface of American culture, and not enough attention to what Americans were actually doing. For all the ambivalence, the spread of gentility was inexorable, as all scholars acknowledge. We need to pay more heed to why it spread, in the face of the undeniable democratic hesitation.

The democratic proclamations of the authors did distinguish American from British manners in altering their context somewhat and, in so doing, gave manners a special role in antebellum America. It has been suggested that the pursuit of gentility and middle-class culture were at odds, a cultural contradiction. But in fact manners served to resolve another, more troubling contradiction: the growing gap between democracy and inequality.[91] Democracy in America rests on the fiction of a classless society. Manners played a role in upholding the system by diverting attention from class divisions, just as the democratic proclamations on the opening pages of antebellum etiquette books served to divert attention from the class-communicating rules within. So manners were essential in republican America. The only alternative was true equality.

To say that manners performed these functions is not to say that the participants or even the authors were fully conscious of them. They may have been only partly conscious, or not at all. One followed the rules because, once learned and internalized, they seemed only proper.[92] Therein lay the game's greatest distraction, for players and spectators alike.

EIGHT

MANNERS FOR ADULTS

We have already seen how, at the age of eighteen, Isaac Mickle was intent on "making his entree into society with becoming flourishes." This was not the only mention of his entrance into the world of adults. Eight months later, on New Year's Day, he reviewed his progress: "During the past twelve months I have begun the study of law; [and] have in a measure come out into company. . . . By the first of these circumstances I have been brought into contact with lawyers, politicians, and other public men, . . . by the second I have been brought into the society of polished, intelligent, and virtuous ladies." Nor were Mickle's embarking on professional training and ceremonious visiting his first forays into the adult world. His birthday reflections the year previous already had a world-weary air: "Could I live my years over again I would keep out of love, out of debt and *out of the newspapers;* or to say all in a few words, I would take the advice of her who has too often advised me to no purpose." This last entry is the most evocative of the ambiguity of this adolescent's position. He refers at once to the frequent publication of his articles in the local newspapers, surely a sign of precocity, and to the advice of his mother, a reminder that he still lived at home. Joseph Kett has described the mixed status of antebellum youth as "semidependence." What stands out most in Mickle's diary, however, is not his lingering dependence but the astonishing degree of his freedom to mix in the world of adults. And he was not alone. Remarking that two of his friends also edited and wrote for local papers, he claimed: "So we young ones have the whole duty of edifying the public on our shoulders." Mickle mentioned his mother only rarely, and when he did, as in the above entry, it is clear how lightly her authority lay upon him. He most frequently notes her indulgence of his whims.[1] In Mickle's world, youth and adults mixed freely, and on nearly equal footing. So did youth and adults in the world constructed by antebellum conduct writers.

The status of youth in antebellum America is a clear illustration of the social and historical plasticity of adolescence. At once child and adult, the adolescent can be construed as, and allowed to be, either. But such liminal figures can be threatening.[2] This is suggested by something quite evident in antebellum conduct advice but not perceivable from Mickle's vantage point, namely, some adults' ambivalence about the high status of youth. The authors who expressed it did not describe this ambivalence directly but conveyed it through a rather curious and unique feature of antebellum advice: nostalgia— a distinct nostalgia for what they assumed had been an unquestioned deference to elders under the old order. As one author wrote: "It cannot be doubted that the majority of the youth of the present day . . . manifest less modesty, less of the becoming spirit of subordination, less respect for age, less of gentle, docile, filial deference for superiors, than were common in the days of our fathers."[3]

In part this nostalgia was simply ill founded, as it rested on a distorted view of the past. But it reflected the present in registering that some real change had occurred in age relations; a "revolution against patriarchal authority" had in fact taken place. This revolution had, and would continue to have, limits. Antebellum conduct writers did not extend the possibility of social equality to young children. Here they mostly continued to prescribe the traditional rituals of subordination. Moreover, in including youth but not children in the world of adults, the writers exacerbated young children's subordination with social exclusion. Nor did the revolution against patriarchal authority entail further erosion of the status of the aged; here the development of a new kind of deference suitable for the weak allowed the authors to prescribe more courteous treatment of the old than in the past. But antebellum conduct writers did confirm and extend the rise in status that youth had begun to enjoy during the revolutionary era. It was just that by voicing mixed feelings about the change in the status of youth, the nostalgic authors also predicted the future. The victory of youth was secure for the moment, but not forever.

AS IN EARLIER periods, antebellum Americans learned how to behave at home, in church, at school, and from books; but schools and books continued to erode the earlier primacy of church and family. To the extent that the family became more private, it both gained and lost influence over the shaping of children. Middle-class children were more sheltered from the sway of the community than in the past; but they were also more isolated from it and thus had to learn its lessons outside the family.[4] While religion continued to be central to the lives of many Americans, the churches' role in conduct instruction declined, for ministers stopped publishing sermons that offered manners instruction or told parents how to train their children. Lay authors took over this role through child-rearing manuals.[5] The role of the school was increasing because more and more children were attending. Elementary schooling was widely available in long-settled areas by the 1820s and 1830s and became even more so during the prewar decades. Schools took over some of the socializing tasks earlier laid on parents and eased the transition for children from the family to new forms of work organization. Children could also take a good bit of conduct instruction directly from books, as at least fifteen different works addressed those under fifteen or sixteen years of age.[6]

Who taught children manners through these various agencies? This is worth asking, as historians have claimed that this period witnessed the reign of mothers as the primary shapers of children through a new system of "gentle nurture." This development was paralleled outside the home by the feminization of the teaching force. But these changes occured gradually, and while the conduct literature clearly reflects a new role for women in child rearing, it also reminds us that men still played a role.[7] Women wrote many of the etiquette books that made up over half of the works for children; but men wrote most of the general advice works.

Socialization within the family would certainly have been reduced for the many youth, especially young men, who left home in their mid-teens. Leaving home was not in itself a departure from the past, when servants and apprentices lived with their masters' families; but in this period many young men left home to live on their own, often in the growing cities. Scholars have noted that this increased mobility led to a tension between the education still offered by parents in the increasingly "domesticated" home and the education offered by "them": the employers, strangers, and corrupters of the outside world. Because young people normally finished their formal schooling by their mid-teens, even that institution ceased to help them negotiate between the family and the world. If the traditional institutions of family, church, and school could offer little guidance to youth, one might expect to find contemporary concern over their formation. And such concern is evident in the flood of advice works that appeared, purporting to guide young men and women in every sphere of life.[8]

Of course, not all youth left home; some studies have found that many middle-class youth lived with their families until marriage. This practice has been described, in the case of young men, as a strategy to give them the education necessary to secure positions in middle-class occupations.[9] Such youth were obviously not fully adult, but prolonged residence at home and lengthy education did not necessarily entail dependence or immaturity. Isaac Mickle lived at home in his late teens (although he had friends who lived on their own in boarding houses), and it did not cramp his style in the least. Nor did it keep him from feeling the need to read an etiquette book.

As in the two earlier periods, antebellum conduct writers directed most of their advice to youth (still defined as those from their mid-teens to early twenties). They devoted forty-five works exclusively to youth and another twenty-four to both youth and adults. When analyzed according to type, however, a new pattern emerges in these antebellum works. Nearly all of the works for youth alone were general advice books. These discussed amusements, employments, religious practice, character, relationships, habits, and morals, in addition to demeanor and deportment, and were intended to direct youth from puberty through the first years of marriage. Almost all of the works that addressed both youth and adults, in contrast, were etiquette manuals. The authors of these works did not explicitly restrict their audience to a particular age group, but the tone and character of their prescriptions indicate that they were addressing both youth and adults (and they did not differ from the few etiquette books that were explicitly directed to youth).

This vagueness in the age address of many antebellum-era etiquette manuals resembles their vagueness in class address and suggests that the authors did not deem families, churches, and schools fully able to meet this society's manners-training needs. For the manuals were really addressed to youth and *uninitiated* adults. Both the etiquette and general-advice writers sometimes referred to the old institutions, regretting that young people were growing up and leaving home without their former comprehensive training, and hinting that the result was a growing need for the kind of information they were offering.[10] Although the etiquette writers did not fear the consequences of the decline of socializing institutions for youth to the same extent as did the writers of advice books, they were responding to, if not taking advantage of, the same felt need. The writers did not perceive the same demand as regarded young children. There they saw their role as supplementary to parental instruction, not as filling a gap. Mrs. Manners told children, for example, that "I do not doubt that your parents or friends, or teachers, may remind you of the very things that I do; but young people are heedless, and cannot be told these things too often."[11]

Nearly fifty antebellum-era conduct works addressed adult readers, and half of these were seemingly intended exclusively for adults. This was double the proportion of adults-only conduct works in the past. Two-thirds of these works were etiquette manuals. It is clear, then, that both in relative and absolute numbers, more conduct advice (and in the form of etiquette) was directed to adults in this period than ever before. For the first time, conduct writers gave adults nearly the same amount of advice as they gave youth, a fact that has been overlooked by historians who have commented on the flood of advice to youth.[12] These authors believed that more persons were reaching maturity without having learned enough manners to feel comfortable in their middle-class roles and thus needed to learn them from books. And because etiquette books were the most accessible and least preachy form of such advice, they were well suited to this fluid class society.

Timing provides further clues about the causes of all this advice to adults. For any instruction directed to all age groups, the advice to children was the oldest or came earliest in the period, followed by the advice to youth alone; the advice to both youth and adults or adults alone was the newest, or came latest. In part, then, as the period wore on, conduct writers were teaching adults what they had earlier taught children. At first glance, this would seem to indicate that minimum standards for behavior were declining, as adults learned what had earlier been children's lessons. When considered together with the class dimension of antebellum etiquette, however, it becomes clear that standards actually remained fairly stable; they were simply being disseminated to a wider audience. The later life stage to which much manners instruction was directed as the period wore on is an indication of the "self-help" nature of manners for the middle class. As one author explained, ". . . it constantly occurs that those who have spent their early lives in acquiring property, find themselves placed in a position in society, new to them, and for which they are not at once prepared. It is the purpose of this little work to exhibit to such as these, as well as to all who are not familiar with them, the rules which regulate society in the United States. . . ."[13] Moreover, the newest advice of the period, the elaborate stage directions for social occasions, was not directed to children at all. Standards were not declining, then; if anything, the rules were becoming more complex as they were codified and disseminated to a broader social group.

Antebellum conduct writers did not address any advice exclusively to the aged. Gone were the seventeenth- and early-eighteenth-century sermons in which ministers advised old people on their proper demeanor. Gone too were the few remarks to old people that lingered on in the religious and general-advice works of the late eighteenth and early nineteenth centuries. In the antebellum era only two works even purported to address all ages. The conduct writers evidently thought that old people did not have to learn any special behavior.

THEY DID PAY some attention to the treatment of old people, which is interesting in light of their nostalgic laments about the decline of deference to elders. Of course, as regarded the aged, the nostalgic authors were simply mistaken about the past; earlier writers had never paid more than lip service to the notion that the young should revere the old. It was the antebellum authors who went furthest in urging the young to defer to the aged, and they ceased insisting that the aged had to earn this deference through proper behavior on their own part. Antebellum authors were able to push deference to the aged because a new type of deference had evolved: as we shall see, the writers reported and prescribed a new "protective deference" that was different from traditional deference in that it was not intended to be paid to the powerful but to the weak. Here again, manners can help to reconcile seemingly contradictory historical interpretations. Some scholars have argued that the antebellum period witnessed increasing expressions of hostility toward the elderly, while others have pointed to a new idealization of the old.[14] Protective deference reflects neither hostility nor idealization but simply continued ambivalence toward old age.

Mixed feelings are immediately evident in advice about spending time with the aged. A few writers encouraged children and youth to mix with old people because such interaction was good for young people; but, as in the past, some assumed that the young would be reticent to do so. More authors suggested that adults and youth devote time to paying various little attentions to the elderly, but more out of kindness than for their own benefit.[15]

Another expression of ambivalence was that recommendations of consideration for age very often got mixed with class and gender concerns, especially in discussions of precedence. A number of authors advised youth and adults to allow the elderly to go first in various situations, for example; but these writers nearly always claimed that sex and class had to be taken into consideration along with age in determining precedence. All agreed that age was to be considered along with rank and general importance in the chief example of precedence discussed: the lining up of guests for the procession to the dining room at a dinner party. But age precedence was generally to be exercised after gender precedence; thus, when guests were announced, the women were named first, although in order of age or rank. Likewise, when interacting with several women, a man was to offer his arm, tip his hat, and speak first to the oldest. Women, too, were to address the eldest female first, as when greeting a group of party guests. Younger persons were always to be presented to their elders during introductions; but here again, age had to be balanced with class and gender considerations.[16]

Some counsels draw our attention to the relative physical weakness of the aged, alerting us that deference to the elderly was often different from traditional deference to superiors. While adults and youth were not to ask peers about their health, for example, they could do so of the aged. The authors also referred to various occasions when young and adult men were to tender an arm to escort an older person. This advice reveals a link in the authors' minds between the kind of deference all were to show old people and that which men were to show women. Indeed, they urged men of all ages to devote time to the elderly by performing little services such as offering them an arm or waiting on them at table; and more often than not, they suggested that these attentions be paid to all women as well. Men were to offer the wall when passing or walking with women or elderly men on the street, and regulate their pace by that of such partners. Youth and adults of both sexes were told to offer the best seats to the aged and to let the aged take the lead in salutations and leave-taking; again these were honors also due women. Similarly, a few writers told adults and youth that it was especially improper to contradict the old, one specifying that men should "show especial deference to the opinions of the aged and of the fair sex." This new kind of deference to the weak developed, as we shall see, as a result of changes in gender relations. But its invention allowed conduct writers, for the first time, to pay more than lip service to the time-honored notion that the elderly should be venerated.

The real and persisting attitude that the aged were as weak in social power as in body occasionally became quite clear. The writers continued to remind readers not to make fun of old people. Some prescriptions to men were even more explicit: "Politeness demands that a gentleman should incommode himself to confer a favor upon a lady, or an aged or weakly person." "There are other persons to whom a lady or gentleman should be especially polite. All elderly persons, the unattractive; the poor, and those whose dependent positions may cause them to fear neglect. . . . A debtor of any kind is to be treated with particular courtesy."[17]

The demand for deference to the aged had been modest to begin with in early America but had waned further with the waning of hierarchy in the revolutionary era. It received a new lease on life in the antebellum era, but not owing to a new appreciation for the aged. Americans had simply developed a technique for accomodating the weak.

NOT ALL THE WEAK could expect even this mock deference, for the authors treated children, the other powerless age group, quite differently. The inequality of children to adults remained stable in this period; only the relation required new treatment in this supposedly democratic age. As in the past, children shared the fate of servants. Instead of the new kind of deference accorded women and the aged, they were simply excluded from the social stage. They received relatively little conduct advice, and, as in the past, most of it consisted of instructions to allow adults to control encounters. And when the authors gave youth but not children new advice that revealed their inclusion in adult society—coupled with some direct suggestions that children be segregated from it—the persisting inferiority of children was only underscored. The conduct evidence calls for a tempering of notions of indulgent American attitudes toward "little innocents." While more affectionate relations with young children had triumphed in the revolutionary era, antebellum manuals suggest that children were regarded as potentially disruptive of middle-class genteel performances. The conduct writers gave adults only a modest amount of conduct advice respecting children; but their advice implies that, as regarded the very young, their nostalgia announced a retreat from the more relaxed child-rearing of the revolutionary era. Some authors now expressed fears that parents had become too soft and lenient with their children and urged them to be loving but firm.[18]

Most of the authors who were nostalgic, however, were addressing youth; and while they were mistaken in lamenting the passing of deference to the elderly, they were dead right in noting the passing of deference to elders on the part of youth. Their own advice confirms this, for, nostalgia notwithstanding, antebellum writers gave youth much scantier and milder advice than they gave children about interaction with adults—advice sometimes similar to that which they gave adults regarding their age superiors. Moreover, they did not discuss the master-servant relation in such a way as to suggest that they construed it as an age relation between youth and adults.[19] The writers likewise gave adults very little advice regarding youth. To be sure, adult concern about the behavior of youth is reflected in the flood of advice directed to them, but the content of that advice was substantially the same as that addressed to adults. The authors sought to teach youth proper adult behavior and not to control them as minors. The manners gap that had developed between children and youth in the revolutionary era only grew wider in the antebellum period, while that between adults and youth became quite narrow.

There were some continuities from the previous era. While a few authors simply encouraged youth to spend time with adults, for example, children were given all of the old instructions to allow adults to control their time. While both children and youth were urged to give place to their elders, children were given more exacting instructions and were also counseled to yield space. And there was a similar gap persisting from the revolutionary era in advice to the two groups on body carriage and facial expression before adults.[20]

The gap widened in advice on conversation with elders. Whereas a few of the earlier authors had urged youth as well as children not to speak unless spoken to, not to interrupt, and to use respectful terms of address when with adults, antebellum authors stopped asking youth to observe these rules. The authors persisted in advising both children and youth not to talk too much with adults. They also persisted in only telling youth not to fall silent. They continued to urge both children and youth to speak to adults in a respectful manner and never to argue. But they added some advice that reflected the new tendency to include youth in the world of adults while excluding children: some writers encouraged youth to confide in their elders, while others warned children not to pester adults with annoying questions.[21] An assumption that youth would interact with adults in social arenas—while children would not—is also disclosed in instructions to youth to give adults precedence in introductions and processions to the dining room at a dinner party.[22]

Traditionally the most important means of expressing deference to adults were salutations and demeanor, and here too specific counsels persisted from the previous era. Both children and youth continued to be told to have a respectful and attentive demeanor, and youth were to mix their reverence with ease. Yet discussions of demeanor and salutations were ambiguous in the sense that they were also the sites, especially in advice to youth, of most of the antebellum nostalgia for past deference. Whereas a few authors reminded young men to remove their hats when they encountered adults in public, for example, others simply lamented the decline of such gestures. With only one exception, authors for children did not express this nostalgia but simply continued to remind them to curtsy or bow and uncover when entering or leaving the presence of adults. That children did in fact perform these gestures is suggested by the descriptions of various memoirists of the curtsies, bows, and uncoverings to adults practiced during their antebellum childhoods.[23]

When examined more closely the antebellum nostalgia passages reveal their authors' attitudes toward the revolution in age relations that had occurred in the previous era. First, both their laments and their actual advice confirm not only that such a revolution had taken place but, at least as far as youth were concerned, was something they accepted. Youth's former obligation to pay deference to adults had been diluted, and the authors assured their readers that they did not wish to see a complete resumption of the old system. As Alcott asserted, "The customs of our ancestors were founded in truth, only they carried them to an unwise extreme." More important, the authors did not generally accompany their laments to youth with much in the way of specific prescriptions that they revere their elders. A good bit of their nostalgia was simply that—they were not giving any direct instructions; they were simply reminiscing![24]

Not only did the authors continue to give youth much less and more relaxed advice about encounters with elders than they gave to children, but often their tone and wording underscored the fact that the revolution against patriarchal authority had been successful. Rather than asserting that reverence was a duty and a proper recognition of their elders' superiority, as had been the habit of their predecessors, antebellum writers often hinted that youth were to defer to elders out of kindness. Timothy Arthur recommended:

> Towards parents the deportment should always be deferential and kind. A young man, who properly reflects upon the new relation now existing between them and himself, will naturally change his manner of address, and be far more guarded than he was before he arrived of age, lest he say or do anything that might cause them to feel that he now considered himself beyond their control.

Another author, who gave young men the general advice to have a deferential demeanor toward those "who are advanced in life and dignified by their station and character," went on to say that the respect shown did not have to be sincere; in another place he told young men to let older persons take the lead in conversations, to make them feel as though they were in control. Robert De Valcourt was even franker: "A teacher stands, in some respects, in the relation of a parent. He is to be treated with just as much reverence and affection as he inspires."[25]

These discussions convey the same impression that Isaac Mickle's references to his mother convey. On the few occasions that he mentioned her, he never failed to do so in exalted terms. But it is clear that his was a reverence inspired by love and courtesy rather than her authority. He was similarly respectful but by no means "aweful" of his guardian Uncle. Witness the tone of his description (at eighteen years) of an important family discussion:

> At the breakfast table this morning, I opened to my uncle my intention of studying law. He asked me if I had a wish to spend some time first at a College. I replied I had not. It was then settled that I should read in Philadelphia, and board at home. My respected mother fully consents to my choice of a profession; and for this, and for countless millions of other kind indulgences to the whims of her son, May God bless her! He alone can requite a mother's love.[26]

THAT MICKLE LEFT it to the Deity to repay his mother's love suggests that, at this stage in his life, he did not feel too bound by her "gentle nurture." The trends in the conduct literature were consistent with his experience. While antebellum conduct writers gave adults advice concerning interactions with children, advice which revolved around parents' duty to teach children to behave properly, they gave adults almost no advice concerning youth. One explanation for the lack of advice about youth is that the authors assumed this chief task would be completed by adolescence. Of course the authors could not have regarded the job as fully accomplished, else they would not have offered their own advice. Antebellum authors assumed that some adolescents had already left home, for a few offered their companionship in the parents' stead. As for youth living at home, the paucity of advice to parents about them implies that parents and youth were to behave as equals and/or that youth were not expected to spend much time at home. Two writers repeated the old advice to parents that a warm and familiar rather than stern and formal manner would encourage their sons and daughters to spend time with them and not be tempted to seek companionship elsewhere, but that was the extent of the advice to adults on behavior with youth.[27]

Not only did the writers give adults much more advice on behavior with children, but they even gave youth some of this advice, which suggests again that youth were closer in status to adults than to children. Mickle drew a similar line between himself and his young cousins when he referred to them, after a visit, as "the delightful children." Both male and female authors wrote about proper adult behavior with children, and, contrary to what we might expect, given historians' emphasis of a new reign of maternal nurture in this period, they generally addressed their suggestions to both parents. There are no significant gender differences in the advice. Perhaps the new recognition of maternal nurture reflected a new valuation of infancy and early childhood (long under feminine sway), whereas fathers were still expected to be fully involved with the school-age children discussed in conduct advice.[28] The only discernible difference was that between the mostly male-authored child-rearing guides and the mostly female-authored etiquette books. Ironically, given scholars' emphasis on gentle nurture, the former stressed that parents needed to train their children, while the latter stressed that parents needed to keep their children from being or becoming social nuisances. The two genres spoke with one voice, however, on the point where these two ideas intersected: that parents should teach their children good manners.

As in the past, in exhorting parents to work on their children's behavior, the authors were implying that parents should spend time with their children. A few continued to urge parents to encourage their children's attendance by allowing freedom in their company, to supervise their children's associations, and to keep them from spending too much time with domestic servants in particular. While these suggestions had also been made by revolutionary-era authors, some antebellum writers specifically recommended something that had only been implied in earlier advice: that children be allowed to take their meals with the family, as this would improve their manners. When compared with antebellum advice to adults and youth concerning dinner parties, however, it is apparent that middle-class Americans drew a clear distinction between family dinners, at which young children were generally welcome, and company dinners, where they were not.[29]

While the writers encouraged parents to spend time with their children, they discouraged parents from promoting interaction between their children and other adults. This was a clear departure from earlier advice. While a few authors implied that one's children, if they were well behaved, could be present occasionally when one received company, others discouraged parents from inflicting their children on guests. One author cheerfully advised, for example, that "If you should happen to be blessed with those lovely nuisances, children, and should be entertaining company, never allow them to be brought in after dinner, unless they are particularly asked for, and even then it is better to say they are at school." Several other writers gave similar advice. A few authors warned parents further not to allow their children to pester visitors, and a number of writers repeated the caution that "to carry children or dogs with you on a visit of ceremony, is altogether vulgar." Some historians have observed this Victorian habit of separating children from adults and suggest that adults were concerned with protecting children from the corruption of the adult world. The argument is that adults increasingly regarded children as pure and innocent, in contrast to older Calvinist notions of their depravity, and wished to shield them from contamination. But the manners evidence suggests a different, or at least an additional, take. These discussions do not reveal much of a preoccupation with childish innocence; the writers seem more concerned with excluding than with protecting children from adult society. The implication was that children were an annoying nuisance and liable to disrupt the performances of middle-class adults.

The suggestions to adults concerning demeanor and talk with children do indicate that the revolutionary campaign to introduce more affection and less formality in parent-child interaction had been successful. Antebellum writers did urge adults to treat children with affection and to have a kind, respectful, and protective manner toward them. As had their predecessors, many authors agreed that excessive reserve and severity would only alienate children; they advised instead that adults be familiar, cheerful, and loving in manner as well as even-tempered in correcting them. Moreover, reflecting the larger cultural conflation of youth and adulthood, antebellum authors also began to address some of these instructions about young children to youth. But whereas antebellum authors accepted the need for warm and loving relations between adults and children, they were now concerned that these not be taken too far. While some authors applauded the fact that stiff formality with children was no longer in fashion, others were ambivalent and wondered whether the pendulum had swung too far in the opposite direction. At least one author claimed outright that American parents now erred on the side of softness; others warned parents against overindulgence.

Some antebellum authors suggested that it was this last concern that caused them to continue recommending corporal punishment of young children. Their discussions had changed little from those of the revolutionary era in the sense that there was disagreement among the authors, yet the majority still recommended the rod as a last resort. Only one male author recommended to both parents the supposed hallmark of nineteenth-century maternal discipline: withdrawal of love through temporary banishment from the parent's presence (exclusion from table or the parlor). But Cotton Mather and Benjamin Rush had each described this method in earlier periods. Reflecting the varied practices recorded in diaries, then, Americans continued to have mixed feelings about juvenile discipline. And some Americans continued to beat their children, now the only group in white society for whom this practice was condoned. All in all, ideas about the treatment of children had not changed that much; their relative inequality simply became more stark with the democratization of the larger society.

TO A GREATER DEGREE than ever before, antebellum advice concerned behavior not with members of different age groups but rather with equals. Behavior with peers was also the subject on which advice to adults and advice to youth was most similar. Most antebellum etiquette was not only part of a single class code but also a single code for all persons who had reached puberty—a code intended to guide their behavior with peers or in general society. Antebellum conduct writers were thus mainly concerned with telling middle-class adults how to behave with other middle-class adults. Historians have long noted that antebellum writers poured down a torrent of advice upon youth. Some have suggested that the writers were conservative and hoped "to bridge the gap between traditional values and new conditions" by promoting "decision of character" in youth. But they have not realized that, as regarded face-to-face interaction, most of the advice for youth was the same as advice for adults.[30] This was the greatest confirmation of the revolution in age relations for youth. The advice to youth was sometimes more elaborate, but very much of it is also found in works for both youth and adults and not infrequently in works intended for adults alone. In contrast, the authors only occasionally gave children the same advice they gave youth, and there were distinct patterns in the distribution of peer advice to children. Antebellum writers gave children much of the old body-control advice but very few of the new stage directions for social life.

Antebellum advice to children thus signals the differentiation of "domestic" from "social" behavior. Instead of introductions, entertainments, and visits, most of the advice to children concerned relations with family members, teachers, or schoolmates and interaction within the household, church, or school. On the one hand this pattern reflects the stable and unchanging nature of conduct advice to children, a trait which in turn affirms that their status had only changed moderately from the early colonial period. The pattern also confirms the increasing age segregation in antebellum-era socializing. In the early colonial period adults might have wished for children to be unseen as well as unheard, but the promiscuous structure of the household and society precluded any such custom. By the antebellum era, middle-class homes often had nurseries where young children spent a good deal of time. In addition, attic or "garret" space was often consigned to children as play area. But confining children to these segregated spaces was not simply, as has been suggested, an expression of the desire to protect them from the outside world. As we have seen, the emphasis in the conduct literature was more on the exclusion than the protection of young children. The very geography of nurseries and garrets supports the latter interpretation, for not only were these spaces in the most remote (highest and farthest back) sections of the house, but they were also sparsely and plainly furnished.[31] The new physical possibility of banishing children to these back regions and then restricting entertainments to adults simply allowed ritual reflection in manners of the persisting inferiority of young children.

That the old social fact of the inferiority of children now occurred in a new context did alter its meaning a bit. When the advice to children is compared with that to youth, it becomes clear that children had become more infantilized in the minds of the conduct writers, who now saw a distinct break in human development at adolescence. Children's dress also reveals a desire to separate children from both young and mature adults. Boys and girls between ages three and nine were dressed in the new androgynous costume for children: pantaloons and frock. Gender differences were also obliterated in children's hair styles, in the same effort to make children look different from everyone else.[32] In this case, then, material culture and conduct literature paint the same picture. The social world was an adult world. Children were not included.

But youth were. The conduct writers said as much themselves, in such statements as the following: "Young people, who just begin to be recognized as companions in the social circle rather than children, may study this book with much advantage." We should not be surprised to find youth mixing with adults in conduct books; wherever scholars have focussed on the actual activities of youth in this era—whether in religion, politics, work, or associational life—they have found them mixing with adults and sharing adult concerns. One scholar has also observed that commercial and then industrial opportunities "made it possible for young people to achieve adult economic status at relatively young ages." To be sure, there were many youth groups; but what is striking, especially compared to the end of the century, is that such groups were run by youth (rather than by adults) and scarcely differed from their adult counterparts, in which we also find youth. Isaac Mickle's experience was similar to what historians have noted of other communities: not only did he mix freely with both youth and adults throughout his mid- and late teens, but also before the age of twenty-one he had founded the Camden Debating Society (a youth group), been elected to the board of the Camden Temperance Society (youth and adults), and regularly indulged his penchant for politics as frequent contributor to and editor of both of Camden's newspapers.[33]

Antebellum conduct works did give the more traditional advice on behavior with peers to children, youth, and adults alike—even some counsels that had mostly been addressed to youth in the preceding era. The authors continued to give some of this advice special emphasis for youth. This was true of the counsels to frequent good company and be careful in choosing friends, for example. Some historians have pointed to this advice as evidence that antebellum writers were trying to protect from the dreaded confidence man all those youth who were moving from countryside to city. But this was among the most traditional of counsels to youth, as evident in seventeenth-century as in nineteenth-century works; and more than ever before, authors also discussed these concerns in works for children and adults.[34] All ages now also received the traditional counsels about the importance of demeanor in shaping others' impressions, the pleas for a modest air, and the reminders to avoid bashfulness and awkwardness.[35] All were now given much of the advice on body carriage. Indeed, children received more of this than of any other peer advice, and much more of it than in the previous period. All were now warned against "odd tricks," unnatural postures, and self-touching, for example, and urged to cultivate gracefulness.[36] Body control was thus important for all ages; the only difference was that the authors gave adults and youth some additional advice explicitly concerning social occasions. While all groups were told how to sit, stand, and walk properly, for example, adults and youth were given special advice pertaining to specific social contexts.[37] While all ages were warned not to grab or poke others, only adults and youth were given instructions on body contact in the form of salutations (handshakes and kisses).[38]

Age patterns in antebellum advice on facial expression and conversation were similar. Most of this advice—much more than in the past—was given to all age groups. Yet in a few places social life required a more elaborate set of rules for adults and youth. To cite just one example, while the authors directed nearly all of their warnings against noise-making in company to children, youth, and adults alike, they only addressed the caution against whispering to others at parties to adults and youth.[39]

In some areas, the authors mixed traditional counsels with new variations, but to the same effect. That is, they gave the traditional advice to all age groups and only gave the newer advice, concerning busy streets and social occasions, to youth and adults. The writers gave all ages the various old counsels to pay attention to their peers, for example; but they only gave adults and youth the new warnings not to be absent-minded when walking down a street.[40] While authors for all ages warned their readers not to intrude where they were not desired, they directed their most frequent warnings against intrusion, those concerning taking others' time by stopping them in the street, to adults and youth.[41] They gave all ages the old reminders not to take the best places in company, but writers for adults and youth added specific advice about seating at dinner parties and visits.[42] And while all ages were to have a courteous demeanor with peers, the writers only reminded adults and youth about the importance of a gracious demeanor when making or receiving visits.[43]

Antebellum authors clearly gave children more body-control advice than had their revolutionary-era predecessors. That they gave children more of this self-control advice could be taken as a sign that antebellum parents were extending the Lockean method of nurturing internal controls to children. Indeed, maternal gentle nurture might simply be the spread of this system to younger age groups, groups increasingly in the care of women. The maternal nurture that has been described for this period, and credited as a strategy "for the reproduction of a middle-class personality," involved the same cultivation of rationality and self-mastery that were integral aspects of both youth nurture and the formation of middle-class culture in the late eighteenth century. But there was not a big difference between the two periods in the extension of body control advice to children; the antebellum era saw mostly a modest elaboration of earlier injunctions. On the whole, it appears that the antebellum authors' chief intent as regarded young children was to maintain their subordination. And the areas where the advice to children was strongest (do not stare, do not laugh, do not talk too much, do not make noise) asked for self-effacement as much as self-control. It is unlikely that the conduct writers had vastly different goals than the earlier advocates of Locke as regarded young children, goals consistent with the legacy of Calvinist influences on both: the parents' first objective was to establish authority. Indeed, the task of preparing youth for independence was dependent on the parents' having first secured influence over the child.[44]

The much bigger change from the revolutionary era in the age distribution of this traditional body-control advice occurred at the other end of the spectrum. In the antebellum period, authors felt obliged to address much more of this advice to adults. This was because they were writing for a broader audience. While in the revolutionary era prosperous elements among the middling sort were challenging the aristocratic monopoly on gentility, in the antebellum period all would-be members of the respectable middle class had to learn the rules. If a foothold in the middle class was not secured until adulthood, so be it. A host of manuals stood at the ready to fill one in. The increasing elaboration and ritualization of social life which occured as the middle class began to draw a line between themselves and the lower class made the newly established clerk and his wife all the more inclined to consult the book before entertaining.

Antebellum writers thus addressed all of the new "stage directions" of the period to adults along with youth, but only rarely to children. They did not advise children as to the specific requirements of behavior in middle-class social life because they did not think children belonged there. Some writers even restricted interaction between children, albeit indirectly, by continuing to give them the old instructions not to go out without their parents' permission and not to loiter in the streets. Other sources suggest that middle-class reformers were particularly disturbed by the presence of poor children at work and at play in city streets. Scholars have argued that they were disturbed because this situation conflicted with the idea that children ought to be protected within the newly privatized family. The manners evidence underscores the social consequences of this desire to protect children; it entailed their segregation from adult life. In contrast, the authors gave adults and youth ample advice on how to behave in street encounters. More generally, they assured adults and youth that constant mixing in society was beneficial to their deportment.[45]

Antebellum conduct writers accordingly directed all the various instructions on how to introduce peers, in person or through letters of introduction, to both adults and youth, but never to children. The authors also gave adults and youth, but not children, the warnings against "cutting" properly introduced acquaintances, and the advice about when it was proper to talk to strangers without introduction.[46] Consistent with the restriction of these access rituals to the social world of adults, some accompanying rules on demeanor and salutation were also prescribed to adults and youth, but only rarely to children. Writers for youth in particular often repeated Chesterfield's advice against indiscriminate familiarity with others, as well as his recommendation of reserve with all but close friends. Antebellum writers added that adults and youth should adopt a reserve with strangers, with new or undesirable acquaintances, in public places, and at large parties.[47] Some of Chesterfield's followers urged youth to attend to their manner of entering a room and greeting company. The writers encouraged both adults and youth, but especially the latter, to enlist a dancing master's help in learning how to perform the necessary gestures.[48] The writers gave both adults and youth, but not children, all their recommendations concerning the gestures to be performed upon introduction to peers.[49] They also gave adults and youth more, and more-specific, advice than they gave children on saluting acquaintances met thereafter.[50] And they almost always confined their discussions of the gestures to be performed upon entering and leaving visits, parties, and balls to works for youth and adults.[51]

The pattern holds in the period's extensive discussions of visiting. The conduct writers nearly always addressed these to both adults and youth, but rarely to children. Many advised adults and youth on the distinctions between ceremonious and friendly visits, when and how to return visits, and how to use calling cards. They also gave both adults and youth all of the advice on proper conduct during visits, both on the part of the visitor and the person receiving the visit. In contrast, only two authors for children even mentioned visiting.[52] It is likely this expectation of greater adult engagement in ritualized social life that accounts for the somewhat more elaborate advice to youth and adults than that to children on proper conversational matter.[53]

As with visits, many conduct writers directed their advice on proper conduct at dinners, evening parties, and balls to both adults and youth. The writers most often directed advice on issuing invitations to these events to adult readers, evidently assuming that adults would host these parties;[54] but they gave both adults and youth all the elaborate advice on the customary proceedings at dinner parties, such as how and when to proceed from room to room and what to do at the dinner table. While most of these counsels are not found in works for children, a number of writers did urge children to be punctual in coming to table, to accept what they were served without comment, to wait for others to begin eating, and to avoid eating too fast or too slow. But these rules rarely referred to company dinners; they were intended for family use.[55] The authors likewise directed the instructions concerning proper behavior at balls or evening parties, whether on the part of guests or hosts, to both adults and youth, and never to children.[56] As if to confirm the exclusion of children from balls and parties, antebellum authors generally confined their discussions of dancing to adults and youth.[57]

When analyzed from the perspective of age relations, antebellum advice for behavior with peers conjures up two different but overlapping worlds: the world of the family and the world of social life. Children, youth, and adults alike needed to learn the basic middle-class body-control instructions for all their interactions, within the family and abroad. To that extent, it is clear that middle-class homes were not strictly divided between "back-stage" and "front-stage" regions; regulated behavior was as necessary between family members as in other relations.[58] But only adults and youth needed to learn the stage directions to guide their gestures and talk in the scenes of middle-class social life. In that world, children (and indeed acknowledgment of family relations in general) were banished to the wings. These features of the system should make us question the characterization of middle-class manners as simply "domesticated" refinement.[59] As will become clearer in the next chapter, they had a larger sphere.

ANTEBELLUM MANNERS show how the questions about age relations raised by the revolution against patriarchal authority were answered in the adolescent republic. The conduct writers gave a fair amount of advice urging deference to the elderly, especially when compared with earlier periods; but this was not a reflection of a rise in the status of the aged. A new variety of deference allowed antebellum authors to recommend gestures to those who had always been socially weak. The authors gave children more traditional deference advice concerning behavior toward adults, while that to youth was often ambivalent or scanty. Likewise, the authors gave adults very little advice concerning their relations with youth as age inferiors, and gave them far more advice, though less than in other periods, regarding children. The pendulum was swinging back in this last relation after the opening of possibilities in the revolutionary era. Some authors expressed fears that parents had become too indulgent and encouraged them to show authority as well as love. Overall, the authors gave children relatively little advice in the antebellum period, and most of it, whether about interaction with superiors or peers, was stable and old-fashioned.

In contrast, there was an outpouring of advice to youth concerning relations with peers. The substance of most of this advice was the same as that addressed to adults. That is, it was not so much designed to secure their deference as youth as it was to teach them proper adult behavior. Many antebellum-era etiquette manuals were addressed to both youth and adults. To a greater degree than ever before the authors were directing their efforts to people who had reached maturity without having been trained in manners. In the end, they gave adults almost as much advice as they gave youth.

When compared with the converging advice to adults and youth, the relatively unchanging advice to children suggests that a certain degree of age segregation was being acknowledged and encouraged in antebellum-era advice. The new social world included both youth and adults on nearly the same footing, but it did not include children. As in the case of class relations, then, antebellum conduct writers confirmed the rise of one group but drew the line at another. Their ambitions for youth were tied to their ambitions for their class, because they focused their attention on youth of their class. Indeed, it is possible that their ambitions for youth were dependent on their class ambitions and not for youth's sake alone, for there were signs of ambivalence about the equality of youth, especially in some authors' nostalgia.

Not all of the conduct writers were nostalgic. Many did not offer judgment or even comment on the revolution against patriarchal authority but merely codified it. Etiquette book authors in particular were simply busy with the task of instructing young and uninitiated adults in the rules of "polite society," to which both now had access. Still, among the nostalgic were some of the most popular advice writers of the day—figures like William Alcott, Timothy Shay Arthur, John Todd, and Eliza Ware Farrar, whose works were reprinted again and again. The nostalgia of these popular authors was so strong, and so unique to this period, that it must have some important meaning. We cannot ignore the fact that, while acknowledging the revolution against patriarchal authority, these authors were clearly annoyed at the freedom with which they believed young people were behaving toward their elders.[60]

Given what historians have told us about the history of adolescence in America, their ambivalence about the revolution against patriarchal authority was a clear indication that the victory of youth would not be secure in the future. The authors themselves gave broad hints that they did not regard the recent changes in age relations as settled once and for all. Alcott wrote, "From the extreme of too much deference for the old, we are fast going to the extreme of paying them too little deference," and asked whether "in passing, as we now are, to the other extreme, it may be worthwhile to inquire whether there is not danger of going too far. . . . Is it reasonable for the young, so generally, to place themselves on a level with the old?"[61]

Observing the situation later in the century, Joseph Kett suggests that adults often use nostalgia to shape their concept of youth and of proper age relations, and to supply justification for the creation of institutions (whether school, family, church, or other) to put their notions into effect. The antebellum ambivalence about youth—itself a reaction to the opening of possibilities for youth that had accompanied the revolutionary era—points to even earlier roots of the modern institution of adolescence.[62] In other words, youth triumphed in the revolution against patriarchal authority and in the following decades, only to cause their elders to scramble to contain this advance as they were scrambling to contain the advances made by women and the "common man." These conduct writers, acting for their class, succeeded in their own time in the latter cases by drawing lines with middle-class etiquette to exclude "the lower sort," and, as we shall see, by cloaking continuing gender inequality with the protective deference of "ladies first." While beyond the scope of this study, exploration of post–Civil War rules for social interaction would likely reveal a similar containing drive with regard to youth. Studies of schools and other institutions for youth, as well as juvenile literature, certainly show such a drive—one which culminated in practices that revealed outright hostility to adult behavior in youth. The fact that there was such an agenda in their nostalgia may be suggested by one antebellum author's rather awkward use of the present tense in his lament: "In the land of our forefathers, domestic government and control have not been sacrificed to mere theories on the development of juvenile manliness and independence. The junior members of a family know and keep their place, and are submissive to a legitimate and necessary authority in the hands of the parent."[63] In thus speaking of the past in the present tense, this author may have been expressing not nostalgia but a utopian vision, not what was but what he wanted to see.

Perhaps it was the unsettling liminality of youth, at once younger and equal, that caused these authors to object to their independence. Their objection probably also reflected a stubborn persistence of hierarchical thinking in family relations. It is quite likely that the authors' discomfort was an unconscious recognition that the Lockean youth nurture experiment failed to meet their needs. Seized by prosperous middling families as a way to prepare sons and daughters for a new world without masters, it had succeeded in creating autonomous individuals. But this ran counter to the growth of the equally important ideal of the close and private family. While Locke had hoped that the granting of filial independence would allow the reorganization of the family on an egalitarian and affectionate basis—that children raised this way would continue to revere their parents when they became adults—the nineteenth-century doubts about the results suggest that his may have been wishful thinking.[64] Young men, at least, were not contained by the embrace of domesticity. Moreover, historians have suggested that perpetuating middle-class status from generation to generation came to require more than simply launching self-directed sons and daughters into the world; indeed, it soon required the opposite, a longer period of dependence and careful preparation for middle-class careers. Perpetuating middle-class status in fact would demand more authority over youth, not less.[65] It would require a more pliable subject—the "awkward adolescent" barely perceptible on the horizon.

NINE

LADIES FIRST?

Isaac Mickle spent a lot of time with other young men. They met in each others' rooms to play music or chess; they stopped in for a chat at the local billiard room or blacksmith's shop; they ran into each other on the street and decided to go for a sail in his boat, a stroll of Philadelphia's Chestnut Street, or a ramble in the woods. They also visited young ladies together. In opting for the last, however, they crossed a boundary. The boundary was not a visible one but it was real. Mickle revealed it rhetorically. While he spent time every day with other young men, he only came "into company" by spending time with women. While his interactions with other young men were casual, spontaneous, and unritualized, his encounters with women were ceremonially framed. This ceremonial boundary did not mean that there was a big gap between the sexes. Mickle spent more and more time with young women in his late teens; sometimes he spent four evenings in a row visiting his friends the Sheppard girls. He came to be as emotionally close to them as to any of his male friends. To a great degree he shared their standards for propriety in behavior.[1] But the activities he describes, mainly visiting them and escorting them various places, were ritualized. They were the stuff of antebellum etiquette books. His ramblings with male friends were not.

If the Sheppard girls had kept diaries, we would probably see that when Mickle entered their parlor, they too were crossing an invisible line. They probably straightened their dresses and changed the subject of their private sisterly chat. We can guess how they behaved, in part from Mickle's diary, but also because the period's advice literature had so much to say about parlor visits. This literature was not concerned with sisters' behavior toward each other, or even toward their female friends. The world discussed in conduct books was the one men and women stepped into when they came together. Mickle's accounts of these encounters confirm the prevalence of conduct book expectations.

Why did antebellum conduct writers focus on this mixed-sex world when early colonial writers had focused on a man's world? Conduct writers always described the social world; it was just that they now saw women in that vision. Recall that they began to see women in the social world in the revolutionary era, but it was still a man's world. In the antebellum era, not only were women part of the picture, but the authors believed that "society" existed only where the sexes came together. Yet the fact that the authors needed to discuss and offer instruction in this realm—that this was the realm of ritualized behavior—suggests that while Mickle's friendships with the Sheppard girls may have been no more problematic than his male friendships, there was still some cultural work to be done here. Americans were trying to solve a cultural conflict when they resorted to elaborate rituals to regulate relations between the sexes.

We have seen how the codifiers of middle-class culture made gentility their own. We have seen how they resolved the revolution in age relations, however temporarily, in favor of youth. The question remained what sort of accommodations they would register for the third group whose unequal status under the old regime was challenged, at least in theory, by the great revolution. What would the fate of women be in "democratic" America? We know, of course, that women did not attain their rightful place in any democracy worthy of the name; even a few contemporaries, the advocates of women's rights, knew that. But the elaborate gender system the middle class devised to camouflage the continuing inequality of women is nonetheless worthy of study in and of itself because of its extraordinary durability. We are still dealing with its effects today. Moreover, we have more to learn about just how this system worked. In particular, the degree to which manners spread a ritual mantle over the cultural contradiction between democracy and gender inequality has not been understood. Scholars have also not appreciated how well the system worked. Ironically, the very rituals necessitated by the difficulty of integrating women into the old world of men ended up allowing considerable intimacy in the new mixed-sex social world.

That the social world depicted by middle-class conduct writers was decidedly mixed sex runs contrary to the assumption of many social historians that antebellum advice books simply presented the ideology of separate spheres packaged for popular consumption. Historians have subjected this ideology to intense scrutiny in recent years. It is a slippery set of ideas, unsatisfactory because reality was obviously more complicated, yet stubbornly persistent—not least because it was invoked by contemporaries as much as by historians. Women were not confined to the home, domestic concerns, and each other's company; men were not purely economic and political animals in the "outside world." We are learning of significant overlap in men's and women's lives—of male domesticity and female political activity, for example. Yet men and women obviously did not have identical rights or experiences. Nor did they view their roles as interchangeable. Linda Kerber is correct in pointing out that for present-day scholars and nineteenth-century Americans alike, the term separate spheres is and was a trope, a metaphor that contemporaries could invoke to indicate their different expectations of male and female experience, expectations grounded in, though not a mirror image of, a more complex reality.[2]

Perhaps it is the power of this trope that has led us and contemporaries to neglect the actual overlap in men's and women's lives. Not only did conduct advisors write women into their social scripts, but also very often they directed women to behave just as they directed men to behave. Yet, as in the revolutionary era, the trend toward gender integration in conduct advice went unremarked. Nevertheless, it was crucial. Indeed, the mixed-sex social world depicted in conduct books suggests that its real-life counterpart (the one we see in Mickle's diary) served to mediate between the more gendered public and private spheres, both real and ideal. To be sure, advice books occasionally proclaimed the spheres, although not as dramatically as has been supposed (works for women, for example, often presented a series of chapters on intellectual and social pursuits before coming to domestic concerns midvolume). There are even hints of separate spheres in the rules for face-to-face behavior. In particular, there is evidence of the "female world of love and ritual," a world of intense female relationships that Carroll Smith-Rosenberg and other historians have described. But both male and female writers were quite emphatic that this "woman's culture" was properly confined to "private times and places." Historians have neglected its larger context; then as now, women lived in a wider social world. If a parallel "male world" of intense homosocial relations existed, it too was not considered "society." One author explained:

> All society . . . is the result of the mutual attraction of the sexes for each other; and social forms, observances, occasions, and amusements . . . are all subordinate to this end—all intended to satisfy this central attraction. There is no society otherwise. Clubs, where men meet to read newspapers, talk politics, dine, and play together, are not society. Tea drinkings, and other exclusive assemblages of the ladies, are not society. These are its severed halves, which require to come together. . . . [T]he love of the sexes for each other, is the first, and the indispensable element of society, and the one to which all others are subordinate.[3]

The social world described by antebellum conduct writers was thus a meeting ground for the sexes. Review of the actual locales depicted in their advice—the writers described specific geographic contexts to a much greater degree than had their predecessors—suggests that this social world also mediated in the sense that it geographically overlapped the public and private spheres. The locations described were, first, the rooms of the home that were consecrated to receiving guests: the parlor (or drawing room) and the dining room. Thus, some sites were domestic, but it was mainly the public areas of private homes that the authors were concerned with regulating. The other locations were public in their sense of the word, that is, areas outside of private residences. The conduct writers often discussed behavior in the street, or "public promenades." They also discussed proper behavior in theaters, public ballrooms, concert and lecture halls, museums, or other "public places of amusement." These spaces, neither truly private (in the sense of familial) nor public (in the sense of state-related) but, rather, social, were the primary locations of the etiquette book world. Every now and then other scenes were mentioned, as when authors gave advice for proper behavior in churches, shops, schools, coaches, boats, or hotels. But the authors never discussed the worlds of work or politics. Nor did they discuss proper behavior in single-sex institutions such as men's and ladies' clubs.[4]

Some antebellum scholars have tended to identify manners with the parlor, and with women, and to neglect their role in social spaces outside the home. Some have also argued that the parlor declined in importance as political and economic activity moved out of homes and into offices in the nineteenth century. But these historians have overlooked the fact that conduct writers, male and female, regarded the parlor and other social spaces as central. While they were actually prescribing behavior in a circumscribed realm of activity, they did not acknowledge this limitation. They spoke in general terms, of manners as the necessary laws of social life, or life in general, or as necessary for smooth human relations. One author, for example, referred to "The laws of etiquette, or those conventional forms of good breeding, which prevail in society."[5] They did not confine their concerns in terms of gender or spheres. They discussed what behavior a person should adopt "in company" or "in society," terms which were not usually gendered. Most advice concerned mixed-sex activities such as visiting, dinner parties, and dances, or behavior in public places where both sexes were expected to resort. Moreover, at these sites the authors often specifically prescribed intermingling between men and women. While gender played a central role in the social order portrayed by antebellum-era etiquette, it did not simply act as a dividing line. The only gender-distancing promoted was that between married couples in company— spouses were to ignore each other.[6] In the authors' minds, women were now fully incorporated in this important third area between the "public" and "private" spheres: the social sphere.

Yet perhaps we should not call the social world depicted in conduct literature another "sphere." Above all, the literature suggests that even those who have followed Jurgen Habermas in exploring an expanded notion of the public sphere have erred in overdichotomizing the public and private. To add a third sphere might compound the syndrome of overcompartmentalizing past lives. The conduct literature can be more useful in simply reminding us of the common humanity and concerns of middle-class men and women. Antebellum manners show us that their gendered concerns and responsibilities were embedded in a larger social matrix. In this as in other ways, manners help us to understand how men and women shared lives together.[7]

To argue that the social world depicted in conduct literature was a mixed-sex world is not to argue that women were regarded as equal to or the same as men. While antebellum authors often gave men and women the same advice, the rules were gendered in some important ways. Gender differentiation did not proceed, however, along the lines essayed in the revolutionary-era. Antebellum authors preserved the revolutionary era requests for modesty in women, but they did not build on them. Their new rules reveal a different tack in responding to the challenge of integrating women in society, and one which helped with both the cultural contradiction this introduced between persisting gender inequality in a supposedly democratic society and the problem of female sexual vulnerability in an individualistic social order. They did so by offering women compensatory privileges and, above all, protection, via the new and ritually efficacious system of "ladies first."

SOME FIRST CLUES about the nature of the system are supplied by the gender of the authors and intended audience of antebellum conduct literature. In contrast to the revolutionary era, with its new interest in the education of women, more antebellum-era conduct works were addressed to men than to women. Even some works ostensibly addressed to both sexes seemed to address only men. The decline in the proportion of works devoted to women underscores the transitional nature of the earlier period, when the place of women in the young republic was a new and important issue. It also suggests that antebellum conduct writers felt a need for greater regulation of male behavior.

While men wrote most of the works addressed to men, the authorship of works for women was divided between men and women. Women wrote the etiquette works for women. Although men wrote more than half of the general advice works for women, the specific rules of female deportment had become the province of female teachers. Writing advice and especially etiquette books was one option for those women—Eliza Leslie, Catherine Sedgwick, and Eliza Farrar are examples—who turned to commercial writing in this period as a way to support their families.[8] Women thus had a hand in the making of the antebellum American manners system. It is equally important to note that men wrote most of the new rules for men.

ONE COULD ARGUE that the relative neglect of single-sex encounters in antebellum conduct advice is actually consistent with a world divided into separate male and female spheres of feeling and activity, in that same-sex interactions might have posed little difficulty and hence required little ceremonial regulation. This was surely the case, but, as suggested above, the few allusions to such worlds show that they were circumscribed in the authors' minds and situated on the margins of the more important mixed-sex social world. Some authors' comments do help to clarify the relationship between separate spheres and the social world when they hint that the latter was feminized to a certain degree. In "bachelor seclusion" or when busy with business, for example, men were allowed to ignore some requirements of ceremony among themselves, while women always had to keep them up.

Most allusions to interaction between women were indirect; we find them between the lines of descriptions of the mixed-sex social world. For example, many writers mentioned the custom whereby women left the table shortly after dessert at dinner parties and retired by themselves to the drawing room, while the men remained behind to drink and smoke. Women were to watch for the hostess to give the signal by rising from her chair. One writer described the scene:

> The time between leaving the dinner table and being joined by the gentlemen is generally a very easy and social one with the ladies; the younger ones walk about; or run upstairs, or play with children, or have some jokes and stories in a corner by themselves, whilst the matrons discourse of their own affairs. If your dress wants any adjusting, this is the time to attend to it. Presently, coffee is handed round, and then the gentlemen come dropping in, the young ones first and the politicians last. . . .

While a few authors condemned this custom, especially at the end of the period, the majority reported and supported it.[9]

We only learn from their language that many authors assumed that many social calls would be made by women to women. For example, some authors for women claimed that "if the call is made in a carriage, the servant will ask if the lady you wish to see is at home," or told women not to quit their bonnets and shawls in entering upon a visit "unless at the express permission of the lady visited." Many of the rules for visiting would thus seem to refer to encounters between women. But this was by no means always the case, and advice to women concerning visits with women does not differ from advice on visiting directed to both sexes, or to men, or to instances in which the sex of the person visited is not clear. It is clear that while women were at liberty to receive male visitors, to make visits accompanied by men, and to interact with male friends and relations encountered in their women friends' parlors, they were not, for social purposes, to call upon men themselves. One author declared that "a lady never calls on a gentleman, unless professionally or officially."[10]

Nor did the authors make any definite statements about contact between men—but their assumptions are again revealing. For instance, the offhand references of a few authors to "a party of bachelors," "a gentleman's party," etc., suggest that they condoned some all-male socializing. Yet all of the much more frequent and extensive discussions of balls and parties and most references to dinners indicate that these were generally mixed-sex affairs and that the authors encouraged participation in them. That only one author gave men advice on how to behave in social calls between men suggests that ceremonial visiting was also regarded as a generally mixed-sex (if not female) activity. Just because the authors did not discuss visits between men does not mean that they did not happen. Recall that Isaac Mickle's male friends dropped in all the time. But he did not regard these as formal social calls, as he did his visits to women or to men who were not friends. The more casual visits among men (and those between intimate women friends) were of the unregulated "friendly" variety that the authors did not spend much time on. Ceremony was not normally required on such occasions, as is revealed by Mickle's jesting description of an early morning visit:

> As I was lying in bed this morning . . . who should pop in but Will Jeffers, my delectable chum, and what should he hold up before my half doubting eyes but a letter from . . . the Secretary of the Navy, acquainting him of . . . his appointment as a midshipman. . . . Jumping upon the floor at hearing this news, I congratulated my friend for his good luck with all the formality of which I was capable; but I suspect my bows and flourishes were more polite than elegant, considering I performed them in my shirt and nightcap.[11]

Some messages about sex segregation at social affairs were mixed. Some authors told men not to stand together at parties but to devote their time to the women present. Yet an equal number of authors for women or for both sexes simply asserted that "gentlemen usually stand in groups" or "walk about the room" together at such events. Even though he had escorted several women to a ball, for example, Mickle managed to take "several strolls into the Champagne room" with his friend Harry Edwards. And more often than not authors for men assumed they would remain at the table for a time after women withdrew at the end of a dinner.[12]

While the writers thus acknowledged some same-sex interaction, they began to limit its place, at least among women, when they discussed body contact. Again, some of their thoughts on this subject were not communicated deliberately but embedded in other advice. These comments reveal an acceptance of touching between women, as when a number of authors told women who wished to show respect for a female visitor to "take her by the hand and conduct her" to a seat of honor. Women could shake hands with female acquaintances, something they could only do with intimate male friends. They could greet female friends with a kiss, though some authors did not want them to do so in public, or, as four writers specified, "in the presence of gentlemen with whom they are but slightly acquainted."[13]

This last qualifier is found in other advice. The authors seemed to expect a certain amount of touching between women but asked them to refrain *before company*. One author thus claimed that "there is a custom among young ladies of holding each other's hands and fondling them before company, which had much better be dispensed with. All kissing and caressing of your female friends should be kept for your hours of privacy, and never be indulged in before gentlemen." Another urged women to "Reserve all fondling and caressing for more private interviews"; and in a list of "certain bad practices," a third author for women included "putting your arm around the neck of another young girl, or promenading the room with arms encircling waists. Holding the hand of a friend all the time she sits beside you; or kissing and fondling her before company." These authors, all female, were not arguing against female body contact but against its display before others, particularly men.[14] While this advice seems to confirm the existence of a "female world of love and ritual," it also suggests that even female authors deemed that world a private one, and one that was not to intrude on the mixed-sex social world.

More touching was allowed between women than between men. Discussions of handshaking reveal that the authors expected at least that much body contact between men, although they often recommended bowing and uncovering instead. But a man was only to take the arm of an elderly man, and the authors never mentioned intimate touching of the sort they alluded to between women.[15]

Ironically, while greater intimacy was expected between women than between men, so was greater ceremony. Some of the rules for behavior at balls and parties, for example, called for women to give other women the precedence. Recall that they were to speak first to the lady of the house on entering such festivities. They were to give their sex the precedence in performing introductions. They were only expected to give up their seats to other (presumably older or higher-ranking) women. They only had to rise to greet another woman at a party; if a man saluted they were to stay seated.[16] Men did not need to observe as many formalities with each other. While the authors told both sexes never to introduce a man to a woman without having previously obtained her permission, for example, several agreed that "This formality is not necessary between men alone." Some authors advised that when two men called on a third for business purposes, each was to introduce the other. When two men were introduced, all other things being equal, the operation was to be performed "with mathematical simplicity and precision," as in "Mr. A., Mr. A'; Mr. A', Mr. A." The few references to social invitations between men suggest that ceremony could be dispensed with here as well; one author claimed that "Invitations to dine from bachelors to a party of bachelors may be less formal."[17]

A man could even relax his body carriage somewhat in the company of male friends. One observed: "Crossing the legs, elevating the feet, lounging on one side, . . . etc., though quite excusable in the *abandon* of bachelor seclusion, should never be indulged in where ceremony is properly required. In the company of ladies, particularly, too much care cannot be exhibited in one's attitudes." This theme of the "abandon of bachelor seclusion" may be confirmation of a realm of intimate male relations that paralleled the female.[18] But it also tells us that ceremonious behavior was most requisite in the company of ladies. This observation is also supported by the occasional suggestions that "businessmen," or adult middle-class males at work, were to be excused from obligations to pay punctilious attention to ceremonial forms. In fact, a few authors hinted at a new obligation to respect each others' "busyness." For example, several warned men not to intrude unnecessarily on the time of other men met in the street, especially during business hours and on business streets. One author added that a man could excuse himself from such an encounter if he had an appointment to meet.[19]

We cannot take this argument too far. Men had many proprieties to observe with each other, even among friends; manners were not only expected of and with women. Some authors reminded men, for example, not to greet male friends noisily or to proclaim their names loudly in public. Others urged men to address each other with some formality, that is, with proper names and the title Mr. Further qualifying "the abandon of bachelor seclusion," several writers warned men not to countenance vice in their talk with other men.[20] Still, it is clear that men had to modify their behavior more when they went "into company"—read mixed-sex encounters—than when they were alone with each other. The presence of women always called for more ceremony. Recall that Isaac Mickle was not concerned with what other men would think of his awkward bow but with what women would think. To this extent, the social world depicted in conduct literature, like some other sites in nineteenth-century culture, had become feminized. But it was not, as we shall see, an extension of women's private or domestic sphere. It lay beyond that sphere.

THE MOST COMPELLING evidence that the world described in antebellum conduct books was not simply an extension of women's sphere but one that represented the full inclusion of women in the old male-dominated social world lies in the writers' continuation of the revolutionary-era trend of giving women more and more of the advice previously and currently given to men about behavior in general society. With only a few exceptions, they addressed most of the new advice to the middle class to both sexes equally. There was no great gender differentiation in this advice; women were mostly told to behave just as men were told to behave, right down to the bow (as we shall see, in most instances it was no longer proper to curtsy). The hints that the social world was feminized, then, were a superficial cover for this great body of similar expectations for men's and women's behavior.

Of course there were some gender distinctions in the rules. The old body-control advice that persisted from the revolutionary era brought with it those earlier authors' attempts to distinguish ideal male and female behavior. Antebellum works thus continued to underscore the importance of modesty in women and self-mastery in men. Men were given more advice than were women on demeanor, body carriage, and facial issues in particular. Usually, this was advice derived or copied from Chesterfield that emphasized the importance of assured carriage and the necessity of avoiding awkwardness. Women needed to take special pains to be modest and to avoid affectation. Relative to the great amount of advice that was given to both men and women in equal proportions, however, these variations appear vestigial. Antebellum-era authors did not build upon them.

Historians have overlooked the convergence of expectations for male and female behavior. They usually argue, from the authors' surface nods to separate spheres and their repetition of revolutionary-era advice, that antebellum conduct books pressed differences between the sexes.[21] But antebellum conduct writers actually pursued a different solution to the problem of integrating unequal women into a "democratic" social world, by granting women special protection in that world. This protectiveness confirms women's continuing status as the weaker sex, however much an integral part of the social world. But the situation had some charms, for weakness had its privileges: women had the right to preside over social events. This was how the social sphere was feminized—women were granted protection wrapped in privilege.

That this privilege was superficial is immediately suggested by rules for the regulation of time and place in general society. In addition to giving both men and women the old suggestions to give time to others by paying attention, for example, antebellum conduct writers also warned women not to keep others waiting.[22] While the writers gave virtually all of their advice on the use of space in encounters to both men and women, here too they urged women not to abuse their privileges. Several authors told women not to regard any seat as their right at public amusements, and not to force themselves into a space that was full or attempt to save seats for latecomers.[23]

Most of the advice on proper demeanor with peers applied to both men and women in general society. Both sexes were to have an attentive, courteous, and agreeable air; any gender differences were usually old ones. They often boiled down to the repetition of Chesterfieldian precepts (such as the importance of making a good first impression, maintaining a real but not too apparent reserve, showing a certain dignity, and hiding one's emotions) more often to men than to women.[24] Yet some authors implied that self-possession was especially important in women, particularly in public. The difference was subtle and, again, dated back to the revolutionary era: both sexes required dignity to elicit others' respect, but men needed this to protect their affairs while women needed it to protect themselves.[25] Antebellum authors warned women more than men against affectation in manner; perhaps this too reflects the continuing influence of the great dissimulator on advice to men.[26]

While antebellum-era authors advised both men and women to be modest in general society, they continued to think a modest demeanor especially important in women. Still, some gender leveling had occurred. Both sexes were warned not to confuse modesty with bashfulness and timidity. Only a few old-fashioned authors continued to argue that the latter were attractive traits in a woman. Some authors continued to urge men to have a proper assurance in the presence of others; many urged men and women to be neither bashful nor bold, embarrassed nor impertinent. For every author who told women to guard against excessive forwardness one can be found who gave the same advice to men.[27]

A few authors continued to tell women to govern their movements with modesty and to avoid motions in public that might attract attention. Some claimed that women especially were judged by their motions, and historians have argued accordingly, but their claims were and are outweighed by the frequency with which the authors preached the same lesson to men. Antebellum conduct works urged both sexes to avoid awkwardness and strive for ease and grace in both manner and motions.[28]

The more specific and elaborate antebellum instructions on body carriage and facial expression sometimes included subtle gender variations, and
occasionally the authors continued to give men a little more advice than they
gave women. Yet here, too, most of the advice, including some that had been
addressed to men alone in the previous era, was now directed to both sexes.
Antebellum authors warned men not to raise their legs and women not to
spread their dresses when sitting, for example, and repeated more of Chesterfield's comments about graceful sitting to men but otherwise addressed their
advice on sitting to both sexes.[29] While some told women that short steps
were mincing and long steps "masculine," and others stressed the necessity of
graceful entrances more often to men, the authors addressed most advice on
proper standing and walking to both sexes.[30] Antebellum conduct writers addressed most of their praise for and advice on dancing to both sexes but
hinted that they thought men needed an extra nudge in this direction. A
number of authors urged men to learn to dance, arguing that it was rude to go
to balls and refuse to participate. Again it seems that these works were in dia-
log with Isaac Mickle's diary. After several years of scorning the art, he finally
got himself to the dancing master.[31] Nearly all of the antebellum-era warnings to the middle class against superfluous motions in the presence of others
were addressed to both sexes, as were virtually all of the instructions on facial
expression. Some authors emphasized the need for modest and unaffected expressions in women, but they dropped the old warnings to women against
"bold looks."[32]

On the whole, it appears that antebellum authors had fallen behind
rather than proceeded beyond their predecessors in distinguishing the sexes
through rules for deportment. Men were still given a few more injunctions
urging control of their bodies, and women were sometimes asked to appear
modest, but otherwise they were to follow the same rules. The gender gap had
actually continued to narrow since the previous era. Even when the authors
repeated old advice, as when a few told women to blush, they nearly canceled
out such special injunctions with all their identical suggestions to men and
women. Perhaps this is why German emigré Francis Lieber marveled about
American girls: "[S]o perfectly self-possessed are they, that blushing is decidedly of little occurrence." The essential similarity in injunctions to men and
women on facial expression is interesting in light of the varying arguments
that historians have made about gender and emotional expression in antebellum America. Some have argued that women were not allowed as broad a
range of emotional expression as men; others have claimed that women were
expected to display more emotion. Yet systematic comparison of the etiquette
prescriptions does not reveal much difference.[33]

The same arrangement—a little more self-control advice for men and a
little more modesty advice for women, but for the most part similar instructions—is evident in the antebellum advice on conversation in general society. While antebellum authors now addressed nearly all of their various denunciations of unnecessary noises to both sexes, for example, they did give
some warnings more frequently to men.[34] They addressed all of their advice

on how much to talk in company to both sexes. They also gave both men and women all the instructions about tone of voice and pronunciation; some authors simply urged women in particular not to raise their voices or pronounce words affectedly.[35] Nor were there significant differences between the sexes in the advice on choice of language.

Most of the advice to the middle class on proper manner and matter in conversation with peers applied to both men and women. Antebellum authors thus stopped asking women to be especially modest and started asking them simply to be courteous and pleasant—just as they had long advised men. The authors did continue to warn women a little more often than men about affectation and exaggeration, while some gave men special warnings against an overbearing manner.[36] But both sexes were to choose conversational topics carefully, avoiding controversial subjects. The writers recommended small talk to men more often than to women, while they urged women more often to choose instructive topics. This contrasts with earlier cautions about learned talk on the part of women. Antebellum authors also began to tell men to avoid professional topics in general company. While these do constitute minor gender differences in the advice on conversational matter, they are consistent with the larger trend of gender integration.[37] All the other counsels on conversational matter, such as warnings against discussing one's own or others' affairs and injudicious flattery, were dispensed to both sexes equally, whereas before they had been addressed more frequently to men. The writers urged both sexes to use humor and wit with caution; they also gave nearly all of the remaining (and traditional) suggestions for keeping conversation pleasant to both sexes equally. Contrary to one historian's claim, they did not warn men against angry talk and the need to avoid disputes any more often than they warned women about these offenses.[38]

Antebellum writers obviously repeated much of the revolutionary-era advice. They thereby maintained at least some of the modest gender differentiation sketched out by the older authors. Historians have stressed these injunctions to modesty in women and self-control in men in their tendency to mate bourgeois culture with separate spheres.[39] What they have not noticed is that this was old advice by the antebellum period, and antebellum authors did not add to it. Instead, they gave women more of the body control advice than they had previously. The self-control gap was continuing to narrow. Moreover, antebellum authors dropped some of the earlier calls for modesty. So they added to the revolutionary-era trend of giving women more and more of the advice that they gave men but not to that of drawing distinctions between the sexes. This pattern is especially clear in the new advice of the antebellum era, the "stage directions" for salutations, introductions, and entertainments; most of this advice was simply addressed to both sexes. Perhaps the most dramatic illustration is found in the new antebellum profusion of salutation rules and their revelation of the birth of the female bow.

Antebellum discussions of salutations were not completely gender-neutral. Reminders of the importance of salutations and the necessity of varying one's salutes under different circumstances were most frequently addressed to men. Women did not take off their hats, whereas some writers told men that they could touch or raise their hats to others, and many required men to remove their hats indoors. There was also a slight gender difference in discussions of the more intimate salutations: rules for handshaking were most often addressed to men while those for kiss-greetings were most often addressed to women. But the most significant feature of these discussions was the revolution in the primary gesture of salutation: women were told that instead of curtsying they should bow, as men did. The elaborate antebellum advice to bow, upon introduction to peers and when meeting or leaving acquaintances thereafter, was thus addressed to men and women alike. A number of authors commented on the change. Some simply pointed out to women that curtsying at introductions was obsolete and had been replaced by the bow: as one author commented, "I notice that ladies bow now, instead of curtseying." Some claimed, regarding salutations in public, that the custom had changed because "the courtesy is not gracefully consistent with locomotion." But since women were to bow even when standing still, the advent of this new advice can be read more simply as one of the more vivid signs of their integration into society, one of the many instances in which they were advised to act as men were advised to act. Only now could an author innocently assert: "We have seen many exquisite bows, both by ladies and gentlemen." It may have been owing to the newness of the gesture for women that, in addition to the instructions to both sexes, four authors felt it necessary to remind women not to bow "hastily, but with slow and measured dignity."[40]

In addition to showing that antebellum conduct writers were continuing to give women more of the advice that they gave men, and were ceasing to try to differentiate proper male and female behavior in the old ways, the new antebellum stage directions are useful in illustrating their alternative strategy. It was in these discussions, especially those concerning introductions and entertainments, that antebellum authors showed that their plan for integrating women in the social world was to make a privilege out of protection. This strategy is evident in advice to women on their proper degree of contact with others in general society. Only a few older writers repeated the traditional advice that women not go out often in public. Most antebellum-era authors revealed instead their assumption that women would have active and public social lives by giving them a good deal of advice on how to conduct themselves in public and by claiming that women exercised a great influence on society in general and men in particular. But antebellum-era authors did continue to believe that being in public posed dangers to women, for they advised women to have protection in the form of an escort. They did not object to women going abroad but to women doing so alone. Accordingly, they discussed at length the issue of proper accompaniment when women took walks, visited, and attended or moved about at balls and parties. Some authors claimed that it was improper for a woman to go alone to a library or a museum, unless for the purpose of studying or working as an artist. All authors agreed that women were not to walk or ride an omnibus alone in the evening. The proper age and sex of the escort depended on the woman's age, her marital status, and the situation.[41]

Antebellum authors assumed that men and women would mix often in general society—indeed, in mandating escorts they were promoting such mixing. They gave both sexes the traditional cautions about choosing company and forming friendships. They also addressed all of the new advice concerning introductions and letters of introduction to both men and women. Yet here too there were occasional intimations of the more protective attitude toward women. Some writers counseled women to accept introductions only from family members and trusted friends. Some explained that a woman "can not shake off improper acquaintance with the same facility as a gentleman can do, and their character is much easier affected by apparent contact with the worthless and dissipated." A related concern is evident in advice to men to reconsider their circle of acquaintance upon marriage. A man's friends were to assume their relationship was terminated when he married, unless he subsequently signaled an intention to continue the friendship by sending them his and his new bride's cards. Some authors recommended that the man give a dinner for his bachelor friends, to ease the dismissal. In addition to limiting the number of persons he would be obliged to entertain when under the financial burden of setting up a new household, a primary purpose of this custom was to allow a man to tailor his acquaintance to those friends who would be suitable for his wife.[42]

Antebellum advisors warned both sexes against "cutting" properly introduced acquaintances. They also expressed ambivalence about contact with strangers in advice to both sexes; they told men and women to refrain from making acquaintance with strangers in public but not to hesitate to render assistance to anyone needing it or converse with fellow-travelers or guests at private parties. While some historians have stressed the vulnerability of female travelers in this period and their need to shrink from interaction with strangers, the conduct literature tends to corroborate those contemporaries who insisted that American women traveled without fear of molestation. Charles Dickens was emphatic on this point: "Nor did I ever once, on any occasion, anywhere, during my rambles in America, see a woman exposed to the slightest act of rudeness, incivility, or even inattention . . . any lady may travel alone, from one end of the United States to the other, and be certain of the most courteous treatment everywhere."[43]

Virtually all of the antebellum instructions on visiting were directed to both men and women of the middle class, which tells us that this was an activity in which both sexes were expected to participate and to behave in similar fashion. Some odd bits of the advice, such as the instructions for keeping account of visits, are found in works for women and works for both sexes but not in works for men, which may indicate that the authors expected women to be a little more involved in ceremonial visiting than were men. But there is no strong pattern here. Another possible gender distinction appears in advice on the timing of friendly visits. While the authors told both men and women that friendly visits could be made at all hours provided one was considerate, some authors for men and for both sexes, but none for women alone, mentioned that close friends could be visited in the evening. One author for

women, on the other hand, objected to evening calls. If there was some suggestion that women would be more involved in making "morning calls," then,
there was equal indication that men would make more evening visits. These
bits of advice might reflect that middle-class men increasingly resorted to a
separate workplace during the day. They should not distract, however, from
the fact that the vast majority of rules for making and receiving visits were intended for both men and women, including rules which suggested that men
often made morning calls. Middle-class men were not complete nine-to-fivers
yet.[44] All of these issues are reflected in Mickle's diary. He mostly visited the
Sheppard girls in the evening, since he was generally occupied reading law in
a law office during the day. But neither he nor his superiors were tied to that
office, and he occasionally called in the afternoon.

Although both men and women made visits, it is clear that most ceremonious visits were made *to* women. But this was not an activity that occurred in
"women's sphere." Visiting was certainly not considered private or domestic
activity. The writers explained that the purpose of visiting was to maintain
acquaintance at a time when urban life was growing more complex. Parlor
visits were typical of the social world in that they were neither public nor private. Some authors claimed, for example, that visits were useful because peo
ple could talk of things that were not appropriately discussed in public. But
private and domestic matters were not appropriate topics during visits; as one
author reminded women: "All conversations about one's household affairs
should be studiously avoided."[45] That visits were most frequently made to
women but were not part of a domestic sphere gives us further clues about the
ways in which the social world was feminized. Historians have long been
aware that northern middle-class women were able to enter the public domain in the antebellum era through associational activity justified by their
role as guardians of morality in the home. We need to recognize as well the
ways in which women pulled quasi-public functions into the home through
ceremonious visiting.

As with visits, antebellum authors directed most of their new advice on
the proper regulation of dinners, evening parties, and balls to both men and
women. Yet here, too, there were gendered elements to a few of the instructions that hint further of the feminization of the social world. More often
than not, for example, the authors suggested that invitations to these events
be sent in the name of the lady of the house. Women were expected to offici-
ate at such functions. Recall that entering guests were to greet their hostess
before all others. The mistress of the house was to see that everyone was well
served at dinner parties and was to signal the end of the meal.[46] These and
other instructions hint that women had won a sort of preeminence in the social world.

Some scholars have emphasized this new female sway in social life. Some
have added it as a class embellishment to portraits of woman's sphere—the
woman as queen of middle-class gentility in the parlor, ready to refine rude
men entering from the rough-and-tumble outside world of men's sphere. Others have stressed that it gave women an important role in class definition, as

they gained at least some control over the undeniable "access" functions of introductions, visits, and invitations.[47] There is truth to these interpretations, but the whole cloth of manners suggests that they are features of a more fundamental pattern. In the context of other rules, female social privilege had two primary functions. On the surface, this privilege—what we might call the ethic of "ladies first"—served as token compensation for men's clear preeminence in the crucial economic and political arenas. Beneath the surface, female privilege seems to have had a gender function that provides a more consistent explanation for specific rules than any class purpose. The specific rules do not add up to any real female control over social life; that was something they shared with men. Rather, the rituals of "ladies first" served above all to protect women in what had long been, but was no longer, a man's world. And the rules took for granted a high level of civility on the part of most men. These compensatory and protective aspects of deference to women are hinted at in advice about male and female behavior in general society, but they are clearest in advice to men and women about behavior toward each other.

ADVICE TO MEN on behavior toward women reveals the most dramatic change of the entire history of manners in America: the inversion of the gender hierarchy. Early colonial conduct writers had openly claimed that women were inferior to men. Revolutionary-era authors were sufficiently ambivalent on this issue to warrant our continuing to treat the relationship between women and men as one between inferiors and superiors. Antebellum-era writers claimed that women were men's social superiors, and thus compel us to reverse the order. Clearly the ideologies of the revolutionary age had made British and American writers uncomfortable with frank assertions of female inferiority after the mid-eighteenth century. As we have seen, revolutionary-era manners were intended to help women assume a new, less unequal social role.

But why did antebellum writers endorse a complete role reversal? Of course the answer is that they did not, really. Antebellum-era advice to men about behavior with women bore only superficial resemblance to advice for class and age inferiors. It was far more elaborate—the most elaborate deference advice of the period. Indeed, deference in antebellum America was mostly something that men were to pay to women. But the kind of deference men were to pay to women was different from that expected of class and age inferiors, and different from traditional deference, because it was something the strong were to pay the weak, not the other way around; it was protective, not awe-inspired. Indeed, the authors no longer needed to tell women how to fend off men's improper advances. They now put the burden on men to restrain themselves. The only parallels to this "protective deference" in other relations are found, as we have seen, in some advice on behavior to the aged.

Not all the specific gallant gestures of the "ladies first" system were new. Diaries and novels suggest that men had long performed at least some of these acts. But these gestures, and the importance of male-female interaction generally, were new to conduct literature. The net effect was that, in contrast to the revolutionary era, antebellum authors gave men more advice on how to behave with women than they gave women on how to behave with men. The relative quantity of advice to the sexes is reflective of its content; the authors expected women to be mostly passive spectators to acts performed by men. Moreover, the meaning of these acts had changed. In the revolutionary era, gallantry was the prelude to seduction. In the antebellum period, it meant protection. It is no coincidence that the rise of "ladies first" in advice books coincided with the decline of the cautionary novel of seduction.

This protective stance has not been sufficiently acknowledged by historians. Even those who recognize it stress that women paid for this protection with dependence.[48] While that is certainly true, scholars have overlooked the extent to which women had a hand in making this system. Not only did they write some of the etiquette books that described it, but new research on a "cult of fear" in the late eighteenth and early nineteenth century suggests a missing link between the seduction fears of the revolutionary era and the protective gallantry of the antebellum decades. Female diaries and letters reveal a rash of public performances of feminine fear, specifically, rather theatrical cries for male protection and assistance on rather trivial occasions. Susan Klepp has observed that through these displays, women could invoke traditional dependency in order to actively renegotiate its terms. These displays of fear likely spurred the calls for protection in antebellum etiquette books.[49]

Scholars have also overlooked the extent to which the system placed demands on men. In the revolutionary era, sexuality was the one area where men were not asked to exercise self-control; the burden of self-restraint was borne by women. But in the antebellum era, the task of protecting middle-class women called for considerable self-restraint and sacrifice on men's part. This did not make women superior, or even equal; but it does help to explain why they subscribed to the bargain. They must have appreciated the work involved for men.

Indeed, men were to pursue opportunities to serve women. Many antebellum conduct writers told men, especially young men, to seek out the company of virtuous women, who would restrain them from bad behavior and polish their manners. Revolutionary-era authors had made similar suggestions, but antebellum writers indicated the new protective rather than seductive character of male-female relations with their advice on how men were to begin to cultivate relationships with women: they urged young men to start by cultivating the friendship of their mothers and, especially, their sisters. Men were to practice with them the gallantry requisite with all women by escorting them and devoting time to doing them favors. Over and over again the authors claimed that for young men to be their sisters' companions would serve both to protect the sisters and to improve their own manners. Practicing at home would make their gallantry habitual. Men's letters and memoirs indicate that they followed these suggestions.[50]

The authors did impose some limits on contact with women. Some pointed out that not all female company was salutary, and warned men to avoid coquettes and loose women; others specified that they did not have "silly, flirting girls" in mind when they recommended female company.[51] In keeping with advice to other inferiors, the authors also suggested that men were to allow women to control their degree of contact. Recall, for example, that a woman's permission had to be obtained before a man could be introduced to her. Men were also to refrain from greeting a woman on the street until she gave a signal of recognition, unless they were intimately acquainted. According to one author, "The reasons are: 1st, she is the superior; 2d if you bow to a lady first, she may not choose to acknowledge you, and there is no remedy; but if she bow to you—you, as a gentleman, cannot cut her." Moreover, a man was never to leave a woman before she had taken leave of him, and it was up to the woman to decide when to leave when a man and woman made calls together. Men were also to be respectful of women's time. They were never to engross a woman for any considerable time at a party or on the street. While these rules resemble those to other inferiors, they had a special protective twist. For example, men were not to converse with persons on the street who were unknown to the woman they accompanied.[52]

Again in harmony with advice to other inferiors, many authors endorsed Lord Chesterfield's suggestion that men were to devote time to women by waiting on them and satisfying their every want and whim. Yet the antebellum versions of this advice stressed protection, and other inferiors were not generally advised to protect their superiors. A few authors made it clear that the new gender deference was a privilege of the weak; as one explained: "Women are physically weaker than men. They are unable to defend themselves from insult or injury, and it would be considered indelicate for them to do so, even if they possessed the power. For these and other reasons, it is only simple politeness, and a sign of good sense, to render any little service. . . ." Another author suggested the proper extent of male service to women when he advised: "Never allow a lady to get a chair for herself, ring a bell, pick up a handkerchief or glove she may have dropped, or, in short, perform any service for herself which you can perform for her." Men were to be especially attentive to and protective of women in public, although a few writers reminded husbands and brothers that the same attention was due at all times to their wives and sisters.[53]

The advice to men to perform services for women was far more elaborate and extensive than related instructions to class and age inferiors, even to domestic servants regarding their employers. The protective nature of men's services to women makes it doubtful that men were given more extensive instructions because they were considered more inferior than other inferiors. Rather, the extent of the advice tells us that proper regulation of the male-female relationship was of much concern, and that the creative function of ritual was being called into play. In other words, men needed much instruction in this area because they were taking on a new role.

The clearest and most novel manifestation of men's duty to protect was their responsibility to escort women in public. Young men were to begin with their sisters. Many authors told men to offer assistance to any unattended woman who appeared to need it, even a stranger. This attention was particularly important toward women encountered while traveling. In the street, a man was to offer his hand or arm whenever there was need, as when a woman got into or out of a carriage or crossed a plank over a puddle. Men were also to offer women an arm when walking or ascending steps together. Although a few authors stressed that a man was only to offer his arm when necessary, all agreed that he was never to fail to do so if it was, for instance, at night, in crowded places, or where the way was rough.[54]

There were many other attentions that men were to pay women in company. They were to offer to carry things and to find women seats. They were to leave the choice of amusements and the destination of excursions to the women of their party. They were even to offer assistance if a woman's shoe became untied. Some authors warned men not to be overassiduous in attending women, thereby degrading themselves and annoying the women. Some also cautioned men not to be overofficious in a woman's defense in public, as women preferred to handle small offenses quietly by themselves. In company, men were not to pay exclusive attention to the same woman but to let their courtesies be general. Still, these cautions must be measured against the huge quantity of advice that instructed men to serve women. Of course the authors generally conceived of male deference to women as something that took place within a middle-class world.[55]

Many examples of the ways in which men were to protect and assist women can be found in the discussions of visits, dinners, parties, and dances. Several authors for men encouraged visits to women; more simply assumed that men would do so. It was appropriate to visit a woman after escorting or meeting her at a party, for example, although it was not proper to bring a friend along without first securing her permission. Some authors observed that men would occasionally accompany women on visits, and told them to render the women every courtesy in entering and leaving. Men were to ask for the mistress, not the master, of the house when visiting. If a woman called at the same time, they were to escort her out if no other men were present and were to take their leave at that time if their own visit had been long enough. Isaac Mickle accordingly noted of a visit to Elizabeth Stivers that "the house beginning to fill up with company, and Angeline Turner starting to go home, the former was the cause and the latter the occasion of my withdrawing." The master of the house was to conduct a female visitor to the door himself and hand her into her carriage.[56]

At dinner parties, a man needed to escort the woman designated by his host into the dining room. Once arrived at the table, he was to bow and sit, after her, by her side. During the meal he had to wait on her, taking care "that the lady has all that she wishes, yet without appearing to direct your attention too much to her plate." Here as elsewhere, he was not to be overofficious in assisting; while he was to serve her, he did not need, several authors specified, to "pare an apple or a pear for a lady unless she desire you."[57]

Men had many attentions to pay to women at parties and balls. Upon entering, they were to lead the woman they escorted to the ladies' dressing room and repair themselves to the men's room to remove their coats and hats.

Then they were to meet their partners at the entrance of the women's room and conduct them into the parlor or ballroom. Isaac Mickle confirmed this itinerary when he reported conversing with George Dallas at a party while both waited for their partners. The chat ended when Mr. Dallas's "daughter appeared at the dressing-room door, and took him off." Recall that a man's first duty upon entering the company, whether accompanied or alone, was to seek out and greet the hostess; meanwhile the master of the house would be busy finding seats for female guests.[58]

Over the course of the evening, the men of the house were to entertain older women and quietly see that all the younger female guests had dancing partners. The male guests whom they asked to dance with wallflowers were supposed to assent to their requests with alacrity. A man was not to pay exclusive attention to the same woman, even one he had escorted. He was instead to introduce friends to her for the purpose of dancing. If a man wished to dance with a woman with whom he was not acquainted at a public ball, he was to ask the master of ceremonies to introduce him. Men were assured that no woman would agree to dance without an introduction. Isaac Mickle reveals the protective function of these rules when he once again obliges us by breaking them. He was at a public ball when the local sheriff and judge came in, both drunk, with exciting news of the Democratic Convention.

> Thereat I was so confounded that I really introduced Watson, in his booziness, to the belle of the room, Miss Doughten. . . . My head was so full of Convention and logrolling and wire-pulling . . . that I really forgot that it was hardly according to Gunter to ask the handsomest girl to dance with the most intoxicated man, in the room. However I got Miss Doughten's attendant, Benjamin H. Browning, to explain and apologize to her, and perhaps the matter will all be right.

It was understood that it was men's prerogative to ask women to dance; the authors only encouraged them to do so politely. But the writers also granted women some latitude. Although women were supposed to dance with any man who asked unless they were already engaged, at least twenty authors told men not to be offended if a woman refused them and then danced with another. If a woman replied she was engaged, a man was to ask her for a later dance, but he was not to ask the woman sitting next to her, lest the latter "feel hurt at being invited after another." On the dance floor, a man was to devote his entire attention to his partner. When the music stopped, he was to reconduct her to her place and thank her for the honor. He was to continue to offer his services after the set, by asking if she desired to promenade or be escorted to refreshments. He was not supposed to leave her until another man came up. At the end of the party he was to offer his arm to the woman he attended, in order to take leave, and then see her home. Some authors advised men who came alone to offer to attend unaccompanied women.

Men were thus to devote time to women in many ways during these social occasions, and all of this advice was new to the antebellum period. Men were also always to yield women the precedence. They generally had to name women first and present men to them when making introductions. They were to wait for women to sit down first in company and see that women were served before them. In these and other ways, then, men were to obey the rule of "ladies first." The few exceptions were necessitated by the pervasive requirement of protection. Men were only occasionally to encourage women to precede or pass before them when walking, for example; they were normally to walk at a woman's side. This rule differed from class and age deference, where superiors were more generally allowed to precede. Men were to precede women if necessary "to clear the way" for their safety and comfort, as when entering a crowded place or a place of public amusement (this rule at least parallels class deference, as servants were to do the same for their employers). A number of authors also told men to precede women in ascending a staircase, if there was not room for two to go abreast (in contrast to the rule for middle-class persons with class superiors).[59]

The rules of place paralleled the rules of precedence. Generally, men were to yield places of honor to women, such as the right-hand or wall side when passing or walking with them, but antebellum authors sometimes modified the traditional rule in the interest of protection. Men were always to give women the wall side of the staircase, for example, because, as one explained, it was farthest from the bannister and therefore safest. If two men were walking with a woman in the street, they were to stand on either side of her; if two women were walking with a man, he could walk between them (the traditional right of superiors) (but some authors considered it best for him to walk on the outside). When passing another man who was walking with a woman, a man was to walk on the woman's unprotected side. A few authors simply advised men to offer a woman either arm, depending on which side was safest. On horseback, men were generally to ride to the "off" or right side of women, though a man could ride between two women and a woman between two men—again, for the women's protection.[60]

Many writers discussed men's duty to secure seats for women. Like other inferiors, men were always to give women the best places. They were never to continue sitting if women lacked seats. This requirement caused Isaac Mickle some chagrin one evening when he accompanied the Sheppard girls to the Baptist church. "I observed on the road to Phoebe that if it were possible I was going to sit in the same pew with them," he wrote, "and sure enough I was just entering one after them when an old lady came along and lo! I had to back out to make room for her. Phoebe had a hearty laugh at my disappointment, and vexed as I was, I had to laugh too." Francis Lieber was a little less amused. Frustrated at the way he was obliged to give place to women at every crowded social event, he resolved "to get up a *Polite anti-ladies thronging-poor-men-out-of-every-chance-of-seeing-any-thing* Society."

The conduct writers also told men (but not other inferiors) to offer their seats to a woman less well-accommodated when traveling, and a number of writers specified that women were to be offered the best seats in a coach. European travelers often remarked on this custom, which they regarded as peculiarly American. Frederic Marryat described a young Englishman who was asked to "give up his place to a *lady*. Aware of the custom of the country, he immediately resigned his seat, and went to look for another." Whether or not a man was to relinquish his seat at a lecture, concert, or play depended on the circumstances. If the seats had not been reserved in advance and he was alone, he had to give his seat to a woman. If he accompanied a woman, he was to stay by her side. Men were always to offer women the front row in box seats, another custom noted by Dickens.[61]

Recall that the places of honor for men at the dinner table were at the sides of the hostess (the upper end of the table) and those for women at the sides of the host. Note the ambivalence of this rule from the gender perspective: while the upper end was the female end—that of the hostess—this was where the most distinguished male guests were placed, not the most distinguished female guests. Otherwise, male guests were to sit at the side of the woman they had accompanied into the dining room, at the place designated by the host or hostess. The "side-by-side" requirements of protective deference were overtaking the old above-and-below-the-salt rule.[62]

Salutations figured prominently in the new deference to women. Men were always to "bow with great politeness" upon introduction to women. It was the woman's prerogative, as a man's social superior, to extend a hand for a handshake. Recall that a man had to wait for a woman's nod of recognition before saluting her on subsequent occasions. This was all standard advice to inferiors, but the authors gave it to men regarding women more frequently than to class or age inferiors. A man was bound to return a woman's salute by bowing and raising his hat entirely off his head. Isaac Mickle reveals the importance of this gesture through his description of yet another awkwardness: "While there [at an auction] I met two of the Sheppards in company with Dr. Burroughs. They introduced me to Mrs. Smalley, the mother of my old school mate. This incident of my meeting these ladies there would not have been recorded here, but for the fact that I bowed so awkwardly to Miss Phoebe that I have been out of humour with myself all day." The next day he recorded: "This evening I called at Sheppards' . . . I entered with a firm intention to atone for my clumsiness in lifting my hat yesterday morning and I hope I succeeded." Like other inferiors, men were generally to remain uncovered if they stopped to converse with a woman, and to bow again on parting.

The writers also gave men a variety of instructions about salutations that they did not give other inferiors; these instructions suggest again the special intensity and protective nature of deference to women. When walking with a woman, a man was not to salute men with whom she was not acquainted, although he was to return the salutes of men who bowed on account of acquaintance with her. Men were to raise their hats to salute male friends accompanied by unfamiliar women. The hat-raising was made necessary by the presence of the women; the customary nod to male friends was not sufficient. If acquainted with both the man and the woman, a man was to bow to the woman first. Salutations also underscored the ritual nature of men's services to women by serving as punctuation for those services. A man was thus to doff his hat or bow when handing a woman into or out of a carriage, for example, or prior to running up the stairs before her.[63]

Protective deference to women is especially clear in these antebellum stage directions for social occasions, but it also seeped into the more traditional body-control advice. It was evident in the authors' extensive discussions of men's proper demeanor in the presence of women, for example, in contrast to the rather scant advice of revolutionary-era authors on this subject. Antebellum writers urged men to be gentle and attentive with all women, even strangers. Their warnings that men should not take their gallantry too far and be urgent, overly familiar, or officiously attentive are more evidence that the new gallantry was of a different sort than the more dangerous gallantry of the old seduction tales. Recall that a number of authors told young men that gallantry was best obtained by practicing at home with their mothers and sisters; several also reminded husbands to be attentive to their wives. Antebellum gallantry thus presents another example of the permeability of the line between the familial and social worlds.[64]

While antebellum authors gave men extensive advice designed to coach them in protective deference, they did not otherwise ask men to carry themselves any differently with women than in general society. The only posture rule that warranted discussion was another sign of deference: men were never to sit in the presence of women who were standing. They were to rise from their seats when women entered the room and to remain standing until all women present were seated, whether in a parlor, dining room, or church pew. In some cases, such as at a dance or during a walk in the country, a man was to refrain from sitting down at all unless the woman he accompanied invited him to. Whenever women in their presence had occasion to rise from their seats, whether to move across a room during a visit or to leave the table at a dinner party, men were to rise and remain standing until the women sat down again or left the room.[65]

Men also did not need to alter their talk much with women. While some authors advised them to "be particular in your discourse to the ladies," the rules for talk with women were little different from rules for talk in general society.[66] The only exceptions were some writers' claims that a loud tone was especially improper in the presence of women and that men should pay extra attention to their language before women. They were to address women correctly, avoiding "all mistimed or unsanctioned use of nick-names and Christian names." Some writers told men that it was especially important not to swear in the presence of women; more urged men not to use immodest language. Men were also to refrain from giving women immodest looks. While some writers continued to make the old claim that a woman's respectability would prevent men from looking "obscenely," the majority addressed men directly and urged them not to stare at women, especially in public.[67]

In revolutionary-era conduct works it had been up to women to inspire proper treatment and forestall improper treatment by men. But antebellum authors told men to watch their own behavior. Men were now asked to exercise self-control in the one area where revolutionary-era authors had let them off the hook. This is especially clear in prescriptions concerning physical closeness and body contact with women. Advice in these areas contradicts two ideas associated with the separate spheres model of nineteenth-century gender relations: the notion of physical distancing between men and women and the notion that chaste relations were guaranteed primarily by beliefs in female sexual passionlessness and moral superiority. Historians of courtship have already questioned the hold of these ideas in their surveys of men's and women's diaries and letters. But even they assume there was a line between private and public behavior, that sexual distancing was the norm in the latter, and that it was a norm supported by conduct advice. It was not.[68]

A few conduct writers did instruct men not to come too close to women. They were to sit "at some distance" when visiting. They needed a woman's permission to sit next to her at a dance. They were to avoid leaning on or over women, passing between them, or coming so close as to disturb their dresses. And they were not to crowd women in door- or passageways.[69] But some of these injunctions applied to men in general society as well. More important, more of the advice to men on behavior with women assumed or required a great deal of physical propinquity.

The rules directing men to sit next to women at the dinner table, for example, obviously called for some closeness. Many other rules assumed not only physical proximity but considerable physical contact. Consider all the admonitions to men to give an arm to a woman they escorted or a hand to a woman needing assistance (and men's diaries amply confirm that they had many opportunities for these gestures, in private homes, at public amusements, and on the street). Contemplate the difficulty of all this arm-tendering if a man did not walk close to a woman's side. To a far greater degree than in the previous era, or even present-day life, then, the social world painted by antebellum advisors is not one of men and women avoiding each other but of men and women clinging to each other. The conduct injunctions belie the notion that Victorian advice literature promoted distancing between the sexes.[70]

Touching between men and women was not confined to the hand-over-arm negotiation of hallways, streets, and staircases. A man would touch a woman if he followed the advice on the proper way to help her mount and dismount a horse. Customarily, one author explained, the woman takes

> the reins in her right hand, and places her left on the shoulder of the gentleman, who stoops before her making a stirrup of his clasped hands. Raising himself gently, the lady is placed in the saddle. The gentleman puts her foot in the stirrup, adjusts her dress, [and] mounts his horse . . . In dismounting, the lady having lifted her foot from the stirrup . . . may be received in the gentleman's arms.

Not only do the authors' many mentions of dancing imply that body contact between men and women was permitted, but some of their instructions mention touching explicitly. A number of authors counseled men to lead a woman gently by simply touching her fingers, rather than rudely grasp her hand "as if it were made of wood." Waltzing required a greater degree of body contact, and the authors warned men that "if a lady dance with you, beware not to press her waist; you must only lightly touch it with the open palm of your hand, lest you leave a disagreeable impression not only on her ceinture, but on her mind." The authors went so far as to instruct men to aid women in putting on coats and fixing disarrayed dress. Several counseled, for example, that should a woman's "shoe become unlaced, or her dress in any manner disordered, fail not to apprise her of it, respectfully, and offer your assistance. A gentleman may hook a dress or lace a shoe with perfect propriety, and should be able to do so gracefully."[71]

But antebellum authors, far more than their predecessors, also asked men to observe some limits on physical contact with women. Recall that handshakes were only to be initiated by women; and men were reminded not to retain a woman's hand any longer than necessary.[72] The authors also urged men not to attempt "personal familiarities" with women. One told men not to nudge women during conversation. Another told men not to put an arm around a woman in a carriage. A third told young men not to seize a young woman by the body or catch hold of her dress. Several authors spoke disapprovingly of kissing games, and urged men not to "abuse the freedom which the laws of the game allows; but if required . . . delicately kiss the hand, the forehead, or, at most, the cheek of the lady." Some authors gave men more general warnings against undue physical intimacy with women. One told boys to "avoid all personal freedoms" with girls. Another advised young men, regarding their lady loves, to "be very certain of the nature of your relation to each other, before you indulge in any personal familiarities." Others told men not to take any physical advantage over the "weaker sex" or frankly urged them not to seduce women. Never before had conduct writers made such demands of men. The older ethic of physical self-control had now expanded to sexuality, at least in the middle-class world. And diaries such as Isaac Mickle's confirm that men internalized these strictures. While some historians of men have noted this ethic of male sexual continence in other nineteenth-century sources, it has not been sufficiently acknowledged in discussions of women's experience.[73] Yet it was crucial in removing barriers to middle-class women's full inclusion in the social world, for it made that world safe.

OF COURSE THIS protective deference was not true deference, for women were not really men's superiors, nor did it come without a price. There are only occasional similarities between antebellum counsels to women about behavior with men and instructions to middle-class adults about behavior with their class- and age inferiors. Men were not so much women's inferiors as their protectors; the deference they were to pay was that of the stronger to the weaker sex. Perhaps this is why the authors constantly felt it necessary to state that women were men's social superiors, while they took the superiority of masters over servants and adults over children for granted. Most of the advice to women consisted of recommendations that they passively and, above all, gratefully, accept men's attentions. Women were to show their appreciation in their demeanor, facial expressions, gestures, and talk. It was important that women accept men's attentions in the right spirit; between the lines of the authors' claims that women were men's superiors were their continual reminders that women did not actually have any right to this deference.

Antebellum authors expected and encouraged women to spend time with men; they especially encouraged sisters to cultivate the companionship of their brothers. Further, antebellum writers pressed women to seek male accompaniment in their social lives. Women were assured, for example, that they could make social calls attended by a gentleman, even one unknown to the party they were visiting. They could also ask an uninvited man as an escort to a ball or party. That the purpose of these rules was to obtain male protection for women is revealed by the fact that men were not allowed the same privileges; moreover, one author prefaced his advice with the admonition, "[I]f possible do not enter a [ball]room alone."[74]

There is a certain irony to this sort of encouragement of contact with men. Underlying the advice to women to have male protection, especially in public, was the suggestion that what such an escort prevented was contact with "bad" men. This presented a problem as regarded young unmarried women: the authors vacillated on the propriety of male escorts for them because the escort himself might pose a danger. Married women were less of a problem; it was expected that they would be escorted by their husbands to social engagements, and they were deemed in less danger on the streets (they were allowed to go visiting by themselves and even to refuse an offer of accompaniment home after an evening visit). But young women always required an escort. Some authors had no problem with their accepting men's offers to accompany them home from a visit or a party, but others were wary of young women's attending such events alone with men. Most preferred that young women be accompanied to balls and parties by their mothers or a male relation "of respectable age."[75]

Some authors showed the same ambivalence when they discouraged young women from spending time alone with men. Several advised young women to decline men's invitations to go out unless another woman was invited. Some claimed that it was not proper for young women to receive male company apart from the rest of the family. Betrothal gave a girl a bit more freedom to be with her fiance; married women and young widows were allowed even more, and could visit and walk alone with men "of good morals."[76]

To deal with the problem of "bad" men, the authors promoted women's right as social superiors to grant or deny men access to their company. They encouraged women to choose male acquaintance on the basis of character. They were to avoid any men who were even suspected of loose morals or impertinent behavior. When Isaac Mickle and his friend Ned King proposed an excursion to the Sheppard sisters, for example, Phoebe took Isaac aside and told him that "she did not like to go with King, since from his character and disposition she feared he might have too many roué acquaintances, especially as he had played [in the orchestra] in the theaters." While Isaac felt "it is too bad for him to have the cold shoulder given him thus," he agreed that King deserved it, "for not having kept better company." It was the woman's prerogative to decide whether to allow a man to visit her and whether (and at what level) to continue an acquaintanceship with him. And antebellum writers reminded women of their right to initiate encounters in public. Of course a woman was not supposed to "cut" a man to whom she had been properly introduced; but while she was obligated to bow, she could also treat him cooly and thereby communicate her disinterest. Women were also to control the duration of encounters with men, whether on the street, at a visit, or during a party. If a man treated a woman disrespectfully, she was to turn away immediately.[77]

While these rules accorded with the superior's traditional right to control the degree of contact with inferiors and had the effect of giving women the right to decide on a man's respectability, it is clear from the way the rules were tailored that their intent was more to protect than to empower women. Some customs took control over contact with men out of women's hands. Most authors claimed that a woman was not entitled to refuse a man's invitation to dance, for example, unless she had already accepted that of another. A number of writers urged women more generally never to do anything to solicit a man's attention; they were to wait to be chosen by men. Recall as well that women could not make social calls to men.[78] Above all, many authors informed women that they should not regard men's favors as a right, and were never to require too much or put men's complaisance to a test. They were to respond to every favor with gracious appreciation. T. S. Arthur echoed many writers when he warned young women:

> By always remembering that they have *no real title* to a preference in every thing, they will be sure to receive with a proper feeling, and a proper acknowledgement of the *kindness*, all polite attentions and preferences that are accorded to them by the other sex. . . . [T]he generous self-denial made for your comfort, at the same time that it is accepted, should always be retained with an air that shows you feel it to be a *favor*, and not a *right* to which you are entitled (emphasis added).

No superior in the early colonial or revolutionary periods was ever given such advice.

To underscore the counsel that women were not to regard men's deference as a right does not deny that men's attentions to women were to be extensive; one author went so far as to recommend that women not do anything without a man's assistance. The fact that another author felt it necessary to assure women that they were allowed to help themselves when refreshments were handed around at a party suggests just how extensive men's attentions were otherwise expected to be.[79] Relative to what they asked men to do for women, the authors gave women little direct advice about attentions they were to pay to men. In fact, some authors told women to withhold from men some of the attentions they owed other women, such as putting aside needlework when they visited, or seeing them to the street door at the end of a call.

The only instances in which the authors advised women to devote time and attention to men were a few admonitions to wives and daughters to provide comforts to husbands and fathers.[80]

Women also had a rather passive role as regarded place and precedence in their encounters with men. They had merely to stand back and receive men's attentions gracefully. They were to allow men to find them seats, but they were never to seem impatient if an assemblage was crowded and their escort needed time. Many authors urged women never to take such courtesy for granted or to claim a place as their right. They deplored some women's habit of standing at the end of a crowded bench at a church, concert, or lecture (or the door of a coach or omnibus) until they forced a man to give them the seat he had acquired by coming early. Moreover, the authors claimed, all men's offers of seats were to be acknowledged with thanks. The only time women had to offer men seats was when men entered the parlor on a visit.[81]

We have seen that the advice to men contradicts the notion of Victorian distancing between the sexes. The same is true of advice to women. Two authors did tell young women not to get too close to young men. Historian Barbara Welter quoted one of them in her pioneer article on "true womanhood": "Mrs. Eliza Ware Farrar, in *The Young Ladies Friend*, gave practical logistics to avoid trouble: 'Sit not with another in a place that was too narrow; read not out of the same book; let not your eagerness to see anything induce you to place your head close to another person's.' If such good advice were ignored, [Welter added] the consequences were terrible and inexorable." The passage from Mrs. Farrar seems unambiguous, and there is more to it. She went on to suggest that if a young man admired a young woman's brooch, she ought to "draw back and take it off for inspection" rather than to allow him to examine it on her person. But Welter's use of this advice is testimony to the need for systematic analysis of conduct literature, because it is almost unique. There is very little other advice like it. In fact, there is evidence that contemporaries positively objected to this sort of advice. One female book reviewer commented on the same passage in Farrar:

> We object to the method and spirit of these directions. . . . In the first place, the style of manners here prescribed implies great want of confidence in the other sex. It presupposes that they are not worthy of trust; that they have neither delicacy nor honour; that they are on the alert to take advantage of the slightest circumstance which they can possibly turn to advantage in prosecuting sinister ends. If such were the race of man, it would be quite wrong to trust young ladies in society at all; the best and most proper expedient would be a grand universal nunnery.

Welter cited Farrar as part of her case for the hold of the ideal of female purity. But in a complete reversal of that argument—that female sexual purity was the lynchpin of Victorian notions of female moral influence—this reviewer went on to suggest that because "Primness and prudishness are so repugnant to the taste of gentlemen," to adopt such behavior would also "rob women of their influence over men." The sentiments expressed in this review are more typical of the conduct literature than Mrs. Farrar's advice. Farrar's admonitions are canceled out by the frequent discussions of "boy-girl-boy-girl" seating at dinner parties, women taking men's arms, and dancing, which implied that women would be in frequent close physical proximity to men. One author thus told women to "walk near" to the side of a man whose arm she took, "only keeping at such a distance as will enable them to walk with ease."[82]

To be sure, antebellum conduct advisors did pay lip service to the ideal of female purity, but their advice added up to a more complex picture. The writers nodded in the direction of purity in their extensive advice to women on proper demeanor with men, for example, but this advice must be considered in context. The most desirable qualities in a woman's manner with men were the "modesty" of the revolutionary era tempered by a new antebellum goal of "self-possession." "Purity" was recommended, but not nearly as often. A modest and dignified demeanor was thought to display a woman's virtue and thereby ensure respectful behavior from men. Some writers continued to recommend a certain reserve with men, especially impertinent men, and many warned women not to be too forward. They were to be civil but not coquettish. To this extent, the demeanor advice did amount to practical instructions to maintain purity. But this was mostly old advice that predated the supposed rise of the ethic of female purity. Many authors also cautioned women not to be too reserved, bashful, or prudish in manner. Some even argued that women did not need to put on any particular manner in the presence of men; it was best to act with the same ease and openness they would have with other women.

Further, antebellum authors devoted considerable space to new advice that women respond to men's courtesies with a civil, kind, and grateful manner. Some authors added that young women were not to pay too much heed to men's attentions; they were a matter of course, not a sign of particular devotion. Thus the revolutionary-era advice that women protect themselves with a modest demeanor can be found in the antebellum period, but it was surrounded by other suggestions that women could look to men more for civility than seduction.[83]

The same mix of ideas—older injunctions to put up a guard lest men behave improperly, new injunctions to receive men's deference with grace, and a prevailing notion that a woman really did not have to put on any particular manner with men—is evident in the authors' few remarks to women about body carriage before men. Reflecting the persistence of older fears, for example, a few authors warned women not to turn their heads from side to side when walking in the street as "this bad habit seems to be an invitation to the impertinent." Revealing new expectations of female social superiority, however, the authors assured women that they did not have to rise from their seats when men entered a room. Overall, it appears that women did not need to pay any special attention to their motions in the presence of men. Antebellum discussions of dancing and horseback riding remind us that women were allowed some freedom of movement before men; only one author cautioned girls that "the sports in which boys usually engage are improper for your sex."[84]

Suggestions about facial expression were similar. Here, too, a woman best behaved naturally. The most frequent recommendations were that they simply smile at men. Reflecting the mix of old and new concerns, they were especially to smile in acknowledgement of men's services; but they were not to smile at men's improprieties. They were to give men grateful looks as thanks for services, but they were not to stare or give men "wanton looks," which dared men "to speak and act in a more free and unguarded manner than they otherwise would have the boldness to do." Note that it was no longer presumed that men would necessarily be bold in the first place.[85]

Antebellum-era conduct writers assumed that women would have many occasions to talk with men, and they claimed here too that women did not need to put on any particular manner; they were simply to converse with the same ease and sociability as they would with other women. Some authors did give the traditional suggestions that speaking in a dignified and modest manner would check men's attempts at improper familiarity. Yet these older cautions were again balanced by the new requests that women be courteous in making requests and never fail to acknowledge men's services with thanks.[86] The Victorian penchant for formality of address shows up in advice for women concerning men, but within limits. Wives were to refer to their spouses by their full names, with the prefix Mr., rather than as "my husband" or "Mr. B." Generally, they were only to use his first name in private. Several authors warned young women not to address men unrelated to them by their first names. But women were not to sprinkle their talk with "sirs" unless the man was aged, or they wished to be very reserved.[87] The writers did not give women any other specific advice regarding choice of language with men beyond warnings against immodest talk. A few authors gave traditional advice that focused on how women should react to men's use of such language; but more antebellum authors asked women themselves to avoid it. As immodesty was a perennial concern regarding talk between the sexes, this trend illustrates gender convergence in conduct rules more than a rise of female purity.[88] Advice to women regarding the matter of their talk with men differed little from advice on talk in general society.[89]

Antebellum conduct advice to women shows the same expectations of body contact between the sexes seen in advice to men. There were restrictions, to be sure. As we have seen, women were to be conservative in arm-taking, in handshaking, and in kissing games. Some authors warned women more generally against taking or allowing "personal familiarities" with men. In contrast to the revolutionary era, however, antebellum writers did not give women more advice than they gave men on these points. Chastity was still important in women, but the real change was the appearance of demands that men control themselves. The sense of danger for middle-class women was much diminished in antebellum advice.[90] The advisors assured women that they had to be grateful for men's restraint, but they could usually count on it.

This new male self-restraint has not received much notice in historians' accounts of female purity. Even historians of men have only just begun to explore its causes. One has suggested that it resulted from a "growing closeness and emotional power of the mother-son bond."[91] Such a connection could help to explain the new deference to women. But the role that manners tended to play in reconciling cultural contradictions suggests that an overarching explanation lies in the struggle to find a place for women in the new order. Protective deference allowed for the ritual cloaking of continuing female inequality while at the same time securing women's allegiance by requiring sacrifices on the part of men for women's safety. Perhaps this is what allowed the authors, to a much greater degree than before, to depict men and women casually hanging on to each other. Perhaps there was more sexual distancing in the earlier period because there was thought to be more sexual danger. To be sure, women continued to be molested in antebellum America. The authors did imply the continued existence of "bad" men, but at least male protection was now part of the code of respectability. That surely added to its appeal.

ANTEBELLUM CONDUCT WRITERS were clearly wrestling with the contradiction between persisting gender inequality and a supposedly democratic society, because their advice, especially their newest and most elaborate advice, revolved around gender. Their gender focus suggests that this was the greatest conflict with which they and their audience had to come to terms. Unlike the middle class and youth, women had not really gained much power; more important, they had no hopes of growing or earning their way out of their position. The only way middle-class northern Americans could integrate women into the democratic social order was to build a ritual monument to gender—to pronounce women as superior to men in the social world but also as needing men's protection. They thus included women in this world but on a protective pedestal. This monument, "ladies first," helped to draw attention away from persisting inequality. In this sense, it served the same function as the trope of separate spheres, another convenient distraction from unequal power relations between men and women.[92]

In fact, the centrality of gender in antebellum etiquette suggests that the elaborate rituals of "ladies first" played an even greater role in cloaking cultural conflict than simply distracting Americans from persisting gender inequality. It appears that focussing on gender also allowed Americans to ignore class. For adherence to "ladies first" was the sine qua non of the middle-class gentleman and democratic manners. A good number of authors linked "ladies first" with democratic America. Eliza Farrar claimed: "It is hardly possible for the protection and the services, needed by the weaker sex, to be given on a better footing than they are in this country." Another author simply declared that "Civility to women characterizes American manners, long may it continue so." And they were not alone. Here was one point on which native-born and foreign commentators agreed.[93] In providing a focus for antebellum "democratic" manners, "ladies first" served as a distraction from both real gender inequality and the class exclusivity of the code.

We have long recognized the gender inequality behind the pedestal (antebellum feminists recognized it right away). What has been overlooked is the way it allowed full integration of women in the social world, and also the fact that this new treatment of women entailed as much or more change in men's behavior as in women's. Both features help to answer a question that historians have not really dealt with: Why did this system suffice for so many women and men, for so long? The answer lies in the bargain made at the moment of female inclusion in the new world of peers. Revolutionary-era fathers and mothers had fretted over the sexual vulnerability of women in the modern world of individual strivers. They could only urge their daughters to arm themselves with modesty. These fears help us to understand the seductive appeal of antebellum protection. Men would control themselves and grant women a sort of social preeminence. While the path they took might seem in hindsight to have been the long way round to equality, perhaps we can understand it better if we recognize the promise of safety that it held out. Yes, this ceremonial compensation for inequality became a tenacious female handicap. In spreading a chivalrous ritual mantle over the cultural contradiction between gender inequality and democracy, it also obscured it for many, then and since. Jurgen Habermas noted the class contradiction at the core of the bourgeois order some time ago, when he pointed out that the equation of bourgeois and "man" was a fiction. "Ladies first" both helped to enact and allows us to see the fiction of gender equality of that same order.[94]

But while a cloak for inequality, we should recognize that this compensatory deference also provided a cover for gender integration and intimacy in the social world, rather than separation and distance. It is hardly a revelation to note that this system has been so hard to root out simply because it was so cozy. And we should not underrate the full social inclusion that the system allowed. Around the rituals of "ladies first" milled men and women who otherwise acted the same. That reminder should steady us now, as we aim to kick away the pedestal once and for all.

Conclusion: Social Ritual and Democracy

A two-tiered system of inequality developed during the antebellum era. Within the social world of middle- and upper-class adult men and women there existed a ritually obscured inequality, while a more open inequality persisted between members of this circle and marginal groups. The few counsels to lower-class servants about behavior in the presence of their masters and those directed to children about behavior with mature adults were the most similar, although to a lesser degree than in earlier periods. These groups were asked to pay traditional deference to their superiors, acts that would symbolize and ritually reinforce the great inequality that existed between them. Compared to earlier periods, however, the traditional deference advice of the antebellum era was muted, and it had evolved to differentiate the two relations to which it continued to apply. Thus the authors justified servants' duty to respect their masters' control of their time by pointing to the contractual basis of this relationship, while they gave children advice about their parents' control of their time that reflected the persisting paternalistic and pedagogical character of this relationship.

Whether middle-class persons interacting with class superiors or youth and adults interacting with the aged, these groups were asked to pay the new, more ceremonial, and, in the latter case, actually "protective" kind of deference to their superiors. Such deference did not symbolically reinforce the actors' inferiority as did traditional shows of deference. The advice to men on proper behavior with women was the chief and most complex example of the new kind of deference, for its ramifications were spelled out in a whole variety of social situations. The advice to middle-class persons regarding class superiors and to youth and adults regarding the aged were more general echoes of this same kind of deference.

With respect to antebellum advice on proper behavior with peers, the lower class and children again prove to have been out-groups, for they were only occasionally given some of this advice, while all of it was dispensed to the middle class, adults and youth, men and women. The scant counsels to lower-class servants and young children only served to set them off from the social world portrayed in antebellum manners. Those few middle-class authors of antebellum-era works who bothered to address members of the serving class took pains to point out that most of the behaviors proper in ladies and gentlemen were not appropriate in them. Children were only given the by now traditional body-control instructions; their segregation from the social world is thus revealed by the authors' failure to give them any of the new stage directions for social life.

That women were very often given the same advice men were given on proper behavior with class and age peers suggests that they, like middle-class persons and youth, had become fully integrated in the social world by the antebellum decades. But the fact that women were sometimes given advice that indicated they had a special "protected" status in the social world reveals that they were not incorporated as men's equals. The persistence of some strains of revolutionary-era gender differentiation—women were to be more modest than were men; men were to pay greater attention to control of their bodies than were women—reinforces this conclusion. In contrast, there were only faint suggestions that middle-class persons and youth were not completely equal partners in society with upper-class persons and mature adults.

Comparison of the advice to different superiors chiefly serves to differentiate class, age, and gender relations. Advice to middle-class masters concerning lower-class servants and to mature adults respecting children were again the most similar, and the existence of both groups of inferiors was to be ignored when middle-class adults entertained their peers. But mature adults were given very little advice on proper behavior with youth, and the advice to women on proper behavior with men bore only superficial resemblance to the advice for other superiors. Clearly class, age, and gender relations were no longer simply perceived as ramifications of the same overarching hierarchical or organic metaphor for society.

Because deference to superiors was no longer the ruling principle in ante-bellum-era manners, it is difficult to compare the statuses of different groups. Lower-class servants and children were obviously on the bottom of the social scale, but it is equally clear that there was no longer a single social ladder. Class, age, and gender relations were all understood to have different bases. While children and servants were to exhibit traditional deference from the margins of the social world, within that world deference now had a different meaning. Because of their political beliefs, the middle-class authors of ante-bellum etiquette wanted to pretend that all within the social world met on a footing of equality. Manners prescriptions reveal that they had little trouble in perceiving middle-class persons as the equals of upper-class persons and youth as the equals of adults. They did run into problems when it came to dis-cussing behavior toward women and aged persons, and thus they endorsed a new kind of deference that would ceremonially compensate those who had al-ways been, and continued to be, actually regarded as weak.

The task of manners in the antebellum era was to resolve the questions raised by the revolutionary-era opening of possibilities for past inferiors. In answering those questions, northern Americans in general and manners writ-ers in particular were wrestling with what the code of conduct should be in a democratic society. There was conflict between what they wanted to profess about the nature of their society and what the powerful among them were ac-tually willing to grant and to accept in terms of equality. It was thus by ex-cluding some and offering token deference to others that northerners were able to avoid acknowledging the continuing reality of inequality. It was thus that manners writers made the limits of democracy very clear, even in the middle-class world they described.

CONCLUSION

I saac Mickle read Chesterfield's *Principles of Politeness* with the expectation that it would turn him into a graceful man. Of course it didn't. Though Mickle read Chesterfield several times, he remained awkward. At fifteen, for example, he recorded upsetting a platter of ham at a table, and exclaimed to his diary: ". . . to think of making such an awkward splash, after having read Chesterfield's *Principles of Politeness*."[1] This was three years before he resolved to return to Chesterfield for help with his bow. Apparently, Chesterfield did not help Mickle much. And Mickle belittled Chesterfield in other diary entries. But he clearly regarded this conduct book as a resource in his social relations. Even though he remained inept, Mickle's diary reflects both the rituals and the preoccupations of antebellum conduct literature.

In proferring the little rules for behavior that we call manners, conduct writers were describing ritual responses to central problems in American culture. It is unlikely that Mickle would have recognized this—would have recognized, for example, the social function of his bow. He simply internalized the standards of his time, so that to him it was just the right thing for a respectable person like himself to do.[2] In fact, it is not even clear that the codifiers of the little rules, the authors of the conduct literature, were aware of the ritual functions of manners. Some betrayed a glimmer of understanding; more were simply meeting their society's demand for digests of the code. Often enough, the code contradicted the statements of purpose they made in their prefaces. With the perspective of hindsight and that provided by the study of other cultures, however, we can read the code and begin to understand how it functioned in past time. Along the way, we can use manners to compare different social relations and follow their evolution over time. We can also hark back to those various individuals who have illustrated for us—through their frustrations, ambitions, and assorted faux-pas—the roles of manners in their lives.

WE BEGAN WITH the hot-headed Governor Dudley and the mild-mannered Samuel Sewall. Despite the differences in their temperaments, behaving like gentlemen and being deferred to as such by their inferiors was of consuming importance to these members of the provincial elite in Puritan New England. Such performances would both enact their traditional hierarchical world view and uphold their power. These magistrates, and their fellow leaders in the ministry, attempted to set themselves off from those below them by adopting and enforcing among themselves a code of gentlemanly behavior akin to that set out in the Continental and British courtesy books on their shelves. They campaigned for deference on the part of the middling and lower sort in their frequent and influential sermons. And they had some success in securing deference, in part because they were able to pursue the same social goals through control of the religious and juridical institutions of their face-to-face society. But they did not get as much deference as they wanted, for several reasons. First, they were claiming a status they would not have been able to attain in the old world. Second, rapid economic change in the mother country was already undermining the traditional foundations of hierarchy. The situation was worsened by the contractual and voluntaristic nature of their particular religious, political, and familial ideology and the leveling material conditions of the New World. Perhaps it was these challenges that continued to spur their quest for deference, for it remained constant, despite their religious preoccupations and despite the ups and downs of the first century of leadership. It appears, too, that they undermined their own campaign, for they insisted on keeping a monopoly on gentility. While they demanded deference, they did not give the populace any further training in courteous behavior, and hence self-control. The people would bow, but only to external pressures.

The desire to maintain inequality in the face of challenges pervaded the elite's discussions of all early New English social relations. While age inequality was both more fundamental and more secure than class inequality in early New England, youth still presented a potential challenge in this land-rich, labor-poor, and youthful society. The conduct literature suggests that the Puritans used the institution of service both to keep adolescents in their place and to create an artificial lower class. That the ambitions of the middle-aged ruling elite were the driving force behind the manners system in early colonial New England is also suggested by the fact that only lip-service was paid to the notion that the aged should be venerated. While Samuel Sewall returned his aged father's hand-kiss, his fellow-magistrate Wait Winthrop felt no need to do so. Early New England was not a gerontocracy.

It was, of course, a patriarchy. Deference to the middle-aged elite was deference to men. Frustrated as she was in obtaining deference during her trip through New England, Madam Knight would agree—as would Mistress Philips, who even tried to bow to a younger minister from her sickbed. Sewall, who recorded everything, did not record any special treatment of women, even those he courted. To the degree that deference was expected in relations between men and women, it was from women to men. This gender inequality is clearest in discussions of marriage, but that was the arena for most of the gendered advice of the period. Gender differentiation was hardly necessary otherwise, for the rest of early New English conduct advice depicted a man's world. But the courtesy-book code for behavior with peers, while clearly for men, was confined to the elite. So the discussions of marriage are important in defining both femininity and masculinity for ordinary folk as well as the special nature of gender inequality. Ordinary men were instructed as women's superiors (to ensure family order), and this may have served to secure their own commitment to hierarchy. Marital roles also had to be considered because they presented a special case in the period's various inequalities. Comparison with class and age relations shows that gender inequality was lesser than these other inequalities, and it was the sexual tie between men and women that made the difference. Women needed to be modest as well as deferential.

In the early colonial period, then, the foremost social function of manners was the social control function. The elite used manners, along with other institutions, to uphold hierarchy—to enforce inequality where it was undergoing challenge. But because the most elaborate manners (the most elaborate self-control instructions) were confined to the elite, this society had to continue to rely heavily on external controls for behavior. That is why local court records have been such a fruitful source for historians. The manners evidence tells us much, especially about the fond wishes of the elite, but in the end that evidence needs to be read along with the other records—those of external coercion.

Manners became more important to northern Americans in the revolutionary era because the elite gradually lost their monopoly on proper behavior. By the mid-eighteenth century, British writers of the middling sort began to offer the secrets of gentility, in concentrated form, to the prosperous and ambitious of their own class. In so doing, they were working out the social and behavioral implications of the great intellectual, economic, and political ferment that was bringing down the old order and giving birth to modern society. Even as these writers and their consumers rejected old notions of ascriptive social status and aristocratic rule, however, they found the kernel of traditional gentility enormously useful for their own ambitions. That kernel was, of course, self-control, the perfect exercise and emblem for self-made men.

Consistent with the larger Enlightenment project, these authors not only borrowed but transformed the code of gentility by dropping old demands of deference for their class and focusing on relations between equals. True to their politics, they were squeamish about overt assertions of inequality. They abhored servility in their own behavior and hesitated to lord it over their inferiors. They concentrated on helping their class acquire the behavior appropriate to a new, more elevated social status by greatly elaborating on the old body-control advice of the original Renaissance treatises. Their works found a ready market among prosperous, educated, and ambitious persons of middling origins in all the northern American towns. We saw how obsessed the young John Adams was with his own and others' body carriage, facial expressions, and demeanor. We saw how Benjamin Rush both fretted over his children's carriage and assured them that hard work was the honorable way to success. These men confirm the message of the conduct literature—that there was a link between the new obsession with body control and the culture that would come to be associated with the middle class.

Manners suggest, then, that the late eighteenth century saw the beginnings of cultural assertion among the more ambitious of the middling sort. These men wanted no masters but themselves, a concern that even found expression in their attitudes toward deportment. Their interest in self-mastery explains the popularity of Chesterfieldian instructions in this vein, despite their concern about the source. It also explains their desire to avoid affectation, another new theme in middling conduct advice. True self-mastery meant that one's behavior would appear "artless." As Chesterfield nagged his son, this required years of practice. Dancing masters were doubtless grateful for the work.

While the middling were destroying hierarchy, however, there were hints that this would be one of the many halfway revolutions of the era. For they did not take pains to include the lower sort; they did not protest servile behavior among servants. They pledged to be more gentle in their dealings with the lower sort but did not pass on the tools for self-mastery. More perniciously, though perhaps unintentionally, in describing a world of peers they were setting up the fiction of a universally middle-class America that has caused so much social blindness ever since.

The bourgeois revolution had age and gender components. To create men who were masters of themselves required changes in child-rearing, or at least the treatment of youth. As confirmed in both the personal writings of men like Rush and John Bartram, and the conduct advice of fathers like Chesterfield, John Locke supplied the recipe. Because the goal was autonomy, there was a turning away from traditional overt controls over youth, whether corporal punishment or the institution of service (now regarded as a class rather than an age relation). How was the new scheme to work in face-to-face relations? The conduct evidence indicates that, in practice, Lockean education was like innoculation. Youth were exposed to adult society in order to develop internal defenses. This was the strategy John Bartram recommended to his children. The patterns in manners suggest that, to a great degree, this meant treating youth like adults. In the end, however, the Lockean scheme required a leap of faith. As parents launched their adolescent children into the world, they could only hope, as Benjamin Rush did, that those self-control mechanisms were in working order.

Lockean child-rearing did not require much change in the treatment of young children, as Locke thought that more overt control was warranted in this relation. The conduct advice in fact reflects considerable stability in expectations and treatment of young children (as it does regarding the aged). A gap was thus beginning to grow between attitudes toward children and attitudes toward youth.

A gap was narrowing in gender relations, contrary to prevailing accounts. Benjamin Rush again serves to illustrate the trend. Rush has long been acknowledged as one of the architects of the "Republican Mother" role for women in the new nation. This association of women with maternity, domesticity, virtue, and exclusion from direct participation in the polity has long been regarded as a stepping stone to a separation of the world into male and female spheres in nineteenth-century thought and practice. But Rush's personal writings tell us something that has been overlooked in this scenario, which is that this effort to distinguish male and female spheres was premised on the inclusion of women in the social vision in the first place. Men like Rush and Adams regarded women as important actors in their social world. They no longer saw women only as wives and were no longer comfortable with simple assertions of female inferiority. They had similar expectations of male and female behavior. All these themes of gender integration in the social world and convergence of expectations for male and female behavior were major motifs in the rules for face-to-face behavior. And this pattern seems the result of a conscious campaign on the part of middling writers, for they expended the most ink on the education of women. The middling were clearly groping for a place for women in the new liberal order.

Inviting women to enter the new social world did raise a problem. As communal controls for behavior were dropped for individualism, women's sexuality brought new risks. Women were now responsible for their own sexual fate, at the same time that they became responsible for their fate on the marriage market. This left them with the tricky task of "obliging, without invitation." The conduct writers could only appeal to the old requirement of female modesty to serve as a woman's armor. Shorn of the old demands that women also defer to men, modesty now stood alone as the chief requirement for female behavior. It was the only way the authors asked women to behave any differently from men.

Men were given somewhat more elaborate advice than were women. It was to men that the period's most extensive instructions for control of the body were addressed. This makes sense, as self-presentation was even more important for middle-class men than for women, faced as they were with ever more competitive market relations. It was still a man's world, indeed increasingly a man's world, in the economic and political realms despite the inclusion of women in the social world. The worlds of family and society, however, were not women's worlds. Men were still very involved in family life. They also continued to hold the reins of power in the intimate realm, for all the burden of sexual self-control lay on women. The unfairness of this double standard gives an unfinished feeling to the revolutionary etiquette of gender relations. The search for a comfortable place for women in the new order would continue.

In this revolutionary age, the way the middling challenged the hegemony of the former elite was to disseminate prescriptions for self-control to those—their own class, youth, and women—who before had only been asked to defer. They lost interest in deference, that is, in using manners to uphold inequality, in all of these relations. The more important social function of manners in this period was its creative function; the middling, youth, and women received new instructions for new behaviors that would allow them to assume new positions in society. We should note that in all three cases this was a transatlantic, or at least an Anglo-American, development, although the results may have appeared more dramatic in the context of the American Revolution. As the cultural ideal of inequality was replaced by its opposite, the possibilities seemed endless.

And yet the great middling revolution found its limits rather quickly. Clues to the future were already evident in the revolutionary era, when despite a desire to soften former inequality it was nevertheless apparent that the bourgeois liberation program did not include servants or young children. The manners solution to the cultural challenge posed by the ideal of equality became very clear in the antebellum decades. Because the middle class had created a world of peers, they were forced to exclude those whom they could not accept as equal: children and servants were banished to the wings.

We saw reflections of the antebellum conduct-book world in Isaac Mickle's diary; Mickle's world, too, was a largely self-referential world of peers. In his world the middling and the wealthy, adults and youth, men and women all met on a footing of equality. Servants, in contrast, were expected to be mere props-, at most, stagehands—for middle-class performances. In his book and the etiquette books, members of the lower classes were almost regarded as members of a different species. Distrust was palpable. Hints here and there make it clear that the increasingly immigrant identity of the serving classes helped to create that alienation.

But how was it to be enacted, in this so-called democracy? As the middling seized the reins of gentility, they used manners to delineate and solidify their new status, to set themselves off from the lower sort. Middle-class authors continued to disseminate all the revolutionary-era body-control demands, only in more elaborately spelled-out versions, for an even broader audience. The revolutionary origins of this advice indicate that its purpose was what it had always been: to help rising individuals acquire a convincing gentility. But the authors made it clear that they did not include the serving class in their broader audience. Moreover, they embedded these older counsels in new antebellum injunctions that raised the hurdle to gentility. These were the extensive instructions for access rituals, such as introductions and salutations, and the elaborate stage directions for such social occasions as visits and dinners. While the authors risked class exclusivity a bit in publishing this advice so broadly, the high material demands of middle-class performances made them too costly for the lower classes. Manners allowed some social mobility, then, but not unlimited social mobility. Antebellum manners thus upheld the fiction of the classless society born with the shedding of hierarchy in the revolutionary era. But because manners served in reality to erect an unspoken barrier to the lower sort, middling conduct writers were effectively pulling the ladder up behind them.

Manners were the ideal tool in this exercise in class consolidation, because they allowed Americans to proclaim democracy while they acted inequality, acted the imperatives of the market. The process was somewhat ironic, as it was only now, decades after declaring independence from Britain, that Americans finally began to desire to carve out a special American social code suitable for a democracy. But the rituals American authors described mostly belie that impulse, as they often resembled the British bourgeois code. This is why Charles Dickens could not tell the difference between a party in Boston and a party in London. In both Britain and America, evolving capitalism was weighing in alongside the democratic revolution in shaping manners.

Perhaps the most striking aspect of Isaac Mickle's diary is the way it reflects his precocity. This adolescent moved in an adult world and was treated as an equal by the adults with whom he interacted. Moreover, he did not appear to be singular in this respect, as his male and female friends shared this experience. Here, too, his diary illustrates the trends evident in the conduct literature. The rise of youth in revolutionary-era manners was sustained in the antebellum decades. The social world of the conduct literature was an adult world, but youth were included whereas children were not. Only youth and adults were given all the newly ritualized advice about various social occasions, while it was thought best that children were segregated from this adult world. This did not really represent change in the treatment of children, for the advice to and about them continued to be remarkably stable and continued to uphold their traditional subordination to adults. But its context changed as the social world came to be defined as an adult world. Continuity within a changing context is also the story of advice to and about the aged. The conduct manuals continued to reflect ambivalence toward the aged; however, now, with the development of deference displays suitable for the weak in the system of "ladies first," the authors finally had adequate gestures to prescribe for treatment of the elderly.

The in-between nature of the life-cycle stage of youth allowed for greater change in their status, and yet that very liminality could be threatening. There are hints that at least some antebellum adults found the youthful freedom and autonomy of their time threatening. Some of the conduct writers were quite nostalgic for what they regarded as the deferential age relations of the old order. These more wistful passages in etiquette books seem to be portents of the "invention of the adolescent" to come at the end of the century. These authors' second thoughts describe the limits of the Lockean experiment. Autonomous youth were not necessarily what were required by the middle-class family as it evolved. The education and socialization necessary to sustain that class status might be more easily dispensed to a more dependent youth.

Both Isaac Mickle and the conduct writers thought that society existed only where men and women came together, signaling that the commitment to gender integration of the revolutionary era was fulfilled in the antebellum period. And yet this full inclusion of women in the social world of peers proved the greatest of the era's cultural challenges. There was a crucial though unremarked narrowing of the self-control gap between men and women as authors increasingly gave both sexes the same advice, especially in their new discussions of social occasions. This advice suggests that we have overlooked an important social world that served as a larger context for any separate spheres. Men and women shared this world; acknowledging it helps us to understand how they lived together. It also helps us to understand the ritualized yet intimate friendships of middle-class Americans like Isaac Mickle and the Sheppard sisters.

Antebellum authors repeated some of the old requests for modest behavior in women, but not all of them. They took a different tack in dealing with both the problem of sexuality and the persisting gap between social equality and political and economic inequality. Their answer was the smoke and mirrors of "ladies first." "Ladies first" served to protect women in the new social world, under the guise of privilege. Female social superiority also served as compensation for continued political and economic inferiority. This system asked much of men; perhaps this was one source of female allegiance to it. Men had to adopt new self-controls in their relationships with women, at least those of their own class. Mickle's diary reveals that his gentility, maturity, and masculinity were all tied up in his internalization of these self-controls. Owing to these new expectations, the world depicted in antebellum conduct advice was far less dangerous for women than that of the revolutionary era. Women could enjoy considerable physical closeness with men without fear of violation. The safety and coziness of the system, and the way it allowed the culmination of gender integration in society, must explain its enduring appeal.

But while men were to serve and protect women, it was clear that the sort of deference they were to pay was different from traditional deference to superiors. Not only were the requisite displays newly protective in nature but, because this deference was not theirs by right, women needed to show gratitude for receiving them. Such beliefs were a world away from Governor Dudley's attitude about the deference he expected from those unlucky carters. Mickle's diary is again useful in helping us see the system in motion (and emotion): while he went to great lengths to serve women, and while his missteps before them left him mortified, he never doubted for a moment that men were in charge.

The middle-class etiquette of the antebellum period was the most elaborate of the three periods of American history examined here, and the etiquette of gender relations was the most elaborate of antebellum manners. These are telling indications of the role of manners in this period. Anthropologists tell us that rituals proliferate when cultural principles are unclear or at odds. This was the case in antebellum America. Growing political democracy was at odds with increasing economic inequality. Rapid urban growth and increasing social and geographic mobility only compounded the confusion for individuals living in American cities. And persisting gender inequality was the most intractable contradiction of all: no promise of social mobility could be held out to women as it was to youth or the middling. The system of "ladies first" provided a ritual solution to these contradictions and confusions. Compensatory deference distracted from persisting inequalities and allowed the inclusion of women (and the aged) in the middle-class social world of peers. Civility to women became the badge of both the perfect gentleman and American manners, thereby distracting from the class-fixing aspects of the code. In this world manners played a crucial role through their communicative function. They allowed Americans to say one thing while nonverbally communicating and clarifying something quite different. Manners communicated status when other avenues for doing so had been shut down by the embracing of democracy.

This story contains some more general lessons about class, age, and gender relations. In terms of class, we are able to follow the first chapters of the continuing American tug-of-war between equality and inequality, both in terms of ideals and material conditions. We learn that middle-class culture and hegemony were long in the making in the Anglo world, and that in the American part of that world its eventual triumph was perhaps evident from the beginning in the social frustrations of the New England elite. We also see the literal underside of the story, as domestic service was transmuted over time from a familial to a class institution. Yet here, too, later developments are at least latent from the beginning, as we see even in Puritan New England a tendency to use the institution of service to reinforce class inequality.

The major shift in the conduct advice for age relations was the rise in status of youth. Whereas until the early eighteenth century the code of behavior for youth was similar to that for young children, by the third decade of the nineteenth century it was in many respects identical to the code for adults. The big lesson of this saga is the liminality of youth. Because of its in-between nature, situated on the cusp of maturity, youth is a plastic age in terms of cultural construction. Indeed, in each period we see reflections of the central concerns of the time in the treatment of youth, whether the need was to reinforce inequality, allow mobility, or create a world of equals among unequals. At the same time, we are reminded of the limits of the social construction of age relations when we examine the fate of the aged and of young children. Manners ask us to draw back from historians' attributions of exotic social constructions and wide swings to the statuses of these groups whose biological immaturity and senescence would always limit the degree of variation. In each period, the scant requests for deference to the aged appear mere side effects—of reverence for biblical injunction in one era or deference to women in another. The central lesson of rules for children is their remarkable stability over two and a half centuries. We are reminded, in the end, that the very young and the very old are simply and literally too weak to ever exercise real social power.

The transition in the etiquette of gender relations was the most dramatic, given the virtual flip-flop from overt discussions of women's inferiority to men in the seventeenth century to the nineteenth-century proclamations of women's social superiority to men. It is clear, however, that deference in the latter period was a protective and compensatory sort that was very different from traditional deference to superiors but did allow Americans to step over the gap between democracy and continued gender inequality. The etiquette of gender relations also reminds us, throughout, that the relationship between men and women will always be a special one because power relations are always crosscut by sexual relations. This is an essential though complicated feature of patriarchy. Thus while one way to read manners is the story of the ever-present need to adapt gender inequality in order to maintain it in different cultural climates, we are also reminded how the sexual ties between men and women always needed to be addressed as well, and always show gender inequality to be more moderate than class or age inequality. In the end there is a feminist lesson as well, for the dramatic flip-flop in manners represented by the rise of "ladies first" is just one more reminder of the great degree to which gender relations are culturally malleable.

WHILE THE MANNERS solutions that we have seen sufficed for the particular cultural conflicts of antebellum society, and while most of them became fundamental in some form to modern American democracy, post–Civil War America did encounter some new challenges for which antebellum solutions were inadequate. Perhaps the biggest challenge was the accelerating growth of wealth inequality. With the advent of huge fortunes like those of John D. Rockefeller, Cornelius Vanderbilt, and J. P. Morgan, the democratic pretensions of the antebellum etiquette book could no longer be upheld. By the turn of the century, there were several thousand millionaires in this country whose existence could no longer be denied. Perhaps, too, Americans had come to accept the social inequality they had long been enacting without admitting it. They were aided by new currents of thought such as "Social Darwinism" and the "Gospel of Wealth" that were supplying new justifications for inequality. All the new fortunes cried out for expression: the answer in terms of manners was found in a new, more overt borrowing from Europe, especially France, and a re-aristocraticization of manners. Middle-class Americans were once again following the elite, whose doings were now described in newspapers' society pages.

All this change is confirmed by change in the literature itself, as postwar Americans began to consume new conduct books by new authors. Newspapers and magazines, especially women's magazines, also began to devote more space to these issues. The rules themselves were new, or at least we see many aristocratic embellishments built onto the old rules. Instructions for table settings and manners, for example, became positively frightening in their complexity. At the other end of the spectrum, new handbooks were generated by demands made on the schools to teach proper deportment to the immigrants flowing in from Europe.[3] And yet, while these late-nineteenth-century manuals would reflect the excesses and preoccupations of their age by flirting with the depiction of a starker class inequality than in the previous era, they were not without their Horatio Alger-esque class-denying moments. The "imperial middle" features of antebellum manners persisted, though somewhat submerged, to be called forth again in the twentieth century.

Another challenge for late-nineteenth-century Americans has already been suggested: the need for longer dependence on the part of middle-class youth. The turn of the century invention of the adolescent would thus be reflected in new discussions of the etiquette of age relations. In time, new institutions for youth would create a youth culture on the nation's campuses that would in turn be codified in the pages of advice works.[4] The constant here was constant change in the status of youth.

The "ladies first" system actually seemed to hold on pretty well, although it was challenged in some ways by feminists and social reformers who did not want to rely on men for protection but instead wished for greater legal and political rights or state-supplied protections. For other elite women, one clearly gendered feature of the conscious abandonment of "democratic" American manners for Continental practices was the growth of chaperonage, although this might also have reflected doubts about the efficacy of male self-control. The "Daisy Miller" parable of the dire consequences of inadequate chaperonage found frequent repetition.[5] Still, "ladies first" never died. Indeed, this aspect of the antebellum manners system lasted the longest, because the problem it addressed has yet to be solved. While the late nineteenth century brought new conditions, new trends, and new conduct works, then, in many ways the basic antebellum responses to the social questions raised by the age of revolution persisted, forming enduring patterns in the weave of American culture.

LOOKING BACK, I find the story of manners in the first half of American history both depressing and hopeful. Manners helped create some of the most shameful and lasting of American blind spots: the mock veneration of the aged and of women, and, worst of all, the fiction of the classless society. But there was that glorious time when ordinary folk tapped into the creative power of manners and used them to assert their worthiness, when women began to be regarded as real fellow actors on the social stage, when youth were allowed to be young adults. Because the revolution only turned out to be partial in reality does not mean its ideals were not worthy. They were, and are, good in themselves. They also made for considerable progress. We must simply remember that their full potential was never reached.

The hope is that this study, like any other inquiry into the workings of our culture, can help us to own up to the ritual evasions of our ideals, at the same time that we justly celebrate the liberating potential of manners. We have opportunities before us, since the social changes of our own time have to be enacted in our own encounters, face to face.

A P P E N D I X

CONDUCT-ADVICE WORKS: AUTHOR/AUDIENCE STATISTICS

		1620–1737	1738–1820	1821–1860
Authors				
Sex	Male	42 (95%)	52 (69%)	56 (52%)
	Female	0 (0%)	10 (13%)	20 (19%)
	Don't Know	2 (5%)	13 (18%)	31 (29%)
Class	Upper	28 (64%)	18 (24%)	0 (0%)
	Middle	9 (20%)	31 (41%)	51 (48%)
	Lower	0 (0%)	0 (0%)	1 (1%)
	Don't Know	7 (16%)	26 (35%)	55 (51%)
Nationality	English	18 (41%)	36 (48%)	10 (9%)
	American	17 (39%)	15 (20%)	81 (76%)
	Italian	4 (9%)	1 (1%)	0 (0%)
	French	2 (5%)	7 (9%)	1 (1%)
	German	0 (0%)	1 (1%)	0 (0%)
	Swiss	0 (0%)	1 (1%)	0 (0%)
	Don't Know	3 (7%)	14 (19%)	15 (14%)
Occupation	Writers	5 (11%)	20 (27%)	20 (19%)
	Courtiers	5 (11%)	10 (13%)	0 (0%)
	Educators	2 (5%)	0 (0%)	11 (10%)
	Dancing Masters	0 (0%)	3 (4%)	4 (4%)
	Doctors	0 (0%)	3 (4%)	0 (0%)
	Businessmen	0 (0%)	1 (1%)	1 (1%)

225

		1620–1737	1738–1820	1821–1860
Authors (continued)				
	Clergymen:	29 (66%)	13 (17%)	19 (18%)
	Protestant	29 (66%)	12 (16%)	10 (9%)
	Catholic	0 (0%)	1 (1%)	0 (0%)
	Clergy/teachers	0 (0%)	0 (0%)	9 (8%)
	Don't Know	3 (7%)	25 (33%)	52 (49%)
Audience				
	Male	12 (27%)	11 (15%)	33 (31%)
Sex	Both Sexes/Male	6 (14%)	10 (13%)	13 (12%)
	Both Sexes	20 (45%)	25 (33%)	28 (26%)
	Both Sexes/Female	0 (0%)	2 (3%)	2 (2%)
	Female	6 (14%)	27 (36%)	31 (29%)
Class	Upper	13 (30%)	8 (11%)	0 (0%)
	Upper and Middle	0 (0%)	19 (25%)	2 (2%)
	Middle	6 (14%)	35 (47%)	94 (88%)
	Middle and Lower	0 (0%)	0 (0%)	6 (6%)
	Lower	5 (11%)	2 (3%)	2 (2%)
	All	20 (45%)	11 (15%)	3 (3%)
Age	Children	4 (9%)	8 (11%)	15 (14%)
	Young Adult	10 (23%)	42 (56%)	45 (42%)
	Young Adult/Adult	12 (27%)	12 (16%)	22 (21%)
	Adult	5 (11%)	6 (8%)	23 (21%)
	Old	2 (5%)	0 (0%)	0 (0%)
	All	11 (25%)	7 (9%)	2 (2%)
Genre	General Advice	41 (93%)	60 (80%)	58 (54%)
	Etiquette	3 (7%)	15 (20%)	49 (46%)

NOTES

INTRODUCTION

Space limitations allow only a sampling of the primary source citations below. For more extensive documentation of the conduct advice works that support any given point, see C. Dallett Hemphill, "Manners for Americans: Interaction Ritual and the Social Order, 1620–1860," Ph.D. dissertation, Brandeis University, 1988.

1. Until the 1980s, historical studies of manners in America were more descriptive than analytical. Useful for background and comparison are Joan Wildeblood's *The Polite World* (London: Oxford University Press, 1965) (largely written for theatrical application) and Esther Aresty's *The Best Behavior* (New York: Simon and Schuster, 1970) (which covers manners in Europe and America since the Renaissance). Robert Davis's dissertation, "Manners and Diplomacy" (Michigan State University, 1967) demonstrates the great preoccupation with matters of etiquette in the diplomacy of the new nation. Most useful is Arthur Schlesinger Sr.'s, *Learning How to Behave* (New York: Cooper Square, 1968) which gives the broad outlines of the history of manners in America. It was the English translation and republication of Norbert Elias's important *The History of Manners*, first published in 1939 (New York: Random House, 1978) that sparked British and American historians to apply the social science theory discussed below to the study of manners. Karen Halttunen uses etiquette books along with other sources in *Confidence Men and Painted Women: A Study of Middle-Class Culture in America* (New Haven: Yale University Press, 1982). John Kasson focuses exclusively on nineteenth-century etiquette works and shows how they guided Americans in a new urban and industrial environment in *Rudeness and Civility: Manners in*

Nineteenth-Century Urban America (New York: Hill and Wang, 1990). Rhys Isaac treats the communicative role of face-to-face performances throughout *The Transformation of Virginia, 1740–1790* (Chapel Hill: University of North Carolina Press, 1982); see also A. G. Roeber, "Authority, Law, and Custom: The Rituals of Court Day in Tidewater Virginia, 1720–1750," *The William and Mary Quarterly*, 3d ser., 37, no. 1 (January 1980): 29–52. Steven Stowe's study of antebellum planter families, *Intimacy and Power in the Old South: Ritual in the Lives of the Planters* (Baltimore: Johns Hopkins, 1987) is useful in exploring the interplay between cultural conventions and individual experience, but the rituals he treats are the more complex processes of the affair of honor, courtship, and coming of age. Most recently, Richard Bushman has examined the connection between manners and material culture in *The Refinement of America: Persons, Houses, Cities* (New York: Random House, 1993), which concentrates on the middle Atlantic region between 1700 and 1850. Bushman is very interested in the aesthetic side of the story—the spread of refinement in terms of taste (what he describes as a "beautifiction program," pp. 96–99). I am more interested in social rituals as a reflection of changing status/power relations. While some of these excellent studies overlap my own, none of them adopts the long-term view that is offered by this study of manners in the northern colonies and states from 1620 to 1860. This study also differs from theirs in its systematic examination and comparison of class, age, and gender relations.

2. Herbert Spencer, *The Principles of Sociology* (New York: Appleton, 1912), 2: 3, 5–6; Peter L. Berger, *Invitation to Sociology* (New York: Doubleday, 1963), pp. 95–99; Erving Goffman, *Interaction Ritual* (New York: Doubleday, 1967; reprint, 1982), pp. 44, 48–49, 90; Erving Goffman, *The Presentation of Self in Everyday Life* (New York: Doubleday, 1959), pp. 1–2, 12, 108, 242, 249; Erving Goffman, *Behavior in Public Places* (New York: Free Press, 1963), pp. 8, 33, 99.

3. One etiquette writer explained, "No work of this kind would pretend to *give laws*; but a simple statement of those which prevail among well-bred people." Her claim was echoed by many authors of etiquette manuals; *Etiquette For Ladies* (Philadelphia, 1838), p. 5. See also Goffman, *Public Places*, p. 5; Elias, pp. 61, 72; Kasson, p. 52. Individual authors themselves made it clear where they were simply reporting accepted customs and where they wished to see change in the accepted customs. The differences in these sorts of prescriptions are accounted for in the analysis.

4. Conduct literature was, to borrow the words of Clifford Geertz, "a story they tell themselves about themselves." See Geertz's "Deep Play: Notes on the Balinese Cockfight," in *The Interpretation of Cultures* (New York: Basic Books, 1973), pp. 448–453.

5. Two interesting examples of the relationship of the culture of such subgroups to the dominant culture are Rhys Isaac's description of the diversity of dance forms in colonial Virginia, p. 356, and Christine Stansell's description of the deportment of New York's "Bowery girls," in *City of Women: Sex and Class in New York, 1789–1860* (Urbana: University of Illinois Press, 1987), pp. 93–95.

6. Kasson adopts a similar, what he calls a "semiotic," approach (see p. 5).

7. See Schlesinger, pp. 6–7, 10. The works of Rhys Isaac and Steven Stowe are highly suggestive regarding the history of manners in the South. On the distinctive social order of the Old South, see Bertram Wyatt Brown's *Southern Honor: Ethics and Behavior in the Old South* (New York: Oxford University Press, 1982). On the book trade see Rosalind Remer, *Printers and Men of Capital* (Philadelphia: University of Pennsylvania Press, 1996), chap. 6.

8. Anthony Benezet, "A Short Account of the People Called Quakers," in

William Penn, *Tender Counsel and Advice* (Walpole, New Hampshire: D. Coolidge, 1805), n.p. On Quaker speech see Richard Bauman, *Let Your Words be Few* (New York: Cambridge University Press, 1983), pp. 43–62, esp. p. 47, and William Penn, *Fruits of a Father's Love* (Philadelphia, 1776), esp. p. 16. On the Quaker elite, see Frederick B. Tolles, *Meeting House and Counting House* (New York: Norton, 1963), pp. 112, 177–178 passim. Penn's own Pennsylvania library included a copy of Richard Brathwait's *The English Gentleman* (London, 1630); Isaac Norris owned Richard Allestree's *The Ladies Calling* (Oxford, 1673).

9. For a useful discussion of the geography of refinement and its spread, see Bushman, pp. 353–401, esp. 383. An interesting example of later change in the West is presented by Mary Ryan's *Cradle of the Middle Class: The Family in Oneida County, New York, 1790–1865* (New York: Cambridge University Press, 1981). She described Oneida County in the late eighteenth century going through patterns experienced in New England a century before; see esp. pp. 35, 51, 59. Oneida only caught up to the East in the antebellum period. On travelers' accounts see Jack Larkin, *The Reshaping of Everyday Life, 1790–1840* (New York: Harper and Row, 1988), pp. 2, 6–9; Warren S. Tryon, ed., *My Native Land: Life in America, 1790–1870* (Chicago: University of Chicago Press, 1952), pp. 299, 321, 333. An instructive contrast is that between Charles Dickens's generally balanced *American Notes* and Mrs. Trollope's nasty *Domestic Manners of the Americans*. Sally Griffiths told me about Daniel Drake.

10. A variety of subjects discussed in conduct works are not considered in this study. In some cases, I have taken a cue from the writers themselves. One subject they occasionally touched on but shied away from, in terms of dispensing "little rules," was courtship. A number of authors echoed the sentiments expressed in *Beadle's Dime Book of Etiquette* (New York, 1859): "Love has a language of its own, and will not thank any book of etiquette for a lesson" (p. 48). Some topics discussed in conduct works—questions of dress and fashion, the use of Americanisms in language, and letter-writing—are not considered in this study because they are either treated elsewhere or do not pertain to face-to-face behavior. Moralistic rules of common decency, of the love-your-neighbor-as-yourself variety, are omitted because they are universal and unchanging. Rules for special occasions—weddings, funerals, "New Year's Visits"—and the advice for preparing for such occasions have been eliminated on the grounds that it is difficult to separate attitudes toward the occasion from statements about the relationships of the people involved. Some rules are not treated because they do not directly pertain to the specific relations under examination here. Thus table manners are only considered where they bear on interaction between persons (i.e., staring at others, helping others, speed of eating, making noise, etc., but not which utensils to use and how to eat various foods). I do not discuss the rules for singing or playing music at parties, as these are too specific and do not directly pertain to the relations at issue. I also ignore toasting and smoking etiquette as both are mostly reflective of contemporary opinions about the consumption of alcohol and tobacco.

11. The work of anthropologists and sociologists suggests that rituals such as those prescribed by manners are most elaborate when principles of social organization are either unclear or at odds. They help people deal with cultural contradictions by making the unclear clear and providing ceremonial bridges over gaps in cultural ideals. On manners as rituals, see Erving Goffman, *Interaction Ritual*, p. 19, and Goffman, *Relations in Public* (New York: Basic Books, 1971), pp. 62–63. My view of the role of interaction ritual in society has been informed by my reading of Max Gluckman, ed., *Essays on the Ritual of Social Relations* (Manchester: Manchester University Press, 1962), especially pp. 38–39, 40, 43; Mary Douglas, *Purity and Danger* (London: Routledge and

Kegan Paul, 1966), especially chapter 9, "The System at War With Itself"; Mary Douglas, *Natural Symbols* (New York: Random House, 1970); Edward Hall, *Beyond Culture* (Garden City, New York: Doubleday, 1976), especially chapter 6, "Context and Meaning"; Sally F. Moore and Barbara Meyerhoff, eds., *Secular Ritual* (1977), especially chapter 1; Moore and Meyerhoff, "Secular Ritual: Forms and Meanings," pp. 1-24. See also Spencer, vol. 2, p. 4; Elias, p. 79; Terence S. Turner, "Transformation, Hierarchy, and Transcendence: A Reformulation of Van Gennep's Model of the Structure of Rites de Passage," in Moore and Meyerhoff, p. 60; Goffman, *Presentation of Self*, p. 245; and Geertz, p. 218.

CHAPTER I

1. Samuel Sewall, *The Diary of Samuel Sewall*, ed. M. Halsey Thomas (New York: Farar, Straus, and Giroux, 1973), 1: 532–535. Timothy Breen interprets this incident as a sign that the colonists thought ill of Dudley's pretensions, and it is true that Dudley was unpopular owing to his part in the hated Andros regime; but Breen only gives the governor's side of the story and does not mention the carters' claims that they did show some deference to the governor. See Breen, *The Character of the Good Ruler: Puritan Political Ideas in New England, 1630–1730* (New York: Norton, 1974), p. 230. As will quickly be evident, most of the discussion that follows considers rank relations in isolation from gender and age relations, and in fact chiefly concerns deference between men. Age and gender relations are treated in chapters 2 and 3.

2. See Breen, especially pp. xii, 36, 217, 270–271, and David Hall's *The Faithful Shepherd: A History of the New England Ministry in the Seventeenth Century* (New York: Norton, 1974), especially pp. 108–115, 130, 132–136, 186–188, 190, 195, 247–248, 273. Of course the New England scene changed dramatically between the early seventeenth and early eighteenth centuries, and the relationship between rulers and the ruled changed along with it. The elite, moreover, was never a static or monolithic group, but was continuously divided between rival groups and individuals. But members of the elite shared a touchiness about deference through the period. See, for example, Edmund Morgan, *The Puritan Dilemma: The Story of John Winthrop* (Boston: Little, Brown, 1958), p. 87; Sewall, 2: 741–742; Breen, pp. 187–188. Here I begin to differ some with Richard Bushman's picture of the emergence of gentility in the eighteenth century in *The Refinement of America*. Bushman sees a close association between material and social change, and links the growth of gentility with "the construction of the great houses" of the eighteenth century. But the New England elite were sticklers for deference and owners of courtesy books (see below) well before great houses were possible. Much of the body of manners that Bushman describes really belongs to a second manners system reflected in works that circulated between 1740 and 1820. See Bushman, pp. 9, 25, 402, and chapters 2 and 3.

3. Perry Miller and Thomas Johnson, eds., *The Puritans: A Sourcebook of Their Writings*, rev. ed. (New York: Harper, 1963), 2: 381; Samuel Eliot Morison, "Precedence at Harvard College in the Seventeenth Century," *Proceedings of the American Antiquarian Society*, n.s., 42 (1932): 377, 379–380.

4. Hall, *Faithful Shepherd*, pp. 68–69, 89, 152; Breen, pp. 65–67; Bushman, pp. 103–110.

5. See Jack Greene, *Pursuits of Happiness: The Social Development of Early Modern British Colonies and the Formation of American Culture* (Chapel Hill: University of North Carolina Press, 1988), pp. 21–22, 30–38; Gordon Wood, *The Radicalism of the American Revolution* (New York: Knopf, 1992), pp. 85–86.

6. Richard Bushman recognizes this function but sees its development at a later date, pp. 207–208, 404.

7. Breen, p. 21.

8. Thomas Goddard Wright, *Literary Culture in New England, 1620–1730* (New Haven: Yale University Press, 1920), pp. 27, 30–31, 35, 61, 278, 282, 286; David Hall, *Worlds of Wonder, Days of Judgement: Popular Religious Belief in Early New England* (New York: Knopf, 1989), p. 44; Gertrude Noyes, A *Bibliography of Courtesy Books in Seventeenth-Century England* (New Haven, 1937), p. 1. For a sampling of the evidence of these works in early New England: Elder Brewster of Plymouth owned a copy of Guazzo; Miles Standish and Governor Bradford of Plymouth owned copies of La Primaudaye. John Harvard bequeathed a copy of La Primaudaye to Harvard Library, along with the *Basilikon Doron.* John Winthrop Jr. owned a copy of Castiglione; Increase Mather, a copy of Osborne. Della Casa and Brathwait's *Gentleman* were both sold in Boston in the early eighteenth century and found in the Harvard Library. Boston book sale catalogs also included *Youth's Behaviour*, Brathwait's *Gentlewoman*, and Allestree's *Ladies Calling.* This evidence contradicts Richard Bushman's assertion that "courtesy manuals were imported into the colonies beginning in the eighteenth century" (p. 31). Two other courtesy works are found in the northern colonies but cannot be documented in New England. Richard Lingard's *Letter of Advice to a Young Gentleman* was reprinted in New York City in 1692, one of the first works issued from that city's press. And William Penn's *Fruits of a Father's Love* was printed early in the eighteenth century in Philadelphia. John Mason, *Gentlefolk in the Making: Studies in the History of English Courtesy Literature and Related Topics from 1531 to 1774* (Philadelphia: University of Pennsylvania Press, 1935; reprint, New York: Octagon Books, 1971), p. 328n (Mason is the best source for a fuller discussion of the history and place of this literature; Bushman offers a convenient summary, see pp. 33–36); Schlesinger, *Learning How to Behave*, pp. 1, 5; Henry M. Dexter, "Elder Brewster's Library," *Massachusetts Historical Society Proceedings* 5 (1889–1890): 67, 71; J. H. Tuttle, "The Libraries of the Mathers," *American Antiquarian Society Proceedings* 20 (1909): 292; Louis B. Wright, "The Purposeful Reading of Our Colonial Ancestors," *ELH, A Journal of English Literary History* 4 (1936–37): 101; Franklin B. Dexter, "Early Private Libraries in New England," *Proceedings of the American Antiquarian Society* 18 (1907): 145; Joshua Moody and Daniel Gookin, *Catalogue of Books* (Boston, 1718); Ebenezer Pemberton, *Catalogue of Books* (Boston, 1717), p. 386; George Curwen, *Catalogue of Books* (Boston, 1718), p. 9; Cotton Mather, *The Diary of Cotton Mather* (New York: F. Ungar, 1957), pp. 231, 262.

9. Hall, *Worlds of Wonder*, pp. 51, 247–248; James Axtell, *The School upon a Hill* (New York: Norton, 1976), p. 136. Two exceptions were courtesy works imported in New England that were addressed to persons below the elite: [Richard Allestree,] *The Whole Duty of Man* (London, 1659), and Caleb Trenchfield, A *Cap of Grey Hairs for a Green Head, or the Father's Counsel to His Son, an Apprentice in London*, 4th ed. (London, 1688). Mason, pp. 85, 147.

10. Schlesinger, pp. 1–3; Axtell, p. 144. Michael Zuckerman argues that "the hierarchy of the pews" in eighteenth-century Massachusetts towns "was an artificial imposition overlaid upon the life of the community" and that specific rankings were often contested and required frequent revision. But these qualifications only underscore the role of such institutions as attempts to impose inequality on an egalitarian social structure. That they were the expression of a vision of what the social order ought to be is made clear when, eventually, with the triumph of new ideas about society, they were simply discontinued. See *Peaceable Kingdoms: New England Towns in the Eighteenth Century* (New York: Norton, 1970), pp. 217–218.

11. An extensive study of these records is Helena Wall's *Fierce Communion: Family and Community in Early America* (Cambridge: Harvard University Press, 1990), p. 4.

12. Sidney George Fisher, *Men, Women, and Manners in Colonial Times* (Philadelphia, 1898), pp. 178–179; Morison, p. 378; Axtell, p. 217.

13. The sumptuary laws of 1634, 1636, and 1639 proscribed the wearing and making of fancy dress for all; no mention was made of rank. For an example of their enforcement see Frederick Johnson Simmons, *Emanuel Downing* (privately printed, 1958), p. 50. These laws were repealed in 1644, and there were no further sumptuary laws until the more elaborate and rank-related statutes of 1651, 1652, and 1662, which remained in force at least through the 1680s. See Nathaniel Shurtleff, ed., *Records of the Governor and Company of the Massachusetts Bay in New England* (Boston: William White, 1853–854), 1: 126, 183, 274; 2: 84; 3: 243–244, 262; 4, pt. 1: 60–61; pt. 2: 41–42; Miller and Johnson, 2: 388; W. H. Whitmore, *Colonial Laws of Massachusetts* (1762; reprint), p. 5, quoted in Morison, p. 378; Axtell, pp. 159–160; George Francis Dow, ed., *Records and Files of the Quarterly Court of Essex County, Massachusetts* (Salem, Mass., 1911–1921), 1: 272–273, 275, 285 [hereafter, *Essex County.*]

14. See, for example, Gary Nash's discussion of the division of wealth at the end of the seventeenth century in Boston, New York, and Philadelphia, in *The Urban Crucible* (Cambridge: Harvard University Press, 1979), pp. 21–25. A survey of the evidence of relative equality of wealth in New England, 1630–1750, can be found in David Fischer, *Albion's Seed: Four British Folkways in America* (New York: Oxford University Press, 1989), pp. 166–174.

15. This campaign is the subject of Richard Gildrie, *The Profane, the Civil and the Godly: The Reformation of Manners in Orthodox New England, 1679–1749* (University Park, Pa: Pennsylvania State University Press, 1994), p. 1 et passim.

16. Cotton Mather, *Diary*, 1: 304, 421, 449, 518, 522–523, 538–539, 548; 2: 187–188; Sewall, 2: 798, 929; see also Ebenezer Turell, *The Life and Character of the Reverend Benjamin Colman, D.D.* (Boston, 1749), excerpted in Miller and Johnson, 2: 540.

17. Hall, *Worlds of Wonder*, esp. pp. 11, 13, 32, 41–43, 58, 67, 69–70, 119, 128–132.

18. Cotton Mather, *The Rules of a Visit* (Boston, 1705), pp. 17–18; Cotton Mather, *A Family Well-Ordered* (Boston, 1699), p. 17.

19. Puritan conduct advice to ordinary folk has been overlooked in recent accounts of manners in early America which assume that manners were restricted to the elite. Richard Bushman's focus on the mid-Atlantic region and on courtesy books causes him to miss the manners instructions in Puritan sermons; see esp. p. 33. See also Kasson, p. 12.

20. Cotton Mather, *Diary*, 2: 751. Such statements contest the recent tendency to view early colonial society as composed only of gentlefolk in wigs and lowly commonfolk in rags, although admittedly there was a greater gap between the elite and everyone else than between the middling and the lower sort; see, for example, Wood, pp. 24 ff.

21. Wadsworth (Boston, 1712), pp. 51–53.

22. Richard Gildrie describes a concerted campaign on the part of New England ministers to reform the behavior of the masses. He claims that they had a big job to do because a rather rowdy "profane" culture had emerged to challenge their authority by the second half of the century. He argues that a better-behaved populace of the mid-eighteenth century was the result of some success on their part, but also of compromise

with the individualistic tendencies of the profane culture (pp. 235–236). But Gildrie may overestimate the degree of cultural contention. Roger Thompson has argued, for example, that popular piety served, to a considerable degree, to rein in misbehavior. See *Sex in Middlesex: Popular Mores in a Massachusetts County, 1649–1699* (University of Massachusetts Press, 1986), pp. 196–198. And while Gildrie acknowledges the dilemma outlined above—that the ministry both wanted to employ manners to improve the behavior of the populace and preserve them as a "sign of distinction" for themselves (pp. 217–218)—he does not recognize the limits this imposed on the success of the clerical reform campaign in preventing the ministry from teaching self-control. Gildrie claims that the reformers stressed the necessity of self-discipline in the commons (pp. 92, 108); but in withholding manners they withheld the tools to its formation. To the extent that the populace did display more refined behavior in the eighteenth century, it probably owed less to the ministers' campaign than to the fact that secularization and the commercial revolution eroded the old notions of hierarchy sufficiently to allow the prosperous to aspire to gentility without benefit of ministerial admonition. As will be discussed in chapter 4, after 1740 middle-class British authors were writing texts that allowed the middling sort to appropriate the old aristocratic code for themselves.

23. Della Casa (London, 1663), pp. 166, 168, 33; Wadsworth, p. 53; see also *Youth's Behaviour* (London, 1661), p. 9; Cotton Mather, *Cares About the Nurseries* (Boston, 1702), p. 11.

24. *Youth's Behaviour,* pp. 7, 9, 13; Eleazar Moody, *The School of Good Manners* (New London, 1754), pp. 2, 13–14, 20–21; Robert Cleaver, *Godly Forme of Household Government* (London, 1598), p. 281. Moody's work is interesting because it represents a compromise between the courtesy works of the elite and the Puritan works intended for all. While fewer than half of early New England children encountered schoolbooks, we cannot assign this one to the elite alone. It is likely that some children of godly families in the middle ranks of society were also exposed to it. The first section appears to have been adapted from an English version of a French courtesy work, but subsequent sections are full of religious matter. Moody's work is also different from the courtesy works in that it was compiled by a New England Puritan. Moreover, other Puritan authors gave some of the same manners instructions that Moody dispensed. So it was not identical to the courtesy works. The first edition appeared in 1715; the edition cited here is the fifth. See R. W. G. Vail, "Moody's School of Good Manners: A Study in American Colonial Etiquette," in *Studies in the History of Culture: The Disciplines of the Humanities* (1942; reprint, Freeport, N.Y.: Books for Libraries Press, 1969), 261–271; Sewall, 1: 526. Richard Bushman recognizes the divided nature of Moody's work but nevertheless treats it as a courtesy work (see p. 31). Two other schoolbooks were similar but contained relatively few etiquette prescriptions: [Henry Dixon et al.] *The Youth's Instructor in the English Tongue,* 8th ed. (Boston, 1746); *A Little Book For Little Children* (Boston, 1702).

25. Castiglione (London, 1561), p. 112; Moody, pp. 10–11; Wadsworth, p. 117; Sewall, 1: 539; *Essex County,* 2: 48.

26. Castiglione, p. 111; Della Casa, p. 33; John Barnard, *Call to Parents and Children* (Boston, 1737), pp. 20, 53; Dixon, pp. 50–51; Moody, pp. 1, 2, 25–26; Wadsworth, p. 52; C. Mather, *Cares,* p. 11; Allestree, *Whole,* pp. 271–272; *Youth's Behaviour,* p. 9.

27. *Little Book,* p. 22; Wadsworth, p. 53; Thomas Doolittle, *Young Man's Counsellor and Old Man's Remembrancer* (London, 1673), pp. 302–303; Richard Steele, *The Husbandmen's Calling* (Boston, 1713), p. 108; Allestree, *Whole,* p. 281; C. Mather, *Family,* p. 70.

28. Cotton Mather, *A Good Master Well-Served* (Boston, 1696), pp. 36–38; C. Mather, *Family*, p. 67; Wadsworth, pp. 111–112, 114, 120; Richard Baxter, *Poor Man's Family Book* (London, 1674), p. 312; William Gouge, *Eight Treatises of Domesticall Duties* (London, 1622), pp. 601, 612; see also Trenchfield, pp. 53–54; Allestree, *Whole*, pp. 323, 325; *Essex County*, 1: 44.

29. Della Casa, p. 161; *Youth's Behaviour*, p. 7; Moody, pp. 10–11, 17, 21; Cleaver, pp. 277–278, 281; W. Gouge, pp. 601–602.

30. W. Gouge, p. 602; Cleaver, p. 280; Moody, pp. 6, 7, 11, 13–15, 18.

31. *Youth's Behaviour*, pp. 9, 17; Della Casa, pp. 153–154; Castiglione, p. 111; Cleaver, pp. 275, 277–278; Moody, pp. 7, 14–16, 18–19; W. Gouge, pp. 596–600; C. Mather, *Master*, pp. 37–38; Wadsworth, pp. 112, 117; C. Mather, *Family*, p. 67; Baxter, p. 312; Allestree, *Whole*, pp. 323, 325. On titles see Norman Dawes, "Titles as Symbols of Prestige in Seventeenth-Century New England," *The William and Mary Quarterly* 6 (winter 1949): 69–83.

32. William Burkitt, *The Poor Man's Help and Young Man's Guide* (Boston, 1725), pp. 18–20; Wadsworth, p. 117; Baxter, p. 312; see also Trenchfield, pp. 38–39, 86.

33. On shared culture see Hall, *Worlds of Wonder*, p. 245.

34. Kenneth Silverman, *The Life and Times of Cotton Mather* (New York: Columbia University Press, 1985), p. 402; Miller and Johnson, 2: 541; Cotton Mather, *Manductio ad Ministerium* (Boston, 1726), p. 11, cited in Gildrie, p. 214; Hall, *Faithful Shepherd*, pp. 190–194, 262–264.

35. Sewall, 2: 246–247; see also pp. 760–761.

36. John Winthrop, *Journal*, James Hosmer ed. (1908), 1: 213–214, cited in Breen, p. 67; see also Breen, pp. 209–210, 218, 220. For other earlier examples of members of the elite correcting each other for unbecoming behavior, see Winthrop, 1: 96, 134; 2: 308.

37. Brathwait, *Gentleman* (London, 1630), pp. 274–275; Castiglione, p. 120; see also *Youth's Behaviour*, p. 13; Brathwait, *Gentlewoman* (London, 1631), p. 51. A concept of elite group consciousness would temper the current notion that "vertical" relationships between superiors and inferiors were the only important relationships in hierarchical societies; see Wood, pp. 23–24. But more evidence is needed to settle this point. On intermarriage, see David Fischer, *Albion's Seed*, pp. 39–41.

38. This aspect of courtesy literature was first noted and explored by Norbert Elias in his path-breaking *History of Manners*.

39. *Youth's Behaviour*, pp. 3, 9, 21; Moody, p. 3; Cleaver, p. 281.

40. Sewall, 1: 180, 360; 2: 622, 730; Winthrop, 1: 313; 2: 77–78.

41. *Youth's Behaviour*, pp. 3, 5, 17; Della Casa, pp. 13, 30–31, 256; Moody, pp. 13–14.

42. Della Casa, pp. 33, 65–66, 68, 258; Guazzo (London, 1581), 1: 156; *Youth's Behaviour*, p. 15; Moody, pp. 1, 14, 26; Cleaver, pp. 90, 277; Barnard, *Call*, p. 20; Wadsworth, p. 53; C. Mather, *Cares*, p. 11; Trenchfield, pp. 46, 77, 103.

43. Della Casa, p. 66; Castiglione, pp. 29, 43.

44. Brathwait, *Gentleman*, pp. 5–7; Della Casa, pp. 240–241; *Youth's Behaviour*, p. 11.

45. *Youth's Behaviour*, pp. 3, 5, 13, 17, 19; Della Casa, pp. 38–39, 68; Brathwait, *Gentleman*, p. 87; Sewall, 1: 592–593; 2: 851.

46. Della Casa, pp. 10, 17, 35–37, 243–244, 255–256; *Youth's Behaviour*, pp. 1, 3, 5, 19; Moody, pp. 11–12, 21.

47. *Youth's Behaviour*, p. 5; Della Casa, pp. 66–67; Guazzo, 1: 156; Benjamin Col-

man, *The Government and Improvement of Mirth* (Boston, 1707), pp. 36–37; Barnard, *Call*, p. 54; Moody, p. 13; Trenchfield, p. 103.

48. Della Casa, pp. 39, 203, 243, 252, 255–256; *Youth's Behaviour*, pp. 3, 5, 15, 19; Moody, p. 21.

49. Della Casa, pp. 67, 161–163; *Youth's Behaviour*, pp. 7, 15; Guazzo, 1: 156; Moody, p. 20; Trenchfield, pp. 103–104. Sewall, 1: 450, 505; see also Demos, *Remarkable Providences*, p. 112.

50. Della Casa, pp. 77–78, 224, 226–227; *Youth's Behaviour*, pp. 3, 15, 17, 19; Brathwait, *Gentleman*, p. 13; La Primaudaye (London, 1586), pp. 132–133; Cleaver, p. 91; Trenchfield, pp. 35, 81; Burkitt, p. 18; Ness, p. 24; *Man's Whole Duty, or The Rule of a Christian's Life* (Boston, 1718), p. 25.

51. Della Casa, pp. 67, 79, 81, 83, 90–91, 177–178, 180, 183, 193, 203, 214, 224–226; *Youth's Behaviour*, pp. 5, 9, 11, 13, 15, 17, 19; Castiglione, p. 150; La Primaudaye, pp. 132–133; Brathwait, *Gentleman*, p. 13; Moody, pp. 14, 16–17, 19–20, 23; *Youth's Instructor*, p. 38; Wadsworth, p. 53; Barnard, *Call*, pp. 53–54; Dixon, p. 53; Burkitt, pp. 18–20; Ness, p. 25; Trenchfield, pp. 41, 43, 46, 81–85, 87–88, 102–103, 110, 113. On disorderly speech see Jane Kamensky, "Words, Witches, and Woman Trouble: Witchcraft, Disorderly Speech, and Gender Boundaries in Puritan New England," *Essex Institute Historical Collections*, 128 (October 1992): 286–309. Examples of members of the elite trying to restrain outbreaks of anger or passion are found in Cotton Mather's *Diary* (see vol. 2, pp. 127, 135, 214, 454–455, 518–519). This evidence would seem to qualify Peter Stearns' assertion that a new concern about anger control developed after 1800, since such a concern was not new in elite-oriented advice; see "Men, Boys, and Anger in American Society, 1860–1940," in J. A. Mangan and James Walvin, eds., *Manliness and Morality: Middle-Class Masculinity in Britain and America, 1800–1940* (New York: St. Martins, 1987), pp. 77–78.

52. Della Casa, pp. 11–15, 36, 244, 255; *Youth's Behaviour*, pp. 1, 17, 19; Moody, pp. 11, 14, 19.

53. Della Casa, pp. 203, 219–221, 223; *Youth's Behaviour*, pp. 3, 15; Brathwait, *Gentleman*, pp. 13, 87; Castiglione, p. 47; Guazzo, 1: 156; La Primaudaye, p. 133; Moody, p. 14.

54. La Primaudaye, p. 132; Guazzo, 1: 156; Della Casa, pp. 67, 86; *Youth's Behaviour*, pp. 9, 11, 13, 15, 17.

55. Della Casa, pp. 185, 203; *Youth's Behaviour*, pp. 5, 11, 15; Moody, p. 16.

56. See, for example, Thompson, *Sex in Middlesex*, esp. pp. 91, 162–164.

57. Wadsworth, p. 105; C. Mather, *Master*, p. 16; Cotton Mather, *Ornaments for the Daughters of Zion* (Cambridge, Mass., 1692), p. 97; W. Gouge, pp. 651–652, 682; Cleaver, pp. 86, 374; see also Trenchfield, pp. 132–134.

58. Guazzo, 2: 97, 105; *Youth's Behaviour*, p. 9; Della Casa, pp. 33, 62–63; La Primaudaye, p. 530; Brathwait, *Gentleman*, pp. 158–159; King James I (Edinburgh, 1599), p. 137; C. Mather, *Ornaments*, p. 97; W. Gouge, pp. 651–652; Cleaver, pp. 90, 277, 374; Wadsworth, p. 53; Moody, pp. 1, 5, 27; Barnard, *Call*, p. 20.

59. Allestree, *Ladies*, pp. 66–67; Brathwait, *Gentleman*, pp. 9, 10; La Primaudaye, p. 530.

60. Della Casa, p. 37; *Youth's Behaviour*, p. 13.

61. W. Gouge, pp. 651, 652–653, 687; Moody, pp. 5, 7, 17; Wadsworth, pp. 106–107; Cleaver, pp. 85, 374; C. Mather, *Master*, p. 15; see also Trenchfield, pp. 133–135; Allestree, *Whole*, p. 327.

62. Guazzo, 2: 98; C. Mather, *Master*, pp. 15–16; Wadsworth, p. 106; W. Gouge, pp. 653, 658–661; *Essex County*, 3: 224.

63. I am endebted to Michael Zuckerman for this observation.

CHAPTER 2

1. Sewall, 1: 430–431. See also Morison, "Precedence at Harvard College," p. 379.

2. John Demos and Philippe Aries have asserted that there was no recognition of adolescence until the nineteenth century; see Aries, *Centuries of Childhood: A Social History of Family Life* (New York: Vintage, 1962), pp. 25–26, 29–30, 239; Demos, *A Little Commonwealth: Family Life in Plymouth Colony* (New York: Oxford University Press, 1970), pp. 145–146; and "The Rise and Fall of Adolescence," in *Past, Present, and Personal: The Family and the Life Course in American History* (New York: Oxford University Press, 1986), pp. 93–94, 98–99. Natalie Davis presents evidence to the contrary in "The Reasons of Misrule: Youth Groups and Charivaris in Sixteenth-Century France," *Past and Present*, 50: 41–75; see also Roger Thompson, "Adolescent Culture in Colonial Massachusetts, *Journal of Family History* (1984), pp. 127–144, and *Sex in Middlesex*. Linda Pollock assails historians who do not recognize past recognition of childhood in *Forgotten Children: Parent-Child Relationships between 1500 and 1900* (Cambridge: Cambridge University Press, 1983), pp. 98–99. Karin Calvert distances herself from the "miniature adulthood" school, yet argues in *Children in the House: The Material Culture of Early Childhood, 1600–1900* (Boston: Northeastern University Press, 1992), pp. 46, 51–52, 150–151, that early Americans did not place much value on childhood. For contemporary evidence of the line separating childhood and youth, see Thomas Shepherd in Miller and Johnson, 2: 715–716, and Ross Beales, "In Search of the Historical Child: Miniature Adulthood and Youth in Colonial New England," *American Quarterly* 27 (1975), 379–398. Many historians have accepted David Fischer's "Gerontocratia" argument: see *Growing Old in America* (New York: Oxford University Press, 1978), especially part 1, pp. 26–77, and *Albion's Seed*, pp. 103–111. On sixty as the dividing line between middle- and old age, see Cotton Mather, cited in Silverman, p. 398; Demos, "Old Age in Early New England," in *Past, Present, and Personal*, pp. 141–142, 154; and Carol Haber, *Beyond Sixty-Five: The Dilemma of Old Age in America's Past* (New York: Cambridge University Press, 1983), p. 8.

3. Scholars have come to recognize a struggle between youth and their elders in the not infrequent court appearances of rowdy youth, especially in the latter part of the seventeenth century: see Axtell, pp. 93–95; Thompson, *Sex in Middlesex* and "Adolescent Culture;" Lawrence Towner, "A Fondness for Freedom: Servant Protest in Puritan Society," *The William and Mary Quarterly*, 19 (1962): 279–297. The ministers responded with considerable public admonition (and not a little private handwringing). Cotton Mather, for example, repeatedly agonized over the misbehavior of youth in general and his son Increase in particular, and sought ways to correct them (see *Diary*, 1: 146; 2: 612, 614–615).

4. On the pervasiveness of the paradigm of the patriarchal family in early American society and politics, see Melvin Yazawa, *From Colonies to Commonwealth: Familial Ideology and the Beginnings of the American Republic* (Baltimore: Johns Hopkins University Press, 1985), parts 1 and 2, especially, pp. 19–20.

5. Lawrence A. Cremin, *Traditions of American Education* (New York: Basic Books, 1977), pp. 12, 14, 19; Bernard Bailyn, *Education in the Forming of American Society* (New York: Norton, 1972), p. 91.

6. Bailyn, pp 16–17; Cremin, pp. 12, 28–29; Axtell, pp. 21–22, 149.

7. C. Mather, *Family*, p. 4; Cleaver, pp. 281–282; see also Moody, pp. 25–28.

8. Cleaver, p. 305. Historians have supposed that teaching by example was a Lockean invention. Here and elsewhere the manners evidence suggests Puritan influence on Lockean thought. See Jay Fliegelman, *Prodigals and Pilgrims: The American*

Revolution Against Patriarchal Authority, 1750–1800 (Cambridge: Cambridge University Press, 1982), pp. 12–13.

9. Axtell, p. 146; Foster Watson, *The English Grammar Schools to 1660: Their Curriculum and Practice* (1908; reprint, London: Frank Cass, 1968), pp. 115–116; Cleaver, pp. 264, 267, 275–278, 281–282; C. Mather, *Family*, p. 17; C. Mather, *Nurseries*, p. 11; Barnard, *Call*, pp. 20, 27; W. Gouge, pp. 530–532; Wadsworth, pp. 51–53; C. Mather, *Diary*, 2: 262 (see also 2: 231); Silverman, p. 265; Cremin, p. 13; Bailyn, p. 18. Axtell reprints a list of conduct rules that schoolmaster and public servant Josiah Cotton intended to teach his children, pp. 151–152.

10. Bailyn, pp. 19, 29, 96; Axtell, pp. 169–176; Cremin, pp. 13, 28.

11. Watson, pp. 98–120, 126–136; Robert Middlekauff, *Ancients and Axioms: Secondary Education in Eighteenth-Century New England* (New Haven: Yale University Press, 1963), pp. 77, 84; Aresty, p. 113; Vail, p. 264.

12. Axtell, pp. 112–116, 207.

13. John Demos and Carol Haber argue that attitudes toward old age were more nuanced than Fischer's "gerontocratia" thesis allows. Demos points out that the frequently repeated prescription to honor old age was often accompanied by descriptions of the physical and moral infirmities of old age that betray near-contempt. Demos suggests that aged persons themselves might have shared this attitude, for "few of them seem to have enjoyed being old"; see "Old Age in Early New England," pp. 142–145, 156–160, 178–179. Haber claims that the exceptions and contradictions to Fischer's rule of veneration were more numerous than he acknowledges, and argues that although active older people could command respect, "age itself guaranteed little power and recognition." Haber believes that age combined with other factors (mainly economic) to determine whether or not one would have high status; see n. 5, p. 130; and pp. 2–3, 5, 9, 16, 26. Fischer acknowledges some of these exceptions and sources of ambivalence but apparently does not believe they undermine his argument (see *Growing Old*, pp. 60–72, 223).

14. Demos, "Old Age in Early New England," p. 171.

15. William Bridge, *A Word to the Aged* (Boston, 1679), p. 5; Benjamin Colman, *The Duty and Honour of Aged Women* (Boston, 1711), pp. 2, 41; Cotton Mather, *Addresses to Old Men, Young Men, and Little Children* (Boston, 1690), p. 4; Benjamin Colman, *The Honour and Happiness of the Vertuous Woman* (Boston, 1716), pp. 5–6; Increase Mather's *Two Discourses . . . The Dignity and Duty of the Aged Servants of the Lord* (Boston, 1716), pp. 51, 53–54, 64, 98; Wadsworth, pp. 52, 93; Barnard, *Call*, pp. 20, 53; Doolittle, pp. 301–302; *Little Book*, p. 23.

16. I. Mather, *Dignity*, pp. 54, 98–100, 102; Wadsworth, p. 93; Colman, *Honour*, pp. 5–6; Samuel Phillips, *Advice to a Child* (Boston, 1729), pp. 23–25; Doolittle, p. 302; C. Mather, *Addresses*, p. 4; Barnard, *Call*, p. 20; Dixon, p. 55. Cf. Fischer, *Growing Old*, p. 37.

17. C. Mather, *Addresses*, pp. 34–35; Colman, *Duty*, pp. 2, 21–22; Guazzo, 2: 172–174; C. Mather, *Tabitha Rediviva* (Boston, 1713), p. 39; Allestree, *Ladies*, p. 217; I. Mather, *Dignity*, p. 124.

18. Colman, *Government*, p. iv; C. Mather, *Addresses*, p. 35. The authors made even greater demands for gravity in aged women; Colman, *Duty*, pp. 11–12.

19. C. Mather, *Addresses*, p. 37; Colman, *Duty*, pp. 24–25; Castiglione, pp. 107–108.

20. In those days of extended childbearing, parental duties could last into old age, but *most* children would reach adulthood before their parents became aged. See Fischer, *Growing Old*, p. 56; Haber, pp. 10–11.

21. W. Gouge, p. 437; Cleaver, p. 349.

22. There was no formal or mandatory retirement system and many magistrates and ministers served till death; but life expectancies were lower than today, and there is evidence of gradual withdrawal from ministerial and official activity on the part of even more powerful figures such as Increase Mather. See Haber, pp. 2, 16, 19, and Demos, "Old Age in Early New England," pp. 166–171. As Demos finds in relation to Hampton, New Hampshire, selectmen, Daniel Scott Smith has found that most office-holders in Hingham, Massachusetts, were men between the ages of 40 and 60. David Fischer acknowledges that "The rulers of that society were younger than today, be-cause of differences in life expectancy. But they ruled with the authority of age, as so many of their titles tell us." ["Ruling elder," etc.] But that middle-aged men ruled with the authority of age does not mean that they ruled with the authority of old age. See Fischer, *Growing Old*, pp. 29, 44–47, 59, 222, 242–243. A similar argument can be made for another index of power, landholding. Philip Greven argues that the first gen-eration of fathers in Andover, Massachusetts held on to their land until death and were rather long-lived, thereby suggesting that old men held power over young men in this society; see *Four Generations: Population, Land, and Family in Colonial Andover, Massachusetts* (Ithaca, N.Y.: Cornell University Press, 1970), pp. 74–99. But his con-clusions have not been replicated in other communities. John Demos, for example, using samples from six New England communities, finds that on average, men's wealth reached a peak in their fifties and declined gradually thereafter, as "men past sixty were deeding away property to their grown children"; see "Old Age in Early New England," p. 137, and *A Little Commonwealth*, pp. 164–170.

23. Cotton Mather only appears concerned to comfort old people and help them prepare for death. See his *Diary*, 2: 135, 344, 461, 476–477, 539, 579, 606, 615, 617, 652–653.

24. David Fischer argues that patriarchy and gerontocracy are overlapping terms, *Growing Old*, p. 252. I do not know of early American evidence that supports the col-lapsing of these terms. Here again I am endebted to Yazawa's clear delineation of the "familial paradigm" of early American society.

25. Robert Middlekauff notes, for example, that early New Englanders were not able to maintain the traditional distinction between writing and grammar schools that prevailed in England, and thus that boys (and a few girls) of various ages were lumped together, pp. 13–19. On age mixing and gradual maturation, see Demos, *A Little Com-monwealth*, pp. 147, 149–150, and "The Rise and Fall of Adolescence," pp. 97–99. On the requirement to live in families, see Thompson, "Adolescent Culture," p. 134, and *Sex in Middlesex*, p. 83. On inheritance, see Greven, *Four Generations*.

26. *Youth's Behaviour*, pp. 9, 13, 17; W. Gouge, pp. 431–435, 437, 602; Moody, pp. 2–7, 10–11, 13–18, 20, 27; Cleaver, pp. 275–277, 280–281; Wadsworth, pp. 91–92; C. Mather, *Family*, pp. 60–61; Dixon, pp. 50–51.

27. Colman, *Honour*, pp. 4–5; Dixon, p. 54; Doolittle, p. 301; C. Mather, *Family*, p. 61; Wadsworth pp. 91–92; W. Gouge, p. 437; Moody, pp. 4–7, 10–11, 13–15, 17–18, 21–22; Cleaver, pp. 277–278, 280–281.

28. See, for example, C. Mather, *Family*, pp. 59–61, 70–71; Doolittle, pp. 301–303; Colman, *Honour*, pp. 4–5; Wadsworth, pp. 51–53, 90–93; W. Gouge, pp. 431, 530; Phillips, *Advice*, pp. 22–23; Barnard, *Call*, pp. 20, 53; Baxter, p. 310; Mather, *Tabitha*, p. 38; *Little Book*, pp. 22, 25; Moody, pp. 1, 25; C. Mather, *Nurseries*, p. 11.

29. Edmund Morgan, *The Puritan Family: Religion and Domestic Relations in Sev-enteenth-Century New England*, rev. ed. (New York: Harper and Row, 1966), pp. 75–78, 109–132; John Demos, *A Little Commonwealth*, pp. 71–75, 107–117; Axtell, pp. 112–

116; C. Mather, *Family*, p. 67; W. Gouge, p. 596. For a review of this institution as re-flected in the court records, see Wall, pp. 97–125. For a very useful discussion of ado-lescent service among English Puritans, see Alan MacFarlane's, *The Family Life of Ralph Josselin: A Seventeenth-Century Clergyman* (New York: Norton, 1970), pp. 146–148, 205–210.

30. Wadsworth, p. 117; Thompson, "Adolescent Culture," pp. 132–133.

31. C. Mather, *Master*, pp. 35–38; Doolittle, pp. 301–302; C. Mather, *Family*, p. 67; Wadsworth, pp. 111–112, 117; W. Gouge, pp. 596–601; Allestree, *Whole*, pp. 323, 325; Baxter, p. 312; Trenchfield, pp. 38–39, 53–54.

32. W. Gouge, p. 602.

33. To this extent the advice corroborates other scholars' recent claims about the unchallenged subordination of children in this society. Helena Wall finds evidence in the court records of neighborly restraint in dealings with others' children that she does not find in other areas and attributes it to "a strong sense of children as the dependents and inferiors—in fact the property—of their parents," pp. 94–95. Karin Calvert finds that adulthood was "the recognized ideal" and childhood defined "as a period of inade-quacy" in her study of material culture (p. 52).

34. Guazzo, 2: 71; Cleaver, p. 305.

35. C. Mather, *Family*, p. 22; Baxter, pp. 304–305; La Primaudaye, pp. 534–535; Wadsworth, p. 56; Barnard, *Call*, p. 34; Cleaver, pp. 295, 297; Doolittle, p. 303; Trenchfield, pp. 183–184; W. Gouge, p. 551; Guazzo, 2: 70–71; Steele, *Husbandman*, pp. 108, 192; Silverman, p. 265. Melvin Yazawa supplies a much needed correction of the predominant depiction of Puritan child-rearing as harshly authoritarian. He re-minds us that will-breaking was supposed to start very early and was not intended to root out the child's will but to break it free from "passion," and, I would add, to incline it toward obedience—hence my term "will-curbing" (pp. 39–42, 249). See also Pol-lock, p. 116.

36. Baxter, pp. 304–305; Guazzo, 2: 70–71, 75–77; C. Mather, *Family*, pp. 17, 28–29; Wadsworth, pp. 51, 53, 57–58, 105–106; Barnard, *Call*, p. 30; Phillips, *Advice*, p. 132; W. Gouge, pp. 530, 532, 682; C. Mather, *Tabitha*, p. 35; C. Mather, *Master*, p. 16; Cleaver, pp. 86, 374; Allestree, *Whole*, p. 327; C. Mather, *Ornaments*, p. 97; C. Mather, *Diary*, 2: 139.

37. Trenchfield, pp. 132–134; Cleaver, pp. 374, 384; W. Gouge, pp. 651–652, 687; C. Mather, *Ornaments*, p. 97; Guazzo, 2: 97, 105; Brathwait, *Gentleman*, pp. 158–159; La Primaudaye, p. 530; Wadsworth, p. 107.

38. Baxter, p. 305; Wadsworth, pp. 56–57, 106–107; Allestree, *Whole*, pp. 298–299, 327; Barnard, *Call*, pp. 33–34; C. Mather, *Family*, p. 25; W. Gouge, pp. 550–551, 556, 652–653; Cleaver, pp. 49, 85, 374; Trenchfield, pp. 134–135; C. Mather, *Master*, p. 15.

39. C. Mather, *Diary*, 1: 536; Wadsworth, pp. 56–57; Cleaver, pp. 49–50, 52, 292; Barnard, *Call*, p. 33; Allestree, *Whole*, pp. 298–299; W. Gouge, pp. 551–552, 556; Cleaver, pp. 50, 52, 292; La Primaudaye, pp. 534–535; C. Mather, *Family*, p. 25; Doolittle, p. 303; Guazzo, 2: 70.

40. See, for example, Sewall, 1: 300; Winthrop, 2: 84–85, 169–170; Barnard in Demos, *Remarkable Providences*, p. 91. Philippe Aries found a general trend of corporal punishment of children and youth of all classes in early modern Europe, pp. 261–262.

41. Wadsworth, p. 106; C. Mather, *Master*, p. 16; W. Gouge, pp. 653, 658–661; Wall, pp. 116–117.

42. Helena Wall argues strongly that "most commonly" "putting out was associ-ated with poverty" (which the Puritans conflated with parental unfitness), pp. 102,

104, 105 et passim. But she examines this institution solely through the lens of court records, which mostly reveal those bindings-out that were a response to family crisis, p. 212, n. 103. Wall herself acknowledges that "the prominence of boys in the records of hiring or putting out may be misleading," and cites Cornelia Dayton's suggestion that "the putting out of girls may have been handled more informally," p. 209, n. 63. She does not acknowledge that elite families also put their children out into other households, perhaps also without court involvement. See, for example, Sewall, *Diary*, 1: 321, 327, 336, 371. It may well be that in Puritan New England, as in old England, there was a net drain of adolescents from poorer toward richer households; see Mac-Farlane, pp. 209–210. On the colleges, see Axtell, pp. 219–230, 235–236; Yazawa, pp. 59–81.

43. Morgan, p. 77; see also Demos, *A Little Commonwealth*, pp. 69–74. In contrast, some other historians, noting elite concern over misbehaving youth, have speculated that parents put their children out to avoid fighting with them. But the institution of service added to rather than reduced generational conflict. Most of the misbehaving youth in the court records were servants, and several historians have claimed that their misbehavior was a form of protest over their treatment: Thompson, *Sex in Middlesex* and "Adolescent Culture," esp. pp. 133–134, 140; Towner, "Servant Protest," pp. 207, 211. Helena Wall describes some of the cases of parent-master conflict, although she interprets it differently, pp. 118–125.

44. Della Casa, pp. 17, 30–31, 35–37, 39, 67–68, 161–162, 240–241, 243, 255–256; Guazzo, 1: 156; *Youth's Behaviour*, pp. 1, 3, 5, 7, 9, 11, 15, 17; Brathwait, *Gentleman*, pp. 5–7; Moody, pp. 3, 11–14, 20–21; Increase Mather, *An Arrow Against Profane and Promiscuous Dancing* (Boston, 1684), pp. 6–7.

45. Castiglione, pp. 33, 150; Della Casa, pp. 38–39, 67, 203, 243, 252, 255–256; Guazzo, 1: 156; *Youth's Behaviour*, pp. 3, 5; Thomas Gouge, *The Young Man's Guide* (Boston, 1742), p. 88; Colman, *Government*, pp. 22, 45; Francis Osborne, *Advice to a Son* (Oxford, 1656), p. 52; Moody, pp. 13, 21.

46. Castiglione, p. 124; Brathwait, *Gentleman*, pp. 249, 253–254; *Youth's Behaviour*, p. 13; Guazzo, 2: 70; Allestree, *Ladies*, p. 196; *Man's Whole Duty*, pp. 24–25; [Christopher Ness,] *Crown and Glory of a Christian* (Boston, 1684), pp. 24, 49; Patrick Ker, *The Map of Man's Misery* (Boston, 1692), pp. 42–43; Trenchfield, pp. 62–63, 66–67, 70–71; *Little Book*, pp. 24–25; Moody, pp. 1–2, 22; Cleaver, p. 76; C. Mather, *Tabitha*, p. 38; Phillips, *Advice*, pp. 120, 132; C. Mather, *Family*, pp. 28–29; Barnard, *Call*, p. 30. C. Mather, *Diary*, 1: 147, 399; 2: 76; Silverman, pp. 268, 291; John Winthrop Jr. to Fitz-John Winthrop, in John Demos, *Remarkable Providences*, p. 139; Leonard Hoar to Josiah Flynt and Thomas Shepherd to his son in Miller and Johnson, 2: 712, 716–717.

47. Phillips, *Advice*, pp. 17, 19–20, 22–25, 132; Cleaver, pp. 354–355; I. Mather, *Arrow*, p. 2; C. Mather, *Addresses*, pp. 72–73; Barnard, *Call*, p. 30; Moody, p. 19; Dixon, p. 52; Thompson, "Adolescent Culture," esp. pp. 133–134, 137–138; and *Sex in Middlesex*, pp. 84–88, 91.

48. Allestree, *Whole*, p. 265; Della Casa, pp. 33, 65–66, 258; Guazzo, 1: 156, 170; 2: 80; *Youth's Behaviour*, p. 15; Castiglione, pp. 108–109; Trenchfield, pp. 46, 103; Allestree, *Ladies*, p. 147; C. Mather, *Addresses*, pp. 76–77; Barnard, *Call*, pp. 20, 53; Cleaver, pp. 277, 354–355; Phillips, *Advice*, p. 117; Colman, *Government*, pp. 36–37; Moody, pp. 1, 14, 28; C. Mather, *Cares*, p. 11.

49. Della Casa, pp. 11–14, 36, 77–78, 185, 203, 219–221, 223–224, 226–227, 255; Brathwait, *Gentleman*, pp. 13, 87, 279–280; Guazzo, 1: 128; La Primaudaye, pp. 132–133; Castiglione, pp. 43, 47; Brathwait, *Gentlewoman*, p. 89; *Youth's Behav-*

iour, pp. 3, 5, 11, 15, 17, 19; Moody, pp. 11, 13–14, 19; Barnard, *Call*, pp. 53–54; Colman, *Government*, pp. ii–iii, 19, 44–52, 55–58, 60, 69; Phillips, *Advice*, pp. 19–20, 117; Ker, pp. 37–38.

50. Della Casa, pp. 67, 79, 81, 83, 177–178, 180, 193, 214–215, 224–226; C. Mather, *Visit*, pp. 18–20, 23–25; Allestree, *Whole*, p. 268; Colman, *Government*, pp. 20, 46–47, 56–58; Phillips, *Advice*, pp. 17, 19–20; Cleaver, p. 355; Barnard, *Call*, pp. 53–54; *Youth's Behaviour*, pp. 5, 11, 13, 15, 17, 19; Moody, pp. 1–2, 5, 14, 16–20, 22–23, 28; Dixon, p. 53; *Little Book*, pp. 24–25; Burkitt, pp. 18–20; La Primaudaye, pp. 132–133, 151; Ness, p. 25; Castiglione, pp. 33, 150; Trenchfield, pp. 43, 45–46, 102–103, 110; Guazzo, 1: 156; T. Gouge, pp. 87, 89–90.

51. Roger Thompson, *Sex in Middlesex*, pp. 53, 83–84, 164–167, 193–195; Lawrence Towner, "Servant Protest," p. 213.

CHAPTER 3

1. This case is presented in Laurel T. Ulrich, *Good Wives: Image and Reality in the Lives of Women in Northern New England, 1650–1750* (New York: Oxford University Press, 1983), pp. 220–221.

2. For emphasis on inequality, see Lyle Koehler, *A Search For Power: The "Weaker Sex" in Seventeenth-Century New England* (Urbana, 1980), and Karlsen, *Devil in the Shape of a Woman*. For emphasis on partnership, see Morgan, *Puritan Family*; Demos, *A Little Commonwealth*; Ulrich, *Good Wives*; and C. Dallett Hemphill, "Women in Court: Sex-Role Differentiation in Salem, Massachusetts, 1636–1683," *The William and Mary Quarterly*, 39 (1982): 164–175.

3. See Ulrich, ch. 2, pp. 35–50, and Hemphill, "Women in Court."

4. Karlsen asserts that gender inequality was "the very model of and for all hierarchical relations," pp. 181, 216. See also Mary Beth Norton's *Founding Mothers and Fathers: Gendered Power and the Forming of American Society* (New York: Knopf, 1996).

5. Cleaver, p. 169.

6. While only a third of the conduct works were specifically addressed to men, a good number of works directed to both sexes or lacking in sex-specification appear from their contents to have been solely or mostly intended for men.

7. Literate gentlewomen, especially after 1700, might have been exposed to seventeenth-century English works in the courtesy tradition. As it is unlikely that these works would have reached the hands of more than a very few elite women before the mid-eighteenth century, however, they should not be given undue stress in the early colonial period. Even if these works did have a wide circulation, it would not have made much of a difference, for the subject of proper female behavior was one where Renaissance courtiers and Puritan ministers saw eye to eye.

8. Wadsworth, pp. 90–92; Osborne, p. 112; Colman, *Honour*, pp. 4–5; C. Mather, *Family*, p. 67; Colman, *Duty*, p. 41; I. Mather, *Dignity*, pp. 100–101; see also Ulrich, pp. 153–156.

9. W. Gouge, pp. 277–279, 364, 596; Doolittle pp. 301, 303; Wadsworth, pp. 25, 34–35; C. Mather, *Tabitha*, pp. 35–36; La Primaudaye, pp. 512–513; Cleaver, pp. 83, 100, 215, 236, 354; see also Castiglione, pp. 16, 207, 263; Guazzo, 2: 33.

10. Thompson, *Sex in Middlesex*, pp. 59, 84–88; Gildrie, p. 72; Hemphill, "Women in Court," pp. 166–170; for examples of mixed-sex socializing, see Sewall, 1: 92, 123, 168, and W. Gouge, p. 279.

11. Sewall, 1: 92, 180, 360.

12. See, for example, Sewall, 2: 990.

13. Brathwait, *Gentlewoman*, pp. 89, 170; Castiglione, pp. 207, 209; La Primaudaye, pp. 514, 517; Cleaver, pp. 82, 101, 169, 236; W. Gouge, pp. 281–282, 285; Wadsworth, p. 25.

14. Cleaver, pp. 82, 84; W. Gouge, pp. 364, 281–285; Wadsworth, p. 25; *Essex County*, 2: 344; 6: 386–387; Wall, p. 73.

15. Castiglione, pp. 207, 263; Cleaver, pp. 354–355; Allestree, *Ladies*, pp. 16, 148; C. Mather, *Ornaments*, p. 73.

16. W. Gouge, pp. 278–279, 284; Cleaver, p. 215; Wadsworth, p. 25.

17. Cleaver, pp. 100, 236, 354–355; Guazzo, 2: 33; Brathwait, *Gentlewoman*, pp. 87, 170, 172; C. Mather, *Ornaments*, p. 12; Castiglione, p. 263; Allestree, *Ladies* pp. 16, 148.

18. Cleaver, p. 355; Castiglione, p. 263; Allestree, *Ladies*, pp. 16, 148; Brathwait *Gentlewoman*, pp. 42–43; C. Mather, *Ornaments*, pp. 13, 73.

19. I. Mather, *Arrow*, pp. 1–3, 6–7, 24; C. Mather, *Addresses*, pp. 71–73; Thompson, "Adolescent Culture," pp. 131–135.

20. C. Mather, *Visit*, p. 20; Barnard, *Call*, p. 53; Della Casa, p. 214.

21. Wadsworth, p. 25; W. Gouge, p. 662; Sewall, 2: 572. For other instances of women corrected for physically abusing their husbands, see Wall, p. 73.

22. Rotundo, *American Manhood*, pp. 2–3, 10–12.

23. W. Gouge, pp. 373, 383, 388; Cleaver, pp. 84, 162; La Primaudaye, p. 507; Guazzo, 2: 27.

24. W. Gouge, pp. 364–365, 371, 387–388; La Primaudaye, p. 509; Wadsworth, pp. 25, 34–36; Guazzo, 2: 27.

25. Guazzo, 2: 27; W. Gouge, pp. 371–373, 375, 382–383; Cleaver, pp. 84, 162, 165, 168; La Primaudaye, pp. 504, 507; Trenchfield, p. 165; Wadsworth, p. 25; *Essex County*, 6: 297; 8: 272–273; Wall, p. 72.

26. W. Gouge, p. 388; Guazzo, 2: 27; La Primaudaye, p. 507.

27. La Primaudaye, p. 504; Cleaver, p. 168; Wadsworth, p. 25; W. Gouge, pp. 389, 662; Sewall, 1: 543; *Essex County*, 1: 57, 128, 158, 414; 5: 377; Wall, p. 77.

28. Stone, "The Rise of the Nuclear Family in Early Modern England: The Patriarchal Stage," in Charles Rosenberg, ed., *The Family in History* (Philadelphia, 1975), p. 40.

29. *Journal of Madam Knight*, in Miller and Johnson, 2: 427; see also Ulrich, pp. 65–66.

30. Philippe Aries notes that contemporary European etiquette manuals also excluded women, in contrast to those of the Middle Ages (p. 381). The early New England evidence may thus fit a larger picture of early modern decline in women's status, first described by Alice Clark in *Working Life of Women in the Seventeenth Century* (New York: Harcourt, 1920).

31. Cleaver, pp. 89–90, 104, 169, 218–219, 236; Brathwait, *Gentlewoman*, pp. 41, 50–52, 84; C. Mather, *Tabitha*, pp. 35, 38; La Primaudaye, pp. 512, 514–516; Castiglione, p. 207; Guazzo, 2: 75, 77; Wall, pp. 54, 73–74.

32. C. Mather, *Tabitha*, pp. 35–36, 39; Cleaver, pp. 90, 100, 236; Colman, *Duty*, pp. 11–12, 21–22; C. Mather, *Ornaments*, p. 12; Castiglione, pp. 206, 210; Brathwait, *Gentlewoman*, pp. 41–42, 50, 52, 82–83, 170, 172; Guazzo, 1: 240, and 2: 75, 80; La Primaudaye, pp. 512, 516; Allestree, *Ladies*, pp. 6, 65–66, 147, 217.

33. Cleaver, pp. 89–91, 101, 169, 236; C. Mather, *Ornaments*, pp. 50, 73; C. Mather, *Tabitha*, p. 35; Brathwait, *Gentlewoman*, pp. 41, 50, 89, 170; Guazzo, 1: 240, and 2: 80; La Primaudaye, pp. 514, 517; Allestree, *Ladies*, pp. 7–8, 147–148; Castiglione, p. 207.

34. Allestree, *Ladies*, pp. 6–7, 147–148; Guazzo, 2: 80; C. Mather, *Ornaments*, pp. 12, 51; Colman, *Duty*, p. 12; Brathwait, *Gentlewoman*, pp. 52, 91.

35. C. Mather, *Ornaments*, pp. 51, 73; Colman, *Duty*, p. 12; Brathwait, *Gentlewoman*, pp. 52, 170; La Primaudaye, p. 517; Allestree, *Ladies*, pp. 6, 13; Castiglione, p. 207; *Essex County*, 2: 212, 4: 214, and 7: 149, 238.

36. This is corroborated by Carol Karlsen's observation that "a lack of deference for male neighbors" was "a common thread running through the sins of many witches," p. 150.

37. For details and citations regarding the elite code, see chapter 1.

38. *Youth's Behaviour*, pp. 5, 9, 11, 15, 17; Della Casa, pp. 81, 83, 90–91, 193, 203, 214; Trenchfield, pp. 41, 81–83, 85, 87, 88; Dixon, pp. 52–55; Castiglione, pp. 107, 111, 150; Moody, pp. 16–17, 20, 23–24; Ker, pp. 34–40; Burkitt, pp. 18–20; La Primaudaye, pp. 149, 151; Allestree, *Whole*, p. 268.

39. *Youth's Behaviour*, pp. 11, 13, 15, 17; La Primaudaye, pp. 132–133; Della Casa, pp. 67, 79, 177–178, 180; Moody, pp. 5, 15, 18–19, 22; Trenchfield, pp. 43, 45–46, 102–103, 110; T. Gouge, pp. 87–89; Brathwait, *Gentleman*, p 13.

40. On the condemnation of anger in women see Karlsen, pp. 129–130. Helena Wall claims that "women were particularly identified with slander and offenses such as malicious gossip, opprobrious language, and verbal abuse of neighbors," but acknowledges that Cornelia Dayton finds that New Englanders did not see slander as a particularly female crime. Both historians claim that gossip was associated with women (Wall, pp. 46 and 191, n. 95). Jane Kamensky also argues for a "connection between disorderly speech and the construction of womanhood," in "Words, Witches, and Woman Trouble: Witchcraft, Disorderly Speech, and Gender Boundaries in Puritan New England," *Essex Institute Historical Collections* 128: (October 1992): 286–309. Advice telling men not to gossip: Ker, p. 26; Doolittle, p. 309; Trenchfield, p. 40; *Youth's Behaviour*, pp. 13, 15, 17.

41. This is not to say that members of the elite did not draw any distinctions between elite and ordinary women—they did. Cotton Mather's and Samuel Sewall's diaries, for example, often refer to gentlewomen as such. But they, like the conduct writers, do not make distinctions between the behavior appropriate to women of different ranks.

42. Laurel Ulrich notes this paradox in other evidence, see especially pp. 37–38, 50; see also Hemphill, "Women in Court."

43. Gildrie, p. 99; Karlsen, passim.

44. See Calvert, p. 44.

45. For the economic argument see Ulrich, ch. 2, pp. 35–50, and Hemphill, "Women in Court." On the prescriptive literature, see Fischer, *Albion's Seed*, p. 84.

46. Ulrich also notes this (pp. 106–111).

47. See, for example, Wall, chap. 3, esp. pp. 78–83.

48. See the contrasting views of Karlsen, p. 150, and Ulrich, p. 8.

49. Karlsen makes a strong case for this argument from her witchcraft evidence (see pp. 150, 153–155, 160, 173).

50. Karlsen makes both arguments about gender inequality, p. 216.

CHAPTER 4

1. John Adams, *Diary and Autobiography*, vol. 1., ed. L. H. Butterfield (New York: Atheneum, 1964), pp. 65, 68–69; for other examples, see vol. 1, pp. 51, 54, 75, 83, 98, 134.

2. Adams claimed of his father and grandfathers that "They were all in the middle rank of People in Society" (*Autobiography*, vol. 3, p. 254). In his *Diary*, he refers to himself as a person of "obscure Birth, and Station" and proudly describes himself as self-made (vol. 1, pp. 167, 352; see also vol. 2, pp. 55, 61). Other examples of Founders of middling backgrounds keenly interested in manners and observing others as a way of acquiring them were William Paterson and Benjamin Rush. Wood, pp. 196–203.

3. Stuart Blumin, *The Emergence of the Middle Class: Social Experience in the American City, 1760–1900* (Cambridge: Cambridge University Press, 1989), pp. 17, 19, 33–35, 37–38, 40, 57; see also Wood, pp. 23–24ff. Bushman argues that the great dividing line dropped to include the middling before the mid-nineteenth century, but does not think it began to do so until the very end of the eighteenth century (pp. xv, 27, 279 passim).

4. Blumin, pp. 30–31, 33, 35, and ch. 3, esp. p. 107 passim. See also Mary Ryan, *Cradle of the Middle Class*, and Karen Halttunen, *Confidence Men and Painted Women*. An important exception is Carroll Smith-Rosenberg, who recognizes a "discursively constituted" middle class in the late eighteenth century: see "Dis-Covering the Subject of the 'Great Constitutional Discussion,' 1786–1789," *The Journal of American History* 79, no. 3 (December 1992): 857–859 passim.

5. See Robert E. Brown, *Middle-Class Democracy and the Revolution in Massachusetts, 1690–1780* (Ithaca: Cornell University Press, 1955) and, especially, Jackson Turner Main, *The Social Structure of Revolutionary America* (Princeton: Princeton University Press, 1965), pp. 42–43, 68; Alice Hanson Jones, *Wealth of a Nation to Be* (New York: Columbia University Press, 1980), pp. 321–322, 324; Thomas Doerflinger, *A Vigorous Spirit of Enterprise: Merchants and Economic Development in Revolutionary Philadelphia* (Chapel Hill: University of North Carolina Press, 1986), pp. 16–17, 32 passim; Gary Nash, "The Social Evolution of Preindustrial American Cities, 1700–1820: Reflections and New Directions," *Journal of Urban History* 13, no. 2 (Feb. 1987): 125–126. In fact, few historians of class deny the existence of a group in the middle in eighteenth-century society, for most acknowledge the frequent references of contemporaries to the term "the middling sort" or people of "middling condition." But most stress the fact that the term "middle class" was not frequently used until the mid-nineteenth century. Blumin, pp. 1, 17–19; E. P. Thompson, "Eighteenth-Century English Society: Class Struggle without Class," *Social History* 3 (1978): 148. In fact, one finds both usages in the 18th century—like the emergence of the middle class, the linguistic transition did not take place overnight. Hence transitional language, such as New York Congressman Melancthon Smith's call for adequate representation of "the middling class" in 1788, "Speech Before the New York Ratifying Convention," in Jack Greene, ed., *Colonies to Nation, 1763–1789* (New York: Norton, 1967), p. 564; see also Benjamin Rush, *Autobiography*, ed. George W. Corner (Princeton: Princeton University Press, 1948), p. 110, and John Seed, "From Middling Sort to Middle Class in Late Eighteenth- and Early-Nineteenth-Century England," in *Social Orders and Social Classes in Europe Since 1500: Studies in Social Stratification*, ed. M. L. Bush (New York: Longmans, 1992), pp. 115, 119–120.

6. On the self-made man as an antebellum image and reality central to middle-class culture, see Ryan, pp. 152–153. Ronald Schultz has similarly argued for eighteenth-century roots of the American working class in *The Republic of Labor: Philadelphia Artisans and the Politics of Class, 1720–1830* (New York: Oxford University Press, 1993), and has no trouble identifying a clear middle-class element in Philadelphia politics, pp. xi–xii, 44–45, 51–60 passim.

7. E. P. Thompson claimed that the middle classes in England remained in a

client or deferential relationship until the last three decades of the century: see "Class Struggle Without Class," pp. 142–143. Thompson argues that class does not exist independent of class struggle (p. 149). This may well be true of the emergence of the working class, but I am suggesting that the process of middle class formation was one of mimesis, not struggle. Why should we expect class formation to be a similar process for all classes? As Thompson himself reminds us, "Class is a historical formation, and it does not occur only in ways prescribed as theoretically proper" (p. 150). In the case of the middle class, perhaps what we see emerging is class without class struggle. Wood makes the point about emulative consumption, while missing it in the case of manners (pp. 135–136). Bushman notes the emulative nature of the middling pursuit of refinement, but he, too, argues for a gentry/commons gulf till the end of the century. This is despite the fact that he, like Wood, also acknowledges that ordinary folk began to acquire "genteel possessions" by midcentury: pp. 28–29, 186, 208–209, 403. He notes that half of the population at midcentury were "knife-and-fork" people (pp. 77–78, 184) and that the new Georgian style of architecture was adopted by many of modest fortune as well as the elite (pp. 113–116).

8. Phillip Dormer Stanhope, 4th Earl of Chesterfield, *Letters to His Son* (New York, 1775).

9. Bushman argues that middle-class Americans adopted aristocratic manners, but he does not recognize the special emphases that differentiated the middling character of revolutionary-era manners from the deferential elite model of the seventeenth century. He only sees middle-class modification (with religion and domesticity) in the nineteenth century: see pp. 38–39, 402–403. So for him, republicans adopting aristocratic etiquette remains a cultural contradiction. He claims gentility was at odds with middle-class values but was borrowed anyway because it "supported class authority" in the eighteenth century: see pp. xvi and xix, 411. He also attributes power to the old aristocracy in "influencing [the] cultural forms" adopted by Americans. He is led to these views because he does not examine closely the truly deferential culture of seventeenth-century Anglo-America and the change in the body of conduct literature and its authors that occurred around the mid-eighteenth century. So he does not see middling authors appropriating aristocratic forms for their own purposes, which were not so much to support class authority as to challenge it by facilitating the rise of the middling. In fact, self-control advice was congenial to middle-class values. Gordon Wood acknowledges that "the enlightened age emphasized new, man-made criteria of gentility," but he, too, fails to see in this the origins of the middling culture of self-improvement. Indeed, he claims that Franklin's *Autobiography* was more a part of nineteenth-century culture and that the Founders of modest origins had patrons and did not advertise the fact of their mobility (pp. 195, 341–342). I think these claims are not sustainable in light of the frank discussions of their middling origins and *lack* of patrons in the writings of Adams and Rush (see ns. 2 above and 11 below) and the simple fact that Franklin wrote his *Autobiography* when he did.

10. Wood discusses the Founders' anger at hereditary aristocracy but does not see the middling campaign at work in their promoting of a natural aristocracy: pp. 180–181, 200, 202. Bushman describes the ambivalence but does not note that the main detractors, people like Mercy Warren and John Adams, had long resented the local elite. I do not think the depth of their ambivalence can be explained without acknowledging the difference between their backgrounds and those of the elite they scorned. Bushman notes that "The multifaceted critiques of gentility did not impede in the slightest the pursuit of refinement," and makes the useful suggestion that the critiques were a means of marking out the bounds of refined behavior (pp. 186–203). But

he, too, does not see that this was part of the middling project. See n. 59 below on slaps at Chesterfield.

11. Rush described his modest background, early education in manners, and lack of family connections or patronage in his *Autobiography*, pp. 25, 27, 30, 79, 85; Benjamin Rush, *Letters of Benjamin Rush*, ed. L. H. Butterfield (Princeton: Princeton University Press, 1951), 2: 860–861.

12. Nash, *Urban Crucible*, passim, esp. p. 384.

13. Five of fifteen sources persisting from the early colonial period were imported or reprinted often enough to be considered significant sources after 1738. Data from these works has been added to those from revolutionary-era sources in the analysis of revolutionary-era rules for behavior.

14. Main, pp. 254–257; Cathy Davidson, "Introduction," *Reading in America: Literature and Social History* (Baltimore: Johns Hopkins, 1989), p. 14; and in the same volume, David Nord, "A Republican Literature: Magazine Reading and Readers in Late-Eighteenth-Century New York," pp. 115–131; Cathy Davidson, *Revolution and the Word: The Rise of the Novel in America* (New York: Norton, 1986), esp. chap. 2, "The Book in the New Republic," pp. 25–27. The Samuel Phillips Savage almanac (1792) is held by the Massachusetts Historical Society.

15. Davidson's analysis of the rise of the novel presents strong parallels to that of middling conduct literature, although the conduct works merely reported and facilitated the process of bourgeois "empowerment," while the novels raised as many questions about the new as about the old order: *Revolution*, pp. 14, 42, 44–45, 218–220. Davidson also reminds us of the deliberation with which printers chose the books they brought out in order to meet the market (pp. 87–91).

16. Jack P. Greene, "Search For Identity," *Journal of Social History*, 3 (1970), pp. 195–219; Davidson, *Revolution*, p. 36; Schlesinger, p. 13.

17. Mason, pp. 107, 253, 286, 297, 369; Virgil B. Heltzell, "Chesterfield and the Tradition of the Ideal Gentleman" (diss., University of Chicago, 1925), abstract in *University of Chicago Abstracts of Theses, Humanistic Series* (1928): 328; Schlesinger, pp. 10–11, 79, n. 14; Frank Luther Mott, *Golden Multitudes: The Story of Best Sellers in the United States* (New York: MacMillan, 1947), pp. 303–304. The most objectionable parts reflected Chesterfield's rather utilitarian attitude toward women. One widely reprinted version was *Principles of Politeness*, arranged by John Trusler, an English minister (he also added a few rules); Aresty, pp. 151–152.

18. Mason, p. 108.

19. Mason, pp. 83–84, 105; Wright, pp. XII, XXII. Erasmus Darwin, an important writer for the emerging middle class in England, recommended three of these works along with those written by and addressed to middle-class persons in his *A Plan for the Conduct of Female Education* (Philadelphia, 1798), p. 183; on Darwin, see Leonore Davidoff and Catherine Hall, *Family Fortunes: Men and Women of the English Middle Class, 1780–1850* (Chicago: University of Chicago Press, 1987), pp. 235, 263, 290. Joan Wildeblood doubts the upper-class exclusivity of this literature in England, pp. 37–38; see also Aresty, p. 142.

20. John Gregory, *A Father's Legacy to His Daughters* (Philadelphia, 1775); Rush, *Letters*, vol. 1, pp. 191–192, 218.

21. John Hamilton Moore, *The Young Gentleman and Lady's Monitor*, 5th ed. (New York, 1787).

22. See Nash, *The Urban Crucible*, pp. 33, 35 passim, and "Social Evolution," p. 134, for the erosion of deference politics in the eighteenth century.

23. Sharon V. Salinger, "Artisans, Journeymen and the Transformation of Labor

in Late-Eighteenth-Century Philadelphia," *The William and Mary Quarterly* 40, no. 1 (January 1983): 62–84; Towner, p. 215; Henretta, "Economic Development and Social Structure," p. 83; Nash, *Urban Crucible,* pp. 258–259, 320–321.

24. Chesterfield, 1775, 1: 121; Walter Raleigh, *Instructions to His Son and to Posterity,* 2d ed. (London, 1632), p. 19; Mrs. M. Peddle, *Rudiments of Taste* (Philadelphia, 1790), pp. 60–61; Moore, p. 237–240, 251–252; Anne Therese, Marquise de Lambert, "A Mother's Advice to Her Son," in *The Young Gentleman's Parental Monitor* (Hartford, 1792), p. 113; Hester Mulso Chapone, *Letters on the Improvement of the Mind* (Boston, 1783), p. 104; William Dover, *Useful Miscellanies Respecting Men's Duty to God and Towards One Another* (Philadelphia, 1753), p. 64; William Homes, *The Good Government of Christian Families* (Boston, 1747), p. 72; Adams, *Diary,* 1: 326.

25. Thomas Gisborne, *An Enquiry into the Duties of the Female Sex* (Philadelphia, 1798), pp. 70, 218 (Davidoff and Hall identify him as an upper-class writer who addressed the middle classes, pp. 112, 170); Gregory, pp. 29–30; Matthew Hale, *A Letter of Advice to His Grandchildren* (Boston, 1817), pp. 137–138, 192, 194–195; *The Polite Lady,* 2d ed. (London, 1769), pp. 60, 62–66; Fenelon, pp. 237–238.

26. L'abbé d'Ancourt, *Lady's Preceptor,* 5th ed. (Woodbridge, New Jersey, 1759), pp. 8, 12; Moore, pp. 237–240; Hannah Webster Foster, *The Boarding School* (Boston, 1798), p. 67; John Griffiths, *A Collection of the Newest Cotillions* (Northhampton, Mass., 1794), p. 11; Dover, pp. 31–32; Francis D. Nichols, *A Guide to Politeness* (Boston, 1810), p. 24.

27. d'Ancourt, p. 9; *The American Academy of Compliments* (Philadelphia, 1796), p. 55; Moody, pp. 13, 20–23; *A Little Pretty Pocket Book* (Worcester, Mass., 1787), pp. 108, 117–118, 121; *A Family Book For Children* (Hartford, 1799), p. 46; [William Green], *The School of Good Manners* (New London, Conn., 1801), pp. 9–10; Giovanni Della Casa, *Galateo* (Baltimore, 1811), pp. 187–189; Hale, p. 193; *The Guide or Counsellor of Human Life* (Springfield, Mass., 1794), p. 41; Adolf Franz vom Knigge, *Practical Philosophy of Social Life* (Lansingburgh, N.Y., 1805), p. 30; *The Polite Academy* 3d ed. (London, 1765), pp. 24–25, 27–28.

28. See, for example, Chesterfield, 1775, 3: pp. 103–104; [William Ramesay], *Gentleman's Companion* (London, 1672), pp. 67–68; d'Ancourt, pp. 8–10, 12, 34; Countess of Carlysle, "Maxims," in Peddle, p. 115; Gregory, p. 29; *Polite Academy,* pp. 3–5, 28; William Cecil, 1st Baron Burghley, *Ten Precepts* (Philadelphia, 1786), p. 189; Hale, p. 193; [Jacob Bailey], *A Little Book For Children* (Portsmouth, N.H., 1758], pp. 5–6; Moody, pp. 10–11, 13, 17, 21; *Little Pretty,* pp. 102, 105–106, 108–112, 118–119; *Family Book,* pp. 41, 43–44, 46; Green, pp. 4, 7–9; *American Academy,* pp. 49–50; Richard Steele, comp., *The Ladies Library* (London, 1714), 1: 233–234; Laban Thurber, *The Young Ladies and Gentleman's Preceptor* (Warren, R.I., 1797), p. 34; Dover, p. 31; James Mott, *Observations on the Education of Children and Hints to Young People on the Duties of Civil Life* (New York, 1816), p. 20; *The Youth's Monitor* (Leominster, Mass., 1799), p. 15; Darwin, p. 95; Bailey, p. 5.

29. Chesterfield, 1775, 2: 83; 3: 103–104; d'Ancourt, p. 7; Ramesay, pp. 67–68; Moore, pp. 225, 265; Hale, pp. 138, 193; John Burton, *Lectures on Female Education and Manners* (New York, 1794), p. 165; Gregory, pp. 29–30; [John Norden], *The Father's Legacy* (London, 1625), n.p. 5; Dover, pp. 31–32, 64; Lambert, "Son," pp. 112–113; William Penn, *Fruits of Solitude,* 8th ed. (Newport, 1749), p. 81; Carlysle, p. 116; *Polite Lady,* p. 71.

30. Jonas Hanway, *Advice from Farmer Trueman, to His Daughter* (Boston, 1810), pp. 96–97, 118–119, 128; Isaac Ambrose, *The Well-Ordered Family* (Boston, 1762), p. 25; Allestree, *Whole,* pp. 271–272, 323, 325; William Penn, *More Fruits of Solitude*

(Newport, 1748), p. 72; Henry Venn, *The Complete Duty of Man* (Worcester, Mass., 1804), p. 246; Robert Dodsley, *The Economy of Human Life*, 7th ed. (Boston, 1752), p. 33.

31. Chesterfield, 1775a, 1: 70; Moore, *Monitor*, 1787, 228; see also *Youth's Monitor*, 1799, p. 11.

32. Chesterfield, 1775, 1: 70-71, 120; George Savile, Marquis of Halifax, *The Lady's New Year's Gift*, 3d ed. (London, 1688), p. 117; Raleigh, pp. 19, 24; [Louis Antoine de Caraciolli], *Advice from a Lady of Quality to Her Children*, 3d ed. (Newburyport, 1784), pp. 78-79; *Polite Lady*, pp. 39, 43; Hale, pp. 136, 143-144; Enos Hitchcock, *Memoirs of the Bloomsgrove Family* (Boston, 1790), p. 177; Peddle, p. 62; Penn, *Fruits of Solitude*, pp. 48, 51; Steele, *Ladies*, 1: 208-209, and 2: 45; Mott, *Observations*, pp. 17, 21; [J. Williams], *Youth's Virtuous Guide* (Boston, 1818), pp. 7-9; [Mrs. Nancy Dennis Sproat], *The Good Boy's Soliloquy* (New York, 1818), p. 29; *The Mirror of the Graces* (New York, 1813), pp. 158-159; Chapone, p. 104; Moore, p. 249.

33. Knigge, pp. 35, 197; Gisborne, pp. 208-218; Hale, p. 195; Thurber, p. 48; Green, p. 7; Norden, n.p.; Jean Baptiste Morvan, l'abbé de Bellegarde, *Politeness of Manners and Behaviour in Fashionable Society* (Boston, 1821), pp. 94, 98; Dover, p. 34. A few authors gave a diluted version of this advice to lower-class readers: Knigge, pp. 193-195; John Barnard, *A Present for an Apprentice* (Boston, 1747), p. 52; Hanway, pp. 117-118, 142.

34. Chesterfield, 1775, 1: 65; 2: 84, 122; 3: 172-173; Phillip Dormer Stanhope, 4th Earl of Chesterfield, *Principles of Politeness* arranged by Trusler (Philadelphia, 1778), pp. 35, 38; Moore, pp. 226, 260, 264, 280; Foster, pp. 67-68; Knigge, p. 31; Moody, pp. 7, 12; *Little Pretty*, pp. 102, 108; Green, pp. 4-6, 8, 10; Della Casa, *Galateo*, pp. 24-25, 37-39, 49, 53, 266-268, 270; Dover, pp. 32, 34; Thurber, p. 24; Rush, *Autobiography*, p. 107.

35. Chesterfield, 1775, 1: 65, 70, 86; Hale, p. 192; Moore, pp. 224, 226, 228, 231; *Polite Academy*, pp. 6-7, 9-11, 17-18, 23-24, 27, 34; *Youth's Monitor*, pp. 11, 14; Green, pp. 4, 7-8; Dover, pp. 31, 33, 36; Moody, pp. 12, 14-15; *Family Book*, p. 44; *Guide or Counsellor*, p. 41; Griffiths, 1794, pp. 11-12; Della Casa, *Galateo*, p. 36.

36. Examples of the advice described in this and the next three paragraphs can be found in the following sources: d'Ancourt, pp. 7, 10-11; Chesterfield, 1775, 1: 39, 65, 70-72, 86-87, 120-121, 148-149, 203-204; 2: 6, 9, 83; 3: 38-39, 101, 104; Phillip Dormer Stanhope, 4th Earl of Chesterfield, *Guide to Men and Manners* (Philadelphia, 1818), pp. 105-106; Halifax, pp. 124-125, 161-162; Penn, *Solitude*, p. 48; Moore, pp. 18-19, 21-29, 203, 224-225, 228-230, 249, 255, 265, 280, 282; Gregory, pp. 72-73; *Polite Lady*, pp. 14-15, 206; Moody, pp. 1, 14, 26; Burton, pp. 70, 163, 165, 169; Norden, n.p.; *Guide or Counsellor*, pp. 41, 57-58; Dixon, p. 52; Della Casa, *Galateo*, pp. 51-53, 264-265, 267-270, 272-273; Tommy Trapwit, *Be Merry and Wise* (Boston, 1762), pp. 12, 14; John Bennett, *Letters to a Young Lady* (Hartford, 1791), 2: 7-8, 27, 42; Bailey, pp. 6-7; Mott, *Observations*, pp. 18, 20; Williams, pp. 3, 5-6; Hitchcock, pp. 74, 79; *The Female Friend* (Baltimore, 1809), pp. 112-113; Hanway, pp. 118, 142; Barnard, *Apprentice*, p. 52. Adams, *Diary*, 1: 71, 83, 172, 242; see also 2: 375; Wood, p. 202; Bushman, p. 371.

37. Chesterfield, 1778, p. 38; Moore, p. 264; Della Casa, *Galateo*, pp. 40, 168-170, 268; Moody, pp. 2-3, 11, 21; *Little Pretty*, pp. 96-97, 107, 119; *Family Book*, pp. 40, 43-44; Green, pp. 7, 9; *Polite Academy*, pp. vi-vii, 5-6, 22-25, 28, 31-33; *Youth's Monitor*, pp. 10-11. Two authors gave young middle-class men and women elaborate instructions for proper standing and walking, advising them in detail on the proper position and motions of the head, arms, and legs: *Polite Academy*, pp. 36-39,

49, and Nichols (a dancing master), pp. 12–13, 22–23. Such lessons were probably the sort the authors anticipated their readers would learn when they studied dancing; for most were content with more general prescriptions on this matter.

38. Chesterfield, 1775, 1: 86; 3: 101, 104; Moore, pp. 224, 229–230; Dover, p. 34; Trapwit, p. 7; [Mrs. Nancy Dennis Sproat], *The Good Girl's Soliloquy* (New York, 1819), p. 29; Griffiths, 1794, p. 12; *Polite Academy*, pp. 19–22; Knigge, p. 31; Della Casa, *Galateo*, pp. 38–39; Moody, p. 12.

39. Chesterfield, 1775, 1: 86, 203; d'Ancourt, pp. 5, 38, 41; Burghley, p. 189; *Polite Academy*, pp. 26, 28, 49; *Polite Lady*, p. 206; Knigge, p. 31; *Little Pretty*, p. 118; Green, pp. 9–10; Della Casa, *Galateo*, pp. 269, 273; *Youth's Monitor*, p. 11; Ahimaaz Harker, *A Companion for the Young People of North America* (New York, 1767), p. 199; *American Academy*, pp. 54–56; Lavater, p. 30; only Barnard recommended bowing among the lower sort: *Apprentice*, p. 52. Chesterfield and d'Ancourt hinted that teaching these gestures was the responsibility of the dancing master. Two authors gave the sort of elaborate instruction in bowing and curtsying that a dancing master would purvey: *Polite Academy*, pp. 37–41, 45–46, 49; Nichols, pp. 13–17, 20–21, 25–26, 32–37.

40. Chesterfield, 1775, 1: 71, 149; 2: 84; 3: 172–173; 1778, pp. 32, 38–39; *Youth's Monitor*, pp. 10–13, 26–27; Della Casa, *Galateo*, pp. 22, 26–27, 39, 171, 179–181, 268; Greene, pp. 4–5, 8; Trapwit, p. 7; Knigge, pp. 29, 31; *Polite Academy*, pp. 23–24; Dover, pp. 31, 34–35; Sproat, *Boy's*, pp. 9, 29; Sproat, *Girl's*, pp. 10, 29; *Little Pretty*, pp. 103, 106–107; Kasson, pp. 124–126; Adams, *Diary*, 1: 93.

41. *Polite Lady*, pp. 114, 207–209; Adams, *Diary*, 1: 83; Chesterfield, 1775, 1: 71, 86, 148; 2: 11, 84; 1778, pp. 38–39; d'Ancourt, pp. 11, 16; Lady Sarah Pennington, "An Unfortunate Mother's Advice to Her Absent Daughters," in *The Lady's Pocket Library* (Philadelphia, 1792), p. 147; Knigge, p. 29; Moore, pp. 18, 99, 224, 228, 235, 265, 267; Hitchcock, p. 74; Bennett, 2: 7, 27; Griffiths, 1794, p. 12; Jean Baptiste Morvan, l'abbé de Bellegarde, "Politeness of Manners and Behavior," in *The Ladies Companion* (Worcester, 1824), p. 27; Moody, p. 13; *Family Book*, p. 44; Dover, pp. 32–33; Trapwit, p. 14; Della Casa, *Galateo*, pp. 24–25, 116, 178–179, 181; *Polite Academy*, pp. vi–vii; Sproat, *Boy's*, p. 9; Sproat, *Girl's*, p. 10; Rush, *Letters*, 2: 1011.

42. Chesterfield, 1775, 1: 148–149; 2: 11, 83; Halifax, pp. 107–108; *Polite Academy*, pp. 19–20, 24–25, 34; Carlysle, pp. 103, 115; Gisborne, p. 79; Johann Caspar Lavater, *Aphorisms on Man* (Philadelphia, 1790), pp. 11–12; *Youth's Monitor*, pp. 9, 26; *Little Pretty*, pp. 108, 113; Green, p. 8; George Brewer, *The Juvenile Lavater* (New York, 1815), p. 104; Trapwit, p. 11; Mott, *Observations*, pp. 20–21; Della Casa, *Galateo*, pp. 180, 267; Kasson, p. 165.

43. Chesterfield, 1775, 1: 93; 2: 9–10, 63–65; 3: 172–173; 1778, p. 38; Moore, pp. 245–246, 265, 280, 282; Knigge, pp. 16, 29–30; *Polite Academy*, pp. 20, 22–25, 31–33, 37–39, 49; Moody, pp. 7, 9, 14, 21; *Family Book*, pp. 42, 44, 46; Griffiths, 1794, p. 12; Della Casa, *Galateo*, pp. 169, 266, 268, 270; *American Academy*, p. 50; Dover, pp. 32, 34–35; *Guide or Counsellor*, pp. 40–41; Bailey, p. 7; Thurber, p. 50; Mott, *Observations*, p. 19; *Polite Lady*, pp. 209–210. Only two writers addressed some of this advice to the lower sort: Barnard, *Apprentice*, pp. 52, 54–55; Hanway, p. 128.

44. Bushman, pp. 83–89. Chesterfield, 1775, 3: 104; 1778, pp. 38–39; d'Ancourt, p. 16; *Polite Academy*, pp. 22–25, 27; Moore, pp. 93–97, 264–265; Carlysle, p. 103; *Family Book*, pp. 42–44, 46; Della Casa, *Galateo*, pp. 23–25, 39, 268; Dover, pp. 31, 33–34; Bailey, pp. 5, 7; Sproat, *Girl's*, pp. 10, 29.

45. Chesterfield, 1775, 2: 6; 3: p. 104; Trapwit, pp. 8–9; Moore, pp. 18, 224, 271, 277–279, 285; d'Ancourt, p. 39; *Polite Academy*, pp. xxi, 22, 31–34; Anne Therese, Marquise de Lambert, "A Mother's Advice to Her Daughter," in *The Lady's Pocket Li-*

brary (Philadelphia, 1792), p. 208; Knigge, pp. 29–30; Penn, *More Fruits*, pp. 43–44; Green, pp. 4–5, 8; Della Casa, *Galateo*, pp. 119–120, 137–138, 143–144, 269–273; *Little Pretty*, pp. 95, 111–113; Griffiths, 1800 ed., pp. 29–30; James Fordyce, *Sermons to Young Women* (Boston, 1767), 1: 134–135; Penn, *Solitude*, p. 51; *Guide or Counsellor*, pp. 41–42; Mrs. Louisa Gurney Hoare, *Hints for the Improvement of Early Education and Nursery Discipline* (New York, 1820), p. 85; Thurber, pp. 35, 85; Hannah More, *Essays on Various Subjects Designed for Young Ladies* (Philadelphia, 1786), p. 17 (Davidoff and Hall describe More as an important writer for the middle class, pp. 167–172); Williams, p. 10; Sproat, *Girl's*, p. 10; Rush, *Letters*, 2: 926–927; Adams, *Diary*, 1: 343, 348.

46. Chesterfield, 1775, 1: 39, 71–73, 148; 2: 11; d'Ancourt, pp. 10–11; Penn, *More Fruits*, pp. 43–44; Moore, pp. 230–231, 234–237, 278; *Polite Lady*, p. 204; *Polite Academy*, pp. vii–viii, 6–8, 31–33; Knigge, p. 30; Fordyce, pp. 135, 137; *Family Book*, pp. 44–45; *Mirror*, pp. 190–191, 203–204; Della Casa, *Galateo*, pp. 74–97, 129, 134, 137–138, 265, 269, 270, 272; Darwin, p. 80; Peddle, p. 68; *Guide or Counsellor*, p. 42; Mott, *Observations*, pp. 18, 20.

47. Chesterfield, 1775, 2: 7, 10, 13; 3: 206; Ramesay, pp. 70, 72; Pennington, p. 147; Moore, pp. 238, 271, 283–284, 286; Foster, pp. 69–70; Griffiths, 1800, pp. 30–31, 33; Della Casa, *Galateo*, pp. 58–61, 69, 101, 264–266, 270–271, 273; Darwin, pp. 80, 91; Lambert, "Son," p. 123; Green, pp. 4, 8–9; Sproat, *Girl's*, p. 10; Dover, pp. 34, 35; John Mellen, *A Discourse Containing a Serious Address to Persons of Several Ages and Characters* (Boston, 1751), p. 39; *Advice to the Fair Sex* (Philadelphia, 1803), p. 49; Charles Atmore, *Serious Advice from a Father to His Children* (Philadelphia, 1819), p. 14.

48. Dover, pp. 32, 33, 35; Moody, p. 16; Mellen, pp. 16, 35, 37; Della Casa, *Galateo*, pp. 57, 127–129, 268, 270, 272–273; Darwin, p. 95; Bailey, p. 4; Thurber, p. 30; Allestree, *Whole*, p. 268; Harker, p. 271; Hannah More, *Strictures on the Modern System of Female Education* (Philadelphia, 1800), 2: 59–60; Dixon, p. 53; Burkitt, pp. 18–20; *The American Ladies Preceptor* (Baltimore, 1810), pp. 42–43; Rush, *Autobiography*, p. 62; see also Adams, *Diary*, 1: 150, 218, 348; 2: 73.

49. Chesterfield, 1775, 2: 7, 10, 13, 64, 83; Ramesay, pp. 70–71, 74; d'Ancourt, pp. 11–12, 17, 34; Moore, pp. 246–247, 263, 265, 271, 274–275, 279–280, 284; *Polite Academy*, pp. xi, xx–xxi, 14, 27, 29–34; Knigge, pp. 16, 30; *Polite Lady*, pp. 88–89, 242–244; Peddle, p. 68; Lambert, "Daughter," p. 208; Della Casa, *Galateo*, pp. 97–99, 103–107, 114–116, 266, 268–271; *Little Pretty*, pp. 95, 100, 113, 115, 117, 119–122; Bennett, 2: 6, 16; More, *Essays*, pp. 18–20; Dixon, pp. 52, 55; Mott, *Observations*, pp. 18–21; Dover, pp. 31, 33–34, 36, 64–65; Bailey, pp. 4–7; Penn, *Father's Love*, p. 17; Adams, *Diary*, 1: 37. Only two relatively obscure writers even attempted to pass on a few of these tips to the lower classes: Burkitt, pp. 18–20; Hanway, pp. 117–118, 138.

50. *Polite Lady*, p. 60, 62–66; Fenelon, pp. 237–238; Hale, pp. 137–138, 192.

51. See Wood, pp. 184–185; Bushman, p. 404; Schultz, pp. 51–60.

52. Raleigh, p. 19; Caraccioli, pp. 78–79; Pennington, pp. 139–140, 170; d'Ancourt, pp. 7, 46; Chesterfield, 2: 83; 1778, p. 37; Moore, pp. 238, 252, 262–263, 265, 268; Gisborne, pp. 218, 278; Hale, pp. 138, 191–192; Carlysle, pp. 97–98; [Benjamin Franklin], *Reflections on Courtship and Marriage* (Philadelphia, 1746), p. 50; Lambert, "Daughter," pp. 209–210; [William Kenrick], *The Whole Duty of a Woman* (Philadelphia, 1788), pp. 53–54; Lambert, "Son," pp. 130, 131; Gregory, pp. 71–72; Knigge, p. 187; Hitchcock, p. 168; Chapone, pp. 104–105, 170; Hoare, p. 83; Mott, *Observations*, pp. 10, 26; Burton, pp. 59–60, 165. Only two writers gave such advice to the lower sort, recommending an affable but not overly familiar demeanor with inferiors: Hanway, p. 118; Barnard, *Apprentice*, pp. 65–67.

53. Foster, pp. 67–68; Carlysle, pp. 113, 115; *Polite Academy*, p. 18; Sproat, *Boy's*, p. 30.

54. Pennington, p. 140; Halifax, pp. 83–84; Ramesay, p. 88; Allestree, *Whole*, p. 327; Fenelon, pp. 218–219; Gregory, pp. 71–72; Steele, *Lady's*, 2: 381, 404, 417–418; *Polite Academy*, pp. xx–xxi, 5, 14–15; Penn, *Solitude*, pp. 67–68; Franklin, p. 50; Venn, p. 188; *Little Pretty*, pp. 100, 102, 113; Chapone, pp. 105, 170; Lambert, "Daughter," p. 209; Dover, pp. 32, 64; Bennett, 2: 29. Barnard, alone, gave similar advice to the lower sort (*Apprentice*, pp. 65–67).

55. See Carroll Smith-Rosenberg, "Domesticating 'Virtue': Coquettes and Revolutionaries in Young America," in Elaine Scarry, ed., *Literature and the Body: Essays on Populations and Persons* (Baltimore: Johns Hopkins, 1988), p. 161; Kasson, p. 195.

56. See Toby Ditz, "The Instability of the Credible Self: Credit and Reputation among Eighteenth-Century Philadelphia Merchants" (unpublished paper presented at the Davis Center Seminar, April 1995), p. 5. On individualism, see Kasson, p. 62. Adams, *Diary*, 2: 76.

57. Halttunen and Kasson describe many of the rules and note their role in the increasingly anonymous urban environment of the antebellum decades. But they neglect the revolutionary-era roots of these rules and exaggerate the ease of reading others in "preindustrial" cities (see Halttunen, pp. 37, 42). Diaries and letters remind us that even though the scale of cities was much smaller, one still encountered strangers on a regular basis in late-eighteenth- and early-nineteenth-century cities. I am indebted to Peter Stearns for some suggestions on these points.

58. On increasing concentration of wealth in long-settled areas, see Nash, *Urban Crucible*, esp. pp. ix–xi, 54–75; James T. Lemon and Gary Nash, "The Distribution of Wealth in Eighteenth-Century America," *Journal of Social History*, 2 (1968): 4, 10–14, 24 (they also claim that middle-class Pennsylvanians were growing more prosperous in the pre-Revolutionary period, p. 15); Jones, esp. pp. 269–272; James Henretta, "Wealth and Social Structure," in Greene and Pole, eds., *Colonial British America* (Baltimore, 1984), pp. 276, 278; see also Thompson, p. 138; Main, pp. 219–220, 229, 233, 283. Bushman explores the material side of this change, by suggesting that gentility could be acquired through purchase of genteel possessions (p. 410). Benjamin DeMott, *The Imperial Middle: Why Americans Can't Think Straight about Class* (New York: William Morrow, 1990).

59. Adams, 1: 93; see also 2: 173, 175; Schlesinger, p. 12; Rush, *Letters*, 1: 190; see also Edmund Hayes, "Mercy Otis Warren versus Lord Chesterfield, 1779," *The William and Mary Quarterly*, 40 (1983): 616–621. Warren's published diatribe against Chesterfield is typical of the concerns others expressed privately. She was mainly outraged by Chesterfield's suggestions that his son take up with Parisian ladies of fashion, suggestions omitted in the digested forms of Chesterfield that began to circulate even as she wrote. She was careful to declare up front that "I have no quarrel with the graces," and acknowledged that "This masterly writer has furnished the present generation with a code of politeness, which, perhaps, surpasses anything of the kind in the English language," p. 618. These contemporary comments disparaging Chesterfield are similar to the contemporary comments disparaging novel reading. Everyone was saying it, but everyone was doing it too.

CHAPTER 5

1. John Bartram, *The Correspondence of John Bartram, 1734–1777*, ed. Edmund Berkeley and Dorothy Smith Berkeley (Gainesville: The University Press of Florida, 1992), pp. 448–449. Konstantin Dierks brought this letter to my attention.

2. See John Locke, *Some Thoughts Concerning Education*, 5th ed. (London, 1705), ed. James Axtell (Cambridge, 1968), p. 195.

3. My thinking here and below has been particularly influenced by Fliegelman's path-breaking *Prodigals and Pilgrims*, esp. pp. 1–15, 33, 38. On the rise of the affectionate and egalitarian family, see Lawrence Stone, *The Family, Sex, and Marriage in England, 1500–1800* (New York: Harper and Row, 1977); Carl Degler, *At Odds: Women and the Family in America from the Revolution to the Present* (New York: Oxford University Press, 1980); Daniel Blake Smith, *Inside the Great House: Planter Family Life in Eighteenth-Century Chesapeake Society* (Ithaca, N. Y.: Cornell University Press, 1980); Nancy F. Cott, "Eighteenth-Century Family and Social Life Revealed in Massachusetts Divorce Records," *The Journal of Social History*, 10 (1976): 2–43; Daniel Scott Smith, "Parental Power and Marriage Patterns: An Analysis of Historical Trends in Hingham, Massachusetts," *Journal of Marriage and the Family*, 35 (1973): 419–428; Wall, pp. 130–131.

4. Rush, *Letters*, pp. 435–436, 535; Calvert, p. 88; Fischer, *Growing Old*, p. 95.

5. Fliegelman recognizes this tension, pp. 57–58.

6. Joseph Kett, *Rites of Passage: Adolescence in America, 1790 to the Present* (New York: Basic Books, 1977), p. 17; Locke, pp. 145, 201; Fliegelman, pp. 36, 80.

7. See Fliegelman, pp. 9–10; Robert Gross, *The Minutemen and Their World* (New York: Hill and Wang, 1976); Wood, pp. 147–148.

8. Yazawa, p. 58.

9. Wood, pp. 149–152. Yazawa argues that Fliegelman overstates the case for change in the revolutionary era because he neglects some Lockean child-rearing inclinations in such figures as Cotton Mather, p. 249. But the conduct literature does suggest dramatic change in attitudes toward youth. Philip Greven, *The Protestant Temperament: Patterns of Child-Rearing, Religious Experience, and the Self in Early America* (New York, 1978), and Pollock both argue for continuity of diverse family forms. Pollock also points out that the indifference toward young children that historians have attributed to premodern society is contrary to our "biological inheritance," pp. 42–43.

10. Rush *Autobiography*, pp. 30–31; Cremin, pp. 23, 30; Axtell, pp. 132, 178, 199, 282; Bailyn, pp. 22, 29–30, 32, 45, 113; Yazawa, pp. 167–190.

11. Cremin, pp. 32–33; Bailyn, pp. 25, 29, 36; Chapone, p. 180. Cf. Kenneth Lockridge, *Literacy in Colonial New England* (New York: Norton, 1974), esp. pp. 4, 28–29, 33–36, 95. See also Ross W. Beales Jr., "Studying Literacy at the Community Level: A Research Note," *Journal of Interdisciplinary History* 9 (1978): 93–102, and David Hall, "The Uses of Literacy in New England, 1600–1850," in William Joyce et al., *Printing and Society in Early America* (Worcester: The American Antiquarian Society, 1983), esp. pp. 42–47.

12. Homes, pp. 71–72.

13. Wood, pp. 195, 197, 202; Adams, *Autobiography*, 3: 257.

14. Della Casa, *Galateo*, pp. x–xi; Nichols, p. 11; *Polite Lady*, p. 272; *Guide or Counsellor*, pp. 38–39.

15. I. Mather, *Arrow*, pp. 24–25; Cotton Mather, *A Cloud of Witnesses vs. Balls and Dances* (Boston, 1700), p. 1; Chesterfield, 1775, 1: 203–204; 2: 6, 38; Williams, p. 3; Locke, pp. 16, 250–251, 310–311; Rush, *Letters*, 1: 251.

16. The conduct literature does not support David Fischer's contention that revolutionary change occurred in attitudes toward old age—from "gerontocratia" to "gerontophobia" (see *Growing Old in America*, parts 1 and 2, esp. pp. 101, 112, 114, 224–225). Rather, it supports Carole Haber's point that Fischer sees big change because he overlooked the negative attitudes of the earlier period; see pp. 5; 131, n. 10.

Haber does see some decline after the colonial era in the economic power of the aged, p. 28.

17. The conduct literature reveals hints of the notion that the experience of the aged was valued in the new republic, as Andrew Achenbaum argues, but these hints were embedded in instructions that reveal a more important (and continuing) ambivalence toward old age. See Achenbaum, *Old Age in the New Land: The American Experience Since 1790* (Baltimore: Johns Hopkins, 1978), pp. 10–11, 18, 25; Samuel Phillips, *A Serious Address to Young People* (Boston, 1763), p. 64; Knigge, pp. 100–101, 103; Job Orton, *Discourses to the Aged* (Salem, 1801), pp. 13–14, 240, 243, 254–255; Atmore, p. 13; Burton, p. 164; Countess of Carlysle, "Maxims," in Peddle, p. 111; Chapone, pp. 90, 92, 185; Bellegarde, 1821, pp. 39–41; Fordyce, p. 122; d'Ancourt, p. 18; Dover, p. 64; Dixon, p. 54; Mellen, p. 17; Brewer, p. 9.

18. See, for example, Adams, *Diary*, 1: 354, 357–358.

19. Knigge, p. 101; Steele, *Ladies*, 2: 362, 372; Orton, pp. 15, 95, 113, 256; Gisborne, pp. 301–302, 304–308; Halifax, pp. 114–116; Bellegarde, 1821, pp. 39–40; Bartram, pp. 449–450.

20. The manners findings thus accord with the revisionist work of Pollock on the status of children in early modern and modern England and America, to the extent that Pollock, too, finds remarkable continuity in the status and care of children between the sixteenth and the nineteenth centuries, et passim, especially pp. 141, 268–271. This is ironic, for Pollock deplores the use of advice literature as a source for the history of childhood. But she dismisses advice literature too easily. Had she applied to it the same systematic analysis that she applies to diaries (something she notes the need for), she would have found that advice regarding children does not falsely indicate change, as she suggests, but is as unchanging as the actual relations she charts (see pp. 43–46, 65 and 290, n. 11; 292, n. 4). Karin Calvert, in contrast, argues that changes in material culture indicate dramatic change after the mid-eighteenth century. She claims that the life stage of childhood itself was newly recognized after 1750, when new, more positive attitudes toward childhood and childishness become evident (part 2, esp. pp. 56, 79–80, 87). Re: youth, see Fliegelman, et passim; Joseph Kett describes the position of youth in this period as "semidependence" and suggests that the balance was shifting toward independence in the early decades of the nineteenth century (pp. 28–31, 604), but his focus is on rural youth and the nineteenth century, whereas the conduct literature, along with Fliegelman's work in other sources, suggests earlier and more dramatic change in the status of youth.

21. See Pollock's review of the literature, especially pp. 8–9, 12, 20. Pollock herself does not see much real change in the eighteenth century (pp. 107, 120, 172).

22. Locke, pp. 145, 201.

23. Rush, *Letters*, 1: 465; Adams, *Diary*, 1: 206–207; Burr, pp. 30–31.

24. Fordyce, pp. 122–123, 164; Burton, p. 36; d'Ancourt, p. 18; Chapone, pp. 90, 92; *Polite Lady*, pp. 57–59; Moody, pp. 5–7, 10–11, 19; *Family Book*, pp. 41, 43, 45; Green, pp. 4–5, 10; *Polite Academy*, pp. 13–14, 17–18, 20–22.

25. Hanway, p. 164; Griffiths, 1794, p. 11; Foster, p. 67; Isaac Taylor, *Advice to the Teens* (Boston, 1820), p. 109; Brewer, p. 8; Moody, pp. 1, 3; *Little Pretty*, pp. 95, 97; *Family Book*, p. 40; *Polite Academy*, pp. 9–11.

26. *American Academy*, p. 55; Hale, p. 193; Penn, *Father's Love*, p. 18; Knigge, p. 30; *Guide or Counsellor*, p. 41; Moody, pp. 2–3, 6, 12–13, 17, 20–21; *Little Pretty*, pp. 96, 101, 107–108, 114, 117–118; Green, pp. 4–7, 9–10; *Polite Academy*, pp. 9–12, 17–18, 21–22, 24–25, 27–28.

27. Chesterfield, 1775, 3: 103–104; Hale, p. 193; Chapone, p. 182; Steele,

Ladies, 1: 233, 237; 2: 1, 2; Burton, pp. 13, 31-32, 34-35, 163-164; Mott, *Observations*, p. 20; Hanway, pp. 96, 119, 164; Phillips, *Serious*, p. 64; Ambrose, pp. 23, 25; Venn, p. 246; Moody, pp. 1-2, 6; *Little Pretty*, pp. 94, 100; Green, pp. 3-4; *Polite Academy*, pp. 5, 14-15, 27, 29-31; Homes, pp. 55, 109, 110.

28. Chesterfield, 1775, 3: 103-104; *American Academy*, pp. 49-50; Griffiths, 1794, p. 11; Moody, pp. 4, 6, 11, 13-15, 17-18; *Little Pretty*, pp. 98-99, 101, 105-106, 108, 110-111, 114-115, 118-119; *Family Book*, pp. 40-41, 43-46; Bailey, p. 6; *Polite Academy*, pp. 5-9, 12-14, 21-22, 28, 31-33; Hale, p. 193; Green, pp. 4, 6-9; Ambrose, p. 23.

29. d'Ancourt, p. 8; Taylor, p. 75; Bailey, p. 6; Sproat, *Girl's*, p. 9; Moody, pp. 2-3, 7, 10, 13, 18; *Little Pretty*, pp. 97, 102, 105, 108-109, 115; *Family Book*, pp. 40, 42-45; Green, pp. 7-8; *Polite Academy*, pp. 3-12, 31-33.

30. Thurber, p. 34; *American Academy*, p. 50; Steele, *Ladies*, 1: 234; 2: 238; Hale, p. 193; Chapone, pp. 183-184. *Polite Lady*, pp. 78-79, 81-82; Fordyce, p. 134; Moody, pp. 2-4, 7, 14-18; *Family Book*, pp. 40-41, 44-45; Green, pp. 5, 7-8; *Polite Academy*, pp. 3, 5-13, 31-34; Hoare, pp. 24, 85.

31. Steele, *Ladies*, 1: 233; d'Ancourt, p. 10; Chesterfield, 1775, 3: 104; Chapone, p. 183; Ambrose, pp. 23, 25; Mott, *Observations*, p. 20; Taylor, p. 75; Moody, pp. 4-5, 15, 18; *Little Pretty*, pp. 99, 111, 115; Green, pp. 4, 6-9; *Polite Academy*, pp. 3-8, 12-13, 31-33; Bailey, p. 5; Homes, pp. 55-56.

32. Chesterfield, 1775, 3: 104; Steele, *Ladies* 2: 2; d'Ancourt, pp. 8, 34; Griffiths, 1794, p. 11; *American Academy*, p. 50; Hale, p. 193; Dodsley, p. 33; Venn, p. 246; Moody, pp. 5-6, 10, 15-16, 20, 22; *Little Pretty*, pp. 99-102, 105, 111-112, 117, 119; *Family Book*, pp. 41, 43-44, 46; Sproat, *Girl's*, p. 9; Homes, p. 55.

33. Dodsley, p. 33; Venn, pp. 187-188; Franklin, p. 50; Steele, *Ladies*, 2: 381, 404, 417-418; Ramesay, p. 88; Allestree, *Whole*, p. 327. On corporal punishment, see Rush, *Letters*, 1: 511-512; Bartram, p. 447; Adams, *Diary*, 1: 9. These condemnations of corporal punishment are stronger and more frequent than the reservations expressed in the earlier period. Cf. Pollock, pp. 143-144, 152-155, 202.

34. Steele, *Ladies*, 2: 165, 231, 237-238, 340-343; Homes, pp. 55-57, 71-72; Harker, pp. 121-124; Mott, *Observations*, p. 10; Hoare, pp. 19, 83-86; *Little Pretty*, p. 12; Burton, pp. 31, 48; Nichols, pp. 22-23.

35. Ruth Bloch, "American Feminine Ideals in Transition: The Rise of the Moral Mother, 1785-1815," *Feminist Studies* 4 (1978): 112-113 et passim; Nancy Cott, *The Bonds of Womanhood: "Woman's Sphere" in New England, 1780-1830* (New Haven: Yale University Press, 1977, pp. 85-87; Linda Kerber, *Women of the Republic: Intellect and Ideology in Revolutionary America* (Chapel Hill: The University of North Carolina Press, 1980), pp. 283-284.

36. Steele, *Ladies*, 2: 136, 178, 198-200, 340, 344-345; Harker, pp. 126-127; Gisborne, pp. 70, 278-280, 282; Fenelon, pp. 43, 57-60, 73; Mott, *Observations*, pp. 10, 12; Caraccioli, p. 186; Homes, p. 85; Hoare, p. 86; Atmore, p. 21; Rush, *Letters*, 1: 465; Fliegelman, p. 15; see also Calvert, pp. 74-75.

37. Norden, n.p.; Steele, *Ladies*, 2: 136, 321-323, 345; Mellen, p. 29; Atmore, p. 20; Mott, *Observations*, p. 3; Hoare, pp. 19, 32-33, 85-86; *Little Pretty*, p. 12; Harker, pp. 126-127; Gisborne, pp. 274, 279-280, 282; Fenelon, pp. 57-60; Allestree, *Whole*, pp. 298-299; Penn, *Father's Love*, p. 28.

38. Allestree, *Whole*, pp. 298-299; Steele, *Ladies*, 2: 136, 161, 342-343; Caraccioli, p. 186; Ramesay, p. 99; Hoare, pp. 19, 32-33, 85-86; Gisborne, pp. 274, 280; Atmore, p. 20; *Little Pretty*, p. 12; Mott, *Observations*, p. 3; Fenelon, p. 61; Bartram, pp. 446-447.

39. *Little Pretty*, p. 12; *American Academy*, p. 48; Allestree, *Whole*, pp. 298-299;

Steele, *Ladies*, 2: 161–162, 318–321; Ramesay, p. 99; Penn, *Father's Love*, p. 28; Mellen, p. 29; Locke, pp. 147–150, 155, 177, 183; Burr, pp. 95, 195; see also Elizabeth Drinker, *The Diary of Elizabeth Drinker*, ed. Elaine F. Crane (Boston: Northeastern University Press, 1991), 2: 1495.

40. Rush, *Letters*, p. 216; Axtell, pp. 235–244; Fliegelman, p. 109; Kett, pp. 54–59.

41. Rush, *Letters*, 1: 585.

42. Fliegelman, pp. 40–41.

43. Fliegelman, p. 80.

44. Raleigh, pp. 19, 24; Penn, *Solitude*, pp. 48, 51; Hale, pp. 136, 143–144, 195; Ramesay, pp. 71, 77; Knigge p. 35; Thurber, pp. 9, 48; Burton, p. 105; Williams, pp. 7, 9; Chesterfield, 1775, 1: 70, 120; Harker, pp. 210–218; Foster, p. 93; Peddle, p. 62; Hanway, pp. 116–118, 142; William Parker Cutler and Julia Perkins Cutler, eds. *Journals and Correspondence of Rev. Manasseh Cutler, LL.D.*, 2 vols. (Cincinnati, 1888), pp. 124–127; Adams, Diary, 1: 118.

45. Bailey, p. 7; Dixon, p. 52; Trapwit, p. 7; Moody, pp. 1–3, 19, 22; *Little Pretty*, pp. 94–95, 97, 115–116, 120; Sproat, *Boy's*, p. 29; Green, pp. 3, 6–7, 10; *Family Book*, pp. 40, 45–46; *Polite Academy*, pp. 6–8, 11, 27, 29–31; Fenelon, pp. 73–74; Gisborne, p. 283.

46. Della Casa, *Galateo*, pp. 37–39, 53, 266–268, 270; Chesterfield, 1775, 1: 65; 2: 122; 3: 172–173; 1778, pp. 35, 38; Moore, pp. 226, 260, 264, 280; Foster, pp. 67–68; *Polite Lady*, p. 93; Dover, p. 34; d'Ancourt, p. 12; Thurber, p. 35; Brewer, p. 9; Moody, p. 12; *Little Pretty*, p. 108; Green, p. 4; *Polite Academy*, pp. 24–26.

47. Dover, pp. 31, 33, 36; d'Ancourt, p. 9; Chesterfield, 1775, 1: 65, 70, 86; Knigge, p. 30; Nichols, pp. 19–20, 33; Della Casa, *Galateo*, pp. 36, 39; Moore, pp. 224, 226, 228, 231; Hale, p. 192; Moody, pp. 2–3, 6, 12–15; *Family Book*, pp. 41, 44; Green, pp. 4, 7–8; *Polite Academy*, pp. 17–18, 23–24, 34; Sproat, *Girl's*, p. 10.

48. Burton, pp. 13–14, 70, 163; Bennett, 2: 6–7, 29; *Little Pretty*, pp. 94, 109, 121; Trapwit, pp. 12, 14; Bailey, pp. 6–7; Hoare, pp. 83, 86; Steele, *Ladies*, 2: 231; Harker, p. 199; d'Ancourt, pp. 7, 10–11; Chesterfield, 1775, 1: 39, 65, 70, 86–87, 120–121; 2: 9, 83–84; 3: 104; Moore, pp. 19, 223–226, 228, 230, 249, 265, 267–268, 282; Peddle, p. 63; *Mirror*, pp. 158–159; Della Casa, *Galateo*, pp. 51–53, 264, 267, 269–270, 273; Griffiths, 1794, p. 12; Gregory, pp. 72–73; Adams, Diary, 1: 118; Philip Schuyler to Stephen Van Rensselaer, 18 September 1781, Schuyler Family Collection, New York State Library; Locke, pp. 245–246.

49. Della Casa, *Galateo*, pp. 182–183, 267–268; Chesterfield, 1775, 1: 70–72, 148–149, 203–204; 2: 6, 38, 83; 1778, pp. 38–39; Moore, pp. 21–29, 228–231, 254–255, 265; Williams, pp. 3, 5–6; *Polite Lady*, pp. 14–15, 206; Peddle, p. 37; Burton, p. 70; *Female Friend*, p. 112; Gregory, p. 57; Halifax, p. 161; Carlysle, p. 105; Kenrick, 1761, p. 23; Hitchcock, pp. 74, 79.

50. Chesterfield, 1778, p. 38; *Youth's Monitor*, pp. 10–11; Della Casa, *Galateo*, pp. 168–170, 268; Nichols, pp. 22–23; Knigge, p. 30; Moody, pp. 2–3, 21; *Little Pretty*, pp. 96–97, 119; Green, pp. 7, 9; *Polite Academy*, pp. vi–vii, 5–8, 24–26, 28, 37–39, 49.

51. Chesterfield, 1775, 3: 101, 104; Moore, pp. 229–230; *Youth's Monitor*, p. 13; Griffiths, 1794, p. 12; Della Casa, *Galateo*, p. 38; Sproat, *Girl's*, p. 29; Moody, pp. 8, 12; *Family Book*, p. 42; Green, p. 5; *Polite Academy*, pp. 19–20.

52. Della Casa, *Galateo*, pp. 22, 38–39, 171, 177, 179–181; Chesterfield, 1775, 1: 39, 71, 149; 2: 84; 3: 104, 173; 1778, pp. 32, 38–39; Moore, pp. 228–229, 254–255, 264, 267, 280; *Youth's Monitor*, pp. 10–12, 27; Dover, pp. 34–35; Knigge, p. 29; Moody, pp. 11–12; *Little Pretty*, pp. 106–107; *Family Book*, pp. 43–44; Sproat, *Girl's*, p. 29; Sproat, *Boy's*, p. 29.

53. Bellegarde, 1824, p. 27; Lavater, pp. 11–12; Della Casa, *Galateo*, pp. 116, 169, 178–181, 266–268, 270, 273; *Polite Lady*, pp. 114, 207–209; Chesterfield, 1775, 1: 71, 86, 93, 148–149; 2: 9–11, 63–65, 83–84; 3: 172–173; 1778, p. 38; Moore, pp. 18, 99, 224, 228, 235, 245–246, 254, 265, 267, 280, 282; Darwin, pp. 86–87, 89; More, *Strictures*, 2: 50; *American Ladies Preceptor*, pp. 40–41; Griffiths, 1794, pp. 11–12; Fordyce, 1: 126; Barnard, *Apprentice*, pp. 52, 54–55; Dover, pp. 32–36; *Little Pretty*, pp. 102, 104, 108, 113, 119; Green, pp. 4, 8; Bailey, pp. 5, 7; Sproat, *Girl's*, p. 10.

54. Lavater, p. 30; d'Ancourt, pp. 5, 38; Della Casa, *Galateo*, pp. 269, 273; Chesterfield, 1775, 1: 86, 203; 3: 39; Moore, pp. 224, 228; Burghley, p. 189; *Polite Lady*, p. 206; Barnard, *Apprentice*, p. 52; *American Academy*, pp. 54–56; *Mirror*, pp. 160–161; Moody, pp. 17, 20–22; *Family Book*, pp. 45–46; Green, pp. 9–10; *Polite Academy*, pp. 5–6, 26, 28. Two works convey the elaborate instructions available from dancing masters: Nichols, pp. 13–17, 20–21, 25–26, 32–37; *Polite Academy*, pp. 37–41, 45–46, 49.

55. Della Casa, *Galateo*, pp. 23–24, 39, 134, 179–180, 267–268; Chesterfield, 1775, 1: 148–149; 2: 11, 83; 3: 104; 1778, pp. 38–39; *Youth's Monitor*, pp. 9–11, 26; Dover, pp. 31, 33–34, 36; Griffiths, 1794, p. 11; Mott, *Observations*, pp. 20–21; Halifax, pp. 107–108; d'Ancourt, pp. 9, 16; Darwin, p. 94; Trapwit, pp. 7, 10–11; *Little Pretty*, pp. 103, 107–109, 117; Green, pp. 4, 8–9; *Polite Academy*, pp. 22–25, 27, 34; Sproat, *Girl's*, p. 10.

56. Lavater, p. 22; Penn, *Solitude*, p. 51; Atmore, p. 12; Della Casa, *Galateo*, pp. 119–120, 137–139, 141–144, 269–273; Chesterfield, 1775, 1: 39, 65, 86; 2: 6; 3: 104; Moore, pp. 18, 224, 271, 277–279, 285; d'Ancourt, p. 39; Chapone, pp. 183–184; Lambert, "Daughter," p. 208; More, *Essays*, p. 17; Knigge, pp. 29–30; Trapwit, pp. 8–9; Moody, pp. 1–2, 14, 16, 18; *Family Book*, pp. 44–45; *Polite Academy*, pp. xxi, 5–8, 22, 31–34.

57. Della Casa, *Galateo*, pp. 52–53, 134, 137–138, 265, 272; Chesterfield, 1775, 1: 39, 65, 72–73, 148; 3: 104; *Youth's Monitor*, pp. 13–15; Kenrick, 1761, pp. 23, 25; Bennett, 2: 28, 41; Darwin, p. 80; *Mirror*, pp. 190–191, 203–204; Moody, pp. 14–15; Green, p. 7; *Polite Academy*, pp. 31–33.

58. *Advice to the Fair Sex*, p. 46; Bellegarde, 1821, p. 75; Della Casa, *Galateo*, pp. 57, 127–129, 268–270, 272–273; Moore, pp. 235–237, 282; *Guide or Counsellor*, p. 42; *Polite Lady*, pp. 195–198; Gregory, pp. 34–35; *American Ladies Preceptor*, pp. 42–43; *Female Friend*, p. 84; More, *Strictures*, 2: 59–60; Mellen, pp. 16, 35–37; *Little Pretty*, p. 112; *Polite Academy*, pp. 31–33.

59. *Advice to the Fair Sex*, p. 49; Raleigh, p. 19; Della Casa, *Galateo*, pp. 57–61, 69, 264–267, 270–271, 273; Chesterfield, 1775, 2: 7, 10, 13; 3: 206; Moore, pp. 238, 271, 283–284, 286; Griffiths, 1800, pp. 31, 33; Darwin, pp. 80, 91; Lambert, "Son," p. 123; Foster, pp. 69–70; Atmore, p. 14; Gregory, p. 31; Moody, pp. 15–17, 19, 24; *Polite Academy*, pp. 8, 29–34; Sproat, *Girl's*, p. 10; Homes, p. 57.

60. *Advice to the Fair Sex*, p. 48; Della Casa, *Galateo*, pp. 104–107, 114–116, 268–270; Chesterfield, 1775, 2: 10, 13, 83; Moore, pp. 263, 265; Penn, *More Fruits*, p. 22; Knigge, p. 16; Gisborne, pp. 79, 197; d'Ancourt, pp. 11, 17; Lambert, "Daughter," p. 208; Bennett, 2: 16; Gregory, pp. 30–31; More, *Essays*, pp. 18–20; Bailey, p. 6; *Little Pretty*, pp. 117, 119, 121–122; *Family Book*, pp. 46–47.

61. Bennett, 2: 6; Burton, p. 169; Bellegarde, 1824, p. 11; Della Casa, *Galateo*, pp. 50, 52–53, 97–99, 101, 103, 266, 269–271; Moore, pp. 246–247, 274–275, 279–280, 284, 286; Dover, pp. 33–34, 36, 64–65; Harker, pp. 199, 246–247; Griffiths, 1794, pp. 11–12 and 1800, pp. 30–31; Mott, *Observations*, pp. 18–19, 21; *Polite Lady*,

pp. 88–89, 242–244; Darwin, p. 92; Mellen, pp. 16, 39; Moody, pp. 1–2, 5, 17–20, 22–23; Green, pp. 3, 6, 8–9; Bailey, pp. 4–7.

62. Sproat, *Girl's*, p. 10; Sproat, *Boy's*, p. 30; Della Casa, *Galateo*, pp. 41, 269; Chesterfield, 1775, 2: 6; Moore, p. 278; Griffiths, 1794, pp. 11–12; 1800, pp. 29–30; Knigge, p. 31.

63. Fliegelman, p. 15.

64. Fliegelman, pp. 34–35, 108–115.

65. Rodney Hessinger, "Problems and Promises: Colonial American Child-Rearing and Modernization Theory," *The Journal of Family History* 21, no. 2 (April 1996): 128.

66. Fliegelman, pp. 260, 262; Rush, *Letters*, 2: 776–777. For an insightful exploration of ambivalent attitudes toward these changes, see Daniel Cohen, "Arthur Mervyn and His Elders: The Ambivalence of Youth in the Early Republic," *The William and Mary Quarterly* 43 (July 1986): 362–380; see also Kett, especially pp. 28–29.

CHAPTER 6

1. Rush, *Letters*, 1: 585; 2: 929. On Republican Motherhood, see Linda Kerber in *Women of the Republic*, chap. 9.

2. For the old view, see Julia Cherry Spruill, *Women's Life and Work in the Southern Colonies* (New York: Norton, 1972); Mary Sumner Benson, *Women in Eighteenth-Century America: A Study of Opinion and Social Usage* (New York: Columbia University Press, 1935; reprint, 1966); Elizabeth A. Dexter, *Colonial Women of Affairs* (Boston: Houghton Mifflin, 1924); Janet Wilson James, *Changing Ideas About Women in the United States, 1776–1825* (New York: Garland, 1981). For the newer view, see Mary Beth Norton, *Liberty's Daughters. The Revolutionary Experience of American Women, 1750–1800* (Boston: Little, Brown, 1980); Kerber, *Women of the Republic*; Marylynn Salmon, *Women and the Law of Property in Early America* (Chapel Hill: University of North Carolina Press, 1986); and Nancy Cott, *The Bonds of Womanhood*. Joan Hoff Wilson offers a dissenting view in "The Illusion of Change: Women and the American Revolution," in Alfred E. Young, ed., *The American Revolution: Explorations in the History of American Radicalism* (Dekalb, Ill.: Northern Illinois University Press, 1976). For examples of some of the newer refining work, see Rosemary Zagarri, "Morals, Manners and the Republican Mother," *The American Quarterly* 44, no. 2 (June 1992): 192–215; Ruth Bloch, "The Gendered Meanings of Virtue in Revolutionary America," *Signs* 13, no. 1 (Autumn 1987): 37–58; and Jan Lewis "The Republican Wife: Virtue and Seduction in the Early Republic," *The William and Mary Quarterly* 44, no. 4: 689–721; Carroll Smith-Rosenberg, "Domesticating 'Virtue.'" Constructions of masculinity among northerners are explored in Anthony Rotundo, "Body and Soul: Changing Ideals of American Middle-Class Manhood, 1770–1920," *The Journal of Social History* 16, no. 4 (Summer 1983): 23–38; "Learning About Manhood: Gender Ideals and the Middle-Class Family in Nineteenth-Century America," in Mangan and Wolvin, eds., *Manliness and Morality*, and *American Manhood*; Toby Ditz, "Shipwrecked, or Masculinity Emperiled: Mercantile Representations of Failure and the Gendered Self in Eighteenth-Century Philadelphia," *The Journal of American History* 81, no. 1 (June 1994): 51–80, and "The Instability of the Credible Self."

3. Jurgen Habermas, *The Structural Transformation of the Public Sphere: An Enquiry into a Category of Bourgeois Society* (Cambridge: Massachusets Institute of Technology, 1989); Joan Landes, *Women and the Public Sphere in the Age of the French Revolution* (Ithaca, N. Y.: Cornell University Press, 1988). I explore these issues further in

"Between Public and Private; Manners, Gender, and the Social Sphere in Antebellum America" (paper presented to the American Historical Association, January 1994). See also Zagarri, p. 210.

4. Axtell, p. 178; James, pp. 284–286; Kerber, *Women of the Republic*, pp. 199–203; Pollock, pp. 246–247; *Essex Gazette*, 19 July 1774, cited in Middlekauff, p. 72; Kathryn Kish Sklar, *Catharine Beecher: A Study in American Domesticity* (New York: Norton, 1976), p. 17; see also Elizabeth Drinker, *Diary*, 2: 1507.

5. New work on female literacy has revised earlier more conservative estimates: see Joel Perlmann and Dennis Shirley, "When Did New England Women Acquire Literacy?" *The William and Mary Quarterly* 48, no. 1 (January 1991): 50–67.

6. Mott, p. 304; Fliegelman claims of Gregory that "few other titles, if any, achieved equivalent wartime success," p. 50; Jared Sparks, ed., *The Works of Benjamin Franklin* (1838), 8: 166–167; cited in James, p. 46. A compilation of several authors, *The Ladies Library* was never reprinted in America but can be found in at least thirty-seven book sale catalogs and library inventories between 1738 and 1799, including the library that Franklin founded with fellow artisans in the 1730s; *A Catalogue of Books Belonging to the Library Company of Philadelphia* (facs. ed. of 1741 cat.) (Philadelphia: The Library Company, 1956). Elizabeth Drinker read Halifax and Kenrick several times; she also read Pierre Joseph Boudier de Villemert, *The Ladies' Friend* (Philadelphia, 1771), Fenelon, and Caraccioli (see her *Diary*.) Chester C. Hallenbeck, "A Colonial Reading List from the Union Library of Hatboro, Pennsylvania," *The Pennsylvania Magazine of History and Biography* LVI (1932): 297, 301, 317; Davidson, *Revolution and the Word*, p. 8; see also Benson, pp. 20, 22–23, 60. Foster recommended Chapone, Bennett, and *The Ladies Library*, pp. 152, 156–157.

7. James, pp. 124–126, 285, 288–290. Zagarri explores the intellectual currents that accompanied the trends in manners that I describe below in her examination of new thinking about women on the part of the civil-jurisprudential school of the Scottish Enlightenment, thereby also stressing the transatlantic nature of the reevaluation of attitudes toward women, pp. 209–210. See also Bloch, "Meanings of Virtue," p. 56 et passim.

8. Davidson, *Revolution and the Word*, p. 32; see also Michael Warner, *The Letters of the Republic: Publication and the Public Sphere in Eighteenth-Century America* (Cambridge: Harvard University Press, 1980), pp. 15–16, and James, pp. 261–272. The evidence does not support Nancy Armstrong's claim that "conduct books of the eighteenth and nineteenth centuries" were "a female genre, often written by women": see "The Rise of the Domestic Woman," in *The Ideology of Conduct*, Nancy Armstrong and Leonard Tennenhouse, eds. (New York: Methuen, 1987), p. 135.

9. Hannah Webster Foster, *The Coquette*, ed. Cathy Davidson (New York: Oxford University Press, 1986), pp. 139–140; on the hidden subversive messages of female novelists, see Davidson, p. 153 et passim, and Carroll Smith-Rosenberg, "Domesticating 'Virtue,'" pp. 166–167.

10. Lewis, "Republican Wife," et passim, esp. pp. 689–690, 693, 697, 699.

11. Boudier de Villemert, pp. 5–6; More, *Essays*, p. 6; *Advice to the Fair Sex*, pp. 17–18; Bennett, 2: 47–48; Fordyce, 1: 60; Gisborne, pp. 241–242; More, *Strictures*, 2: 36–38; Jonathan Swift, "Letter to a Very Young Lady on Her Marriage," in *Reflections on Courtship and Marriage* (Philadelphia, 1746), p. 62. On female influence over men, see Jan Lewis, "The Republican Wife," pp. 700–702 et passim; cf. Rush, *Selected Writings*, p. 384. Among the more entertaining of revolutionary-era accounts of male-female interaction is the extended description of flirtation between Sally Wister and American officers quartered in and around her house, described in her diary of 1777,

Sally Wister's Journal (Philadelphia, 1902); see also Ellen Rothman, *Hands and Hearts: A History of Courtship in America* (Cambridge: Harvard University Press, 1987), pp. 23–24.

12. Della Casa, *Galateo*, p. 274; *Female Friend*, p. 83; *Advice to the Fair Sex*, pp. 25–27; d'Ancourt, p. 42; Chapone, p. 188; *Polite Lady*, pp. 197–198; Foster, pp. 103, 105; *Mirror*, pp. 159–160; Bennett, 2: 101; on the novelists, see Davidson, *Revolution and the Word*, p. 113.

13. Kenrick, 1761, p. 25; Fordyce, 1: 73–74, 164; *Polite Lady*, p. 113; Burton, p. 103; *Female Friend*, pp. 82, 112–113; Gregory, pp. 112–113; Halifax, p. 162; Steele, *Ladies*, 1: 63; Gisborne, p. 132, 134; Sarah Eve, "Extracts from the Journal of Miss Sarah Eve," *Pennsylvania Magazine of History and Biography* V, 1881, p. 203; Wister, et passim. Adams, *Diary*, 1: 195–196. Beyond these occasional uses of the terms *public* and *private*, revolutionary-era conduct writers did not limn a very spatially differentiated social world. The sense of place was much greater in antebellum works.

14. Fordyce, 1: 60, 73–74; 2: 192–193; Gregory, pp. 29–30, 35–37, 43, 78; Bennett, 2: 27–28, 47–48, 96, 98–99, 102–103; Gisborne, pp. 79, 135, 192–193; *Mirror*, pp. 156–160; Halifax, pp. 96, 98–99, 102–104; d'Ancourt, pp. 8, 20–21, 42; *Polite Lady*, pp. 214–216, 219; Chapone, p. 188; Swift, pp. 56–57, 66; Foster, pp. 98, 103; *Female Friend*, pp. 83–84, 94–95, 97, 183–186; Hanway, p. 152; *American Ladies Preceptor*, pp. 20–21, 41, 44; Bellegarde, 1821, pp. 76, 105–108, 135; Steele, *Ladies*, 2: 80, 86, 116–128; Franklin, pp. 37–39; Venn, p. 215. Eliza S. Bowne, letter to Moses Porter, 18 March 1801, in *A Girl's Life Eighty Years Ago*, Clarence Cook, ed. (New York, 1887), p. 47.

15. Ulrich, *Good Wives*, pp. 103–105; John D'Emilio and Estelle Freedman, *Intimate Matters: A History of Sexuality in America* (New York: Harper and Row, 1988), pp. 44–45. Nancy Cott claims that such writers as Gregory and Fordyce were recommending a modesty that was really just an act for men's pleasure, while British Evangelicals like Gisborne and More were beginning to recommend passionlessness; see "Passionlessness: An Interpretation of Victorian Sexual Ideology, 1790–1850," *Signs* 4, no. 2 (Winter 1978): 224–226, and see also Davidson, *Revolution and the Word*, pp. 126–127. But there are no big differences in the advice for face-to-face behavior given in these different works.

16. Halifax, p. 103; Steele, *Ladies*, 1: 197, 207; Gregory, pp. 28–29, 57–60; d'Ancourt, pp. 19–20, 23; Boudier de Villemert, pp. 6, 65; Swift, p. 57; Gisborne, p. 79; *Female Friend*, pp. 94–95, 98, 183–184, 186; *American Ladies Preceptor*, pp. 21, 41; Bellegarde, 1821, pp. 76, 107–108; Kenrick, 1761, p. 25; Fordyce, 1: 69–70; *Polite Lady*, p. 215; Bennett, 2: 28, 99, 103; Burton, p. 110; Darwin, p. 95; *American Academy*, p. 55.

17. Steele, *Ladies*, 2: 80, 86; Homes, p. 50; Franklin, pp. 34, 37–39; Boudier de Villemert, p. 6; Swift, pp. 57, 66; *American Ladies Preceptor*, pp. 21, 41; Gregory, pp. 29–30, 37, 57; Bennett, 2: 27–28, 48; Gisborne, p. 79; Foster, p. 98; *Female Friend*, pp. 97, 184.

18. Halifax, pp. 112–113; Dodsley, p. 27; d'Ancourt, pp. 8, 19–20, 42; *Polite Academy*, p. xiii; *Polite Lady*, pp. 195–198, 214–215; Gregory, pp. 29–30, 34–35, 58–60, 77–78; Bennett, 2: 27–28, 99; Burton, pp. 103, 110; Darwin, p. 95; Foster, pp. 103, 105; *Female Friend*, pp. 84, 94–95, 98; *American Ladies Preceptor*, pp. 41–43; Bellegarde, 1821, pp. 105, 107–108, 135.

19. Gregory, pp. 43–44; Kenrick, 1761, pp. 26–27; Halifax, p. 103; d'Ancourt, pp. 8, 20–23; Foster, pp. 103, 105; *Advice to the Fair Sex*, pp. 25–27; *American Ladies Preceptor*, p. 44; Bellegarde, 1821, pp. 107–108, 135; Swift, p. 57; *Female Friend*, pp. 185–186.

20. Lewis argues that the era's seduction tales were more "a discourse about politics that had implications for women" (namely, symbolic explorations of the fate of virtue in the new republic), but the conduct writers were offering concrete warnings to women, and warnings that are echoed in other sources (not to mention that at least some of the seduction novels were based on true stories); Lewis, personal communication and "Republican Wife," pp. 716–720. Stansell's research in court records and other sources from New York City reveal that "male license for sexual aggressiveness increased" in the late eighteenth century, "especially toward women in public," who were "fair game;" pp. 23–27. Davidson insists that the problem of seduction was indeed the main story of the seduction novels, even though they may also have had metaphorical functions: *Revolution and the Word*, pp. 105–109; on the salience of seduction tales for the marriage decision (although she thinks these issues were not addressed by the conduct books), see pp. 114–123. Some historians see the period's rise in premarital pregnancy rates as female declarations of independence from parental control. At the least it is clear that old communal controls were gone; see Daniel Scott Smith and Michael Hindus, "Premarital Pregnancy in America, 1640–1971: An Overview and Interpretation, *Journal of Interdisciplinary History* 5 (1975): 537–570; Gross, pp. 100–101, 184–185; Fliegelman, p. 120; for an overview, see D'Emilio and Freedman, pp. 44–45.

21. Adams, *Diary*, 1: 51, 54, 75.

22. Raleigh, pp. 19, 24; Della Casa, *Galateo*, p. 266; Penn, *More Fruits*, p. 19; Chesterfield, 1775, 1: 70, 120–121; Dover, pp. 63–64; Moore, pp. 237–240, 251–252; Hitchcock, pp. 177–178; Steele, *Ladies*, 1: 208; 2: 45, 178; Chapone, p. 104; Peddle, p. 63; Burton, p. 105; Foster, p. 93; Hanway, pp. 117–118, 142; *Little Pretty*, pp. 94, 120; Green, p. 3.

23. Knigge, p. 35; Ramesay, p. 77; Ezra Sampson, *The Brief Remarker* (Hudson, New York, 1818), p. 150; Penn, *Solitude*, pp. 48, 51; Penn, *More Fruits*, p. 19; Dover, pp. 34, 64; Norden, n.p., Steele, *Ladies*, 1714, 1: 63; 2: 47; Dodsley, pp. 26, 28; d'Ancourt, p. 46; Fordyce, 1: 73–74, 164; Boudier de Villemert, pp. 9–10; Gregory, pp. 26, 112–113; Burton, pp. 103, 105, 149; *Female Friend*, pp. 82, 112–113. A systematic study needs to be done to determine the currency of this expectation; Elizabeth Drinker, for one, reported that she was "no great goer abroad at any time," *Diary*, 1: 390.

24. Della Casa, *Galateo*, pp. 24–25, 36–39, 53, 266–268, 270; Chesterfield, 1775, 1: 65, 70, 86; 2: 122; 3: 172–173; 1778, pp. 35, 38; Moore, pp. 224, 226, 228, 231, 260, 264, 280; Knigge, p. 31; Green, pp. 4, 8; d'Ancourt, pp. 9, 12; *Polite Lady*, p. 93; Foster, pp. 67–68; Hanway, p. 128; *Youth's Monitor*, pp. 11, 14; Dover, pp. 31, 36; Sproat, *Girl's*, p. 10; *Little Pretty*, pp. 108, 110, 112; *Polite Academy*, p. 34; Nichols, pp. 19–20.

25. Chesterfield, 1775, 1: 71, 149, 203–204; 3: 38–39, 104, 173; 1778, pp. 32, 38–39; Moore, pp. 228–229, 254–255, 264, 280; Barnard, *Apprentice*, p. 52; *American Academy*, pp. 54, 56; Knigge, pp. 13, 29–31; Della Casa, *Galateo*, pp. 22, 39–40, 168–171, 177, 179–181, 268–269, 273; Steele, *Ladies*, 1: 235; d'Ancourt, pp. 38, 41; Bennett, 2: 8; *Polite Lady*, p. 206; *Polite Academy*, pp. vi–vii, 5–6, 22–23, 26, 28, 36–41, 45–46, 49; Nichols, pp. 13–17, 20–23, 25–26, 28–29, 31–37; Kenrick, 1761, pp. 23–24; *Little Pretty*, pp. 97, 106–107, 118–119; Sproat, *Boy's*, pp. 9, 29; Sproat, *Girl's*, p. 29.

26. Green, pp. 4, 8–9; Chesterfield, 1775, 1: 71–72, 149; 2: 83; 3: 104; 1778, pp. 38–39; Moore, pp. 93–97, 230, 234–237, 254, 264–265, 278; Dover, pp. 31, 33–34, 36; *Guide or Counsellor*, pp. 41–42; Della Casa, *Galateo*, pp. 23–25, 39, 74–97, 129, 134, 179–180, 265, 267–270; Steele, *Ladies*, 1: 233, 237; d'Ancourt, pp. 10–11, 16;

Carlysle, pp. 103, 115; Darwin, p. 94; *Female Friend*, p. 112; Hanway, p. 49; *Family Book*, pp. 42–44, 46; *Youth's Monitor*, pp. 9–11, 13; Fordyce, 1: 137.

27. Ramesay, pp. 70–71; *Family Book*, pp. 41, 45–46; Chesterfield, 1775, 2: 7, 13, 64; Moore, pp. 246–247, 274–275, 279, 284, 286; Green, pp. 3, 6, 8–9; Della Casa, *Galateo*, pp. 50, 57, 97–99, 101, 103, 266, 269–271, 273; Steele, *Ladies*, 1: 258–267; 2: 179; *Polite Lady*, pp. 88, 242–244; More, *Essays*, p. 62; Pennington, p. 147; Burton, p. 169; Darwin, p. 92; Foster, pp. 55–56, 70; *Advice to the Fair Sex*, p. 49; Sproat, *Girl's*, p. 10. On historians' association of women and gossip, see Ditz, "Instability," pp. 32–33.

28. Sproat, *Girl's*, p. 29; *Polite Academy*, pp. 19–22; Chesterfield, 1775, 3: 101, 104; and 1778, p. 32; Moore, pp. 229–230, 255; Dover, p. 34; Knigge, p. 31; Moody, pp. 8, 12; *Little Pretty*, pp. 103, 107; Green, p. 5; Sproat, *Boy's*, p. 9; Della Casa, *Galateo*, p. 173.

29. Della Casa, *Galateo*, pp. 24–25, 116, 178–179, 181; Chesterfield, 1775, 1: 71; and 1778, pp. 38–39; *Youth's Monitor*, pp. 11–12; Dover, p. 33; Knigge, pp. 29–31; d'Ancourt, p. 16; Kenrick, 1761, p. 23; *Polite Academy*, pp. vi–vii; Darwin, p. 78; Bellegarde, 1821, p. 63.

30. Steele, *Ladies*, 1: 258–267; James Forrester, *The Polite Philosopher* (New York, 1758), p. 24; *Polite Academy*, pp. xx–xxi; Bennett, 2: 29; Foster, pp. 55–56; Barnard, *Apprentice*, pp. 54–55; Della Casa, *Galateo*, p. 266; Chesterfield, 1775, 2: 63–65; Moore, pp. 245–246; *Youth's Monitor*, pp. 18–19; Knigge, pp. 16, 197.

31. Della Casa, *Galateo*, pp. 169, 268, 270; Chesterfield, 1775, 1: 93; 2: 9–10; 3: 172–173; and 1778, p. 38; Moore, pp. 265, 280, 282; Moody, pp. 7, 9, 21; *Polite Academy*, pp. vi–vii, 22–23, 31–33, 37–39, 49–51; Knigge, pp. 29–30; Dodsley, pp. 27–28; Fordyce, 1: 69–70; Bennett, 2: 41; Hanway, pp. 48–49, 128; Chapone, pp. 183–184; Darwin, p. 89; Lambert, "Daughter," p. 208; More, *Strictures*, 2: 50; *American Ladies Preceptor*, pp. 40–41.

32. Chesterfield, 1775, 1: 86, 148–149; 2: 11, 83–84; Moore, pp. 99, 224, 254, 265, 267; *Little Pretty*, pp. 108, 112; Dover, pp. 32, 36; Barnard, *Apprentice*, p. 52; Lavater, pp. 11–12; d'Ancourt, pp. 9, 11, 16; Fordyce, 1: 126; Chapone, p. 148; Darwin, pp. 86–87, 94; Hanway, p. 138; Bellegarde, 1824, p. 27; Halifax, pp. 107–108; *Female Friend*, p. 112; Pennington, p. 147.

33. *Polite Lady*, pp. 14–15, 203, 205–206; Bennett, 2: 8, 28–30; Williams, p. 11; Burton, p. 70; Halifax, p. 161; Gregory, p. 57; Peddle, p. 37; *Female Friend*, p. 112; Della Casa, *Galateo*, p. 267; Fenelon, p. 73; Sproat, *Girl's*, p. 10; Chesterfield, 1775, 1: 39, 72, 148, 203–204; 2: 6, 38, 83–84; and 1778, p. 15; Moore, pp. 228–230, 265, 267; Sproat, *Boy's*, p. 30.

34. Penn, *Solitude*, p. 51; Dover, p. 33; Chesterfield, 1775, 1: 39, 65, 86; 2: 6; Moore, pp. 18, 224, 271, 277, 279, 285; *Guide or Counsellor*, pp. 41–42; Moody, pp. 2, 16; Della Casa, *Galateo*, pp. 137–139, 141–144, 269–273; Steele, *Ladies*, 1: 56, 180–181, 184, 234; Fordyce, 1: 134–135; *Polite Lady*, pp. 78–79, 81–89; Chapone, pp. 183–184; Carlysle, p. 118; Lambert, "Daughter," p. 208; More, *Strictures*, 2: 50; *American Ladies Preceptor*, pp. 40–41.

35. *Little Pretty*, pp. 111, 115; Sproat, *Boy's*, p. 10; Della Casa, *Galateo*, pp. 134, 137–138, 265, 270, 272; Chesterfield, 1775, 1: 39, 73, 148; 2: 11; Moore, pp. 230–231, 234, 235; Knigge, p. 30; Steele, *Ladies*, 1: 180, 237; Dodsley, p. 28; Kenrick, pp. 23, 25; *Polite Lady*, p. 204; More, *Essays*, p. 46; Peddle, p. 68; Bennett, 2: 24, 28, 41; Sproat, *Girl's*, p. 10.

36. Chesterfield, 1775, 2: 10; Moore, pp. 223, 282; Dover, pp. 33, 35; Mellen, pp. 35, 37; Green, pp. 3, 8; Della Casa, *Galateo*, pp. 57, 127, 129, 268, 270, 272–273; Steele, *Ladies*, 1: 180; d'Ancourt, p. 11; Gregory, pp. 34–35, 58–60; Darwin, p. 93;

More, *Strictures*, 2: 59–60; *Advice to the Fair Sex*, p. 46; *Female Friend*, p. 84; Belle-garde, 1821, pp. 75, 77.

37. Dover, pp. 31, 33, 36; *Little Pretty*, pp. 121–122; Green, pp. 3, 9; Chesterfield, 1775, 2: 10, 13, 83; Moore, pp. 263, 265, 271, 277; Knigge, pp. 16, 30; Della Casa, *Galateo*, pp. 104–107, 114–116, 268–271; Steele, *Ladies*, 1: 57, 237; 2: 178; Fordyce, 1: 131; Gregory, pp. 30–31; Bennett, 2: 16; More, *Strictures*, 2: 53; *Advice to the Fair Sex*, p. 48; *American Ladies Preceptor*, p. 41.

38. Chesterfield, 1775, 2: 7, 10; 3: 104, 206; Moore, pp. 238, 271, 283–284, 286; Raleigh, p. 19; Ramesay, pp. 70, 72; Lambert, "Son," p. 123; Green, pp. 4, 8–9; Penn, *Father's Love*, pp. 18, 26; Della Casa, *Galateo*, pp. 58–61, 69, 264–267, 270–273; Steele, *Ladies*, 1: 56; d'Ancourt, p. 43; Gregory, p. 31; More, *Essays*, p. 16; Bennett, 2: 29; Gisborne, p. 196; Darwin, pp. 80, 91; Peddle, p. 63.

39. Ramesay, pp. 70, 77, 100; Barnard, *Apprentice*, p. 52; Chesterfield, 1775, 1: 39, 65, 70–71, 86–87, 121, 149; 2: 9, 11, 83–84; 3: 104; Moore, pp. 16–19, 21–29, 223–225, 228–230, 238, 249, 255, 280, 282; Della Casa, *Galateo*, pp. 51–53, 264–265, 270, 272–274; *Polite Lady*, pp. 78–79, 203, 205, 207, 212, 214, 245; Fordyce, 1: 69–71, 127, 164; 2: 182–183, 218; d'Ancourt, pp. 5, 7, 10–11, 25, 36; Gregory, pp. 26–28, 72–73, 112; Bennett, 2: 7, 16, 23–24, 26, 28–29, 41–43, 47; Carlysle, pp. 103, 105–106; Chapone, pp. 148, 183; More, *Essays*, pp. 46, 62; Gisborne, pp. 192–193, 196; Caraccioli, p. 176; *Female Friend*, pp. 183–184; Burton, p. 110; Darwin, pp. 77–80, 86–87; Steele, *Ladies*, 1: 56, 179, 234; 2: 43, 168–169; Adams, *Diary*, 2: 133, 188; 3: 164; Elias Boudinot, *Journey to Boston in 1809* (Princeton, 1955), pp. 35, 41, 63.

40. See Carroll Smith-Rosenberg, "Domesticating 'Virtue,'" pp. 166, 178; Toby Ditz, "Shipwrecked," esp. pp. 54, 66, 79–80, and "Instability," pp. 32–35.

41. On control of the body as a nineteenth-century concern, see Rotundo, "Body and Soul," pp. 25–27, 29–32, and "Learning About Manhood," p. 47; Rotundo acknowledges that the ideal of self-made manhood began to grow in the late eighteenth century in *American Manhood* (p. 3) but deemphasizes the importance of the body before the mid-nineteenth century (p. 222).

42. Other scholars also see signs of growing female autonomy in this period. Susan Klepp explores an increasingly calculating attitude of women toward fertility in "Revolutionary Bodies: Women and the Fertility Transition in the Mid-Atlantic Region," *Journal of American History*, 85 (1998): 910–945. Konstantin Dierks describes female self-improvement for the marriage market in "The Feminization of Letter-Writing in Early America, 1750–1800," paper presented at the Second Annual Conference of the Institute of Early American History and Culture, June 1996.

43. Armstrong argues that "the modern individual was first and foremost a female" but does not cite much evidence from conduct books and neglects to examine conduct advice to men. I do not find the emphasis on the domestic ideal that she attributes to these works in their discussions of face-to-face behavior. See "The Rise of the Domestic Woman," pp. 103, 107 et passim. I am similarly uncomfortable with Smith-Rosenberg's suggestion that the middle-class woman "produced her class:" see "Discovering the Subject," pp. 859–861. For the association of middle class formation and separate spheres, see Mary Ryan, *Cradle of the Middle Class*, pp. 15, 239 et passim; Blumin, p. 187. Amanda Vickery notes and criticizes the association of separate spheres with the rise of the middle class in both American and British women's historiography, but she too assumes that separate spheres reigned in advice books; see her valuable review essay, especially with regard to Davidoff and Hall's influential *Family Fortunes*: "Golden Age to Separate Spheres? A Review of the Categories and Chro-

nology of English Women's History," *The Historical Journal*, 36, no. 2 (1993): 383–414. Rotundo notes the connection between male ideals and economic change in "Learning About Manhood," p. 36; he associates both with rising individualism in *American Manhood:* pp. 3, 15–18, 20.

44. Rush, *Letters*, 1: 525. Cf. Bushman, p. 271.

45. Chesterfield, 1775, 3: 105. Some of the overtly negative comments about women were expurgated from the collections of Chesterfield's advice that circulated subsequently, thus disguising the motivations of this seeming champion of gallantry.

46. Chesterfield, 1775, 1: 70; 2: 122; 3: 105; and 1778, p. 15; Moore, p. 226; Della Casa, *Galateo*, pp. 187–190, 192–193, 265; Lambert, "Son," p. 123; Caraccioli, p. 93; Knigge, pp. 30, 153; Taylor, pp. 75, 117, 122–123, 125; Green, pp. 5, 7, 9; Nichols, pp. 17–18; Franklin, pp. 18, 20, 37–39; Forrester, pp. 38, 40, 51; Raleigh, pp. 21–22; Ramesay, p. 94; Homes, p. 48; Venn, p. 215.

47. Forrester, pp. 39–40; Knigge, pp. 152–153; Della Casa, *Galateo*, p. 270; Chesterfield, 1775, 1: 198–199; 3: 105; and 1778, pp. 15, 22; Moore, p. 238; *Youth's Monitor*, p. 15; Taylor, pp. 75, 117; Franklin, pp. 18, 20–22, 34; Ramesay, p. 94; Barnard, *Apprentice*, pp. 18–19; Lambert, "Son," p. 125; Venn, p. 215; Bellegarde, 1821, p. 75.

48. Forrester, pp. 38–40; Knigge, p. 152; Taylor, pp. 117, 121–122, 124–128. Rush, *Letters*, 1: 464, 622. See Zagarri on these ideas among Scottish Enlightenment thinkers, p. 201.

49. *Guide or Counsellor*, p. 176; Cornelia Dayton, "Taking the Trade: Abortion and Gender Relations in an Eighteenth-Century New England Village," *The William and Mary Quarterly*, 48, no. 1 (January 1991): 21–22, 39 et passim; Rodney Hessinger, "'Those Insidious Murderers of Female Innocence'": (paper delivered at the Third Annual Conference of the Omohundro Institute of Early American History and Culture, June, 1997).

50. See Lewis, "The Republican Wife"; on women as companions in contemporary thought, see Zagarri, pp. 200–201.

51. I am indebted to Michael Zuckerman for this point.

52. Zagarri explores the intellectual manifestations of this change in her description of the Scottish Enlightenment discussion of male-female mixing in the "fourth stage" of history achieved with mercantile society (see esp. pp. 199–200). On modesty, see James, pp. 62–63; on fears, Stansell, pp. 21–22.

CHAPTER 7

1. Isaac Mickle, *A Gentleman of Much Promise: The Diary of Isaac Mickle, 1837–1845*, ed. Philip Mackey (Philadelphia: University of Pennsylvania Press, 1977), 1: 150–151.

2. Wood, pp. 271, 275, 286, 345.

3. John Kasson also makes this argument (see esp. pp. 67–69) but suggests that manners also encoded democratic opportunity (see pp. 7, 257, et passim). I am less convinced of the latter reading.

4. *The Perfect Gentleman* (New York, 1860), p. 8; *The Art of Pleasing* (Cincinnati, 1855), pp. vi–vii; Samuel R. Wells, *How to Behave: A Pocket Manual of Republican Etiquette* (New York, 1856), pp. vii–viii. Only Hitchcock alluded to Republican equality before 1820, p. 168.

5. In addition, six works of the revolutionary era were printed continuously dur-

ing the antebellum era (each had more than five post-1820 editions) and thus were considered in the analysis of antebellum-era rules for behavior. They were Dodsley, Gregory, Chesterfield, Chapone, Burghley, Bennett.

6. Kasson discusses the "multiple routes" that led to the role of etiquette advisor, pp. 48–50.

7. Schlesinger, p. 22.

8. On books in middle-class culture, see Bushman, pp. 282–283ff. Kasson discusses the marketing of conduct literature, pp. 44–45..For a sampling of reviews see "Dangers and Duties of Young Men," *The Christian Examiner* 41 (September 1846): 259–26off; review of *My Son's Manual, The Maine Monthly Magazine* 1 (April 1837): 471–472; review of *The Laws of Etiquette, The New York Mirror* 13 (June 4, 1836): 390; review of Eliza Leslie's *The Behaviour Book, The Literary World* 12 (May 28, 1853): 436–439. John Neagle, "Memorandum of Articles Loaned" (unpublished entries between November 1836 and October 1838), John Neagle Collection, Historical Society of Pennsylvania.

9. Edward Pessen, *Jacksonian America: Society, Personality, and Politics,* rev. ed. (Homewood, Ill., 1978), pp. 79–97, and *Riches, Class, and Power Before the Civil War* (Lexington: D.C. Heath, 1973); Jones, pp. 278–279, 283–285.

10. *The Art of Good Behavior* (New York, 1845), pp. viii–ix; de Valcourt, *The Illustrated Manners Book* (New York, 1855), p. 9; Eliza Ware Farrar, *The Young Lady's Friend* (Boston, 1836), p. 319; *Art of Pleasing,* p. vii; *Etiquette at Washington* (Baltimore, 1849), p. 7; Cecil B. Hartley, *The Gentleman's Book of Etiquette and Manual of Politeness* (Boston, 1860), p. 4; Catherine Maria Sedgwick, *Means and Ends, or Self-Training* (Boston, 1839), p. 15.

11. Wells, pp. 124–126; *The Laws of Etiquette,* 2d ed. (Philadelphia, 1836), p. 10. Halttunen also cites this passage, but gives the impression that most conduct writers admitted the contradiction between their democratic proclamations and undemocratic advice, p. 95. They did not.

12. *The Habits of Good Society* (New York, 1860), p. 299; two works claimed to be addressed to the upper class as well as the middle class—Joshua Comstock, *The Whole Duties of Men and Women* (Georgetown, D.C., 1822), and William Cobbett, *Advice to Young Men* (London, 1829)—but these were relatively unimportant works and it is doubtful that they were read by upper-class readers any more often than were the other works primarily addressed to the middle class. Bushman notes of some privileged antebellum children that they showed "fewer signs of self-conscious effort to be properly polite and polished" than had their parents, pp. 213–214.

13. For discussions of the upper class, see Douglas T. Miller, *Jacksonian Aristocracy: Class and Democracy in New York, 1830–1860* (New York: Oxford, 1967); Pessen, *Riches, Class, and Power;* and Blumin, pp. 234–237. Bushman suggests that while the wealthy looked down on the middling, they acknowledged their gentility, pp. 233–234. Re: Mickle, see his diary, 1: 27, 33, 36, 39, 78, 100, 111, 115–116, 155, 161; 2: 480–481. For new work that suggests unique features of an upper-class culture, see Dan Kilbride, "'Your Appropriate Sphere as a Lady': Upper-Class Women and the Public Sphere in Antebellum Philadelphia" (paper presented to the Philadelphia Center For Early American Studies Seminar, November 1995). Kilbride suggests that upper-class families disdained the emphasis on self-control of middle-class civility and pursued a more relaxed (though more hierarchical) code that harked back to the old aristocratic system. He suggests that this code was learned within the family and at exclusive boarding schools: pp. 6–13, 21, 25. Kilbride acknowledges the hegemony of the middle-class code, however, when he describes this elite culture as a "counterculture," p. 27.

14. Bushman argues that gentility spread gradually to the middle class between 1775 and 1850, and emphasizes the latter date, pp. 227–228. I think the date should be pushed back. Part of the difference may be attributable to my urban versus his rural (Dover, Delaware, in this section) focus.

15. Kasson makes similar claims about the class address of his sample of nineteenth-century works, p. 57. Jack Larkin, *The Reshaping of Everyday Life, 1790–1840* (New York: Harper Collins, 1988), pp. 125–126, 139–140, 145; Blumin, pp. 107, 157–158, 161, 163, 189. Bushman provides an extended discussion of the spread of gentility as evidenced by middle-class architecture and furnishings in his chap. 8, esp. pp. 251, 273–275.

16. Contemporary journalists even began to report on the "lowlife" of the antebellum city, for the benefit of middle-class readers from whom it was hidden. This study cannot treat these lower classes, with their different subcultures. For working-class culture in antebellum New York, see Stansell's *City of Women*; on the above points see pp. 41, 44, 64–65, 75; Blumin, pp. 233–234, 252; Kasson, pp. 74–80; Bushman, pp. 365–366, 370.

17. Indeed, reviewers recommended these works to employers. Review of Robert Roberts, *The House Servants' Directory, The Critic* 1 (3 January 1829): 157; review of *Plain Talk and Friendly Advice to Domestics, The National Era* 10 (13 March 1856): 42.

18. Ronald Zboray, "Antebellum Reading and the Ironies of Technological Innovation," in Davidson, ed., *Reading in America*, pp. 190–191, 194–196.

19. Larkin, p. 222; Kasson, p. 140.

20. While in reality both the servant and the supervising employer were increasingly likely to be female, the conduct literature reflects the fact that either *could* be male, and that servants would interact with superiors of both sexes. Faye Dudden, *Serving Women: Household Service in Nineteenth-Century America* (Middletown, Conn.: Wesleyan University Press, 1983); and Stansell, p. 155. As domestic service was the largest paid occupation for women, for them the overlap between lower class and serving class was considerable.

21. Chesterfield, 1775, 1: 71, 121; *The Polite Present* (Boston, 1831), p. 44; *The Young Man's Own Book* (Philadelphia, 1832), pp. 128, 141; *Advice to a Young Gentleman* (Philadelphia, 1839), pp. 70–73; *A Juvenile Guide* (Canterbury, N.Y., 1844), p. 57; *The Book of Manners* (New York, 1852), p. 103; D. Mackellar, *A Treatise on the Art of Politeness, Good Breeding, and Manners* (Detroit, 1855), p. 97; Henry Lunettes [Margaret Cockburn Conkling], *The American Gentleman's Guide to Politeness and Fashion* (New York, 1857), pp. 78, 333; Emily Thornwell, *The Lady's Guide to Perfect Gentility* (New York, 1856), pp. 72–73, 111; William Buell Sprague, *Letters on Practical Subjects to a Daughter*, 3d ed. (New York, 1834), p. 145; *The Boy's Manual* (New York, 1837), p. 181; Samuel Miller, *Letter from a Father to His Sons at College* (Philadelphia, 1843), pp. 261–262.

22. Chesterfield, 1775, 3: 104; Comstock, p. 128; *The Child's Instructor and Moral Primer* (Portland, Me., 1823), p. 21; Cobbett, 1, no. 37; *Young Man's Own*, pp. 108, 180; Abiel A. Livermore, *Lectures to Young Men on Their Moral Dangers and Duties* (Boston, 1846), p. 95; Timothy Shay Arthur, *Lectures to Young Men on Their Duties and Conduct in Life* (Boston, 1847), pp. 153–154; Mackellar, pp. 96–97; de Valcourt, pp. 250, 277–278; Count Alfred d'Orsay [Charles William Day], *Etiquette, or a Guide to the Usages of Society* (New York, 1843), p. 46; *Ladies' and Gentlemen's Letter Writer and Guide to Polite Behaviour* (Boston, 1859), p. 74; C. Hartley, p. 189; Robert Walsh, *Didactics* (Philadelphia, 1836), 2: 10.

23. *Young Man's Own*, p. 181; Mme Celnart [Elisabeth Bayle-Mouillard], *The*

Gentleman and Lady's Book of Politeness and Propriety of Deportment (Boston, 1833), p. 70; d'Orsay, pp. 46, 51; *A Guide to Good Manners* (Springfield, Mass., 1847), p. 36; George Winfred Hervey, *The Principles of Courtesy* (New York, 1852), p. 206; Eliza Leslie, *The Behavior Book* (Philadelphia, 1853), pp. 65–66; *Art of Pleasing*, p. 27; Thornwell, pp. 80–81; *Perfect Gentleman*, pp. 211–212. On British practice, see Leonore Davidoff, *The Best Circles: Society Etiquette and the Season* (London: Croom Helm, 1973), pp. 41–42.

24. *Laws of Etiquette*, 2d ed., p. 64; *A Manual of Politeness* (Philadelphia, 1837), p. 147; *Etiquette for Ladies* (Philadelphia, 1843), p. 11, hereafter cited as *Etiquette for Ladies2*; *True Politeness: A Hand-book of Etiquette for Ladies* (New York, 1847), p. 5; *True Politeness: A Hand-book of Etiquette for Gentlemen* (New York, 1848), p. 5; *The Book of Politeness* (Philadelphia, 1850), p. 15; Mrs. L. G. Abell, *Woman in Her Various Relations* (New York, 1851), p. 140; *Ladies' and Gentlemen's Letter*, p. 23; *Perfect Gentleman*, pp. 227–228; Henry P. Willis, *Etiquette and the Usages of Society* (New York, 1860), p. 8; *Chesterfield's Letter Writer and Complete Book of Etiquette* (New York, 1860), p. 8; *Beadle's Dime Book of Practical Etiquette* (New York, 1859), p. 20. In re: Britain, see Davidoff, *Best Circles*, p. 41.

25. *Guide to Good Manners*, p. 37; Celnart, pp. 69–70, 165; *Young Man's Own*, pp. 110–111, 181; Frances Parkes, *Domestic Duties* (New York, 1828), p. 67; *Etiquette for Ladies* (Philadelphia, 1838), p. 51; d'Orsay, pp. 12–13; [E. C., The Baroness de Calabrella], *The Ladies' Science of Etiquette* (New York, 1844), p. 22; *True Politeness/Ladies*, pp. 46–47; Hervey, pp. 127, 197; de Valcourt, p. 132; *Lunettes*, pp. 162, 172, 176; *The Handbook of Etiquette* (New York, 1860), p. 19; Willis, p. 26; *Habits*, p. 364. In re: Britain, see Davidoff, *Best Circles*, p. 47.

26. *Young Man's Own*, p. 180; Celnart, pp. 50, 69, 165–166, 174; *Art*, pp. 18, 27–28; Hervey, pp. 128, 207; Wells, pp. 85–86, 101; *Perfect Gentleman*, p. 175; Nancy Dennis Sproat, *The School of Good Manners* (New York, 1822), p. 24; *A Juvenile Monitor* (New Lebanon, N.Y., 1823), p. 4; *Polite Present*, pp. 12, 18–19; *Chesterfield's Letter*, p. 26; *Beadle's*, p. 16.

27. De Valcourt, pp. 104, 122; Wells, pp. 67–68; Willis, p. 8; *Habits*, pp. 327, 337; C. Hartley, p. 86; *True Politeness/Gentlemen*, p. 10; Leslie, 1853, pp. 65–66; *Perfect Gentleman*, pp. 211–212; Moody, pp. 11, 21; Burghley, p. 189; Celnart, p. 56; *Manual*, p. 144.

28. Robert Roberts, *The House Servant's Directory* (Boston, 1827), pp. x, xii, 78–79; Matthew Carey, *The Philosophy of Common Sense* (Philadelphia, 1838), pp. 33–34; *Plain Talk and Friendly Advice to Domestics* (Boston, 1855), pp. 124, 186; Dudden, pp. 178–180, 198–201; Stansell, p. 167.

29. Roberts, pp. 54, 62–63, 69, 79, 142–143; *Plain Talk*, pp. 18, 37, 43–44, 124, 127, 131–137, 149, 186–189, 194; Carey, pp. 33–34; Celnart, pp. 16–17; *Manual*, p. 140; Thornwell, p. 83; Florence Hartley, *The Ladies' Book of Etiquette and Manual of Politeness* (Boston, 1860), pp. 242–243; *Beadle's*, p. 19; *Young Man's Own*, p. 94; Dwight, p. 181; Calabrella, p. 42; *Chesterfield's Letter*, p. 46. John Kasson has pointed out that the scant regard paid to the feelings of inferiors amounted to asking them to pay "emotional deference" to superiors, another hidden injury of class perpetrated by manners, p. 181.

30. Dudden, pp. 45–71, et passim. Stansell reports that "by 1855, 74 percent of New York's domestics were Irish; only 4 percent were native born whites," pp. 155–157, 166.

31. Chapone, pp. 104–105; *Young Man's Own*, p. 142; *Boy's Manual*, p. 181; Celnart, p. 58; Harvey Newcomb, *How to Be a Lady* (Boston, 1847), p. 44; Sprague 1834,

p. 145; *Advice to a Young Gentleman*, p. 74; Thornwell, pp. 72–73; Leslie, 1853, p. 66; *Habits*, p. 317.

32. *Polite Present*, pp. 39–40; George Peck, *Formation of a Manly Character* (New York, 1853), p. 151; C. Hartley, pp. 69, 321; *Laws of Etiquette*, 1st ed. (1836), pp. 106–107; Lunettes, p. 343; Timothy Titcomb, Esq. [Josiah Gilbert Holland] *Titcomb's Letters to Young People, Single and Married* (New York, 1858), p. 24; Hervey, p. 213.

33. Parkes, p. 60; Celnart, pp. 16–17, 64; *Laws of Etiquette*, 2d ed., pp. 94, 189; *Etiquette for Ladies2*, p. 46; Leslie, 1853, p. 31; *Art of Pleasing*, pp. 25, 46; Lunettes, pp. 158, 160; Willis, p. 46; de Valcourt, p. 132. A reviewer chastised William Alcott, who was exceptional in this regard: "The author . . . has some very weak and trite observations upon the custom in all civilized society, of employing household servants; and he would fain have everybody wait on themselves," review of *The Young Wife*, *New York Mirror* 13 (9 January 1838): 223. On servants and middle-class social life, see Davidoff, *Best Circles*, p. 69; Stansell, pp. 158–159, 161; Dudden, pp. 46–47, 78–79, 108–113, 115, 118, 123.

34. Lunettes, pp. 103–104; *Laws of Etiquette*, 2d ed., pp. 142, 187; *Handbook*, p. 31; F. Hartley, p. 242; Leslie, 1853, pp. 104, 141; Farrar, pp. 231–241; Dudden, pp. 89–90; Ryan, p. 207; Stansell, p. 162.

35. *Manual*, pp. 140–141; *Etiquette for Ladies*, p. 94; Thornwell, pp. 82–83; F. Hartley, pp. 90, 94–95, 242–243, 290; *Handbook*, p. 8; *Laws of Etiquette*, 2d ed., pp. 156–157, 187, 190; *Etiquette for Ladies2*, pp. 27, 45–46; d'Orsay, p. 18; *True Politeness/Gentlemen*, pp. 48–49; *Ladies' and Gentlemen's Letter*, p. 45; *Perfect Gentleman*, p. 176; *Chesterfield's Letter*, pp. 30, 46; Halttunen, pp. 106–107; Davidoff, *Best Circles*, p. 42; Dudden, pp. 177–178.

36. Celnart, p. 17; Farrar, pp. 236–241, 243, 344; *Laws of Etiquette*, 2d ed., pp. 150, 157, 181–189; *True Politeness/Ladies*, p. 51; *Etiquette at Washington*, 1849, p. 71; de Valcourt, pp. 133, 139; *Habits*, p. 291; *Beadle's*, pp. 41–42; Titcomb, pp. 216–218; Carey, p. 30; Newcomb, *Lady*, p. 43; Abell, pp. 154–155.

37. Lydia Howard Sigourney, *Letters to Young Ladies* (Hartford, 1833), p. 48; James Alexander, *The Merchant's Clerk Cheered and Counselled* (New York, 1856), p. 30; Sproat, *School*, p. 45; *The Young Lady's Own Book* (Philadelphia, 1832), pp. 221, 238; Lydia Howard Sigourney, *The Boy's Book* (New York, 1843), p. 96; Theodore Dwight Jr., *The Father's Book* (New York, 1834), pp. 166, 181–182; Celnart, pp. 15–17; *Manual*, pp. 139–140; Artemus Muzzey, *The Young Maiden* (Boston, 1840), p. 93; *American Gentlemen's Everyday*, p. 22; Wells, pp. 64–65; C. Hartley, p. 204; Willis, pp. 30, 46–47; Lunettes, pp. 103–104. On salutations: Comstock, p. 105; *Laws of Etiquette*, 2d ed., p. 61; *True Politeness/Gentlemen*, p. 10; Leslie, 1853, p. 66; Lunettes, p. 130; cf. Kasson, p. 141.

38. Dudden, pp. 194–198, 234–235 et passim; Stansell, p. 155.

39. Halttunen, pp. xv–xvii, 10, 34, 37, 42, 51, 192–193, et passim; Kasson, pp. 70, 72, 93, 165, et passim; Blumin, p. 179. Halttunen acknowledges the influence of Chesterfield over the body-control advice of antebellum manuals (p. 96), but she neglects the fact that Chesterfieldian advice itself persisted, along with its explicitly instrumental message. She recognizes that the body-control demands were at odds with the call for sincere performances but argues that the latter generated some of the more important features of the antebellum code in order to deal with the conflict (pp. 92–93, 99, 101, 122, 189). I read the evidence differently, because I do not find any marked fear of hypocrisy or concern for sincerity in the writers' discussions of specific face-to-face behaviors. Kasson also describes the fear of the confidence man (pp. 99–111), but sincerity is not central to his argument. Bushman acknowledges the

continuity of the code from the eighteenth to the nineteenth century, but because he does not perceive its middle-class cooptation in the revolutionary era, he regards it as still "aristocratic," and therefore somewhat alien, in the nineteenth century; see, pp. 208, 290–291, 301–302.

40. *Polite Present*, pp. 11–12, 29, 56–57; Sigourney, *Ladies*, 1833, p. 85; Parley, pp. 102–103; Austin, p. 80; Anna Fergurson, *The Young Lady* (Lowell, 1848), pp. 56–57; Porter, p. 125; Frost, p. 207; William A. Alcott, *The Young Man's Guide* (Boston, 1833), p. 68; *American Gentleman's Everyday*, pp. 22, 31; Mackellar, p. 98, 103–104; C. Hartley, pp. 20, 79, 307; F. Hartley, pp. 11, 90, 94–95, 285; Willis, pp. 30, 32, 39; Lunettes, p. 128; Wells, pp. 81, 100; Kasson, pp. 80–82.

41. C. Hartley, p. 68; Farrar, p. 334; *Manual*, pp. 68–69, 142; Hervey, p. 207; F. Hartley, pp. 283–284; *The Well-Bred Boy* (Boston, 1844), p. 86; *Ladies' Indispensable*, p. 124; Mackellar, p. 99; *Polite Present*, p. 11; *Juvenile Guide*, pp. 78, 114; *Ladies' and Gentlemen's Letter*, p. 81.

42. Chesterfield, 1775, 1: 65, 70; Sedgwick, *Means*, p. 162; *Young Man's Own*, pp. 114–115, 180; Harvey Newcomb, *How to Be a Man* (Boston, 1847), p. 96; *Habits*, p. 338; C. Hartley, p. 305; *Polite Present*, pp. 5, 29, 32–33; *Laws of Good Breeding*, pp. 16, 27; Abell, p. 129; *True Politeness/Gentlemen*, p. 60; *Art*, p. 33; d'Orsay, p. 50; *Etiquette at Washington*, 1849, p. 73.

43. Celnart, pp. 50–53, 83, 109; Farrar, pp. 323–325, 334–335, 368, 406; de Valcourt, pp. 73, 181, 207; Abell, pp. 116, 129–130, 136, 167; *Young Man's Own*, pp. 117, 155, 166; Sedgwick, *Morals*, pp. 15–16, 18; Hervey, pp. 133, 207; Sproat, *School*, pp. 7, 24–25; Matthew Hale Smith, *Counsels* (Washington, 1846), p. 58; C. Hartley, pp. 21–22, 37, 52, 66–67, 73–74, 100, 185, 203, 296; *Book of Manners*, pp. 145, 175, 190–191; *Ladies' and Gentlemen's Letter*, pp. 76, 79–80, 114.

44. A. Fergurson, pp. 22, 26–27, 55–56; John Todd, *The Student's Manual* (Northampton, Mass., 1835), pp. 228–229, 234–235, 238–242, 246; Charles Butler, *The American Gentleman* (Philadelphia, 1836), pp. 174–175; *My Son's Book* (New York, 1839), pp. 101, 108; *Art of Pleasing*, pp. 13–14, 18–19; *Ladies' Vase* (Lowell, Mass., 1843), pp. 9–11, 13, 59–62; *Chesterfield's Letter*, p. 41; *Habits*, pp. 42, 301; Harvey Newcomb, *The Young Ladies' Guide* (Boston, 1841), pp. 244–245; Daniel Wise, *The Young Lady's Counsellor* (New York, 1851), p. 208; Edward Ferrero, *The Art of Dancing* (New York, 1859), pp. 91, 106; Peck, pp. 154–158, 160–162; C. Hartley, pp. 31–32, 191–192, 304–305, 319, 321; F. Hartley, pp. 148–149; Parley, pp. 120–121. On front and back stage concerns, see Kasson, pp. 165–166; Bushman, p. 256 ff; Halttunen, p. 104; Karen Lystra, *Searching the Heart: Women, Men and Romantic Love in Nineteenth-Century America* (New York: Oxford University Press, 1989), pp. 17–18. Both Kasson and Halttunen acknowledge the "dissimulation" in Chesterfield's advice but downplay its persistence in antebellum works: Kasson, p. 116; Halttunen, p. 94. Halttunen does not acknowledge that demands for a natural and easy behavior originated with Chesterfield, pp. 99–101.

45. *Young Man's Own*, pp. 158, 172; Farrar, pp. 275, 308, 331–333; *Laws of Etiquette*, 2d ed., pp. 207–208; Walsh, 2: 9; *Etiquette For Ladies*, pp. 72–73, 143–144; *Advice to a Young Gentleman*, p. 270; d'Orsay, p. 52; Mrs. Kate C. Maberly, *The Art of Conversation* (New York, 1846), pp. 9, 44; *True Politeness/Ladies*, pp. 8, 13; Timothy Shay Arthur, *Advice to Young Ladies* (Boston, 1848b), pp. 135–138, 141, 147–148; Newcomb, *Man*, pp. 173–174; *Guide to Good Manners*, pp. 10, 16, 24, 95–96.

46. Sprague, 1834, p. 102; *Young Lady's Own*, pp. 178, 250; William A. Alcott, *The Young Woman's Guide to Excellence* (Boston, 1840), pp. 97–100; Calabrella, pp. 5, 13–14; Abell, pp. 114, 135, 168, 177; *Ladies' Vase*, p. 18; Porter, pp. 122, 125; Mackel-

lar, pp. 95–96, 111, 137–138; de Valcourt, pp. 106, 147, 181–182, 205; *Guide to Good Manners*, pp. 10, 16, 18, 24, 63–65, 76; *Polite Present*, pp. 26–27, 37; William Hosmer, *The Young Ladies Book* (Auburn, N. Y., 1851), p. 36; *Boy's Manual*, pp. 171–172; *My Son's Book*, pp. 94, 101, 108; *Manual*, pp. 24, 48, 57–58, 78, 101–114.

47. *Juvenile Monitor*, pp. 8, 12; Sedgwick, *Morals*, pp. 24–25; Celnart, pp. 66, 69, 77–79, 83, 86; *Manual*, pp. 54–55, 78, 101; Miller, p. 49; *Art*, pp. 21, 32, 34; Newcomb, *Lady*, pp. 98, 106; *Book of Manners*, pp. 92, 176, 202; Lunettes, pp. 335–337, 341–344; de Valcourt, p. 55; Mackellar, p. 98–99, 116; Thornwell, pp. 84–87, 103, 110; Willis, pp. 16, 20–21, 41, 44; C. Hartley, pp. 52–53, 82, 84, 319; F. Hartley, pp. 99, 101–103, 107, 151–152, 283, 287.

48. Sproat, *School*, p. 43; *Polite Present*, pp. 10, 18–19; Farrar, pp. 333, 341; *Manual*, pp. 24–25, 56–57, 67–68, 101; *Etiquette for Ladies*, pp. 33, 44–45, 135, 139; *Canons*, pp. 86–87; *My Son's Book*, pp. 108, 117; *Well-Bred Girl*, pp. 14, 127; *Juvenile Guide*, pp. 91–92, 94; *Art*, pp. 17, 19; *Manners*, pp. 58–61; Wells, pp. 44–45; de Valcourt, pp. 55, 378–379, 401; Lunettes, pp. 128, 334–335, 344; Frost, p. 205; *Habits*, pp. 282–283, 309–310; F. Hartley, pp. 111, 114, 151–152.

49. Ferrero, pp. 107, 110; *Young Lady's Own*, p. 149; *Etiquette for Ladies*, pp. 72–73, 154, 156–157; Charles William Day, *Hints on Etiquette and the Usages of Society* (Boston, 1844), pp. 152–153; *True Politeness/Ladies*, pp. 39–40; Arthur, *Men*, p. 84; *American Gentleman's Everyday*, pp. 13–14; *Art of Pleasing*, pp. 60–61; *Ladies' and Gentlemen's Letter*, p. 52; C. Hartley, pp. 92, 95, 104–105, 224–225; F. Hartley, pp. 168, 170, 202; *Perfect Gentleman*, pp. 233, 239–240; Elias Howe, *Howe's Complete Ballroom Handbook* (Boston, 1858), pp. 4, 6, 9, 13; *Chesterfield's Letter*, pp. 24, 31, 43; de Valcourt, pp. 369–370, 400, 403, 406. For more on dancing, see Larkin, pp. 239–244.

50. Sproat, *School*, pp. 7, 24, 41; *Polite Present*, pp. 7–11, 30–32, 34–37, 45, 49, 57–58; *My Son's Book*, pp. 103, 116–117; *Juvenile Guide*, pp. 61, 93–94, 104, 115–116; Sedgwick, *Morals*, p. 17; Sedgwick, *Means*, p. 164; *Art*, pp. 21, 28, 31–32, 34; *Laws of Good Breeding*, pp. 15–16, 27; Mackellar, pp. 98–99, 104, 111, 115, 118–119, 125–126, 138; *Ladies' Indispensable*, pp. 125–126; Hervey, p. 129; Lunettes, p. 343; Wells, pp. 74–75, 136; *Beadle's*, pp. 16–18, 43–44; F. Hartley, pp. 108, 151–152, 283; C. Hartley, pp. 37–38, 305–307.

51. *Polite Present*, pp. 11–12, 15, 31, 34, 44–46, 58; Sproat, *School*, pp. 6, 24, 26, 45; *Young Man's Own*, pp. 158, 160, 162, 165; Celnart, pp. 83–84, 86, 88–89, 97, 185; Butler, pp. 131, 173, 175; *Juvenile Guide*, pp. 62–63, 67–68, 79, 91, 93, 99, 103, 116, 118; William Andrus Alcott, *The Young Mother* (Boston, 1836), pp. 251–252; Mackellar, pp. 98, 111, 117, 126, 129, 137–138; *Book of Manners*, pp. 87, 89, 152, 159–161, 176, 193, 201; Abell, p. 110, 122–123, 131, 134–136, 138, 157, 161; Lunettes, pp. 103, 128–129, 167, 349; de Valcourt, pp. 107, 184, 215–216, 268, 326, 410; *Beadle's*, pp. 26, 44–45, 53, 56–57; F. Hartley, pp. 41, 56, 100, 113, 149, 151, 153, 174, 184, 210, 284, 286; C. Hartley, pp. 25, 79, 100, 106, 224, 295–296, 306, 318–321; *Perfect Gentleman*, pp. 222–223.

52. Ralph Waldo Emerson, *The Conduct of Life* (Boston, 1860), pp. 156, 158; Farrar, pp. 333, 388, 406; Sedgwick, *Means*, pp. 160, 162; Abell, pp. 136, 156, 161, 166; Thornwell, p. 153; de Valcourt, pp. 189, 232, 249, 410; *Ladies' and Gentlemen's Letter*, pp. 56, 114–115; F. Hartley, pp. 100, 154, 174, 184; *Young Man's Own*, pp. 81, 156, 168, 172; Celnart, pp. 83, 96; *Juvenile Guide*, pp. 58, 80, 92, 102, 104, 120; *Guide to Good Manners*, pp. 34, 92; *Habits*, pp. 284, 301; *Handbook*, pp. 15, 28; *Perfect Gentleman*, pp. 218, 222; Sedgwick, *Morals*, p. 15. That this was old advice challenges Kasson's assertion that an interest in reading character from appearances was new to the period, p. 98.

53. *Young Man's Own*, pp. 135–136; *Laws of Etiquette*, 2d ed., p. 28; *Manual*, pp. 57–58, 212–213; *Advice to a Young Gentleman*, pp. 82, 84, 134; Ferrero, p. 105; *My Son's Book*, p. 144; *Well–Bred Boy*, p. 93; Newcomb, *Man*, pp. 107–108, 132; Newcomb, *Lady*, pp. 107–108, 132; A. Ferguson, p. 135; *Book of Manners*, pp. 80, 188; Theodore Dwight, *The Father's Book* (Springfield, Mass., 1834), p. 113; *Mother's Friend*, p. 29; *Habits*, p. 309; *Beadle's*, pp. 56–57. Halttunen claims that advice writers called for an "open countenance," and cites Alcott, but he was idiosyncratic in this (as in other areas). She acknowledges the advice described above, attributing it to an unusually cynical "anonymous writer," but the passage she cites, from Chesterfield, was frequently repeated. She suggests that this advice was intended to protect one from strangers in antebellum streets, whereas sincerity was to be practiced in the parlor, but this advice was not confined to streets, and it predates the "anonymous" antebellum city. In a seeming turnabout, Halttunen later acknowledges that conduct books asked for "complete command of all facial expressions": see pp. 52, 54–55, 97. Kasson acknowledges the eighteenth-century roots of these rules but suggests, I think incorrectly, that the importance of emotion management was increasing in his period. Unlike Halttunen, he does recognize the "instrumental" stance toward feelings that the advice suggests; see pp. 147, 180.

54. *Polite Present*, pp. 3–4, 10–13, 15, 18, 35–36, 44–46, 57–58; Sproat, *School*, pp. 7, 24–26; James Mott, *Brief Hints to Parents on the Subject of Education* (Philadelphia, 1824), p. 14; *Juvenile Guide*, pp. 59–63, 79–80, 91–93, 103, 115–118; Austin, pp. 72–73, 80, 166–168, 192, 285, 360–363; Maberly, pp. 9–11, 14, 17, 25, 28–30, 35–36, 45, 52–53, 55, 59, 62; *Book of Manners*, pp. 31–32, 87, 89, 92, 144–145, 148, 152, 159–161, 176, 187–191, 193, 200–201; de Valcourt, pp. 164–183, 188, 190–191, 211, 214–215, 217, 224, 234, 247, 268, 410; *Ladies' and Gentlemen's Letter*, pp. 31–32, 62–63, 66, 68–69, 80, 113–115; *Well-Bred Girl*, pp. 22, 122–127; Eliza Poole Sandford, *Woman, in her Social and Domestic Character* (Boston, 1833), p. 16; *Etiquette For Ladies2*, pp. 34, 37–39; F. Hartley, pp. 12–14, 17, 41, 56, 100, 107–108, 113, 149–153, 168, 182, 190, 284, 291; *Young Man's Own*, p. 57, 117, 121–122, 124–127, 155, 157–167, 172–173, 176, 178; Alcott, *Man's*, 1833, pp. 68–69, 80–81, 182; *My Son's Book*, pp. 109–110, 113, 116–117; C. Hartley, pp. 17, 20, 22, 24, 26, 53–54, 189, 205, 208, 295, 306–308.

55. *Etiquette for Ladies*, pp. 58–59; *Laws of Good Breeding*, pp. 27, 40; Abell, p. 123; Leslie, 1853, pp. 56–57, 61–65, 307; F. Hartley, p. 286; *Laws of Etiquette*, 2d ed., pp. 211, 217; *Perfect Gentleman*, pp. 207, 215–217; C. Hartley, p. 308; Lunettes, pp. 252–253; *Polite Present*, pp. 29, 35; *Art*, pp. 31–32, 34, 36; d'Orsay, pp. 34–35, 46; de Valcourt, pp. 122, 209–210, 262, 500; *Handbook*, pp. 14, 28; Willis, pp. 8, 11, 19, 21; Mickle, 2: 238, 299.

56. *Child's Instructor*, p. 33; Sproat, *School*, pp. 6, 25–27, 45–46; Farrar, pp. 272–274, 375, 382; *Young Lady's Own*, pp. 18, 178–179, 183–187, 201–202; Margaret Coxe, *The Young Ladies' Companion* (Columbus, Ohio, 1839), pp. 19–20, 40, 49; William A. Alcott, *The Young Wife* (Boston, 1837), pp. 202, 334; *Etiquette For Ladies2*, pp. 32–34, 48; Abell, pp. 130, 133–134, 136–137, 198; Leslie, 1853, pp. 114, 131–132, 200, 308; *Young Man's Own*, pp. 58, 60, 126–128, 133, 136, 153–154, 158–160, 163, 167–169, 173–179; *Letters to a Younger Brother* (Philadelphia, 1838), pp. 149–152; William A. Alcott, *The Young Husband* (Boston, 1839), pp. 318–320; Todd, pp. 199, 202, 206, 210, 213, 214–217, 222–225; *Perfect Gentleman*, pp. 203–206, 214, 220, 224–226, 241; C. Hartley, pp. 11–13, 19–22, 24–27, 93, 100, 205–208, 318–320; Austin, pp. 73–75, 164–166, 169–170, 199, 364–366, 373; Maberly, pp. 12, 14–16, 19, 21–25, 29–33, 43, 47, 51–56, 59–62, 64; *Book of Manners*, pp. 87, 145–146, 149–156,

186, 188–189, 191–194, 198; Valcourt, pp. 124, 187–188, 191–192, 194–199, 202, 204–205, 208, 217, 227, 284, 499, 501; Wells, pp. 63, 76–77; Mickle, 1: 253.

57. Halttunen, pp. 46–47; Kasson, pp. 113–115 (Kasson does not acknowledge that the body rules themselves were not new, 123–124).

58. Most explorers of these rules have taken a cue from the conduct writers themselves and noted their theatricality. See Halttunen, p. 101; Kasson, p. 176; Davidoff, *Best Circles*, p. 88.

59. Blumin, pp. 178, 193–218, et passim; Kasson, p. 72; Bushman, pp. 353–370; Pessen, *Riches, Class, and Power*, pp. 169–204, 222–242, 245.

60. Larkin, pp. 125–126; Davidoff, *Best Circles*, pp. 15, 21, 41; Kasson, pp. 43, 137. On class vs. caste see E. Digby Baltzell's classic work, *The Protestant Establishment: Aristocracy and Caste in America* (New York, 1964). Halttunen suggests that the elaborate rules developed in response to the period's demands for sincere performances. She argues that these framing devices demanded tact of the participants, which allowed them to deny the theatricality of their behavior (p. 101). Yet without other evidence, it seems just as likely that the elaborate rules were simply intended to instruct the self-made.

61. The source for these comparisons is Davidoff's *Best Circles*: see pp. 14, 18, 22–23.

62. Davidoff, *Best Circles*, pp. 14, 21, 101–102; Bushman, p. 414.

63. Kasson, pp. 7, 57, 257; Davidoff, *Best Circles*, p. 36; Schlesinger, pp. 27–48; Bushman, pp. 417–418.

64. Comstock, pp. 47, 117–118; Cobbett, 1, no. 36; *Young Man's Own*, pp. 68–69, 74, 140–141; *Laws of Etiquette*, 2d ed., pp. 132–133; *Boy's Manual*, pp. 184, 217–220; Austin, pp. 120–124, 279–280; *Letters to a Younger Brother*, pp. 101, 107, 110; *Advice to a Young Gentleman*, pp. 81, 277; *My Son's Book*, pp. 57–65; Alcott, *Man's*, 1839, pp. 355–357; Miller, pp. 255–256, 258; Livermore, pp. 43–44; Smith, pp. 16, 48–50; Newcomb, *Man*, pp. 49–50, 172–174, 176–180; Newcomb, *Lady*, pp. 172–174; Arthur, *Men*, pp. 59, 133–134; Frank Fergurson, *The Young Man* (Lowell, 1848), p. 81; Alexander, pp. 9–12; Lunettes, pp. 78, 333; Porter, pp. 32, 35.

65. Cf. Halttunen, pp. 111, 116.

66. *Laws of Etiquette*, 2d ed., pp. 65–70; *Manual*, pp. 147–148; *Etiquette For Ladies2*, pp. 11–12, 19; d'Orsay, pp. 5–7; *Art*, pp. 22–24; *True Politeness/Gentlemen*, pp. 5–6, 32, 38; *Laws of Good Breeding*, pp. 22, 28; *Etiquette at Washington*, 1849, pp. 20, 25–28, 30; *Ladies' Indispensable*, p. 124; *Book of Manners*, pp. 194–195; Leslie, 1853, pp. 56–58; Durang, *Fashionable*, p. 17; Wells, pp. 66–67; F. Hartley, pp. 48–49, 77; C. Hartley, p. 86; Willis, pp. 6, 8; *Beadle's*, pp. 20–21; Mickle, 1: 180–181; Davidoff, *Best Circles*, p. 41.

67. *Laws of Etiquette*, 2d ed., pp. 93–94; *Manual*, pp. 148–149; *Etiquette for Ladies*, pp. 12–14; d'Orsay, pp. 8–10; *Etiquette at Washington*, 1849, pp. 21–25; Abell, p. 141; *Book of Manners*, p. 200; Hervey, p. 250; Leslie, 1853, pp. 171–173; de Valcourt, p. 106; Thornwell, pp. 91; *Perfect Gentleman*, pp. 229–230; *Chesterfield's Letter*, pp. 9–11; see also Mickle, 1: 232.

68. *Laws of Etiquette*, 2d ed., pp. 70–72, 100–101, 193, 195; *Manual*, pp. 61, 146, 149; *Canons*, pp. 69–70; *Etiquette For Ladies2*, pp. 12, 18–19; *Art*, pp. 20, 23; Maberly, p. 45; *True Politeness/Gentlemen*, pp. 7–8, 60; *Etiquette at Washington*, 1849, p. 30; *Ladies' Indispensable*, p. 123; de Valcourt, pp. 107, 116; Wells, pp. 68, 90; Lunettes, pp. 172–174, 253–254; *Handbook*, pp. 7, 11, 26–27, 30; F. Hartley, pp. 37–39, 41; C. Hartley, pp. 202–203; Willis, pp. 7–9, 36–37, 48; Mickle, 1: 133; Dickens, pp. 112, 290; Davidoff, *Best Circles*, p. 42.

69. *Laws of Etiquette*, 2d ed., p. 62; *Etiquette for Ladies*, p. 11; d'Orsay, p. 6; *Laws of Good Breeding*, pp. 22–23; Arthur, *Ladies*, pp. 135–138; *True Politeness/Ladies*, p. 13; *True Politeness/Gentlemen*, p. 14; *Etiquette at Washington*, 1849, pp. 28–29; Hervey, p. 201; Wells, p. 69; F. Hartley, p. 113; *Perfect Gentleman*, pp. 228–229; *Handbook*, p. 13; *Habits*, pp. 314–317; *Chesterfield's Letter*, pp. 7–8; see also Mickle, 1: 62.

70. Sproat, *School*, p. 7; *Juvenile Guide*, pp. 66, 130; de Valcourt, p. 269; Wells, pp. 100–101; C. Hartley, pp. 68, 74, 83, 197–198; Celnart, p. 57; *Laws of Etiquette*, 2d ed., pp. 61–62; *Manual*, pp. 143–144; *Etiquette For Ladies2*, p. 26; *Art*, pp. 18–19; *Guide to Good Manners*, p. 25; *Art of Pleasing*, p. 22; Thornwell, p. 81; Lunettes, pp. 128–130; Willis, pp. 32–33; *Habits*, p. 313; *Beadle's*, p. 44.

71. Kasson, pp. 137–138; Celnart, p. 70; Sedgwick, *Means*, p. 164; *Guide to Good Manners*, p. 9; *Book of Manners*, pp. 69, 191; de Valcourt, pp. 182, 400; C. Hartley, pp. 186, 209, 319; *Young Man's Own*, p. 162; Howe, p. 5; *Boy's Manual*, p. 171; *Advice to a Young Gentleman*, p. 138; Ferrero, p. 118; *Habits*, p. 310; Frost, p. 205; Mickle, 2: 252.

72. Celnart, pp. 56, 68, 84, 175–176; *Laws of Etiquette*, 2d ed., pp. 60–62, 66–67, 208; *Etiquette for Ladies2*, pp. 13, 17–18, 24–25; Calabrella, pp. 3–4, 18; *Art*, pp. 21, 23, 32; *True Politeness/Ladies*, pp. 7, 13, 29; *True Politeness/Gentlemen*, pp. 7, 13–14; *Book of Politeness*, pp. 11–12, 15, 19; *Ladies' Indispensable*, p. 124; Hervey, pp. 201–202, 205–206; de Valcourt, pp. 103–104, 119, 122, 124–125, 146–147, 495–496; Thornwell, pp. 80, 85, 91–92, 94–95, 110–111; Wells, pp. 67–69, 71, 81, 100–101; *Habits*, pp. 313–318, 320–321, 323–324, 326–327, 337; C. Hartley, pp. 86, 92, 94, 101, 215–216, 227; Willis, pp. 8, 11–12, 32, 47; *Beadle's*, pp. 20, 45; Mickle, 1: 142, 151. Kasson and Larkin assume that Americans did invariably shake hands upon introduction, but they both cite only the British traveler Captain Marryat. I think more evidence is necessary to determine how customary it was for strangers to greet each other this way. See Kasson, p. 142; Larkin, pp. 155–156; and Marryat, p. 99.

73. Mickle, 1: 169, 239; 2: 252, 299, 336; see also Blumin, pp. 212–213, 217, 239–240; Larkin, p. 265.

74. The discussion of visiting in this and the four paragraphs following is based on: Parkes, pp. 53–55; Farrar, pp. 389–392, 394–395; *Etiquette for Ladies*, pp. 36–38, 40–42, 55, 73–74; *Well-Bred Girl*, p. 125; *Etiquette for Ladies2*, pp. 19–21; *True Politeness/Ladies*, pp. 27–31, 42; F. Hartley, pp. 59, 79, 81, 83; *Laws of Etiquette*, 2d ed., pp. 74–76, 81, 84–86; *True Politeness/Gentlemen*, pp. 28, 31; *Perfect Gentleman*, p. 246; C. Hartley, pp. 75–78, 81–83, 87, 309; Celnart, pp. 60–62, 64–67, 187; d'Orsay, pp. 18–19, 37–38; *Laws of Good Breeding*, pp. 27–29; *Etiquette at Washington*, 1849, pp. 31–33, 58–59, 72; *Art of Pleasing*, pp. 24–26, 62; de Valcourt, pp. 123–124, 126; Wells, pp. 70–72; *Habits*, pp. 330–331, 333–334, 336, 338; *Beadle's*, pp. 13–15, 17, 70; and *American Gentleman's Everyday*, pp. 18–19. John Kasson attributes intricate calling card etiquette to the late nineteenth century (pp. 173–174), but it was a common topic in antebellum guides. On British visiting practices, see Davidoff, *Best Circles*, pp. 43–45. See also Halttunen, p. 112.

75. Kasson, pp. 173–174; see also Halttunen, pp. 102–103.

76. Farrar, pp. 275, 392; Calabrella, pp. 16, 18; *True Politeness/Ladies*, p. 28; Leslie, 1853, pp. 47–48; F. Hartley, p. 84; *Young Man's Own*, p. 149; *Laws of Etiquette*, 2d ed., pp. 74–75; *American Gentleman's Everyday*, p. 17; C. Hartley, pp. 77, 82; Celnart, pp. 60–61, 67; Hervey, p. 251; *Art of Pleasing*, p. 25; Wells, p. 71; *Habits*, p. 331; Willis, p. 14; Kasson, p. 170.

77. *Laws of Etiquette*, 2d ed., pp. 77–78; *Etiquette for Ladies*, pp. 36, 42–43; *Well-

Bred Girl, p. 125; *True Politeness/Ladies*, pp. 29–30; Thornwell, pp. 83–85; F. Hartley, p. 83; *True Politeness/Gentlemen*, pp. 29–30; C. Hartley, pp. 79–83; Celnart, pp. 67–69; *Book of Politeness*, p. 11; *Etiquette at Washington*, 1850, pp. 41–42; *Art of Pleasing*, p. 26; Wells, p. 73; *Chesterfield's Letter*, p. 15; *Beadle's*, p. 14. Halttunen notes how other instances of "tact" enabled middle-class persons to support each other's genteel performances, p. 107.

78. Dickens, p. 109, 143.

79. Farrar, pp. 341, 368; *Etiquette for Ladies*, pp. 49–50, 69; Abell, p. 107; Leslie, 1853, pp. 58, 300; Thornwell, p. 95; *Laws of Etiquette*, 2d ed., pp. 77, 87–88, 136; *True Politeness/Gentlemen*, p. 49; *American Gentleman's Everyday*, pp. 50–52; *Art of Pleasing*, p. 57; *Perfect Gentleman*, pp. 167–168, 232, 249; C. Hartley, pp. 50, 196; Celnart, p. 164; d'Orsay, pp. 13, 39; *Etiquette at Washington*, 1849, pp. 49, 66–67; 1850, p. 99; *Book of Manners*, pp. 189, 196; de Valcourt, pp. 119, 126, 132, 232, 410; Wells, pp. 73–74, 85, 89, 104; Durang, *Fashionable*, p. 23; *Handbook*, pp. 18–19; *Beadle's*, pp. 40–41.

80. Parkes, pp. 67–68; Farrar, pp. 341–342, 348–349; *Etiquette for Ladies2*, pp. 47, 49–50; *True Politeness/Ladies*, pp. 46–47, 49–50; Abell, pp. 107–108, 111; Thornwell, pp. 98, 104; F. Hartley, pp. 98, 103, 107, 285; *Young Man's Own*, p. 156; *Laws of Etiquette*, 2d ed., pp. 139, 147, 152, 168; *Well-Bred Boy*, p. 30; *True Politeness/Gentlemen*, pp. 45–46; Hervey, pp. 227, 229; C. Hartley, pp. 50–51, 56–57; Celnart, pp. 164–165, 169; *Laws of Good Breeding*, pp. 16, 29–30; *Etiquette at Washington*, 1849, pp. 68, 71; de Valcourt, pp. 132, 138–139, 152, 154; *Chesterfield's Letter*, pp. 26–28, 45; *Habits*, pp. 295, 364. For an excellent discussion of table manners, see Kasson, pp. 182–212. He points out that it was in this period that most urban middle-class homes acquired separate dining rooms.

81. Farrar, p. 361; *Manual*, pp. 52, 61, 67; *Etiquette for Ladies2*, pp. 17–19, 25, 27; *True Politeness/Ladies*, pp. 33, 36–37; Thornwell, pp. 94–95, 111; Willis, pp. 15, 23–24; *Handbook*, p. 40; F. Hartley, pp. 48–49, 51, 167; *Laws of Etiquette*, 2d ed., pp. 98, 175–176; *Canons*, pp. 69–70, 208; *Guide to Good Manners*, pp. 75–77; *True Politeness/Gentlemen*, pp. 33, 37–39; Mackellar, p. 123; *Perfect Gentleman*, pp. 212, 232–233, 248; C. Hartley, pp. 92, 94, 97, 223; *Etiquette at Washington*, 1849, pp. 51–52; Wells, pp. 90, 93.

82. *Plain Talk*, pp. 123–124, 133, 200, 204; Roberts, pp. 70–71, 75; *Beadle's*, p. 47; Leslie, 1853, p. 86.

83. Carey, pp. 33–34; *Plain Talk*, pp. 128, 131, 133, 186, 188; Roberts, pp. xiii, 75.

84. Bushman, pp. 352, 403. Bushman does not take these highly codified staging rules into account. And his own evidence shows that refinement invaded religion, not the other way around, see pp. 321–326. See also Wood, pp. 349–351.

85. On anomie, see Davidoff, *Best Circles*, pp. 17, 23, 33. C. Hartley, p. 66 (see also *Canons*, pp. 62–63; Leslie, 1853, p. 101); Halttunen, pp. xv–xvii, 10, 29, 32, 37, 192. I do not think middle-class liminality presented as much of a crisis as Halttunen suggests. She regards the rituals as a symptom of the problem; I regard them as the solution.

86. On the vicious circle, see Halttunen, pp. 195–196. Bushman highlights "gentility's involvement in the material environment," and explores the connections between the spread of manners, consumption, and capitalism, see pp. xviii–xix, 407–409. Blumin finds "a hardening of class boundaries along a manual–nonmanual fault line," p. 121. Similar to my argument about the conduct writers' treatment of class, he finds a discrepancy between antebellum pronouncements denying the existence of classes and lauding manual labor and the pervasive scorning of those who

worked with their hands that can be read between the lines of newspaper, journal, and advice book discussions of these matters; pp. 121–130. On divergence between manual and non-manual workers' lifestyles, see his chap. 5, pp. 140–191.

87. Blumin, p. 257; Kasson maintains that conduct writers "attempted a balancing act between the requirements of a democratic polity and the demands for social distinction," p. 257. I think the latter prevailed. Halttunen acknowledges that the rituals served as barriers of exclusion in an otherwise classless society, but for her this was the by-product of the desire for sincere performances, pp. 194–195. I think polished performances for the sake of class distinction were being preached from the start—whether the authors owned up to it or not.

88. A few romantic reformers arguably made the situation even worse because they said they hoped to refine the rude, but they were deluding themselves. Their inevitable failure only reinforced the pretense that lower status was an individual's own fault. Kasson, p. 216; Bushman, pp. xv, 278–279, 421–424, 432–433.

89. Davidoff, *Best Circles*, p. 21 and chap. 4, "Change and Decline."

90. Halttunen argues that antebellum attacks on "etiquettish" behavior are evidence of the middle-class demand for sincere performances. She claims that middle-class Americans were highly concerned about the vulnerability of their genteel performances, and this made them reaffirm continually the sincerity of their every act. She asserts that this sense of vulnerability was especially great because "many middle-class Americans were attempting to pass for more than what they were," pp. 117–118. But this argument is too strong. The period's diaries and popular literature do not betray insecurity on this scale. The instructions were indeed very elaborate to accomodate the socially mobile, but they were also intended to guide and reassure. And once learned and practised, one's refinement began indeed to seem "natural," or at least one's "second nature," and the vulnerability passed. See Bushman, pp. 327, 335, although he, too, overemphasizes middle-class ambivalence toward refinement (p. 313). Halttunen claims that there was a growing acceptance of the theatricality of middle-class behavior after the 1850s and attributes this to middle-class self-confidence (pp. 152–153, 163, 166, 186, 196, 205). But there was nothing said in the latter period about manners as a mask for inner character that Chesterfield did not say (and Ben Franklin did not practice) a century earlier. Halttunen cites Anna Mowatt's play "Fashion" as evidence of a new ability of the middle class to laugh at their own efforts to acquire gentility after the midcentury (pp. 154–157). But such satires began much earlier, with the middling campaign for gentility. Royall Tyler's "The Contrast" (1787) is a good example. The middling were always capable of some self-deprecation in their pursuit of gentility. As Bushman points out, this was a useful way of curbing the excesses of the project. More important, it was a way to deny one's own labors in the garden of gentility. On the meaning of claims for a new American code see Kasson, p. 63 (only he thinks they did offer a unique code; see pp. 61, 64).

91. Bushman, pp. 413, 434. For Bushman, gentility was a cultural system, surprisingly strong in republican America but at odds with, and weaker than, capitalism or democracy, pp. 446–447. I think it was the glue that allowed them to coexist.

92. Davidoff, *Best Circles*, pp. 17–18.

CHAPTER 8

1. Mickle, 1: 92, 118, 126, 150; 2: 251–252, 353; Kett, pp. 28–31.

2. Halttunen also notes the potentially threatening liminality of mobile youth, pp. 27, 32.

3. Livermore, pp. 22, 94; Miller, pp. 44–45; Muzzey, *Man's*, p. 86; Todd, 1835b, p. 230; Alcott, *Boy's*, pp. 70–71; Alcott, *Familiar*, pp. 17, 229–241; *Beadle's*, p. 54; Coxe, pp. 220–221; Farrar, pp. 202–203; Ferris, p. 6; Smith, p. 115.

4. Cremin, pp. 46, 55.

5. Ministers did contribute to conduct instruction through other literary genres, but their contribution was smaller than in earlier periods and more secular in tone.

6. Cremin, pp. 50–51; Pessen, *Jacksonian America*, p. 6; Katz, pp. 11, 13. Some authors made their age address very clear, e.g., Newcomb, *Lady:* "for girls and misses, between the ages of eight and fifteen"; Sedgwick, *Means*, p. 13: 10–16 years.

7. For discussions of maternal nurture, see Robert Sunley, "Early Nineenth-Century American Literature on Child Rearing," in *Childhood in Contemporary Cultures*, Margaret Mead and Martha Wolfenstein eds. (Chicago: University of Chicago Press, 1955), pp. 150–153, 158–159, 162–163; Ryan, pp. 100–101, 103–104, 154, 161, 232. As late as 1840, 60 percent of Massachusetts teachers were male, although by 1865, 86 percent were female; Katz, p. 12.

8. Cremin, p. 46; Larkin, pp. 58–59; Halttunen, p. 1, et passim; Kett, pp. 30, 94–95, 102, 108; Kasson, p. 54; Ryan, p. 165.

9. Ryan, pp. 178–179.

10. *My Son's Book*, p. 7; see also *Art*, p. ix, and Sigourney, *Boy's*, p. 99.

11. Richards, p. 62.

12. See n. 8.

13. *Etiquette at Washington*, p. 7; see also *Habits*, p. 24; *Handbook*, p. 23; *Art*, p. ix; *Chesterfield's Letter*, p. iii; d'Orsay, 1844, p. 7; *Canons*, p. 3.

14. Fischer, *Growing Old*, pp. 115–116, 225; Achenbaum, pp. 34–37.

15. Chapone, p. 90; *Advice to Young Gentlemen*, pp. 94–96; Abell, p. 115; Alcott, *Wife*, p. 268; *Well-Bred Boy*, p. 83; de Valcourt, p. 299; *Etiquette For Ladies2*, pp. 17, 39–40; C. Hartley, p. 309; Coxe, p. 232; Wells, p. 108; *Beadle's*, p. 20; Parkes, pp. 60–61; Celnart p. 79.

16. d'Orsay, pp. 12–13; *Laws of Good Breeding*, pp. 22, 29; Abell, pp. 107–108, 116, 140; *Ladies' Indispensable*, p. 125; Hervey, pp. 197, 207; *Perfect Gentleman*, pp. 175, 227–228; Lunettes, pp. 131, 159, 172, 176, 250; F. Hartley, pp. 48, 77; Willis, pp. 8, 26; *Habits*, p. 364; Thornwell, p. 85; C. Hartley, pp. 67, 70; Roberts, p. 62; Celnart, pp. 69–70, 172; *Art of Pleasing*, p. 23.

17. Calabrella, pp. 10, 23, 25; Celnart, pp. 50, 56, 70, 77–78, 105, 168, 171–172; Hervey, pp. 127 128, 197, 204–205; Thornwell, pp. 79–80, 84–85, 102; Lunettes, pp. 77, 131, 134, 163; de Valcourt, pp. 152, 264–265; 6, 33; C. Hartley, pp. 51, 66–67, 71–73, 185, 202, 309; Coxe, pp. 230–231; Austin, pp. 74, 80, 192; Wells, pp. 101, 133; *Handbook*, p. 29; F. Hartley, pp. 150, 284; Farrar, pp. 211–212; Sigourney, *Ladies*, 1833, pp. 16–17, 48; *Advice to Young Gentlemen*, pp. 141–142, 200; Arthur, *Men*, pp. 153–154; *Manners*, pp. 46, 96. The manners evidence fits Carole Haber's observation that the infirmities of old age received increasing emphasis over the nineteenth century, p. 4.

18. In her analysis of diaries, Pollock also found general continuity in child rearing between the 16th and 19th centuries, with a slight increase in discipline in the early 19th century, pp. 184, 199–200, 268, et passim.

19. The two authors of works for servants each only made one reference to the possibility that the servants they addressed and discussed might be young; Roberts, p. xii; *Plain Talk*, p. 128.

20. Sproat, *School*, pp. 6, 24, 27, 42–45; *Child's Instructor*, pp. 32–33; *Juvenile Monitor*, pp. 3–4, 12–13, 19; *Polite Present*, pp. 3–7, 10, 12–141, 16–19; *Well-Bred Girl*, pp. 18–19; *Well-Bred Boy*, pp. 14, 17, 93; Sedgwick, *Morals*, pp. 9, 19; Newcomb, *Lady*,

pp. 26, 32, 49, 52–55; Newcomb, *Man*, pp. 32, 45, 48, 52–55; Farrar, pp. 210–212, 296, 346; Abell, pp. 115, 168, 233; Leslie, 1853, p. 292; *Beadle's*, pp. 16, 65, 68; Coxe, pp. 229–230; *True Politeness/Ladies*, p. 33; Thornwell, p. 86; Sedgwick, *Means*, p. 160; *Juvenile Guide*, pp. 96, 98, 103, 117; Sigourney, *Ladies*, 1833, pp. 85–86; Peck, p. 158; Miller, p. 49.

21. Sprague, 1822, p. 42; 1834, p. 113; *Young Man's Own*, pp. 127, 180–181; Coxe, pp. 221, 227, 229; Smith, p. 12; Miller, p. 48; Wise, *Lady's*, p. 206; *Young Lady's Own*, p. 251; Farrar, pp. 210–211; Wells, p. 58; *Manual*, p. 81; *Laws of Good Breeding*, p. 69; Sproat, *School*, pp. 25–27, 42, 44, 46; *Juvenile Monitor*, pp. 3, 4, 19; *Polite Present*, pp. 4–6, 10, 13, 14–18, 21–22; *Juvenile Guide*, pp. 79, 96, 116–118, 120, 129; Newcomb, *Man*, pp. 28–29, 52–53; *Well-Bred Girl*, pp. 18–19, 123; Leslie, 1853, pp. 291–293, 307; *Beadle's*, pp. 65, 68.

22. *Lunettes*, p. 162; Parkes, p. 67; Farrar, p. 369; Abell, p. 116; *Beadle's*, p. 41; *Art*, p. 22; *Guide to Good Manners*, p. 35.

23. Chesterfield, 1775, 3: 104; Comstock, p. 128; Celnart, pp. 9–10; Todd, pp. 223, 230–231, 235; *Laws of Etiquette*, 2d ed., pp. 131, 206–207; Arthur, *Men*, pp. 138, 142–143, 153–155; A. Fergurson, pp. 26–27; Peck, pp. 154–158; Sproat, *School*, pp. 5–6, 25, 46; *Juvenile Monitor*, p. 3; *Polite Present*, pp. 4–5, 10–11, 16–17, 22–23; Dwight, pp. 117, 164; Alcott, *Boy's*, pp. 65, 69–71; *Juvenile Guide*, p. 129; Sedgwick, *Morals*, p. 9; Newcomb, *Lady*, pp. 26, 32, 45; Newcomb, *Man*, pp. 24, 32, 45; Manners, p. 112; de Valcourt, p. 122; Miller, pp. 45, 47–48; Alcott, *Familiar*, pp. 229–233; Livermore, p. 94; Larkin, pp. 156–157.

24. Alcott, *Familiar*, pp. 17, 229–241; Alcott, *Boy's*, p. 103; Coxe, p. 221; Farrar, pp. 202–203; Miller, p. 45; Todd, p. 230.

25. Arthur, *Men*, 1848 ed., pp. 100, 104; Celnart, pp. 9–10; *Advice to a Young Gentleman*, pp. 142, 200; de Valcourt, p. 256.

26. Mickle, 1: 126; see also 2: 481.

27. Comstock, p. 161; de Valcourt, pp. 253–254.

28. Mickle, 1: 165. See n. 7 for works on maternal nurture. While this study is confined to works that gave direct advice on face-to-face behavior, it is significant that the child-rearing advice examined here was not directed primarily to mothers. There were a couple of mother's guides, but there was also a father's guide; and these works gave their respective audiences the same advice. More important, most writers addressed their parent-to-child conduct advice to "parents." It is possible that the reign of maternal nurture has been a little exaggerated owing to a focus on maternal organizations and magazines. Of course the very appearance of these institutions in the antebellum decades does signal a new recognition of the mother's role, but the focus may have been on infancy and early childhood. The long-run view suggests that with "gentle nurture," antebellum women simply became full partners in the Lockean child-rearing venture.

29. This and the next three paragraphs are based on the following sources: Comstock, pp. 44–47, 160; Mott, *Brief*, pp. 3–5, 7–8, 14; *Mother's Friend*, pp. 29, 35, 43–54, 97–99; Dwight, pp. 112–114, 116–117, 134, 163–164, 166–167, 178; *Laws of Etiquette*, 2d ed., p. 156; Carey, pp. 30, 37–39, 41; *Laws of Good Breeding*, pp. 30, 70–71; Abell, pp. 235–236; Isaac Ferris, "Men of Business: Their Home Responsibilities," in *Man of Business Considered in his Various Relations* (New York, 1857), pp. 6, 8–11, 13, 15, 18–19; *Handbook*, p. 22; Alcott, *Mother*, pp. 305–306, 330–331; Alcott, *Husband*, p. 244; *Etiquette For Ladies*, p. 43; Leslie, 1853, pp. 31, 291–292; *Beadle's*, pp. 42, 65, 68, 70; Willis, pp. 41, 47; F. Hartley, pp. 84, 148; de Valcourt, pp. 157–158, 253–254, 270; Todd, pp. 230–231; Coxe, pp. 220–221; Smith, pp. 106, 109–111, 115. To youth:

Farrar, pp. 226–228; *Boy's Manual*, pp. 240–241; *Juvenile Monitor*, p. 5; *Juvenile Guide*, p. 78; Sigourney, *Ladies*, 1833, p. 48. Cf. Calvert, pp. 7–8, 104–105, 127, 152; Ryan, p. 159; Pollock, pp. 162–164, 185, 199–200; see also Sunley, pp. 159–163.

30. Kett, pp. 95, 102, 105, 107; see also Halttunen, pp. 1–13.

31. Calvert, pp. 7–8, 67–68, 104–105, 130–131, 133–134, 142, 152.

32. Calvert, pp. 7, 101–103, 109.

33. *Chesterfield's Letter Writer*, p. iv; C. Hartley, p. 4; Arthur, *Men*, p. 154; see also *Advice to Young Gentlemen*, pp. 68, 70; *Beadle's*, 1859, p. 10; *Guide to Good Manners*, p. 98; *My Son's Book*, p. 101; Kett, pp. 42, 44, 144; Ryan, pp. 108, 128–130, 135; Mickle, pp. xvi, xxiii–xxiv, and 155–156.

34. Comstock, pp. 117–118; *Laws of Good Breeding*, p. 69; *Handbook*, pp. 13, 27; *American Gentleman's Everyday*, p. 54; *Book of Manners*, pp. 103, 188; Sprague, 1822, p. 5; Cobbett, 1, no. 36; *My Son's Book*, pp. 57–65; Sigourney, *Ladies*, 1835, p. 105; *Letters to a Younger Brother*, pp. 101, 107, 110; A. Fergurson, pp. 11–12; *Boy's Manual*, pp. 184, 217–220; Peck, pp. 149–150, 154, 163; Newcomb, *Young Ladies*, p. 256; Porter, pp. 32, 35; Alexander, pp. 9–12, 29; *Child's Instructor*, p. 33; *Polite Present*, pp. 20, 44; Newcomb, *Man*, pp. 49–50, 172–174, 176–180; Newcomb, *Lady*, pp. 172–174; Halttunen, pp. 3–6, 11–13.

35. *Art of Pleasing*, pp. 13–14, 18; *Etiquette For Ladies*, pp. 14–15, 31, 33–34; Maberly, pp. 8, 43, 47, 51, 57, 60; *American Gentleman's Everyday*, pp. 12–13; *Book of Manners*, pp. 26–27, 31–32, 69, 89, 92, 186–187, 193; C. Hartley, pp. 19, 215, 305–307, 320–321; *Young Man's Own*, pp. 114–116, 122, 148, 150–151, 163; Alcott, *Man's*, 1833, pp. 64–66; Butler, pp. 172–173, 179; Austin, pp. 188, 190–191, 290–292, 360–361; *My Son's Book*, pp. 94, 101, 108; *Advice to a Young Gentleman*, pp. 52–54; Alcott, *Woman's*, pp. 97–100; *Guide to Good Manners*, pp. viii, 9–10, 23, 63–65; Hosmer, p. 36; de Valcourt, pp. 148, 156, 180–182, 299; Alexander, pp. 29–30; Cobbett, 1, p. 37; Sigourney, *Boy's*, pp. 97–98; *Polite Present*, pp. 26–27, 32–37, 45; *Well-Bred Girl*, pp. 122, 124.

36. Abell, pp. 114, 129–130, 138, 157, 167, 177; *Perfect Gentleman*, pp. 169, 215, 221, 250; *Habits*, pp. 42, 285–286, 309; *Manual*, pp. 24–25, 55–57, 63–64, 101–114; Mackellar, pp. 98–99, 111, 115, 118–119, 125–126, 138; F. Hartley, pp. 108, 151–152, 283; C. Hartley, pp. 37–38, 305–307; *Young Man's Own*, pp. 109, 114–115, 144, 155, 158, 162, 168; Celnart, pp. 83–86, 91; Farrar, pp. 337, 347, 362–363; *My Son's Book*, pp. 103, 116–117; *Guide to Good Manners*, pp. 18, 24, 63–65, 91–92; Wells, pp. 43–44, 136; *Polite Present*, pp. 7, 9–11, 30–37, 45, 49, 57–58; *Juvenile Guide*, pp. 61–62, 93–94, 104, 115–116; Newcomb, *Man*, pp. 57, 96, 100–101, 105–106; Newcomb, *Lady*, pp. 57, 98, 101–102, 106; Sproat, *School*, pp. 7, 24.

37. d'Orsay, p. 33; Abell, pp. 115, 130, 167–168; *Perfect Gentleman*, pp. 168–169, 222; *Habits*, pp. 42, 282–284, 292–293, 309–310; *Book of Politeness*, pp. 13–14; *Etiquette for Ladies*, pp. 24, 33, 44–45, 133, 135, 138; *Lunettes*, pp. 335–337, 341–344; *Manual*, pp. 24–25, 54–57, 67–68; Thornwell, pp. 84–87, 103, 110; F. Hartley, pp. 77, 80, 99, 101–103, 107, 151–152, 283; *Young Man's Own*, pp. 109, 115–116, 144; *Art*, pp. 17, 19, 21, 32, 34; de Valcourt, pp. 53, 55, 133, 141, 156, 234, 378–379, 401, 490–492; Celnart, pp. 29–30, 69, 77–79, 83, 85–86; *My Son's Book*, pp. 108, 117; Sproat, *School*, pp. 7, 24, 41–43; *Juvenile Monitor*, pp. 8, 12, 15, 18; Newcomb, *Lady*, pp. 98, 106–107; Newcomb, *Man*, p. 96; *Polite Present*, pp. 3–4, 10, 18–19, 32; *Manners*, pp. 58–60.

38. *Ladies' and Gentlemen's Letter*, pp. 76, 79, 80, 114; Abell, pp. 116, 136, 174; *Art of Pleasing*, pp. 20, 21, 31; Thornwell, pp. 79, 87; *Lunettes*, p. 335; C. Hartley, pp. 37, 66–67, 74, 100, 203, 296; *Book of Manners*, pp. 145, 191; Leslie, 1853, p. 125;

Young Man's Own, p. 166; de Valcourt, pp. 73, 181, 207; Celnart, pp. 50, 52, 83, 109; Farrar, pp. 269, 323, 324, 325, 334, 368, 406; *Juvenile Monitor,* pp. 6–7; *Well–Bred Girl,* pp. 33–34; Parley, p. 126; Sedgwick, *Means,* p. 162. On salutations, see the citations in n. 51.

39. See chap. 7, ns. 51–56.

40. *Etiquette at Washington,* 1849, p. 62; *Art of Pleasing,* pp. 18–19; *Habits,* p. 284; *Book of Manners,* pp. 65, 72–73, 187; *Etiquette For Ladies2,* p. 35; *Lunettes,* p. 128; *Chesterfield's Letter,* pp. 32, 39; Mackellar, p. 98, 103–104; *Young Man's Own,* pp. 109, 131, 155, 168–169; Sigourney, *Ladies,* 1833, p. 85; Wells, p. 100; *Guide to Good Manners,* pp. 10, 33–34; de Valcourt, p. 189; *Juvenile Monitor,* p. 7; *Well–Bred Boy,* pp. 86, 90–91; Sedgwick, *Morals,* p. 18; Newcomb, *Man,* p. 53.

41. *Laws of Etiquette,* 2d ed., pp. 61–62; *Laws of Good Breeding,* pp. 26, 45; *Art of Pleasing,* p. 22; *Habits,* p. 313; *Manual,* pp. 143–144; *Etiquette for Ladies2,* p. 26; Thornwell, pp. 81, 91–92; *Lunettes,* pp. 128–129, 132; C. Hartley, pp. 68, 83, 197–198; *Art,* pp. 18–19; *Guide to Good Manners,* p. 25; de Valcourt, pp. 118, 269; Wells, pp. 100–101; *Juvenile Guide,* 1844, pp. 66, 78, 130; Sproat, *School,* p. 7; *Well-Bred Boy,* p. 90.

42. d'Orsay, pp. 13–14, 50; Calabrella, p. 23; *Book of Politeness,* p. 12; *Habits,* pp. 338, 364; *Perfect Gentleman,* pp. 175, 213–214, 249; Parkes, p. 67; *True Politeness/Gentlemen,* pp. 48, 60; *Beadle's,* p. 40; C. Hartley, pp. 53, 305, 319; Celnart, pp. 165–166; Farrar, pp. 343, 406; *Art,* pp. 27–28, 33; *Guide to Good Manners,* pp. 10, 79; *Polite Present,* pp. 5, 29, 31–33; Sedgwick, *Means,* pp. 161–162; Sedgwick, *Morals,* p. 19; Newcomb, *Man,* p. 96; *Well-Bred Boy,* p. 93.

43. See chap. 7, n. 44 for general requests for a courteous demeanor; *Laws of Etiquette,* 2d ed., p. 80; d'Orsay, p. 47; Calabrella, p. 18; *Book of Politeness,* p. 11; *Canons,* p. 208; Thornwell, p. 83; C. Hartley, pp. 84–85; *Chesterfield's Letter,* p. 15; Parkes, p. 53; *Young Lady's Own,* p. 251; Celnart, p. 67; A. Fergurson, pp. 135–136; Wells, pp. 62–63, 69.

44. Ryan, pp. 154, 161, 232; Daniel T. Rodgers argues that classroom management methods, child-rearing advice, and children's fiction were all increasingly geared to the cultivation of self-control after 1830, but his evidence points mostly to a new insistence on orderly behavior in children, and this can be read as insistence on subordination as much as self-control. Certainly the conduct literature does not support his argument for dramatic change in child rearing from the previous era. See his "Socializing Middle-Class Children: Institutions, Fables, and Work Values in Nineteenth-Century America," reprinted in N. Ray Hiner and Joseph M. Hawes, *Growing Up in America: Children in Historical Perspective* (Chicago: University of Illinois Press, 1985), pp. 122–125.

45. Sproat, *School,* pp. 44–45; *Child's Instructor,* p. 32; *Polite Present,* pp. 5, 17–18; Newcomb, *Lady,* pp. 49, 72; *Handbook,* p. 32; *Beadle's,* p. 10; C. Hartley, p. 215; *Advice to a Young Gentleman,* pp. 68, 97; de Valcourt, p. 300; Stansell, pp. 202–205, 208.

46. See chap. 7, ns. 66–69.

47. Abell, pp. 140, 173; *Laws of Etiquette,* 2d ed., pp. 207–208; *Art of Pleasing,* pp. 18, 60–61; *Perfect Gentleman,* pp. 228–229; *Etiquette For Ladies,* pp. 72–73, 143–144; *True Politeness/Gentlemen,* pp. 8, 14; Mackellar, pp. 108–109, 137; F. Hartley, pp. 113, 285; C. Hartley, pp. 204, 209, 319–320; Sprague, 1834, pp. 19, 26, 106; *Young Man's Own,* pp. 148, 158, 172; Farrar, pp. 275, 308, 331–333; Muzzey, *Maiden,* pp. 125, 204–206; *Advice to a Young Gentleman,* pp. 142, 270–271; *Guide to Good Manners,* pp. 10, 16, 24, 95–96; Peck, pp. 142, 144; Porter, p. 38; Newcomb, *Lady,* p. 173; Newcomb, *Man,* p. 173.

48. *Laws of Etiquette*, 2d ed., p. 203; d'Orsay, p. 6; *Art of Pleasing*, p. 18; Howe, p. 5; *Habits*, p. 310; *Book of Manners*, pp. 69, 191; C. Hartley, pp. 209, 319; *Young Man's Own*, p. 162; Celnart, p. 70; *Guide to Good Manners*, p. 9; de Valcourt, pp. 182, 400–401, 498; *Boy's Manual*, p. 171; *My Son's Book*, p. 108; *Advice to a Young Gentleman*, p. 138; Frost, p. 205; cf. Sedgwick, *Means*, p. 164 (for children). For specific instructions see *Manual*, pp. 50–52, 76; Durang, *Ballroom*, pp. 26–29; Ferrero, pp. 118–120.

49. See chap. 7, n. 71.

50. Abell, pp. 129, 136; *Habits*, pp. 312–318, 320–321, 323–324, 327; *Laws of Etiquette*, 2d ed., pp. 60–62, 208; *Laws of Good Breeding*, pp. 15, 22–23, 25, 27; *True Politeness/Gentlemen*, pp. 11–14; *True Politeness/Ladies*, pp. 7, 11, 13; *Etiquette For Ladies*, pp. 11, 59, 145–146; *Manual*, pp. 143–146; Willis, pp. 7, 11–12, 32, 47; Celnart, pp. 54, 56, 84; Todd, p. 246; *Art*, pp. 18, 32; de Valcourt, pp. 119, 122, 124–125, 495–496; Wells, pp. 69, 81, 100–101; *Polite Present*, p. 18; *Well-Bred Boy*, p. 90; Sedgwick, *Morals*, pp. 14–15; *Manners*, p. 63; Sigourney, *Boy's*, p. 97.

51. Calabrella, p. 18; *Book of Politeness*, pp. 11–12; *Ladies' Indispensable*, p. 124; Thornwell, p. 85; *Lunettes*, p. 160; *Art*, p. 21; *Laws of Etiquette*, 2d ed., pp. 98–99; *Etiquette at Washington*, 1849, pp. 51, 53; *Art of Pleasing*, pp. 26, 54–56, 62; *Handbook*, pp. 26, 40, 43; *Etiquette For Ladies2*, pp. 17–18, 25; *Book of Manners*, pp. 190, 200; Durang, *Fashionable*, pp. 16 22; C. Hartley, pp. 92, 94, 101, 215, 227; F. Hartley, pp. 58, 98; Celnart, pp. 68, 175–176, 187; Farrar, pp. 342, 361–362; de Valcourt, pp. 119, 401, 407; Wells, pp. 71, 90; *Well-Bred Girl*, pp. 22, 34.

52. *Laws of Etiquette*, 2d ed., pp. 74–78, 81, 84–86; Calabrella, pp. 10–11, 15–19, 33; *Etiquette at Washington*, 1849, pp. 31–33, 58–59, 72, 74; Abell, pp. 144–147; Hervey, pp. 249–251; *Habits*, pp. 330–331, 333–334, 336, 338; *Etiquette for Ladies*, pp. 24, 26–27, 36–38, 40–43, 55, 73–74; *True Politeness/Ladies*, pp. 27–33, 42; *True Politeness/Gentlemen*, pp. 28, 30–31, 33; *Beadle's*, pp. 13–17, 20, 70; Willis, pp. 12–14, 15–16, 30, 45; *Young Man's Own*, pp. 149, 180; Celnart, pp. 60–62, 64–69, 77–80, 187; Farrar, pp. 275, 389–392, 394–395; de Valcourt, pp. 123–127, 153; Wells, pp. 63, 70–73; A. Ferguson, pp. 135–139; *Child's Instructor*, pp. 21–22; *Well-Bred Girl*, p. 125.

53. *Art of Pleasing*, pp. 14, 18, 35, 39, 40, 55, 59; *Laws of Good Breeding*, pp. 27, 40, 48, 69; *Handbook*, pp. 13–14, 28–31; *Perfect Gentleman*, pp. 203–204, 207, 215–217, 219–220, 226, 246; *True Politeness/Ladies*, pp. 8, 12, 22–23; *True Politeness/Gentlemen*, pp. 8, 13, 21; *Chesterfield's Letter*, pp. 8, 11, 14, 19–21, 23, 47–48; *Lunettes*, pp. 158, 161, 252–253, 295–296, 300, 304; *Young Man's Own*, pp. 58, 116, 126–128, 133, 147, 169, 173–179; *Young Lady's Own*, pp. 18, 179, 185–187; de Valcourt, pp. 122, 124, 181, 187, 192, 194–198, 204, 209–210, 227, 262, 284, 499–501; Wells, pp. 63, 68, 76–77, 94; *Polite Present*, pp. 14, 18, 21, 27, 29, 35; *Well-Bred Boy*, pp. 86–87, 89–90, 92; Parley, pp. 102–103; *Well-Bred Girl*, pp. 126–127.

54. *Laws of Etiquette*, 2d ed., pp. 77, 136–137; d'Orsay, pp. 18–19, 39; *Etiquette at Washington*, 1849, pp. 49, 66–67; Abell, p. 107; *Perfect Gentleman*, pp. 167, 232, 249; *Etiquette for Ladies*, pp. 49–50; *Canons*, p. 70; *True Politeness/Gentlemen*, pp. 48–49; *Book of Manners*, p. 196; Leslie, 1853, p. 58; *Beadle's*, p. 40; Willis, p. 18; C. Hartley, p. 50; Farrar, p. 341; de Valcourt, pp. 405, 410; Wells, pp. 74, 89.

55. Calabrella, p. 22; *Laws of Good Breeding*, pp. 16, 29–30; Abell, pp. 107–108, 111; Hervey, pp. 227–230; *Etiquette for Ladies2*, pp. 47, 49–50; *Chesterfield's Letter*, pp. 26–28, 45; Celnart, pp. 164–165, 169; Farrar, pp. 341–342, 348–349; *Art*, pp. 27–29; *Guide to Good Manners*, pp. 79, 81, 91; Sproat, *School*, pp. 27–28; *Polite Present*, pp. 6–7, 49–50; *Mother's Friend*, p. 98; *Well-Bred Boy*, p. 30; Alcott, *Boy's*, pp. 34, 36; Newcomb, *Man*, pp. 52–55; Newcomb, *Lady*, pp. 52, 54–55; *Manners*, p. 18.

56. See chap. 7, n. 81.

57. See chap. 7, n. 49.

58. Cf. Halttunen, pp. 104, 109.

59. Cf. Bushman, p. 281.

60. See, especially, *Beadle's*, p. 54; Coxe, pp. 220, 227, 229–232; Livermore, pp. 94–95; Smith, p. 12; A. Fergurson, p. 28; Wells, p. 57.

61. Alcott, *Boy's*, p. 103; Farrar, pp. 202–203; Alcott, *Familiar Letters*, pp. 17, 234.

62. Kett, p. 60. Examples of nostalgic discussions of adolescence can also be found in the present; see Allan Bloom, *The Closing of the American Mind* (New York: Simon and Schuster, 1987), and in the last few pages of an essay that is the best introduction to the history and historiography of adolescence, John Demos's "The Rise and Fall of Adolescence," in *Past, Present, and Personal*, pp. 107–109. Historians can thus use nostalgia to probe the intentions of the youth shapers of any given period. Interestingly, in describing the youth of today, these two authors mourn the passing of very different youths.

63. Ferris, "Men of Business," p. 6; Kett, p. 126–127, 143, 167, 171, 210, et passim; Rodgers, p. 131.

64. Fliegelman, pp. 33, 83.

65. Ryan, pp. 178–179, 239; Larkin, p. 71.

CHAPTER 9

1. For an example of Mickle's equation of "company" with women, see vol. 2, pp. 251–252. Mickle's diary is consistent with the conduct literature in suggesting an interpretation of male-female relations that falls between Carroll Smith-Rosenberg's argument—that there were "severe social restrictions on intimacy between men and women" and that men were "an other or out group, . . . socialized to different behavior and coached to a proper formality in courtship behavior," in "The Female World of Love and Ritual," *Signs* 1 (Autumn 1975): 9, 21—and Ellen Rothman's rejection of that argument and insistence that men and women were constantly together, pp. 23, and 319, n. 14. To situate the argument another way, Mickle's diary reveals the male spheres of association that Rotundo describes in *American Manhood* (in many ways the male counterpart of Smith-Rosenberg's argument for women); but Mickle did not have any intense "romantic friendships" with other men such as Rotundo describes, p. 172; "Body and Soul," p. 13. Interaction with women is mostly confined to discussions of family, courtship, and marriage in Rotundo's schema, while it was not so confined in Mickle's diary or antebellum conduct prescriptions. Nor does Mickle's diary show a world of men who were only "coached to a proper formality" by women and for women, as he appears to have internalized similar standards of propriety and applied them to relations with men as well as women. He sometimes complained about improper female behavior; see 1: 110; 2: 478 of his diary.

2. For reviews of the historiography of separate spheres, see Linda Kerber, "Separate Spheres, Female Worlds, Woman's Place: The Rhetoric of Women's History," *The Journal of American History* 75, no. 1 (June 1988): 9–39, and Vickery, "From Golden Age to Separate Spheres." On female political activity see Elizabeth Varon, "Tippecanoe and the Ladies Too: White Women and Party Politics in Antebellum Virginia, *The Journal of American History* 82, no. 2 (September 1995): 494–521; on male domesticity, see Laura McCall, "Gender in Fiction: The Creations of Literary Men and Women" (paper delivered at the Social Science History Association, November 1991)

and "'The Reign of Brute Force is Now Over': A Content Analysis of Godey's Lady's Book," *Journal of the Early Republic* 9 (Summer 1989): 217–236.

3. de Valcourt, p. 287; cf. Rotundo, *American Manhood*, p. 145. For the place of domestic concerns in advice books see the tables of contents of William Alcott's *Young Woman's Guide*, Harvey Newcomb's *How to Be a Lady*, and *The Young Lady's Own Book*. Smith-Rosenberg, "Female World," pp. 1–29. Rotundo describes some male worlds that existed outside the mixed-sex social world of conduct books, such as those of "boy culture," and "romantic friendships" among young men, as well as "the male sociability of the middle-class work world" in *American Manhood*.

4. The conduct literature thus challenges descriptions of nineteenth-century social visions as sharply divided between "home" and "the streets" (see Ryan, p. 233). Karen Hansen has discovered a similar mixed–sex social world in the papers of New England working-people: see "Making the Social Central: An Introduction," chapter 1 of *A Very Social Time: Crafting Community in Antebellum New England* (University of California Press, 1995). Karen Halttunen also identifies a "middle social sphere" in the middle-class parlor; but I do not think the social world was limited to the parlor (p. 59).

5. Bushman, pp. 440–446 (though Bushman gives a broader discussion of "the geography of refinement" in chap. 11); Blumin, pp. 182–185; Arthur, *Men*, 85.

6. Celnart, pp. 14, 165–166; Calabrella, pp. 23, 41; d'Orsay, pp. 13–14; *Etiquette at Washington*, 1849, p. 66; 1850, pp. 99–100; Wells, p. 86; Thornwell, p. 99; *Beadle's*, pp. 40, 50, 53; *Art*, p. 35; de Valcourt, pp. 108–110, 132, 410, 501; Durang, *Fashionable*, p. 21; Howe, p. 11.

7. The conduct literature thus presents a gender critique of both Jurgen Habermas and his feminist critics, because both overdichotomize the public and private; in addition to Habermas, see the essays by Mary Ryan and Geoff Eley, in Craig Calhoun, ed., *Habermas and the Public Sphere* (Cambridge: Massachusetts Institute of Technology Press, 1990). Laurel Ulrich cautioned me about adding another sphere.

8. John Kasson finds a few more female than male authors in his 1830–1910 sample of advice books, which suggests that the role of women continued to grow after midcentury (pp. 48–49). On female writers see Mary Kelley, *Private Woman, Public Stage: Literary Domesticity in Nineteenth-Century America* (New York: Oxford University Press, 1984), and Susan Coultrap-McQuinn, *Doing Literary Business: American Women Writers in the Nineteenth Century* (Chapel Hill: University of North Carolina Press, 1990).

9. Farrar, p. 348; *Etiquette for Ladies2*, pp. 52–53; *Art*, p. 29; Abell, pp. 111, 113; *Art of Pleasing*, p. 53; *Habits*, p. 365; *Etiquette at Washington*, 1849, p. 72; de Valcourt, p. 136; *Beadle's*, p. 42.

10. *Young Lady's Own*, p. 251; *Manual*, p. 49; *Etiquette For Ladies2*, pp. 12, 20; Calabrella, pp. 17–18; *True Politeness/Ladies*, pp. 29–30; Leslie, 1853, pp. 31, 33, 38, 48–50, 112, 116; Thornwell, pp. 82–84; *Habits*, p. 338.

11. *Laws of Etiquette*, 2d ed., p. 167; Calabrella, p. 21; *Lunettes*, pp. 176, 336; *Perfect Gentlemen*, p. 167; C. Hartley, pp. 51, 84–85. Rotundo argues, in contrast, that many dinners were "stag" affairs, *American Manhood*, pp. 197, 199. His examples seem to be from the end of the century. Mickle, 1: 83–84.

12. Celnart, pp. 175, 183; *Etiquette for Ladies*, p. 69; Thornwell, p. 95; *Art of Pleasing*, pp. 53–55, 57; *Canons*, p. 73; *Perfect Gentleman*, pp. 177–178, 248; *Handbook*, p. 42; C. Hartley, p. 100; *Laws of Etiquette*, 2d ed., pp. 154–156, 167; *Guide to Good Manners*, p. 81; Mickle, 2: 502.

13. Celnart, p. 78; *True Politeness/Ladies*, pp. 7, 12; *Book of Politeness*, p. 15; Well-

Bred Girl, p. 22; *Etiquette for Ladies2,* p. 17; *Ladies' and Gentlemen's Letter,* p. 37; Thornwell, p. 86; de Valcourt, pp. 124–125, 147, 495–496; Manners, p. 63; Leslie, 1853, p. 57.

14. Farrar, p. 269; *Well-Bred Girl,* pp. 33–34; Abell, pp. 173–174; Manners, p. 63; Leslie, 1853, p. 304; de Valcourt, p. 273; F. Hartley, p. 56.

15. *Laws of Etiquette,* 2d ed., pp. 66–67, 208, 219–220; *Art,* pp. 17–18, 23; *True Politeness/Gentlemen,* p. 7; Mackellar, p. 126; Wells, p. 69; Lunettes, p. 129; *Chesterfield's Letter,* p. 42; C. Hartley, p. 71. See Rotundo, *American Manhood,* pp. 82–85, for a discussion of the permissibility of unritualized touching between men.

16. Celnart, pp. 77–78, 175; Farrar, pp. 342, 361; *Etiquette for Ladies2,* pp. 10, 17–18; *True Politeness/Ladies,* pp. 5–6, 32–33, 36–37; Abell, pp. 107–108, 140; F. Hartley, pp. 77, 167; *Etiquette for Ladies,* pp. 24–25; A. Ferguson, pp. 136–137; Thornwell, pp. 84–86, 88; *Handbook,* p. 13; *Art of Pleasing,* p. 55.

17. *Laws of Etiquette,* 2d ed., pp. 65, 67–68; Wells, p. 67; Lunettes, p. 254; *Etiquette at Washington,* 1849, pp. 49–50; *Perfect Gentleman,* p. 167.

18. Lunettes, p. 336; see also Miller, p. 49. Rotundo also suggests this, from evidence in men's letters, in "Romantic Friendship: Male Intimacy and Middle-Class Youth in the Northern United States, 1800–1900," *The Journal of Social History* 23, no. 1: 1–25. But his examples, like Smith-Rosenberg's of the "female world," are mostly of "private" relationships that need to be viewed in their wider social context.

19. Lunettes, pp. 128–129; C. Hartley, pp. 197–198; *Laws of Good Breeding,* p. 45.

20. *Laws of Etiquette,* 2d ed., pp. 208, 211; de Valcourt, p. 122; Willis, p. 11; *Advice to a Young Gentleman,* p. 271; Arthur, *Men,* p. 152; Peck, pp. 148–149.

21. See, for example, Suzanne Lebsock, *The Free Women of Petersburg: Status and Culture in a Southern Town, 1784–1860* (New York: Norton, 1985), p. 49. For a rare acknowledgment of nineteenth-century convergence in gender norms, see Karen Lystra's *Searching the Heart: Women, Men, and Romantic Love in Nineteenth-Century America* (New York: Oxford, 1989), p. 128. Lystra's is one of the more powerful cases for setting aside the separate spheres paradigm.

22. On paying attention to others, see ch. 7, n. 43. Farrar, pp. 320, 327, 330, 411; Porter, pp. 129, 177; Leslie, 1853, pp. 74, 76–77, 89; F. Hartley, pp. 35, 301–302; Coxe, p. 285; Abell, p. 134; Celnart, p. 37.

23. Here and below, where antebellum conduct works addressed a certain category of advice to both sexes, the reader can refer to the relevant sections of the discussion of behavior between middle-class peers in chapter 7 for details and citations. As a rule, only gender variations are documented in this chapter. Farrar, pp. 318, 320, 325; Austin, p. 285; Porter, pp. 129–130; Leslie, 1853, p. 69; Arthur, *Ladies,* p. 144.

24. *Boy's Manual,* pp. 170–171; *My Son's Book,* pp. 101, 108, 144; Peck, pp. 142, 144, 160–162; *Art of Pleasing,* pp. 13–14, 16, 18; *Manual,* pp. 63–64; Farrar, pp. 275, 333; Walsh, 2: 9; *Etiquette for Ladies,* pp. 72–73, 143; Newcomb, *Lady,* p. 173; Porter, p. 38; *Young Man's Own,* pp. 158, 172; *Laws of Etiquette,* 2d ed., pp. 207–208; *American Gentleman's Everyday,* pp. 9, 20; Mackellar, pp. 108–109, 137, 140; C. Hartley, pp. 204, 209, 304–305, 319–320; *Handbook,* p. 13; *Guide to Good Manners,* pp. viii, 9, 15–16, 23–24, 95–96; *Book of Manners,* pp. 69, 74, 87; de Valcourt, pp. 182, 299. Patricia Cohen emphasizes women's need for a reserved demeanor in public and while traveling; but she does not acknowledge strictures to men; see "Safety and Danger: Women on American Public Transport," in Dorothy Helly and Susan Reverby, eds., *Gendered Domains: Rethinking Public and Private in Women's History* (Ithaca: Cornell University Press, 1992), pp. 109–122. My argument is closer to Kasson's, although he, too, underplays the demands made of men, pp. 117–136.

25. Comstock, pp. 16, 83; Sprague, 1834, p. 102; Sigourney, *Ladies*, 1835, p. 48; *Ladies Vase*, p. 18; *Art*, p. 19; Abell, pp. 114–115, 131, 135; F. Hartley, pp. 34, 90, 95, 99, 168, 183, 185, 286; *Habits*, pp. 282, 302; *Young Man's Own*, pp. 158, 162; *Laws of Etiquette*, 2d ed., pp. 28, 204–205; *Advice to a Young Gentleman*, pp. 124, 129; *My Son's Book*, p. 108; d'Orsay, p. 30; Durang, *Ballroom*, p. 7; Peck, pp. 141–142, 147; Mackellar, pp. 111, 137–138; *Chesterfield's Letter*, pp. 19, 30, 48; Maberly, p. 44; de Valcourt, pp. 106, 147–148, 205, 219–220; *Art of Pleasing*, pp. 14–15.

26. Sprague, 1822, p. 38; *Young Lady's Own*, p. 18; Austin, pp. 290, 361; Sedgwick, *Means*, p. 164; Muzzey, *Maiden*, p. 125; Calabrella, p. 13; Porter, p. 123; Thornwell, p. 74; F. Hartley, pp. 20, 148–149; *Canons*, p. 58; *American Gentleman's Everyday*, p. 11; *Perfect Gentleman*, p. 219; *Manual*, pp. 43, 124–134; Celnart, p. 84; Maberly, pp. 43–44, 56, 64; de Valcourt, pp. 182, 410.

27. *Child's Instructor*, pp. 30–32; *Young Lady's Own*, pp. 15–16, 148, 178, 250; Sandford, pp. 13–14; Celnart, pp. 31, 84–86; *Etiquette for Ladies*, pp. 14–15, 31, 34; Alcott, *Woman's*, pp. 97–100; Newcomb, *Lady*, pp. 48, 95–96; Porter, pp. 122–123, 142; Daniel Wise, *Young Lady's Counsellor* (New York, 1851), p. 222; F. Hartley, pp. 41, 149–150, 152, 168, 170, 210; *Book of Manners*, pp. 26–27, 31–32, 186, 193; *Advice to a Young Gentleman*, pp. 52–54; *Laws of Etiquette*, 2d ed., p. 131; Sigourney, *Boy's*, pp. 97–98; Alexander, pp. 29–30; *Young Man's Own*, pp. 148, 150–151, 163; Alcott, *Man's*, 1833, pp. 64–66; Mackellar, pp. 95–96; Lunettes, pp. 73, 78; C. Hartley, pp. 186, 215, 320–321.

28. Comstock, pp. 83–84; Celnart, pp. 84–86; *Etiquette for Ladies*, pp. 30–33, 132–135, 139; *Well-Bred Girl*, p. 124; Abell, pp. 114, 168, 177; F. Hartley, pp. 149–152, 173–174; *Chesterfield's Letter*, p. 43; *Young Man's Own*, pp. 114–116, 149, 162; *Boy's Manual*, pp. 171–172; *My Son's Book*, p. 101; *Book of Manners*, pp. 89, 92, 186–187; Peck, pp. 142, 147, 161–162; *Art of Pleasing*, pp. 13–15; C. Hartley, pp. 92, 305–307; *Manual*, pp. 24–25, 56–57, 63–64, 67, 101–114; *Guide to Good Manners*, pp. 16, 18, 24, 63–65; Wells, pp. 43–44; Ferrero, pp. 106–107; Kasson, pp. 124, 128.

29. Celnart, pp. 66, 83, 86; *Manual*, pp. 54–55, 101; *Etiquette for Ladies*, p. 33; *Art*, pp. 32, 34; Newcomb, *Lady*, pp. 98, 106; Abell, pp. 115, 129, 167–168; F. Hartley, pp. 99, 101–103, 107, 151–152, 283; *Perfect Gentleman*, pp. 168–169, 222; Willis, pp. 20–21, 41, 44–45; *Habits*, pp. 42, 284, 292–293, 309–310; *Young Man's Own*, pp. 109, 115–116; d'Orsay, p. 33; Miller, p. 49; Newcomb, *Man*, p. 96; *Laws of Good Breeding*, pp. 40, 46; *Book of Manners*, pp. 92, 202; Mackellar, p. 98–99, 116; Lunettes, pp. 335–337, 341–343; *Juvenile Monitor*, pp. 8, 12, 15; de Valcourt, pp. 55, 133, 141, 156, 234, 490–492.

30. Newcomb, *Lady*, pp. 106–107; *Child's Instructor*, p. 33; Celnart, pp. 29–30, 85–86; *Etiquette for Ladies*, pp. 33, 44–45, 135, 139; *Etiquette for Ladies2*, p. 25; *Manners*, pp. 58–61; Wells, pp. 44–45; Thornwell, p. 78; F. Hartley, pp. 111, 114, 151–152, 154; *Chesterfield's Letter*, pp. 43–44; *Habits*, pp. 282–283, 309–310; *Boy's Manual*, p. 171; *Manual*, pp. 24–25, 67–68; *My Son's Book*, pp. 108, 117; Frost, p. 205; *Art*, pp. 17, 19; Lunettes, pp. 334–335; *Perfect Gentleman*, p. 215; *Guide to Good Manners*, p. 92; de Valcourt, pp. 55, 378–379, 401.

31. *Young Lady's Own*, p. 149; Celnart, p. 186; *Etiquette for Ladies*, pp. 72–73, 154, 156–157; *True Politeness/Ladies*, pp. 39–40; F. Hartley, pp. 168, 170, 202; *Laws of Etiquette*, 2d ed., pp. 176–178; *Boy's Manual*, p. 170; d'Orsay, pp. 28–29; Frost, p. 205; *True Politeness/Gentlemen*, p. 35; Arthur, *Men*, pp. 84–85; *Laws of Good Breeding*, p. 33; *American Gentleman's Everyday*, pp. 13–14; *Book of Politeness*, pp. 18–19; Howe, pp. 4, 6, 9, 13; C. Hartley, pp. 91–92, 95, 104–106, 224–225; *Perfect Gentleman*, pp. 233,

239–240; de Valcourt, pp. 400, 406; *Handbook*, p. 42; *Young Man's Own*, p. 116; Mickle, 1: 59, 67; 2: 359, 428, 461, 478, 485, 488, 495, 500.

32. See chap. 7, ns. 50–53; Comstock, pp. 84–87; *Etiquette For Ladies*, pp. 14, 16, 33; *Well-Bred Girl*, p. 127; *Chesterfield's Letter*, p. 44; Ferrero, p. 105; Muzzey, *Maiden*, p. 125. Cf. Kasson p. 162.

33. Lieber, in Tryon, p. 86. For women's narrower range, see Kasson, pp. 162, 180; in contrast, see Lystra, p. 126. See also Halttunen, pp. 57, 80.

34. Newcomb, *Lady*, p. 93; Abell, p. 130; Leslie, 1853, pp. 304, 306; Farrar, p. 337; F. Hartley, p. 108; *Young Man's Own*, pp. 109, 155, 158; *My Son's Book*, pp. 116–117; *Well-Bred Boy*, p. 86; *Art*, pp. 19, 34; Mackellar, pp. 99, 125–126; *Perfect Gentleman*, pp. 215, 250; *Polite Present*, pp. 7, 10–11, 18, 35–36, 57–58; *Juvenile Guide*, pp. 61, 115–116; *Guide to Good Manners*, pp. 91–92; *Book of Manners*, pp. 159, 176, 190; *Ladies' and Gentlemen's Letter*, pp. 32, 114; Wells, p. 136; *Chesterfield's Letter*, pp. 39–40.

35. Austin, pp. 360–361; Newcomb, *Lady*, p. 40; *True Politeness/Ladies*, p. 20; Abell, p. 154; F. Hartley, pp. 152, 190; Sigourney, *Ladies*, 1833, pp. 83–84; Sedgwick, *Means*, p. 236; *Etiquette for Ladies2*, p. 38; Maberly, p. 28; *Young Man's Own*, pp. 121–122; *Advice to Young Gentlemen*, p. 178; *Book of Manners*, p. 187; de Valcourt, pp. 168–179, 217; *Habits*, p. 301; *Handbook*, p. 31.

36. *Young Lady's Own*, p. 18; *Well-Bred Girl*, pp. 126–127; Sedgwick, *Means*, pp. 202, 234–236; Newcomb, *Lady*, p. 201; F. Hartley, p. 149; Sigourney, *Ladies*, 1833, p. 88; Farrar, p. 376; *Ladies' Vase*, pp. 41–45; A. Fergurson, pp. 46–48; Titcomb, p. 139; Alcott, *Man's*, 1833, p. 182; Alcott, *Boy's*, p. 102; Newcomb, *Man*, p. 201; de Valcourt, p. 199; Maberly, pp. 61, 64; C. Hartley, pp. 20, 27, 205, 208; Lunettes, p. 298; *Perfect Gentleman*, p. 224.

37. Sigourney, *Ladies*, 1833, pp. 86, 88; Sprague, 1834, p. 117; Farrar, pp. 276, 299; Alcott, *Wife*, p. 334; Newcomb, *Lady*, p. 205; Abell, p. 198; F. Hartley, pp. 18, 153; Todd, pp. 199, 210; de Valcourt, pp. 124, 181, 188, 194–195, 208; *Boy's Manual*, p. 131; *Book of Politeness*, pp. 11, 22; C. Hartley, p. 21; Wells, p. 77; Willis, p. 21; *Young Man's Own*, pp. 127–128, 169, 174, 175; *Advice to a Young Gentleman*, pp. 169, 171; *Manual*, pp. 90–94; *My Son's Book*, pp. 102–103; *Art of Pleasing*, pp. 40, 47; Ferrero, p. 96.

38. Kasson, pp. 160–161. My findings are consistent with those of Peter Stearns, who argues that before 1860 demands to suppress anger were identical for both sexes: see "Men, Boys and Anger in American Society," in Mangan and Walvin, eds., p. 79.

39. See, for example, Ryan, pp. 155, 218, et passim; Kasson, p. 128.

40. *Etiquette for Ladies*, pp. 10–11, 59, 134, 145–146; *Art*, pp. 17–18, 23, 32, 34; *True Politeness/Ladies*, pp. 7, 13; *Book of Politeness*, pp. 4, 13, 15, 19; Willis, pp. 7–8, 11–12, 22, 32, 34, 41, 47; *Laws of Etiquette*, 2d ed., pp. 60–62, 66–67, 208, 220; *True Politeness/Gentlemen*, pp. 7, 13–14; Lunettes, pp. 128–130, 166; *Handbook*, pp. 13–14; *Ladies' Indispensable*, pp. 123–124; de Valcourt, pp. 103–104, 118–119, 124–125, 146–147, 182, 232, 235, 247, 400, 495–496; *Habits*, pp. 310, 313, 318, 320–321, 323–324, 327, 337; Celnart, pp. 56, 70, 84; Hervey, pp. 134, 201–202, 205–206; Wells, pp. 67–69, 80–81, 100, 104; *Perfect Gentleman*, pp. 208–211, 221, 241–242; Smith, pp. 47, 58–59; *Etiquette for Ladies2*, p. 24; *Young Man's Own*, p. 162; *Manual*, pp. 50, 143–146.

41. Parkes, pp. 335–336; *Young Lady's Own*, pp. 15, 148, 241–246; Celnart, pp. 29–31, 169, 183–184; Farrar, pp. 296–297, 332, 366, 371; Abbott, p. 65; *Etiquette for Ladies*, pp. 43–46, 54–55, 69–70; *True Politeness/Ladies*, pp. 37, 40–41, 53, 64; Arthur, *Ladies*, p. 155; *Guide to Good Manners*, p. 75; Abell, pp. 115, 299; Hervey, p. 130; Leslie, 1853, pp. 38, 68, 70–71, 93–94, 97–99; 1854, p. 310; de Valcourt,

pp. 158–159, 299–300; Thornwell, pp. 78–79, 95–96; Howe, p. 12; Ferrero, pp. 109–110; *Handbook*, pp. 12, 41; F. Hartley, pp. 40, 114, 168, 170, 172, 176, 191; *Perfect Gentleman*, p. 247; *Chesterfield's Letter*, p. 48. Stansell claims that working-class girls walked the streets without male protectors and that bourgeois commentators remarked on this, pp. 86–89, 183.

42. *Etiquette for Ladies*, pp. 9–10; *Art*, p. 34; *True Politeness/Ladies*, pp. 6–7; Arthur, *Ladies*, pp. 135–138; *Etiquette at Washington*, 1849, pp. 27, 59–60; 1850, pp. 34–36; de Valcourt pp. 238–239; Thornwell, pp. 109–110; d'Orsay, pp. 11, 19; *True Politeness/Gentlemen*, p. 51; *Book of Politeness*, p. 20; Abell, pp. 212–213; *Perfect Gentleman*, p. 238; C. Hartley, p. 86; Willis, pp. 30, 62.

43. See Cohen, "Safety and Danger;" Dickens, pp. 111, 192; Lieber, in Tryon, p. 82.

44. Alcott, *Wife*, p. 330; *Etiquette at Washington*, 1849, p. 33; *Canons*, p. 198; C. Hartley, pp. 77–78, 82 (this last author, at the end of the period, was explicit: "[I]n this country, where almost every man has some business to occupy his day, the evening is the best time for paying calls"; but even he proceeded to give men advice concerning morning visits). Cf. Ryan, who claims that "separate spheres" was based on a certain real sexual segregation entailed by the separation of home and workplaces, pp. 232–233. Rotundo suggests that early-nineteenth-century middle-class men engaged in a fair amount of visiting in connection with their work (*American Manhood*, pp. 196–197); the manuals suggest that they engaged in social visits as well.

45. *Etiquette at Washington*, 1849, pp. 32–33; see also Halttunen, pp. 102–110.

46. *Etiquette at Washington*, 1849, pp. 49–50, 72; *Perfect Gentleman*, pp. 167, 233, 248–249; *True Politeness/Ladies*, pp. 52–53; Thornwell, pp. 94, 103; *Etiquette for Ladies2*, pp. 49–50, 52–53; *Etiquette for Ladies*, p. 54; Abell, pp. 107, 111; *Art of Pleasing*, p. 53; Celnart, p. 169; *Art*, p. 29; *Book of Politeness*, p. 13; Hervey, p. 230; C. Hartley, pp. 50, 57–58.

47. Blumin, pp. 182–183; Bushman, pp. 440–441; Davidoff, *Best Circles*, pp. 15, 21, 41–42.

48. Davidson, *Revolution*, p. 135. Hannah Webster Foster's *The Coquette*, for example, is full of male gallantry, but with the aim of seduction rather than protection. Patricia Cohen does not acknowledge the ethic of male protection in stressing the dangers of travel for women; see "Safety and Danger." More generally, Rotundo claims that it was women's role to curb male behavior (*American Manhood*, p. 25). Kasson stresses the way that male aid served to "ritualize women's subordination to men," pp. 132–136. While she claims that the deportment of the "Bowery girl" was "a studied departure" from bourgeois standards of female decorum, Stansell also observes the emergence of a protective ethic between working-class men and women; see pp. 93–96, 99–100.

49. Susan Klepp, "'Heroines whose courage had risen superior to sex': Women, Fear, and Autobiography in the Early Republic" (paper presented to the conference on Festive Culture and Public Ritual in Early America, April 1996), esp. pp. 3, 6.

50. *Young Man's Own*, pp. 128, 290–296, 303–305; Alcott, *Man's*, 1833, pp. 210–211, 213, 217–218, 229; *Manual*, pp. 11, 95; *Boy's Manual*, pp. 85–86, 125–126; *Letters to a Younger Brother*, p. 34; Austin, pp. 180, 200; *Canons*, p. 49; Arthur, *Men*, pp. 146–147, 149; Newcomb, *Man*, pp. 38–39; F. Ferguson, pp. 83–87, 90; *Laws of Good Breeding*, p. 48; *Manners*, p. 96; Mackellar, pp. 158, 160; Wells, p. 59; Alexander, p. 32; *Lunettes*, pp. 96, 457; Titcomb, p. 24; C. Hartley, pp. 186, 191–192; see also Mickle, 1: 169. Rotundo finds the brother-sister bond very important in his study of men's letters: see *American Manhood*, pp. 93–94.

51. Comstock, pp. 30, 34; *Young Man's Own*, pp. 290, 292, 296, 297; Wise, *Man's*, p. 240; Peck, p. 154; Lunettes, p. 343.

52. *Laws of Etiquette*, 2d ed., pp. 60–62, 67; Art, pp. 18, 22; *Laws of Good Breeding*, pp. 22, 25, 45; *Etiquette at Washington*, 1849, pp. 27–28; de Valcourt, pp. 103–104, 118; Wells, pp. 67, 71, 101; Lunettes, pp. 132, 161–162, 253; Ferrero, pp. 95–96; *Beadle's*, pp. 20, 45; *Handbook*, pp. 11, 13; Willis, pp. 6, 11–12, 32–33; *Guide to Good Manners*, p. 25; *Art of Pleasing*, pp. 22–23; Hervey, p. 206; *Perfect Gentleman*, pp. 210, 251–252; *Habits*, p. 313.

53. *Young Man's Own*, pp. 109, 112, 305; Celnart, pp. 189, 191; Alcott, *Man's*, 1833, p. 218; Austin, p. 192; *Advice to a Young Gentleman*, p. 144; Art, pp. 25, 33; Sedgwick, *Morals*, p. 19; Abell, p. 127; Manners, pp. 46–47; de Valcourt, pp. 103, 248; Wells, pp. 59–60, 76; Lunettes, pp. 133, 348; *Ladies' and Gentlemen's Letter*, pp. 75, 82; C. Hartley, pp. 68, 186, 191–192; Carey, p. 3; F. Fergurson, p. 117.

54. *Young Man's Own*, p. 295; Lunettes, pp. 133, 163, 167, 348; Alcott, *Man's*, 1833, p. 218; Arthur, *Men*, p. 147; Manners, pp. 45–46, 48; Wells, pp. 68, 96; C. Hartley, pp. 67, 69–73, 163, 176–178, 199, 295–296, 299; Walsh, 2: 23; *Laws of Etiquette*, 2d ed., pp. 71–72; Canons, p. 66; *Guide to Good Manners*, p. 36; *True Politeness/Gentlemen*, p. 8; Hervey, pp. 205, 213; Leslie, 1853, pp. 67, 70; *Chesterfield's Letter*, pp. 9, 33; Celnart, pp. 51, 69, 160, 171; Manual, pp. 62, 142; Thornwell, p. 80; *Beadle's*, pp. 45–46.

55. *Young Man's Own*, pp. 112, 296; Celnart, pp. 159, 171, 180; *Book of Politeness*, pp. 14, 16; Hervey, pp. 128, 133, 205, 213; Manners, p. 47; de Valcourt, pp. 236, 248, 407; Wells, pp. 91, 95–96, 107, 112; Lunettes, pp. 163, 173; C. Hartley, pp. 69–70, 178, 186, 202, 298–299, 321; Willis, pp. 22, 32, 36, 53; *Ladies' Indispensable*, p. 123; Alcott, *Man's*, 1833, pp. 218–219; *Advice to a Young Gentleman*, p. 144; *True Politeness/Gentlemen*, p. 36; *Ladies' and Gentlemen's Letter*, pp. 41, 53; *Laws of Etiquette*, 1st ed., p. 106; 2d ed., p. 115; Maberly, p. 41.

56. Canons, p. 70; *True Politeness/Ladies*, p. 30; Alcott, *Familiar*, pp. 277–278; *Etiquette at Washington*, 1849, p. 45; 1850, p. 44; *Ladies' Indispensable*, pp. 123–124, 127; Wells, p. 71; Lunettes, pp. 157, 159–162; *Chesterfield's Letter*, p. 12; C. Hartley, pp. 75–77, 81, 227; Celnart, pp. 65, 80; *Laws of Etiquette*, 2d ed., p. 76; Art, p. 21; *True Politeness/Gentlemen*, p. 28; de Valcourt, p. 153; *Perfect Gentleman*, p. 246; *Habits*, p. 336; Mickle, 2: 306.

57. Parkes, p. 67; *Laws of Etiquette*, 2d ed., pp. 139, 150–151; d'Orsay, pp. 12–14, 17; Art, pp. 27–29; *True Politeness/Gentlemen*, pp. 43, 45–47; Hervey, pp. 227, 230; Wells, pp. 85–88; Lunettes, pp. 171, 176, 340; C. Hartley, pp. 51–53; Celnart, p. 168; de Valcourt, pp. 132–133, 135, 139; *Beadle's*, p. 41; Willis, pp. 27, 30.

58. Examples of the rules discussed in this and the following two paragraphs are found in: Celnart, pp. 175, 183–186; *Laws of Etiquette*, 1st ed., pp. 113–114; 2d ed., pp. 98–99, 172, 174–176, 178–179; Canons, pp. 65–66, 68–69, 73; Art, pp. 24–27, 37; Durang, *Ballroom*, pp. 5–8; *Guide to Good Manners*, pp. 76–78; *Etiquette at Washington*, 1849, pp. 42–45, 51–52; de Valcourt, pp. 102, 405–407; Durang, *Fashionable*, pp. 16–18, 21–22, 189; Howe, pp. 3, 5–10, 12–13; C. Hartley, pp. 92–97, 100–101, 104–105, 223–225, 227; *Perfect Gentleman*, pp. 233, 239–241, 248, 252; d'Orsay, pp. 74–75, 77–78; *True Politeness/Gentlemen*, pp. 6, 34–40; *Laws of Good Breeding*, pp. 32–34; *Art of Pleasing*, pp. 55, 57–59, 61; Wells, pp. 90, 92–94; *Beadle's*, pp. 31–32, 35, 37; *Handbook*, pp. 12, 40–43; *Chesterfield's Letter*, pp. 22–24, 30–32; Mickle, 2: 428, 502.

59. *Laws of Etiquette*, 2d ed., pp. 64, 217; d'Orsay, pp. 6, 13; Art, pp. 20, 22, 34; *True Politeness/Gentlemen*, pp. 5, 63; *Etiquette at Washington*, 1849, pp. 27, 51, 73; de Valcourt, pp. 104, 121, 411; *Art of Pleasing*, pp. 23, 47; Lunettes, pp. 131, 161–163,

172, 250; *Ladies' and Gentlemen's Letter*, p. 23; *Beadle's*, pp. 20, 32; *Perfect Gentleman*, pp. 227, 248; *Chesterfield's Letter*, pp. 8, 12, 33; C. Hartley, pp. 51, 67, 184, 189, 202, 295; *Handbook*, pp. 11–12; Wells, pp. 67, 71, 102, 104; Celnart, p. 173; Hosmer, p. 135; Hervey, pp. 126–127, 133, 197, 205.

60. Celnart, pp. 50, 69, 80, 173–174; *Laws of Etiquette*, 2d ed., p. 221; *Canons*, p. 82; *True Politeness/Gentlemen*, pp. 43, 63–64; *Art*, p. 18; *Laws of Good Breeding*, pp. 13, 30; *Book of Politeness*, p. 13; Hervey, pp. 204–205, 207; *Art of Pleasing*, pp. 22, 46; de Valcourt, pp. 121, 132, 422; Wells, pp. 100, 102; *Lunettes*, pp. 131–132, 163; *Beadle's*, pp. 19, 45–46, 62; Ferrero, p. 99; *Handbook*, pp. 14, 19; *Chesterfield's Letter*, pp. 26, 33; C. Hartley, pp. 66–67, 72–73, 161; *Perfect Gentleman*, pp. 218, 249, 251; *Manual*, p. 54; Howe, p. 7.

61. *Young Man's Own*, p. 112; Celnart, pp. 159, 174, 183, 189, 190–191; *Laws of Etiquette*, 2d ed., pp. 191–192; 1st ed., pp. 106–107, 113; Austin, p. 192; *Art*, pp. 24–25, 33; Sedgwick, *Morals*, p. 19; *Etiquette at Washington*, 1849, pp. 45–48; *Book of Manners*, p. 201; Hervey, p. 128; *Manners*, p. 47; de Valcourt, pp. 233, 248; Wells, pp. 105, 107; *Lunettes*, pp. 162, 167, 173; *Beadle's*, p. 32; C. Hartley, pp. 70–71, 84, 185–186, 202–203, 223, 225, 294–296, 299; *Handbook*, pp. 14, 43; Willis, pp. 35–37; Mickle, 1: 62; 2: 295; Marryat, p. 264; Dickens, pp. 110, 112; Lieber in Tryon, pp. 82–85; Martineau, pp. 89–90, 106.

62. Parkes, p. 67; Celnart, p. 165; d'Orsay, pp. 13–14; *Art*, pp. 27–28; *True Politeness/Gentlemen*, p. 48; *Etiquette at Washington*, 1849, p. 68; Hervey, p. 227; *Book of Manners*, p. 197; de Valcourt, pp. 132, 411; Wells, pp. 85–86; *Lunettes*, p. 176; *Ladies' and Gentlemen's Letter*, pp. 43–44; *Handbook*, p. 20; *Chesterfield's Letter*, pp. 26–27; *Perfect Gentleman*, pp. 175, 249.

63. *Manual*, pp. 78, 143–145; *Laws of Etiquette*, 2d ed., pp. 60, 62, 71, 205–206; *Lunettes*, pp. 130–132, 172, 348; de Valcourt, pp. 103–104, 118–120, 236–237; Wells, pp. 67–68, 101–102; *Handbook*, pp. 11, 13–14; Willis, pp. 7–9, 11, 31–33; C. Hartley, pp. 68–69, 74, 189, 202, 209–210; d'Orsay, pp. 5–6, 27, 45; *Guide to Good Manners*, pp. 25, 36; *True Politeness/Gentlemen*, pp. 11–12, 60, 62; *Laws of Good Breeding*, pp. 14, 25, 27, 33; *Etiquette at Washington*, 1849, pp. 45, 73; Hervey, pp. 205–206; *Beadle's*, pp. 19–20, 31, 44–46; Mickle, 1: 237–238.

64. *Polite Present*, pp. 39–40; *Young Man's Own*, pp. 109, 294–296, 304–305; Alcott, *Men*, 1833, pp. 217–219; Farrar, p. 402; Carey, p. 3; *Advice to Young Gentlemen*, p. 144; Alcott, *Boy's*, p. 106; Newcomb, *Man*, pp. 38–39, 50; F. Fergurson, pp. 83–84, 86–87, 117, 119; *True Politeness/Gentlemen*, pp. 8, 35; Abell, p. 209; Hervey, pp. 204–205, 213; *Manners*, pp. 42, 46–48, 94–96; Peck, pp. 150–151; de Valcourt, pp. 236–237, 251, 256; Durang, *Fashionable*, p. 189; Wells, pp. 59–60, 76, 108; C. Hartley, pp. 36–37, 66, 68–69, 100, 176, 178, 186, 191–192, 224, 321.

65. Celnart, p. 66; *Laws of Etiquette*, 2d ed., pp. 204, 218–219; *Manual*, p. 78; *True Politeness/Gentlemen*, p. 62; *Etiquette at Washington*, 1849, p. 45; 1850, pp. 105–106; Hervey, p. 127; *Book of Manners*, p. 202; *Art of Pleasing*, pp. 47, 53; *Lunettes*, pp. 160, 162, 173, 344; C. Hartley, pp. 51, 84; *Handbook*, p. 22.

66. For a sampling, see *Young Man's Own*, pp. 112, 294, 304–306; *Laws of Etiquette*, 2d ed., p. 114; Maberly, pp. 34, 40–41, 57; Newcomb, *Man*, p. 50; *True Politeness/Gentlemen*, p. 24; *Book of Manners*, p. 192; F. Fergurson, pp. 117–118; de Valcourt, pp. 194, 327; *Lunettes*, pp. 161, 307–308, 354–355; *Ladies' and Gentlemen's Letter*, pp. 75–76, 82; *Beadle's*, pp. 26, 44; C. Hartley, pp. 27, 93, 100, 186, 191–192, 319; Ferrero, p. 99; *Handbook*, p. 29; Peck, p. 153; *Manual*, pp. 79–80, 95; d'Orsay, p. 34; Wells, p. 76; Alcott, *Man's*, 1833, p. 212.

67. *True Politeness/Gentlemen*, p. 19; *Laws of Good Breeding*, p. 38; *Lunettes*,

pp. 134, 303, 308; C. Hartley, pp. 22, 26, 100, 185, 194, 295; Willis, p. 8; *Canons,* p. 153; Smith, p. 47; *Young Man's Own,* p. 290; Alcott, *Man,* 1833, p. 213; *Boy's Manual,* p. 235; Austin, pp. 167, 192; *Art,* p. 43; F. Fergurson, p. 83; de Valcourt, pp. 235, 249; Wells, p. 105; *Beadle's,* pp. 18, 44; *Perfect Gentleman,* p. 218.

68. The classic cases for the ideology of female purity are made in Barbara Welter, "The Cult of True Womanhood," *American Quarterly* 18 (1966): 151–174, and Nancy Cott, "Passionlessness." For revisions by courtship historians, see Lystra, pp. 5–6, 17–18, 58, 88, 91; and Rothman, pp. 122–138.

69. Celnart, pp. 50–51, 66, 108, 176; *Etiquette at Washington,* 1849, p. 45; Hervey, pp. 127, 205; Ferrero, p. 99; Wells, p. 90; Lunettes, pp. 134, 172; Howe, p. 5; *Beadle's,* pp. 32, 44; C. Hartley, pp. 67, 84, 185, 225; *Perfect Gentleman,* p. 218.

70. Celnart, pp. 51, 69, 80, 160, 165, 169, 171–172; *Laws of Etiquette,* 2d ed., pp. 139, 179, 192, 221–222; *Canons,* p. 66; *True Politeness/Gentlemen,* pp. 39–40, 43, 60, 64; *Laws of Good Breeding,* pp. 25–26, 30; Hervey, pp. 205, 207, 213, 227; de Valcourt, pp. 120, 132, 153, 235–236; Wells, pp. 79, 85, 96, 102; Lunettes, pp. 133–134, 162–163; Howe, pp. 5–6, 7; *Beadle's,* pp. 37, 40–41, 43, 45–46; C. Hartley, pp. 51, 57, 67, 69–70, 71, 93–94, 163, 178, 223, 225, 227, 295, 298; *Perfect Gentleman,* pp. 175, 218, 248–249, 252; *Handbook,* pp. 8, 13–14.

71. *Manual,* p. 62; *Art,* pp. 18, 37–38; *Book of Politeness,* pp. 14, 16–17; de Valcourt, pp. 236, 406, 422; *Beadle's,* p. 62; C. Hartley, pp. 72, 106, 160–162; d'Orsay, pp. 28–29; *True Politeness/Gentlemen,* p. 37; *Etiquette at Washington,* 1849, p. 44; Howe, p. 4; 72. *Ladies' and Gentlemen's Letter,* pp. 52, 54; *Handbook,* p. 42; *Perfect Gentleman,* pp. 239–241; *Chesterfield's Letter,* pp. 24, 31; *Ladies' Indispensable,* p. 123.

72. *Art,* pp. 18, 21; *Guide to Good Manners,* p. 76; de Valcourt, pp. 103–104; Mackellar, p. 123; Lunettes, pp. 130, 159–160; *Habits,* pp. 313, 326–327; C. Hartley, pp. 74, 202; Wells, p. 68; Willis, p. 8.

73. Celnart, p. 180; de Valcourt, pp. 236–237, 295, 499; Wells, p. 91; Lunettes, p. 308; C. Hartley, pp. 36, 71; *Chesterfield's Letter,* p. 22; Sedgwick, *Morals,* p. 23; Comstock, pp. 31–34; see Mickle, 1: 110; 2: 478. Some historians have argued that the ethic of male sexual self-control was accompanied by an expectation of male sexual aggression. The conduct literature accords with Rotundo's suggestion that the former applied to middle-class relations, while the latter might have pervaded a more exploitive approach to women of lower social status. Still, his subjects were apparently constrained by "a moral taboo on seduction" even with "chippies." He does remind us that some bourgeois young men must have visited prostitutes. See Charles Rosenberg, "Sexuality, Class, and Role in Nineteenth-Century America," *American Quarterly,* 35, no. 2 (May 1973): 131–153; Rotundo, "Body and Soul," pp. 26–27; *American Manhood,* pp. 120–127; Rothman, p. 138; Robert Griswold, *Family and Divorce in California, 1850–1890: Victorian Illusions and Everyday Realities* (Albany, N.Y.: SUNY Press, 1982), pp. 114–119.

74. *Young Lady's Own,* p. 209; Farrar, pp. 218, 221–222; A. Fergurson, p. 21; Arthur, *Ladies,* p. 113; Newcomb, *Young Ladies',* p. 307; *True Politeness/Ladies,* pp. 29–30, 37; *Etiquette for Ladies2,* p. 12; *Guide to Good Manners,* p. 75; Thornwell, pp. 93–94; *Ladies' and Gentlemen's Letter,* p. 24; *Handbook,* p. 7; Willis, pp. 12, 15.

75. F. Hartley, pp. 34, 40, 114, 168, 176, 191; Celnart, pp. 29–31, 183; *Etiquette for Ladies,* pp. 43–46, 69; Leslie, 1853, pp. 38, 70–71, 97, 310; de Valcourt, pp. 158–159; Thornwell, pp. 78–79, 95; *Chesterfield's Letter,* p. 48; *True Politeness/Ladies,* pp. 40–41; *Beadle's,* p. 35; Ferrero, pp. 109–110; *Art of Pleasing,* p. 57; Howe, p. 12; Parkes, pp. 335–336; Farrar, p. 371; Abell, p. 117; *Handbook,* p. 41.

76. Comstock, p. 139, 143–144; Abbott, p. 65; Farrar, pp. 294–297; Arthur,

Ladies, p. 155; Wise, Lady's, p. 248; Hosmer, p. 35; Abell, pp. 197–198; de Valcourt, p. 290; Willis, pp. 56–57, 63; F. Hartley, p. 172; Celnart, p. 29; Calabrella, p. 19.

77. Young Lady's Own, p. 253; Farrar, pp. 308–309, 370–371; Austin, pp. 282–283, 295; Arthur, Ladies, pp. 135–138, 145, 147–148; Book of Manners, p. 56; Leslie, 1853, pp. 66–67, 99–100, 112–113; Abell, pp. 116–117; Thornwell, pp. 80–81; Art of Pleasing, p. 22; True Politeness/Ladies, pp. 8, 11–12; de Valcourt, p. 103; Titcomb, p. 120; Habits, pp. 312, 316; Celnart, p. 30; Calabrella, p. 4; F. Hartley, pp. 38, 113, 168; Mickle, 3: 306, 308.

78. Celnart, p. 184; Manual, p. 61; Well-Bred Girl, pp. 23–24; Calabrella, p. 31; True Politeness/Ladies, pp. 38–39, 41; Etiquette at Washington, 1849, p. 43; Durang, Fashionable, p. 16; Thornwell, pp. 96, 146; Howe, pp. 12–13; Beadle's, pp. 34–35; Ferrero, pp. 107–108; F. Hartley, pp. 167–168; Sprague, 1834, pp. 146–147; Ladies' Vase, p. 129.

79. Celnart, p. 160; Walsh, 2: 23; Farrar, pp. 325, 372, 403; Coxe, p. 52; Sedgwick, Means, p. 153; Newcomb, Young Ladies', p. 307; Etiquette for Ladies2, p. 61; Art, p. 25; True Politeness/Ladies, p. 40; Arthur, Ladies, pp. 142, 144–145; Etiquette at Washington, 1850, p. 69; Abell, p. 117; Leslie, 1853, pp. 68, 89, 93–94, 98–99; 1854, p. 310; Wells, pp. 96, 108; Thornwell, pp. 146–147; F. Hartley, pp. 34, 291.

80. Parkes, p. 60; Celnart, p. 80; Etiquette for Ladies2, 1843, p. 17; Beadle's, p. 16; F. Hartley, p. 80; Abbott, p. 68; de Valcourt, p. 326; Wells, p. 61.

81. Wells, p. 108; True Politeness/Ladies, p. 63; Leslie, 1853, pp. 89, 300; Etiquette at Washington, 1849, pp. 47–48; Farrar, p. 320; Austin, pp. 285–286; Sedgwick, Morals, p. 20; Arthur, Ladies, pp. 142–144; Porter, p. 131; Abell, p. 151; A. Fergurson, p. 136; Thornwell, pp. 85, 110.

82. Welter, p. 155; Farrar, p. 293; Leslie, 1853, p. 305; Review of The Young Lady's Friend, Godey's Lady's Book, XVI (1838): 247–248; cf. Cott, "Passionlessness," p. 225; Book of Politeness, p. 14. On dinner seating: Celnart, p. 165; Etiquette at Washington, 1849, p. 66; Ladies' Indispensable, p. 125; Book of Manners, p. 197; de Valcourt, p. 132; Wells, pp. 85–86; Thornwell, p. 99; Handbook, p. 20; Chesterfield's Letter, pp. 26–27.

83. Comstock, pp. 124, 139, 141; Sprague, 1834, p. 147; Young Lady's Own, pp. 15–16, 253; Sandford, pp. 13–14; Farrar, pp. 290–291, 293–294, 308, 403; Alcott, Wife, pp. 202–203; Etiquette for Ladies, pp. 11–12, 141–143; Austin, pp. 294–296; Coxe, p. 52; Muzzey, Maiden, pp. 204–206; Newcomb, Young Ladies', pp. 307–308, 310; Sedgwick, Morals, pp. 20, 22; Arthur, Ladies, pp. 134–138, 141–142, 145, 147–148; Abell, pp. 127, 193; Hosmer, p. 36; Leslie, 1853, pp. 100, 114; de Valcourt, pp. 147–148, 299, 309–310; Wells, pp. 108, 112; Thornwell, pp. 146–147; F. Hartley, pp. 19–20, 34, 38, 150, 291.

84. Celnart, pp. 30, 175; Calabrella, pp. 19–20; Etiquette for Ladies2, p. 48; Book of Politeness, p. 17; Art of Pleasing, pp. 47, 55; Thornwell, pp. 84, 109; Handbook, p. 7; Young Lady's Own, pp. 147, 149; Austin, p. 336; True Politeness/Ladies, p. 39; F. Hartley, pp. 168, 191–192; Newcomb, Lady, p. 48.

85. Farrar, p. 291; Ladies' Vase, pp. 127–128; F. Hartley, p. 19; Carey, p. 6; Abbott, p. 68; Art, p. 26; Smith, p. 78; True Politeness/Ladies, p. 40; Leslie, 1853, pp. 89, 114, 301; de Valcourt, p. 326; Wells, pp. 96, 107–108; Coxe, p. 52; Thornwell, pp. 87, 146; Cobbett, III, p. 90; Comstock, pp. 124, 141; Chesterfield's Letter, p. 56.

86. Celnart, p. 30; Farrar, pp. 291, 332, 403; Arthur, Ladies, pp. 135–136, 141–143; F. Hartley, pp. 19–20, 41, 56, 156, 170, 176; Sigourney, Ladies, 1833, pp. 96, 98; Calabrella, pp. 4, 19, 31; Leslie, 1853, pp. 68, 89, 99, 100, 114; Thornwell, pp. 78–79, 96, 111, 146; True Politeness/Ladies, p. 8; Newcomb, Lady, p. 48; Coxe, pp. 51–52,

53; Sedgwick, *Means*, p. 153; Newcomb, *Young Ladies'*, p. 307; *Ladies' Vase*, pp. 127–128; Sedgwick, *Morals*, p. 20; *Etiquette at Washington*, 1849, p. 47; Abell, pp. 117, 194; Wells, pp. 96, 107, 108.

87. Celnart, p. 107; Coxe, pp. 52–53; Calabrella, p. 26; *Art*, p. 34; *Laws of Good Breeding*, p. 40; Abell, p. 123; de Valcourt, p. 500; Thornwell, pp. 147, 151; Wells, p. 81; F. Hartley, pp. 13, 286; Willis, p. 47; *Handbook*, p. 28.

88. Cobbett, III, p. 90; Coxe, p. 53; *Young Lady's Own*, p. 15; Alcott, *Wife*, p. 202; *Etiquette for Ladies*, p. 16; *True Politeness/Ladies*, pp. 22–23; Arthur, *Ladies*, p. 135; Wise, *Man's*, p. 240; de Valcourt, p. 299; *Chesterfield's Letter*, p. 56.

89. For a sampling, see Sigourney, *Ladies*, 1833, p. 96; Newcomb, *Young Ladies'*, p. 307; Arthur, *Ladies*, pp. 136, 140–141; Wise, *Lady's*, pp. 248–249; Leslie, 1853, pp. 113–114, 302; Celnart, p. 30; Farrar, pp. 214, 299–300; Alcott, *Wife*, p. 202; Calabrella, p. 6; *Young Lady's Own*, pp. 185–187; Sprague, 1822, pp. 59–61; Coxe, p. 52; *Etiquette For Ladies2*, p. 62; Hosmer, p. 37; Thornwell, p. 146; Parkes, p. 38; Austin, pp. 283, 295–296; Comstock, p. 142.

90. *Art*, pp. 19, 38; *Book of Politeness*, pp. 14–15, 17; Thornwell, pp. 109, 147; F. Hartley, pp. 113, 191–192; Farrar, pp. 293–294, 296; Leslie, 1853, pp. 67–68, 304, 310; Coxe, p. 52; *Etiquette For Ladies2*, pp. 13, 26; *True Politeness/Ladies*, pp. 7, 39–40, 63; *Laws of Good Breeding*, pp. 25–26; *Handbook*, p. 8; *Etiquette for Ladies*, pp. 10–11, 144–146; de Valcourt, pp. 147, 499; *Chesterfield's Letter*, pp. 22, 47, 55; *Habits*, p. 327; Wells, p. 91; Newcomb, *Young Ladies'*, p. 307. Cf. Patricia Cohen's finding of "a rising preoccupation with sexual danger for women in public in the 1830s": "Safety and Danger," p. 119.

91. Rotundo, "Body and Soul," pp. 30–32.

92. Kerber, "Separate Spheres," pp. 30, 39.

93. Farrar, pp. 402–403; Sedgwick, *Morals*, p. 20; Wells, p. 108; Walsh, 2: 23; *Laws of Good Breeding*, p. 11.

94. Habermas, pp. 84–87, 124–125.

CONCLUSION

1. Mickle, 1: 30.

2. Davidoff, *Best Circles*, pp. 17–18.

3. This sketch of postwar manners draws heavily from Schlesinger, pp. 27–34, 41–43; on table manners, see also Kasson, pp. 189, 202–204.

4. Schlesinger, pp. 52, 54.

5. Schlesinger, pp. 44–45.

BIBLIOGRAPHY OF CONDUCT
WORKS CITED

Editions listed are the earliest editions of each work that were available to the author. Multiple editions are only noted where used (because changes in the text supplied additional data).

Abbott, John S. C. *The School Girl, or the Principles of Christian Duty Familiarly Enforced*. Boston: Crocker and Brewster, 1840.

Abell, Mrs. L. G. *Woman in Her Various Relations: Containing Practical Rules for American Females*. New York: W. Holdredge, 1851.

Advice to a Young Gentleman, on Entering Society. Philadelphia: Lea and Blanchard, 1839.

Advice to the Fair Sex; in a Series of Letters. Philadelphia: Robert Cochran, 1803.

Alcott, William Andrus. *The Boy's Guide to Usefulness*. Boston: Waite, Pierce and Company, 1844.

———. *Familiar Letters to Young Men on Various Subjects*. Buffalo: Derby and Company, 1849.

———. *The Young Husband*. 1st ed. Boston: G. W. Light, 1839.

———. *The Young Man's Guide*. Boston: Lilly, Wait, Colman, and Holden, 1833; 13th ed. Boston: Perkins and Marvin, 1839.

———. *The Young Mother, or Management of Children in Regard to Health*. 1st ed. Boston: Light and Stearns, 1836.

———. *The Young Wife*. 1st ed. Boston: G. W. Light, 1837.

———. *The Young Woman's Guide to Excellence*. 1st ed. Boston: G. W. Light, 1840.

Alexander, James. *The Merchant's Clerk Cheered and Counselled*. New York: A. D. F. Randolph, 1856.

[Allestree, Richard.] *The Ladies Calling*. Oxford: "at the Theater," 1673.

[————.] *The Whole Duty of Man*. London: T. Garthwait, 1659.

Ambrose, Isaac. *The Well Ordered Family*. Boston: S. Kneeland, 1762.

The American Academy of Compliments, or the Complete American Secretary. Philadelphia: Deshong and Folwell, 1796.

American Gentleman's Everyday Handbook, or Modern Letter-Writing, Etiquette, Dreams, Songs. Philadelphia: Henry F. Anners, 1849.

The American Ladies' Preceptor. Baltimore: Coale; Philadelphia: Watson, 1810.

Ancourt, L'abbé d'. *Lady's Preceptor, or a Letter to a Young Lady of Distinction Upon Politeness*. 5th ed. Woodbridge, New Jersey, 1759.

The Art of Good Behavior, and Letter Writer on Love, Courtship, and Marriage. New York: C. P. Huestis, 1845.

The Art of Pleasing, or the American Lady and Gentleman's Book of Etiquette. Cincinnati: H. M. Rulison, 1855.

Arthur, Timothy Shay. *Advice to Young Ladies on Their Duties and Conduct in Life*. Boston: Phillips, Sampson and Company, 1848.

————. *Advice to Young Men on Their Duties and Conduct in Life*. Philadelphia: J. E. Potter and Company, 1847.

Atmore, Charles. *Serious Advice from a Father to His Children*. Philadelphia: Cunningham, 1819.

Austin, John Mather. *A Voice to Youth, Addressed to Young Men and Young Ladies*. Utica, New York: Grosh and Hutchinson, 1838.

[Bailey, Jacob.] *A Little Book for Children, Containing a Few Rules for the Regulation of Their Tho'ts, Words, and Actions*. Portsmouth, New Hampshire, 1758.

Barnard, John. *Call to Parents and Children*. Boston: Fleet for D. Henchman, 1737.

Barnard, Sir John. *A Present for an Apprentice*. Boston: Rogers and Fowle, 1747.

Baxter, Richard. *Poor Man's Family Book*. 1st ed. London: R. W. for Nevill Simmons, 1674.

[Bayle-Mouillard, Elisabeth; see Mme Celnart.]

Beadle's Dime Book of Practical Etiquette. New York: Irwin P. Beadle and Company, 1859.

Bellegarde, Jean Baptiste Morvan, l'abbé de. *Politeness of Manners and Behavior in Fashionable Society*. Boston: Charles Ewer, 1821; also in *The Ladies Companion*. Worcester, Massachusetts: The Spy Office, 1824.

Bennett, John. *Letters to a Young Lady*. 2 vols. Hartford: Hudson and Goodwin, 1791.

The Book of Manners: A Guide to Social Intercourse. New York: Carlton and Porter, 1852.

The Book of Politeness. Philadelphia, New York, Boston, and Baltimore: Fischer and Brother, 1850?

Boudier de Villemert, Pierre Joseph. *The Ladies Friend; Being a Treatise on the Virtues . . . of the Fair Sex*. Philadelphia: Dunlap, 1771.

The Boy's Manual: Comprising a Summary View of the Studies, Accomplishments, and Principles of Conduct Best Suited For Promoting Respectability and Success in Life. New York: Appleton and Company; Philadelphia: G. Appleton, 1837.

Brathwait, Richard. *The English Gentleman*. London: Haviland for Bostock, 1630.

————. *The English Gentlewoman*. London: Michaell Sparke, 1631.

Brewer, George. *The Juvenile Lavater*. New York: Forbes for M'Dermut and Arden, 1815.

Bridge, William. *A Word to the Aged*. Boston: Foster for Griffen, 1679.

Burghley, William Cecil, 1st Baron. *Ten Precepts*. Philadelphia: Dobson, 1786.

Burkitt, William. *The Poor Man's Help and Young Man's Guide*. Boston: Green for Eliot, 1725.

Burton, John. *Lectures on Female Education and Manners*. 1st Amer. ed. New York: Campbell, 1794.

Butler, Charles. *The American Gentleman*. Philadelphia: Hogan and Thompson, 1836.

[Calabrella, E. C., Baroness de.] *The Ladies' Science of Etiquette*. New York: Wilson and Company, 1844.

The Canons of Good Breeding, or the Handbook of the Man of Fashion. Philadelphia: Lea and Blanchard, 1839.

[Caraccioli, Louis Antoine de.] *Advice from a Lady of Quality to Her Children*. 3d ed. Newburyport, 1784.

Carey, Matthew. *The Philosophy of Common Sense, Containing Practical Rules for the Promotion of Domestic Happiness*. Philadelphia: Carey and Hart, 1838.

Carlysle, Countess of. "Maxims." In Mrs. M. Peddle, *Rudiments of Taste, in a Series of Letters from a Mother to Her Daughter*. Philadelphia: Spotswood, 1790.

Castiglione, Baldassar. *The Book of the Courtier*. London, 1561.

Celnart, Madame [Elisabeth Bayle-Mouillard]. *The Gentleman and Lady's Book of Politeness and Propriety of Deportment*. 1st American ed. Boston: Allen and Ticknor, 1833.

Chapone, Hester Mulso. *Letters on the Improvement of the Mind, Addressed to a Young Lady*. Boston: Hedge for Green, 1783.

Chesterfield, Phillip Dormer Stanhope, 4th Earl of. *Letters to His Son*. 3d ed. New York: Rivington and Gaine, 1775; *Principles of Politeness*. Abridged ed. Philadelphia: Bell, 1778; *Guide to Men and Manners*. Abridged ed. Philadelphia: Benjamin Warner, 1818.

Chesterfield's Letter Writer and Complete Book of Etiquette. New York: Dick and Fitzgerald, 1860.

The Child's Instructor and Moral Primer. Portland, Maine: A.W. Thayer, 1823.

Cleaver, Robert. *A Godly Forme of Householde Government*. London: Creede, 1598.

Cobbett, William. *Advice to Young Men and (Incidentally) to Young Women in the Middle and Higher Ranks of Life*. London: the author, 1829.

Colman, Benjamin. *The Duty and Honour of Aged Women*. Boston: B. Green, 1711.

———. *The Government and Improvement of Mirth*. Boston: B. Green, 1707.

———. *The Honour and Happiness of the Vertuous Woman*. Boston: B. Green, 1716.

Comstock, Joshua. *The Whole Duties of Men and Women*. Georgetown, D.C.: J. Comstock, 1822.

[Conkling, Margaret Cockburn; see Henry Lunettes]

Coxe, Margaret. *The Young Ladies Companion*. Columbus, Ohio: I. N. Whiting, 1839.

Darwin, Erasmus. *A Plan for the Conduct of Female Education*. Philadelphia: Ormrod, 1798.

[Day, Charles William; see Count Alfred d'Orsay]

Day, Charles William. *Hints on Etiquette and the Usages of Society*. Boston: Otis Broaders, 1844.

Della Casa, Giovanni. *Galateo, or a Treatise on Politeness and Delicacy of Manners*. Baltimore: B. Edes for George Hill, 1811.

———. *The Refin'd Courtier, or a Correction of Indecencies in Civil Conversation*. London: J. G. for R. Royston, 1663.

[De Valcourt, Robert.] *The Illustrated Manners Book, a Manual of Good Behavior and Polite Accomplishments*. New York: Leland, Clay, 1855.

[Dixon, Henry et al.] *The Youth's Instructor in the English Tongue*. 8th ed. Boston: Henchman, 1746.

Dodsley, Robert. *The Economy of Human Life*. 7th ed. Boston: Fowle, 1752.

Doolittle, Thomas. *Young Man's Counsellor and the Old Man's Remembrancer*. London: Thomas Parkhurst, 1673.

Dover, William. *Useful Miscellanies Respecting Men's Duty to God and Towards One Another*. Philadelphia: James Chattin, 1753.

Durang, Charles. *The Ballroom Bijou and Art of Dancing . . . With Rules of Polite Behavior*. Philadelphia: Turner and Fisher, 1848.

———. *Fashionable Dancer's Casket, or the Ballroom Instructor*. Philadelphia, Baltimore, and New York: Fisher and Brother, 1856.

Dwight, Theodore Jr. *The Father's Book, or Suggestions for the Instruction and Government of Young Children*. Springfield, Massachusetts: G. and C. Merriam; New York: Leavitt, Lord and Company; Boston: Crocker and Brewster, 1834.

Emerson, Ralph Waldo. *The Conduct of Life*. 1st ed. Boston: Ticknor and Fields, 1860.

Etiquette at Washington, Together with the Customs Adopted by Polite Society in the Other Cities of the United States. Baltimore: J. Murphy, 1849; 2d ed. Baltimore: J. Murphy, 1850.

Etiquette For Ladies, with Hints on the Preservation, Improvement, and Display of Female Beauty. Philadelphia: Carey, Lea and Blanchard, 1838.

Etiquette for Ladies: A Manual of the Most Approved Rules for Conduct in Polished Society, for Married and Unmarried Ladies. Philadelphia: J. and J. L. Gihon, 1843. (Cited as *Etiquette For Ladies2*.)

A Family Book for Children. Hartford: Babcock, 1799.

[Farrar, Eliza Ware.] *The Young Lady's Friend*. Boston: American Stationers Company, 1836.

The Female Friend, or the Duties of Christian Virgins, to Which is Added, Advice to a Young Married Lady. Baltimore: Keatinge, 1809.

Fenelon, François de Salignac de la Mothe, Archbishop. *A Treatise on the Education of Daughters*. Trans. T. F. Dibdin. Albany: Backus and Whiting, 1806.

Fergurson, Anna. *The Young Lady, or a Guide to Knowledge, Virtue, and Happiness*. Lowell, Massachusetts: N. L. Dayton, 1848.

Fergurson, Frank. *The Young Man, or a Guide to Virtue, Knowledge, and Happiness*. Nashua, New Hampshire: J. M. Fletcher; Lowell, Massachusetts: N. C. Dayton, 1848.

Ferrero, Edward. *The Art of Dancing, with a Few Hints on Etiquette*. New York: Dick and Fitzgerald, 1859.

Ferris, Isaac. "Men of Business: Their Home Responsibilities." In *Man of Business Considered in His Various Relations*. New York: Randolf, 1857.

Fordyce, James. *Sermons to Young Women*. Boston: Mein and Fleeming, 1767.

Forrester, James. *The Polite Philosopher*. 15th ed. New York: Parker and Weyman, 1758.

Foster, Hannah Webster. *The Boarding School*. Boston: Thomas and Andrews for Bingham, 1798.

[Franklin, Benjamin.] *Reflections on Courtship and Marriage*. Philadelphia: Franklin, 1746.

[Frost, John.] *The Young Mechanic*. 2d ed. New York: Saxton and Miles; Boston: Saxton, Pierce and Company, 1843.

Gisborne, Thomas. *An Enquiry into the Duties of the Female Sex*. Philadelphia: J. Humphreys, 1798.

[Goodrich, Samuel Griswold; see Peter Parley]

Gouge, Thomas. *The Young Man's Guide*. Boston: F. Draper for J. Blanchard, 1742.

Gouge, William. *Eight Treatises of Domesticall Duties*. London: T. Haviland for William Bladen, 1622.

[Green, William.] *The School of Good Manners, Containing Rules for Children's Behaviour in Every Situation of Life*. New London: Connecticut: Samuel Green, 1801.

Gregory, John. *A Father's Legacy to His Daughters*. Philadelphia: for Aikman of Annapolis, 1775.

Griffiths, John. *A Collection of the Newest Cotillions, to Which Is Added, Instances of Ill Manners to Be Carefully Avoided by Youth of Both Sexes*. Northampton, Massachusetts, 1794; Worcester, Massachusetts, 1800.

Guazzo, Stefano. *The Civile Conversation*. Trans. George Pettie. 1581. Reprint, New York: AMS Press, 1967.

The Guide or Counsellor of Human Life. 1st ed. Springfield, Massachusetts, 1794.

A Guide to Good Manners: Containing Hints on Etiquette, Business, Morals, Dress, Friendship, Weddings, Balls, Dinners, Parties, Compliments, and Letter Writing. Springfield, Massachusetts: John M. Wood, 1847.

Habits of Good Society: A Handbook for Ladies and Gentlemen. 1st Am. ed. New York: Rudd and Carleton, 1860.

Hale, Sir Matthew. *A Letter of Advice to His Grandchildren*. Boston: Wells and Lilly, 1817.

[Halifax, George Savile, Marquis of.] *The Lady's New Year's Gift, or Advice to a Daughter*. 3d ed. London: for Matthew Gillyflower and James Partridge, 1688.

The Handbook of Etiquette, Being a Complete Guide to the Usages of Polite Society. London, New York: Cassell, Petten and Golpin, 1860.

[Hanway, Jonas.] *Advice from Farmer Trueman, to His Daughter*. Boston: Munroe and Francis, 1810.

Harker, Ahimaaz. *A Companion for the Young People of North America*. New York: Holt, 1767.

Hartley, Cecil B. *The Gentleman's Book of Etiquette and Manual of Politeness*. Boston: G. W. Cottrell; Philadelphia: G. G. Evans, 1860.

Hartley, Florence. *The Ladies' Book of Etiquette and Manual of Politeness*. Boston: G. W. Cottrell; Philadelphia: G. G. Evans, 1860.

Hervey, George Winfred. *The Principles of Courtesy: With Hints and Observations on Manners and Habits*. 2d ed. New York: Harper and Brothers, 1852.

Hitchcock, Enos. *Memoirs of the Bloomsgrove Family . . . Containing Sentiments on a Mode of Domestic Education, Suited to . . . the United States*. 2d ed. 2 vols. Boston: Thomas and Andrews, 1790.

Hoare, Mrs. Louisa Gurney. *Hints for the Improvement of Early Education and Nursery Discipline*. 1st Amer. ed. New York: Collins and Company, 1820.

[Holland, Josiah Gilbert; see Timothy Titcomb, Esq.]

Homes, William. *The Good Government of Christian Families*. Boston: D. Henchman, 1747.

Hosmer, William. *The Young Ladies Book, or Principles of Female Education*. Auburn, New York: Derby and Miller, 1851.

Howe, Elias. *Howe's Complete Ball-room Handbook*. Boston: Brown, Taggard and Chase, 1858.

James Stuart, King of England. *Basilikon Doron*. Edinburgh: Robert Waldegrave, 1599.

A Juvenile Guide, or Manual of Good Manners. Consisting of Counsels, Instructions and Rules of Deportment, for the Young. Canterbury, New York, 1844.

A Juvenile Monitor, Containing Instructions for Youth and Children; Pointing Out Ill Manners, and Showing Them How to Behave in the Various Conditions of Childhood and Youth. New Lebanon, New York, 1823. (Later revised and expanded as *A Juvenile Guide*, above.)

[Kenrick, William.] *The Whole Duty of a Woman*. 2d ed. Boston: Fowle and Draper, 1761; Philadelphia: Crukshank, 1788.

Ker, Patrick. *The Map of Man's Misery*. Boston: Phillips, 1692.

Knigge, Adolf Franz Friedrich Ludwig Freiher vom. *Practical Philosophy of Social Life*. 1st Amer. ed. Trans. P. Will. Lansingburgh, New York: A. Penniman of Troy for Penniman and Bliss, 1805.

Ladies' and Gentlemen's Letter Writer and Guide to Polite Behaviour. Boston: G. W. Cottrell, 1859.

Ladies' Indispensable Assistant. New York: F. J. Dow and Company, 1851.

Ladies' Vase, or Polite Manual for Young Ladies. Lowell, Massachusetts: N. L. Dayton; Boston: Lewis and Sampson, 1843.

Lambert, Anne Therese, Marquise de. "A Mother's Advice to her Daughter." In *The Lady's Pocket Library*. Philadelphia: Mathew Carey, 1792.

Lambert, Anne Therese, Marquise de. "A Mother's Advice to Her Son." In *The Young Gentleman's Parental Monitor*. Hartford: Patten, 1792.

La Primaudaye, Pierre de. *The French Academy, Wherein Is Discoursed the Institution of Maners and Whatsoever Els Concerneth the Good and Happie Life of All Estates and Callings*. Trans. T. B. C. London: Edmund Bollifant for G. Bishop and Ralph Newbery, 1586.

Lavater, Johann Caspar. *Aphorisms on Man*. Philadelphia: Spotswood, 1790.

The Laws of Etiquette, or Short Rules and Reflections for Conduct in Society. 1st ed. Philadelphia: Carey, Lea and Blanchard, 1836; 2d ed., Philadelphia: Carey, Lea and Blanchard, 1836.

The Laws of Good Breeding, or the Science of Etiquette for Ladies and Gentlemen. Cincinnati: Hayward James, 1848.

Leslie, Eliza. *The Behavior Book*. Philadelphia: W. P. Hazard, 1853; 4th ed. Philadelphia: W. P. Hazard, 1854.

Letters to a Younger Brother, on Various Subjects, Relating to the Virtues and Vices, Duties and Dangers of Youth. Philadelphia: American Sunday School Union, 1838.

[Lingard, Richard.] *Letter of Advice to a Young Gentleman Leaving the University Concerning His Behaviour and Conversation in the World*. New York, 1696.

A Little Book for Little Children. Boston: Green, 1702.

A Little Pretty Pocket Book. 1st Worcester ed. Worcester, Massachusetts: Isaiah Thomas, 1787.

Livermore, Abiel Abbott. *Lectures to Young Men on Their Moral Dangers and Duties*. Boston: James Munroe and Company, 1846.

Lunettes, Henry [Margaret Cockburn Conkling]. *The American Gentleman's Guide to Politeness and Fashion*. New York: Derby and Jackson, 1857.

Maberly, Mrs. Kate Charlotte. *The Art of Conversation, with Remarks on Fashion and Address: Together with General Rules to Be Observed in Intercourse with Society*. New York: Wilson; Brother Jonathan Press, 1846.

Mackellar, D. *A Treatise on the Art of Politeness, Good Breeding and Manners, with Maxims and Moral Reflections*. Detroit: George E. Pomeroy, 1855.

Manners, Mrs. [Cornelia Holroyd Bradley Richards.] *At Home and Abroad, or How to Behave*. 1st ed. New York: Evans and Brittan, 1853.

Man's Whole Duty, or the Rule of a Christian's Life. Boston: B. Green for B. Eliot, 1718.

A Manual of Politeness, Comprising the Principles of Etiquette, and Rules of Behavior in Genteel Society, for Persons of Both Sexes. Philadelphia: Marshall and Company, 1837.

Mather, Cotton. *Addresses to Old Men and Young Men and Little Children*. Boston: R. Pierce for N. Buttolph, 1690.

————. *Cares About the Nurseries*. Boston: Green for Eliot, 1702.

————. *A Cloud of Witnesses vs. Balls and Dances*. Boston: Green and Allen, 1700.

————. *A Family Well-Ordered*. Boston: Green and Allen, 1699.

————. *A Good Master Well-Served*. Boston: Green and Allen, 1696.

————. *Ornaments for the Daughters of Zion*. Cambridge: Phillips, 1692.

————. *The Rules of a Visit*. Boston: T. Green, 1705.

————. *Tabitha Rediviva*. Boston: J. Allen, 1713.

Mather, Increase. *An Arrow Against Profane and Promiscuous Dancing*. Boston: S. Green for J. Brunning, 1684.

————. *Two Discourses Shewing, I, That the Lord's Ears are Open to the Prayers of the Righteous, and II, The Dignity and Duty of the Aged Servants of the Lord*. Boston: Green for Henchman, 1716.

Mellen, John. *A Discourse Containing a Serious Address to Persons of Several Ages and Characters*. Boston: Edes and Gill, 1751.

Miller, Samuel. *Letter from a Father to His Sons at College*. Philadelphia: Grigg, 1843.

The Mirror of the Graces. New York: C. Wiley for I. Riley, 1813.

Moody, Eleazar. *The School of Good Manners*. 5th ed. New London: T. and J. Green, 1754.

Moore, John Hamilton. *The Young Gentleman and Lady's Monitor*. 5th ed. New York: Gaine, 1787.

More, Hannah. *Essays on Various Subjects Designed for Young Ladies*. Philadelphia: Young, Stewart and M'Culloch, 1786.

————. *Strictures on the Modern System of Female Education*. 2 vols. Philadelphia: Dobson, 1800.

The Mother's Friend, or Familiar Directions for Forming the Mental and Moral Habits of Young Children. New York: Leavitt, Lord, and Company; Boston: Crocker and Brewster, 1834.

Mott, James. *Observations on the Education of Children and Hints to Young People on the Duties of Civil Life*. New York: Wood, 1816.

————. *Brief Hints to Parents on the Subject of Education*. Philadelphia: B. and T. Kite, 1824.

Muzzey, Artemus B. *The Young Maiden*. Boston: William Crosby and Company, 1840.

————. *The Young Man's Friend*. Boston: James Munroe and Company, 1836.

My Son's Book. New York: F. W. Bradley and Company, 1839.

[Ness, Christopher.] *Crown and Glory of a Christian*. 3d ed. Boston: Green for Griffen, 1684.

Newcomb, Harvey. *How to Be a Lady: A Book for Girls, Containing Useful Hints on the Formation of Character*. Boston: Gould, Kendall and Lincoln, 1847.

————. *How to Be a Man: A Book for Boys, Containing Useful Hints on the Formation of Character*. Boston: Gould, Kendall and Lincoln; Cincinnati: George S. Blanchard; New York: Sheldon and Company, 1847.

————. *The Young Ladies' Guide to the Harmonious Development of Christian Character*. 3d ed. Boston: James B. Dow, 1841.

Nichols, Francis D. *A Guide to Politeness*. Boston: Lincoln and Edmunds, 1810.

[Norden, John.] *The Father's Legacy*. London: John Marriot, 1625.

Orsay, Alfred, Count d' [Charles William Day.] *Etiquette, or a Guide to the Usages of Society, with a Glance at Bad Habits*. New York: Wilson, 1843.

Orton, Job. *Discourses to the Aged*. Salem: J. Cushing for T. C. Cushing, 1801.

Osborne, Francis. *Advice to a Son, or Directions for Your Better Conduct Through the Various and Most Important Encounters of This Life*. Oxford: H. Hall for Thomas

Robinson, 1656. Reprinted in *Advice to a Son*. Ed. Louis Wright. Folger Shakespeare Library; Ithaca, New York: Cornell University Press, 1962.

Parkes, Frances. *Domestic Duties*. 1st Amer. ed. from 3d London ed. New York:
Harpers, 1828.

Parley, Peter [Samuel Griswold Goodrich]. *What to Do, and How to Do it, or Morals
and Manners Taught by Examples*. New York: Wiley and Putnam, 1844.

Peck, George. *Formation of a Manly Character: A Series of Lectures to Young Men*. New
York: Carlton and Philips, 1853.

Peddle, Mrs. M. *Rudiments of Taste, in a Series of Letters from a Mother to Her Daughter*.
Philadelphia: Spotswood, 1790.

Penn, William. *Fruits of a Father's Love*. 6th ed. Philadelphia: Crukshank, 1776.

————. *Fruits of Solitude*. 8th ed. Newport: Franklin, 1749.

————. *More Fruits of Solitude*. Newport, 1748.

Pennington, Lady Sarah. "An Unfortunate Mother's Advice to Her Absent Daughters, in a Letter to Miss Pennington." In *The Lady's Pocket Library*. Philadelphia:
Matthew Carey, 1792.

The Perfect Gentleman, or Etiquette and Eloquence. New York: Dick and Fitzgerald, 1860.

Phillips, Samuel. *Advice to a Child, or Young People Solemnly Warn'd Both Against Entic-
ing, and Consenting When Enticed to Sin*. Boston: J. Phillips, 1729.

————. *A Serious Address to Young People*. Boston: Kneeland, 1763.

Plain Talk and Friendly Advice to Domestics with Counsel on Home Matters. Boston:
Phillips, Sampson and Company, 1855.

The Polite Academy. 3d ed. London: Baldwin and Collins, 1765.

The Polite Lady, or a Course of Female Education. 2d ed. London: Newbury and Carnan,
1769.

The Polite Present, or a Manual of Good Manners. Boston: Munroe and Francis, 1831.

Porter, James. *The Operative's Friend, and Defence, or Hints to Young Ladies, Who Are
Dependent on Their Own Exertions*. Boston: Charles H. Pierce, 1859.

Raleigh, Sir Walter. *Sir Walter Raleigh's Instructions to His Son and to Posterity*. 2d ed.
London: Benjamin Fisher, 1632. Reprinted in *Advice to a Son*. Ed. Louis Wright.
Folger Shakespeare Library; Ithaca, New York: Cornell University Press, 1962.

[Ramesay, William.] *Gentleman's Companion, or a Character of True Nobility and Gentility in the Way of Essay*. London: E. Okes for Rowland Reynolds, 1672.

[Richards, Cornelia Holroyd Bradley; see Mrs. Manners]

Roberts, Robert. *The House Servant's Directory*. Boston: Munroe and Francis; New
York: Charles S. Francis, 1827.

Sampson, Ezra. *The Brief Remarker*. Hudson, New York: Stone and Cross, 1818.

Sandford, Eliza Poole. *Woman, in Her Social and Domestic Character*. Boston: Leonard
C. Bowles, 1833.

Sedgwick, Catherine Maria. *Means and Ends, or Self Training*. Boston: Marsh, Capen,
Lyon and Webb, 1839.

————. *Morals of Manners, or Hints for our Young People*. New York: Wiley and Putnam, 1846.

Sigourney, Lydia Howard. *The Boy's Book*. New York: Turner, Hughes and Hayden,
1843.

[————.] *Letters to Young Ladies*. Hartford: Canfield, 1833; 2d ed. Hartford: Watson,
1835.

Smith, Matthew Hale. *Counsels, Addressed to Young Women, Young Men, Young Persons
in Married Life, and Young Parents*. Washington: Blair and Rives, 1846.

Sprague, William Buell. *Letters on Practical Subjects to a Daughter*. Hartford: Huntington and Hopkins, 1822; 3d Amer. ed. New York: Appleton, 1834.

[Sproat, Mrs. Nancy Dennis.] *The Good Boy's Soliloquy, Containing His Parents' Instructions Relative to His Disposition and Manners*. New York: Samuel Wood and Sons, 1818.

[————.] *The Good Girl's Soliloquy, Containing Her Parents' Instructions Relative to Her Disposition and Manners*. New York: S. Wood and Sons; Baltimore: S. Wood, 1819.

————. *The School of Good Manners*. New York and Baltimore: Samuel Wood and Sons, 1822.

Steele, Richard. *The Husbandman's Calling*. Boston: B. Green for N. Buttolph, 1713.

[Steele, Sir Richard, comp.] *The Ladies Library*. London: Jacob Tonson, 1714 (for vols. 1 and 2); 7th ed. London: Strahan, 1772 (for vol. 3).

Swift, Johnathan. "Letter to a Very Young Lady on Her Marriage." In *Reflections on Courtship and Marriage*. Philadelphia: Franklin, 1746.

Taylor, Isaac. *Advice to the Teens*. Boston: Wells and Lilly, 1820.

Thornwell, Emily. *The Lady's Guide to Perfect Gentility*. New York: Derby and Jackson, 1856.

Thurber, Laban. *The Young Ladies' and Gentleman's Preceptor: or, Eighteen Moral Rules*. Warren, Rhode Island: Phillips, 1797.

Titcomb, Timothy, Esq. [Josiah Gilbert Holland]. *Titcomb's Letters to Young People, Single and Married*. 1st ed. New York: Charles Scribner, 1858.

Todd, John. *The Student's Manual, Designed by Specific Directions to Aid in Forming and Strengthening the Intellectual and Moral Character and Habits of the Student*. 2d ed. Northampton, Massachusetts: J. H. Butler, 1835.

Trapwit, Tommy. *Be Merry and Wise, or the Cream of the Jests, and the Marrow of Maxims for the Conduct of Life*. Boston: Fowle and Draper, 1762.

Trenchfield, Caleb. *A Cap of Grey Hairs for a Green Head, or the Father's Counsel to His Son, an Apprentice in London*. 4th ed. London: Samuel Manship, 1688.

True Politeness: a Hand-book of Etiquette for Gentlemen. New York: Leavitt and Allen, 1848.

True Politeness: a Hand-book of Etiquette for Ladies. New York: Leavitt and Allen, 1847.

Venn, Henry. *The Complete Duty of Man, or a System of Doctrinal and Practical Christianity*. 1st Amer. ed. Worcester, Massachusetts: Goodridge, 1804.

Wadsworth, Benjamin. *The Well-Ordered Family*. Boston: B. Green for N. Buttolph, 1712.

Walsh, Robert. *Didactics: Social, Literary, and Political*. 2 vols. Philadelphia: Carey, Lea and Blanchard, 1836.

The Well-Bred Boy, or New School of Good Manners. Boston: T. H. Carter, 1844.

The Well-Bred Girl, an Addition to the Hints on Good Manners Contained in the Well-Bred Boy. Boston: W. Crosby, 1841.

Wells, Samuel R. *How to Behave: A Pocket Manual of Republican Etiquette*. New York: Fowler and Wells, 1856.

[Williams, J.] *Youth's Virtuous Guide*. Boston: printed for J. Williams, 1818.

Willis, Henry P. *Etiquette, and the Usages of Society*. New York: Dick and Fitzgerald, 1860.

Wise, Daniel. *The Young Lady's Counsellor*. New York: Carlton and Porter, 1851.

————. *The Young Man's Counsellor*. New York: Carlton and Porter, 1850.

The Young Lady's Own Book. Philadelphia: Key, Meikle and Biddle, 1832.

The Young Man's Own Book. Philadelphia: Key, Meikle and Biddle, 1832.

Youth's Behaviour, or Decencie in Conversation Amongst Men. Trans. Francis Hawkins. 7th ed. London: W. Lee, 1661.

The Youth's Monitor, or a Collection of Thoughts on Civil, Moral, and Religious Subjects, Selected From Different Authors. Leominster, Massachusetts, 1799.

INDEX

Absent-mindedness, 143
Access rituals, 147, 218
Adams, Abigail, 86
Adams, John, 72, 80, 93, 94, 99, 116
  on affectation, 76–77
  on good company, 73, 98
  interest in manners of, 65, 79, 85, 86, 216
  middling origins of, 65–66, 244 n. 2
  on women, 109, 113, 217
Adolescence, 177, 178
  historical plasticity of, 89, 161
  invention of, 223
  liminality of, 161
  recognition of, 236 n. 2
  See also youth
Adults
  behavior with age peers, 93, 171–176
  behavior with the aged, 35, 211
  behavior with children, 39–40, 60, 95, 96,
    166, 168–169, 211
  behavior with youth, 39–40, 60, 96, 166,
    168–169
  conduct advice for, 163
Advice books, 163
  See also conduct advice literature
Affectation, 68, 76–77, 82, 99, 117, 144, 190,
  216
Affectionate family, 97, 102, 119
Affective individualism, 88
Age relations
  compared to class relations, 214
  importance to Puritans of, 37, 44–45, 61
  social construction of, 8, 32, 89, 221
Age segregation, 37, 171, 176
Aged, the, 36
  conduct advice to, 92–93, 164

contact of youth with, 164–165
continuity of advice regarding, 217, 219
deference to, 164, 219, 221
demeanor with, 35–37
status of, 35–37, 92, 93, 176
veneration of, 214
weakness of, 165–166
  See also deference to the aged; gerontoc-
    racy; old age
Age-mixing, 37, 238 n. 25
Alcott, William, 132, 117
Alger, Horatio, 223
Allestree, Richard, 17
American manners, compared to British, 147–
  148, 158
American Revolution, 125, 130
  See also revolutionary era
Anger, 190, 235 n. 51, 284 n. 38
  in members of the elite, 14–15
  in men, 57, 115
  in women, 57, 115, 243 n. 40
  in youth, 44
Anglicization, 70, 107
Apprenticeship, 73, 90
  See also master-servant relations; masters
    and mistresses; servants; service
Arm-tendering, 197, 202
Arthur, Timothy Shay, 168, 177
Artificial behavior, 144
Associations. See company; good company
Attention, 75, 99, 114, 143, 188
Awkwardness, 76, 95, 99, 117, 200

Bachelors, 184, 186
Back stage, 176
Bad company, 43–44

Printed in the United States
23772LVS00001B/116